The Future of Representative D

C000264064

The Future of Representative Democracy poses important questions about representation, representative democracy and its future. Inspired by the last major investigation of the subject by Hanna Pitkin over four decades ago, this ambitious volume fills a major gap in the literature by examining the future of representative forms of democracy in terms of present-day trends and past theories of representative democracy. Aware of the pressing need for clarifying key concepts and institutional trends, the volume aims to break down barriers among disciplines and to establish an interdisciplinary dialogue among scholars. The contributors emphasise that representative democracy and its future is a subject of pressing scholarly concern and public importance. Paying close attention to the unfinished, two-century-old relationship between democracy and representation, this book offers a fresh perspective on current problems and dilemmas of representative democracy and the possible future development of new forms of democratic representation.

SONIA ALONSO is Senior Fellow at the Social Science Research Centre Berlin (WZB).

JOHN KEANE is Professor of Politics at the University of Sydney and Research Professor at the Social Science Research Centre Berlin (WZB).

WOLFGANG MERKEL is Director of the research unit 'Democracy: Structures, Performance, Challenges' at the Social Science Research Centre Berlin (WZB) and Professor of Political Science at the Humboldt-Universität zu Berlin.

The Future of Representative Democracy

Edited by

Sonia Alonso, John Keane, Wolfgang Merkel

with the collaboration of Maria Fotou

CAMBRIDGE
UNIVERSITY PRESS

CAMBRIDGE UNIVERSITY PRESS
Cambridge, New York, Melbourne, Madrid, Cape Town,
Singapore, São Paulo, Delhi, Tokyo, Mexico City

Cambridge University Press
The Edinburgh Building, Cambridge CB2 8RU, UK

Published in the United States of America by Cambridge University Press,
New York

www.cambridge.org
Information on this title: www.cambridge.org/9780521177030

First published 2011

Printed in the United Kingdom at the University Press, Cambridge

A catalogue record for this publication is available from the British Library

Library of Congress Cataloguing in Publication data
The Future of Representative Democracy / [edited by] Sonia Alonso,
John Keane, Wolfgang Merkel; with the collaboration of Maria Fotou.
    p. cm
Includes bibliographical references and index.
ISBN 978-0-521-17703-0 (pbk.)
1. Representative government and representation.
2. Democracy. I. Alonso, Sonia (Alonso Sáenz de Oger) II. Keane,
John (John Charlick), 1949– III. Merkel, Wolfgang, 1952– IV. Fotou,
Maria.
JF1051.F88 2011
321.8–dc22
2010049736

ISBN 978-1-107-00356-9 Hardback
ISBN 978-0-521-17703-0 Paperback

Contents

Figures

Tables

Contributors

SONIA ALONSO was awarded her PhD by the Autonomous University of Madrid and the Juan March Institute. She is currently Senior Research Fellow at the Social Science Research Centre Berlin (WZB) and, before this, she has done research and teaching in various universities: University Carlos III of Madrid, St Antony's College (Oxford University), Royal Holloway College, and University of Salamanca. Her main research interests involve the analysis of political devolution, party competition in decentralised states, minority nationalism and ethnic conflict. She is the author of a forthcoming volume with Oxford University Press: *Challenging the State: Devolution and the Battle for Partisan Credibility*.

DAVID BEETHAM is Professor Emeritus of Politics at the University of Leeds, a Fellow of the Human Rights Centre at the University of Essex and Associate Director of the UK Democratic Audit. He has travelled internationally in his capacity as consultant on democracy assessment, and is a leading contributor to the field of human rights. He is author of many books on democracy, including *Democracy and Human Rights*; *Democracy: A Beginner's Guide*; *Parliament and Democracy in the Twenty-first Century*; and *Assessing the Quality of Democracy: A Practical Guide*.

KLAUS VON BEYME studied political science, history and sociology at the universities of Heidelberg, Munich, Paris and Moscow, and is now Professor of Political Science Emeritus at the Faculty of Economic and Social Sciences of the University of Heidelberg and a member of the Berlin-Brandenburg Academy of Sciences. His major research fields are comparative politics and political theory and his latest publication is *Die Faszination des Exotischen* (2008).

DRUDE DAHLERUP is Professor of Political Science at the University of Stockholm. Vice-Chair of the Danish Government's Council for European Politics from 1993 to 2000, she has also served in various research bodies in Denmark and Norway while leading a series of projects, such as the Quota Project in collaboration with International IDEA. Her main research focuses on women in politics, gender quotas and social movements, especially the women's movement and feminist theory. She has recently edited the volume *Women, Quotas and Politics* (2006).

ROBYN ECKERSLEY, having previously been a public lawyer, is now Professor in the School of Social and Political Sciences at the University of Melbourne. Her work focuses on environmental politics, political theory and international relations theory and her 1992 book was one of the first to argue for an ecocentric political theory. She has recently co-edited (along with Andrew Dobson) the book *Political Theory and the Ecological Challenge* (2006).

MARIA FOTOU, educated in the fields of literature, politics and international relations in Athens and London, was until recently a Research Fellow at the Centre for the Study of Democracy (CSD) at the University of Westminster. She was the European Research Manager of *The Future of Representative Democracy* project. Currently a doctoral candidate at the London School of Economics and Political Science, her principal research interests include photography, cinema and the ethics and politics of hospitality.

JOHN KEANE, born in Australia and educated at the universities of Adelaide, Toronto and Cambridge, is Professor of Politics at the University of Sydney and Research Professor at the Social Science Research Centre Berlin (WZB). In 1989 he founded the Centre for the Study of Democracy (CSD) in London and was recently a Leverhulme Major Research Fellow. His current research interests include the future of global institutions, communications and media decadence, fear, violence and democracy, the origins and future of representative government and the philosophy and politics of Islam. His latest publication is *The Life and Death of Democracy* (2009).

WOLFGANG MERKEL is Professor of Political Science at the Humboldt-Universität zu Berlin and member of the Berlin-Brandenburg Academy of Sciences, and is also the Director of the research unit 'Democracy: Structures, Performance, Challenges' at the Social Science Research Centre Berlin (WZB). His research focuses on political regimes, democracy and transformation, parties and party systems, comparative public policy, social justice and reform of the welfare state. He has recently edited (along with Sonja Grimm) *War and Democratization: Legality, Legitimacy and Effectiveness* (2009).

MICHAEL SAWARD is Professor of Politics at the Open University, and was Head of the Department of Politics and International Studies from 2004 to 2007. He has published widely in areas that are the focus of his research: the practical enactment of democratic values, rethinking the meaning of representation, re-engaging the study of political parties with democratic theory, and the terms and practices of citizenship. He plays a leading role in the EU Framework 7 funded programme ENACT (Enacting European Citizenship), and has recently edited the four-volume collection *Democracy: Key Concepts in Political Science* (2007).

PHILIPPE SCHMITTER is an Emeritus Professor at the European University Institute in Florence and also a Visiting Professor at the Central European University in Budapest. His current work focuses on the political characteristics of the emerging Euro-polity, on the consolidation of democracy in Southern and Eastern countries, and on the possibility of post-liberal democracy in Western Europe and North America. Member of many research committees and advisory boards, he has co-written (along with Alexander H. Trechsel) *The Future of Democracy in Europe: Trends, Analyses and Reforms* (2004).

NADIA URBINATI is Nell and Herbert M. Singer Professor of Contemporary Civilization and Professor of Political Theory at the Department of Political Science of Columbia University. Winner of the 2008–9 Lenfest/Columbia Distinguished Faculty Award, Nadia Urbinati specialises in modern and contemporary political thought and the democratic and anti-democratic traditions. She has recently published *Representative Democracy: Principles and Genealogy* (2006; paperback 2008) and co-edited an anthology of Giuseppe Mazzini's essays on democracy, nation building and international relations.

GREGOR WALTER-DROP is an Assistant Professor at the Center for Transnational Relations, Foreign and Security Policy at the Otto Suhr Institut for Political Science at the Freie Universität Berlin. Before joining the Freie Universität in October 2006, he served as Head of Curriculum Development at the Hertie School of Governance in Berlin. His research focuses on globalisation and governance as well as foreign policy analysis. He has recently published *Internetkriminalität – Eine Schattenseite der Globalisierung* (2008).

BERNHARD WESSELS is Senior Research Fellow at the Social Science Research Centre Berlin (WZB), and deputy director of its research unit 'Democracy'. He is a member of the planning committee of the *Comparative Study of Electoral Systems* (CSES), the steering committee of the EU 7th FP Project *PIREDEU – Electoral Democracy in Europe*, and co-director of the *German Longitudinal Election Study 2009–2017*. His main research fields are comparative studies on political representation and electoral behaviour. He is co-author of *Policy Representation in Western Democracies* (1999), and co-editor of *The European Parliament, the National Parliaments, and European Integration* (1999). He has recently co-edited *Wahlen und Wähler* (2005) and *Die Bundestagswahl 2005* (2007).

MICHAEL ZÜRN is a member of the Berlin-Brandenburg Academy of Sciences, and is the director of the department 'Transnational Conflicts and International Institutions' at the Social Science Research Centre Berlin (WZB). Before his move to the WZB and appointment as Dean of the Hertie School of Governance in Berlin, he was co-director of the DFG-Special Research Project, 'State in Transformation'. His research focuses on themes related to globalisation, its regulation through international institutions and their normative foundations, and his publications include *Law and Governance in Postnational Europe* (2005).

Acknowledgements

These reflections on representative democracy and its future are a product of the first systematic research programme on the subject for several decades. Planned during 2006, the framework of *The Future of Representative Democracy* project was first discussed in detail at an international colloquium held in December 2007, at the Social Science Research Centre Berlin (WZB). Following months of intensive correspondence and exchange of materials, the contributors met for a second time, during October 2008, at the Lisbon headquarters of the Calouste Gulbenkian Foundation. The Lisbon discussions proved vital in clarifying agreements and disagreements, and in re-shaping each contribution and the book as a whole. The end result we believe to be distinctive on four counts. First, this book is marked by a strong sense of the historicity of representative democracy, and of the general importance of the past for the present and future of democracy in representative form. Second, the book displays a strong awareness of the pressing need for clarifying key concepts such as representation, citizenship and democracy. Third, the contributors to the volume recognise the genuine advantages of breaking down barriers among research disciplines, as well as the utility of fostering a dialogue among scholars of political sociology and political theory, electoral studies and international relations, comparative political science and media and gender studies. Finally, the contributors to this volume are gripped by a strong sense that the subject of representative democracy and its future matters – that the neglected topic of democracy and representation is of worldwide scholarly and political importance.

The team efforts were assisted by many individuals and institutions. For generous financial and infrastructural support, we wish to thank the Calouste Gulbenkian Foundation; the Centre for the Study of Democracy (CSD) at the University of Westminster; the European Science Foundation; the Major Research Fellowship scheme of the Leverhulme Trust (UK); and the Social Science Research Centre Berlin (WZB). For helpful advice about the project and incisive critical running commentaries on our work in progress, we offer special thanks to Frank Ankersmit, Mark Warren and André Freire.

Our warmest gratitude is extended to the Programme Director of *The Future of Representative Democracy* project, Maria Fotou. Without her creative and tireless efforts this volume would certainly not have happened. Based at the Centre for the Study of Democracy, she worked during a three-year period to develop a strong communication network among editors and contributors. She also translated texts from various languages; provided comments and edited early drafts of a number of contributions; and helped prepare a website that contains additional scholarly materials for readers who are interested in pursuing the subject in further directions (see www.thefutureofrepresentativedemocracy.org). We thank her sincerely for her many intelligent contributions to the project – and her cheerful resilience during its most challenging moments.

Editors' introduction: Rethinking the future of representative democracy

Sonia Alonso, John Keane and Wolfgang Merkel

The fusion of representation and democracy

The invention of representative democracy is often said to be among the distinctive achievements of modern politics. It came as no easy victory. In its European homeland, it took seven centuries (and quite a few rebellions and revolutionary upheavals) to consolidate representative institutions. Church hierarchies had to be resisted in the name of true religion. Monarchs had to be brought under the control of assemblies. Legislatures then had to be subjected to democratic election, and in turn these democratic elements had to be grafted onto pre-democratic institutions of representation. The model of representative democracy that resulted is today familiar – within the European region, the United States, Chile, Japan, India and other countries – as a cluster of territorially bound governing institutions that include written constitutions, independent judiciaries and laws. These institutions guarantee such procedures as periodic election of candidates to legislatures, limited-term holding of political offices, voting by secret ballot, competitive political parties, the right to assemble in public and liberty of the press.

Compared with the previous assembly-based forms of democracy associated with the classical Greek world, representative democracy was different. The ancient world knew nothing of representation; it did not even have a word for it. The citizens of Athens, for instance, thought of their democracy as direct and participatory. Besides, it was highly exclusive and restricted to less than one-third of the population, with foreigners, slaves and women excluded from the *demos* (Meier 1995). Representation as a political language and set of institutions sprang in various and conflicting ways from the fields and towns of medieval Europe, but initially it had little or nothing to do with the egalitarian ethos of democracy. The practical fusion of democracy and representation did not begin to take place until the late sixteenth-century acts of resistance to monarchy in the Low Countries. It dates especially from

1

the time of the great American and French revolutions of the last quarter of the eighteenth century and the struggles they unleashed for the extension of the suffrage during the next two centuries (Pitkin 1967 and 2004; Dahl 1989; Keane 2009).

The invention of representative government and its subsequent democratisation was something of a marriage of convenience. The marriage was supposed to serve the cause of both representation and democracy by improving the effectiveness and legitimacy of government. It was certainly of epochal political importance. It greatly expanded the geographic scale of institutions of self-government; it also fundamentally altered the meaning of democracy. Representative democracy came to signify a type of government in which people, in their role as voters faced with a genuine choice between at least two alternatives, are free to elect others who then act in defence of their interests, that is, represent them by deciding matters on their behalf. Much ink and blood was to be spilled in defining what exactly representation meant, who was entitled to represent whom and what had to be done when representatives snubbed or disappointed those whom they were supposed to represent. But what was common to the new age of representative democracy that finally matured during the early years of the twentieth century was the belief that good government was government by representatives of the people.

Often contrasted with aristocracy and monarchy, representative democracy was praised by a wide spectrum of political writers and public figures. Thomas Jefferson, the Marquis de Condorcet and James Mill were among the best known defenders of the view that representative democracy was a way of governing better by openly airing differences of opinion – not only among the represented themselves, but also between representatives and those whom they are supposed to represent. Representative government was also hailed as an effective new method of apportioning blame for poor political performance; a new way of encouraging the rotation of leadership, guided by merit. Right from the beginning, some critics thought of it as a form of elected aristocracy, but that rather understated another claimed advantage of representative democracy: that it cleared space for political minorities and competition for power that in turn enabled elected representatives to test out their political competence in the presence of others. For those who disliked the restricted (male, property-owning) franchise and who therefore found these arguments suspect, the earliest champions of representative democracy also offered a more pragmatic justification of representation. It was seen as the practical expression of a simple reality: that it wasn't feasible for all of the people to be involved all of the time, even if they were so inclined, in the business of government. Given that reality, the people must delegate the task of government to representatives who are chosen at regular elections. The job of these representatives is to watch over the expenditure of public money, domestic and foreign policies, and all other actions of government. Representatives make representations on behalf of their constituents to the government and its bureaucracy. Representatives debate issues and make laws. They decide who will govern and how – on behalf of the people.

From the time of the birth of representative democracy, not everyone agreed that democracy could or should become representative. Jean-Jacques Rousseau was among the first to argue against the whole idea that democracy could become representative, in his view on the ground that the sovereign will of the whole people could never be authentically represented. According to Rousseau, either the representation of the will of the whole people was identical with that will, in which case it was an unnecessary redundancy; or it was not identical with that will and, hence, a rotten fiction. Parallel complaints against representative democracy subsequently resurfaced many times, for instance in the early decades of the twentieth century in the controversies over the future of parliaments (Schmitt 1923). According to these complainants, examined in Chapter 1 of this volume by Nadia Urbinati, democracy is inimical to representation. Democracy cannot be turned into representative democracy because representation entails an illegitimate transfer of power from the principal (the *demos*) to the agent (the representative). Such a transfer of power is impossible if those who are represented are in fact to remain sovereign. The only way for the sovereign body to keep its sovereignty is to interpret representation exclusively as an act of mere delegation, as a contract in which the representative receives an imperative mandate from the represented. According to such thinking, representative democracy is therefore a contradiction in terms: democracy, the direct form of decision making among equals par excellence, is combined with indirect decision making that supposes a hierarchy of competence, that is, representation.

These arguments still seem to have bite in some political circles. They are today making a comeback, as exemplified by the theorists and advocates of 'deep' or 'participatory' democracy and 'citizens' participation' and 'community involvement'; and, in a different and inverse way, by those who deem representative government to be a way of limiting the democratic impulse and controlling the masses. Contemporary works, such as those by Sheldon Wolin (2004: 599–602; 2008: 259–92) and Bernard Manin (1997: 237–8) argue clearly in this direction, admittedly with altogether different consequences. Wolin sees the egalitarian, power-levelling spirit of democracy as tied to no specific institutional form. It is episodic, an ephemeral process, a fugitive that can grip citizens' lives only in small-scale settings. Representation is the enemy of democracy in this sense. It frustrates collective action by splintering the *demos* and by disconnecting the exercise of power from its rightful source; an active *demos* is replaced by political professionals who protect powerful particular interests. Representation makes a mockery of the power-principle of democracy, majority rule: 'majorities are artifacts manufactured by money, organization and the media'. By contrast, but from within the same critical perspective, Manin carefully examines the historical evolution of the key features of modern democratic institutions. Considering representative democracy as a consciously chosen alternative to popular self-rule, Manin sees representation as a tempering device, as an experiment in amalgamating democratic and aristocratic components. Representative democracy is a balanced system of government. Although it is a substitute for the democratic principle of selection by lot, a principle that provides all individuals with an equal chance of governing, representative mechanisms centred on elections enable citizens periodically to remind representatives of their presence, to ensure (says Manin) that 'the chambers of government are not insulated from their clamour'. Yet elections produce definite 'aristocratic effects'; they reserve public office for 'eminent individuals whom their fellow citizens deem superior to others'.

Among the prominent arguments offered by all contributors to this book is the proposition that the critics of representative democracy, past and present, have failed to recognise that the grafting of representation onto democracy irreversibly changed the original meaning of both. Representation, once conceived by Hobbes and other political thinkers as simply equivalent to the actual or virtual authorisation of government, had to make room for equality, accountability and free elections. For its part, at least in theory, democracy had to find space for the process of delegation of decisions to others and, hence, open itself up to matters of public responsiveness and the public accountability of leaders. Democratic representation is a process of representing the interests and views of electors who are absent from the chambers and forums where decisions are made. Representatives decide things on behalf – and in the physical absence – of those who are affected. But that is only half of the complex, dynamic equation. For under conditions of democracy, those who are rendered absent from the making of decisions periodically step forward and make their presence felt by raising their hands in public, or by touching a screen or placing a cross on a ballot paper in private. Under democratic conditions, representation is a process of periodically rendering or making present what is absent; it is not simply (as Burke supposed) an act of delegation of judgements to the few trustees who make decisions on behalf of those whom they represent. Representation (ideally) is the avoidance of *misrepresentation*. Representation is accountability, an ongoing tussle between representatives who make political judgements and the represented, who themselves also make political judgements. The upshot of this dialectic is that representative democracy is a distinctive form of government that simultaneously distinguishes and links together the source of political power – the people or *demos* – and the use made of political power by representatives who are periodically chastened by the people whose interests they are supposed to serve (Maravall 2008: 12).

The act of responsibly deciding things on behalf of people under democratic conditions can be seen not only as an admission of the inescapability of representation in human affairs and, thus, the impossibility of so-called direct democracy. Something more is at stake: democratic representation can be seen as a marked improvement upon the key limitation of so-called direct democracy. In order to work, so-called direct democracy presumes the existence of a small political community of educated citizens with much time for politics and – a big presumption – a high degree of social and cultural homogeneity of the so-called sovereign people. On that basis, government and society are supposed to be identical, or at least capable of identification; the political representation of social interests is rendered redundant because citizens iron out their differences through ongoing deliberations and decisions that have the effect of renewing their political community. Representative democracy, by contrast, abandons the ancient fiction of a (potentially) homogeneous *demos*; it rejects the ideal of a general will in favour of the acceptance of a dynamic plurality of wills and judgements that are permanently contested and contestable, through processes of publicity, open election and the political representation of diverse social interests.

The contributors to this volume express different understandings of both representation and democracy, but they are nevertheless persuaded that a form of democracy based upon representation is the only type of government that gives open expression to the diversity that it makes possible in the first place. Quite often, those who analyse representative democracy present 'thin' accounts of its mode of operation by concentrating exclusively on the electoral procedures that enable the process of delegation of decision making to representatives. Elections are regarded as the essence of representative democracy, which is seen as an elitist form of government in which 'we are ruled by others,

but we select them and we replace them with our votes' (Manin *et al.*
1999: 4–5). The approach of this volume is different. It favours a 'thick'
understanding of democracy and representation by showing that representative democracy is based in fact not just on elections but on three
core elements: the open public expression of social needs and interests;
the appointment of representatives through free and fair election; and
the temporary granting of powers by the represented to representatives
who make laws within the framework of a written constitution. From
this perspective, representatives receive their political mandate from
the represented, through free and meaningful and lawful periodic elections. Yet from the perspective of representative democracy, elections
do not put an end to the representative process, as a narrowly electoral
conception of democracy would have us believe.

There are three reasons for this. First, the election of representatives
is a dynamic process subject to what can be called the disappointment
principle (Keane 2008). Elections are a method of apportioning blame
for poor political performance – a way of ensuring the rotation of leadership, guided by merit and humility, in the presence of electors equipped
with the power to trip leaders up and throw them out of office if and
when they fail, as often they do. Every election is as much a beginning
as it is an ending. The whole point of elections is that they are a means
of disciplining representatives who disappoint their electors, who are
then entitled to throw harsh words, and paper or electronic rocks, at
them. If representatives were always virtuous, impartial, competent and
responsive then elections would lose their purpose. Second, and obviously linked to the disappointment principle, is the fact that the process
of delegation that takes place through elections is plagued by a difficulty that is the subject of continuing controversy among the analysts
of representative democracy: whether elections are mainly a retroactive
means of punishing and rewarding governments, or whether instead
they are primarily a prospective mechanism for selecting good politicians (Fearon 1999). If elections are mainly a retrospective mechanism
then the conclusion follows that they are an ineffective way of continuously holding the elected accountable. A vast literature has clearly
demonstrated this ineffectiveness (Powell and Whitten 1993; Maravall
1999; Stokes 2003; Achen and Bartels 2004; Maravall and Sánchez-
Cuenca 2008) even though, as much empirical evidence also shows,
voters try hard to judge politicians retrospectively and their programs
prospectively (Manin *et al.* 1999). There is a third reason why elections
are not the be all and end all of representative democracy: the ability
of representatives to define and interpret the interests of the many they
represent depends upon a process of permanent contact and deliberation

between representatives and the represented. Representation always has a vicarious dimension: it implies a relationship between the representative and the represented that goes well beyond a pure and simple face-to-face contract.

Representation – ideally conceived – is an act of delegation whereby the represented grant to representatives the task of defending their interests, all the while insisting that they remain directly accountable to the represented for their actions. Political representation is not a process of issuing political mandates. Representatives do not receive direct daily instructions from the many they represent, and for that reason the former necessarily define and interpret the interests of the latter. It is this representative dimension that unavoidably stands at the heart of representative democracy – and that provides grist to the mill of its many critics, both old and new. In this respect, 'free and fair elections' and the time lapsed between elections matter greatly. So, too, does the access of citizens to their representatives; the free circulation of information and the level of information that is available to citizens; their participation in the deliberation of political issues; and, by no means of least importance, the ability of citizens to respond to the representative claims made by their representatives. The more pluralistic and high quality are the sources of information, and the more citizens participate in public life, the more representatives can be held accountable to the represented (Bühlmann *et al.* 2008).

A crisis of representative democracy?

The contributions to this book by David Beetham, Philippe Schmitter and Bernhard Wessels make clear that the three core elements of representative democracy – freedom of public expression, the electoral mandating of representatives and their lawmaking powers – are nowadays articulated through institutions that have become familiar fixtures in the house of representative democracy. These institutions include free media, electoral systems, political parties and parliaments. Because acts of political representation are inherently interpretative in character, and because they involve not just individuals but relationships among different groups, the existence of political parties is fundamental to the process of representation. So too are parliaments, which are supposed to resemble a marketplace of ideas and interests, the institutional space where political parties engage in a permanent process of contestation, mediation and compromise. The contributions of Sonia Alonso, John Keane, Michael Saward and Michael Zürn and Gregor Walter-Drop further remind us that representative democracy is also supposed to operate within the power container of states with clearly demarcated territorial boundaries, ruling over a population that functions (according to many observers) as a political community, the nation.

It is today still widely believed that the historic synthesis of democracy and representation served the cause of democracy by improving its practicability, effectiveness and legitimacy in larger territorial states. Given that in 1941 there were only eleven representative democracies left on the face of the earth, this is no small political achievement. Of course, there has always been a gap between the bold ideals of representative democracy and its complex, multi-layered and defective real world forms. Some contemporary observers (Fukuyama 2006) draw from this discrepancy the conclusion that expressions of dissatisfaction with 'liberal' representative democracy are normal; even that they are healthy reminders of the precious contingency of a form of good government that has no serious competitors. Other observers (Rosanvallon 1998; Crouch 2004; Ginsborg 2005) draw the opposite conclusion: euphoria is unwarranted, they say, because the mechanisms of representation that lie at the heart of existing democracies are under severe stress, and are triggering public concerns about the future of representative democracy itself. In democratic systems as different as the United States, India, Australia, Germany, Great Britain and Argentina, these analysts point to evidence of a creeping malaise – to signs that the core institutions of representation are either being trumped by increasing concentration of power in the executive branch of government; or sidelined by unaccountable bodies; or suspected or rejected outright by citizens and unelected representatives who cannot identify with these core institutions.

Several broad types of diagnosis of what is currently happening to representative democracies are examined in this volume. Some analysts point to the growing power of so-called guardian institutions and of processes of unelected representation – neo-corporatism in labour relations and economic policy, the rise of independent central banks and advisory councils of experts in the field of government are examples – that have begun to supplant elected government bodies (Pitkin 2004: 339). Others claim that the political asymmetry in the representation of interests and groups is hollowing out democracy's core principle of political equality (Crouch 2004; Dahl 2006). Still other observers draw upon Eurobarometer and other opinion polls in support of the view that several core institutions of representative democracy (elections, parties, parliaments) are losing public legitimacy. They point out that formal membership of political parties has dipped sharply (Dalton 2004; Schmitter and Trechsel 2004) and that voter turnout at elections is becoming more volatile, at least in those countries where it is optional. It is also noted that levels of trust in politicians and government are generally in decline; and that citizens have begun to spot the deformation of policy making by the private power of banks and other organised business interests, and by lobbyists. When considered together, these disparate trends have encouraged some analysts to conclude that representative democracy is breeding political disaffection. Others have argued that its ideals are themselves now under siege, even that we are heading towards an epoch of 'post-democracy'.

These claims about the decline, decay or disappearance of representative democracy have a sense of urgency about them, but how plausible are they? Among the distinctive features of this volume is that it launches a considered investigation of claims that representative democracy is breeding disaffection and may be in terminal decline. The research contributions presented below aim to evaluate the performance of present-day representative democracies by reconsidering not only their founding core principles, but also by using these principles to measure their current performance – and their possible twenty-first-century transformation into forms of democratic representation that defy textbook accounts of representative democracy.

There are certainly plenty of indicators in support of claims about an impending malaise of representative democracy. As already noted, elections, parties and parliaments, among the core institutions of representative democracy, are failing in the eyes of many citizens. The volatility of electoral turnouts is rising, albeit at different rates in different countries. Many citizens do not see elections as sufficiently robust instruments of control over their representatives. Electoral laws are sometimes manipulated in order to favour or guarantee particular outcomes; there are plenty of recorded cases where elections are so manipulated that they are emptied of real content. Despite the fact that citizens remain strongly interested in public affairs, they tend to be ill informed about the particular activities and policies of governments and their representatives. Political parties meanwhile find it increasingly difficult to attract the support of citizens. Membership figures have dropped dramatically and they are no longer major employers or protectors of the welfare of citizens. The corruption of party financing is ubiquitous. Cartel parties have corrosive effects by manoeuvring other political parties from the centres of electoral competition (Katz and Mair 1994). There is evidence, as David Beetham explains in Chapter 5, that parliaments are becoming increasingly unpopular, as a result, among other things, of their connection with party shenanigans, extreme partisanship (in the sense of sectarianism) and 'money politics'.

Bernhard Wessels reminds readers that not all these indicators apply to all countries, or with the same intensity. His reminder serves to highlight the point that the institutions of representative democracy are threatened not only by endogenous forces but by exogenous factors as well. Contemporary representative democracies are evidently not performing according to their own declared standards and values. Governments are failing to deliver the economic and social goods citizens expect. Economic and social inequalities have for some time been increasing throughout the OECD region – a trend that has assumed worldwide proportions with the onset of the global economic downturn. In addition, immigrants and ethnic minorities continue to be excluded from fair representation and decision-making processes; their demands and everyday problems are often neglected. Women remain grossly under-represented in political and, particularly, economic institutions. As the case of the United States after 9/11 shows, human rights are still sometimes abused in democratic polities; this is especially true in young and 'defective' electoral democracies where the rule of law is weakly developed (Merkel 2004). All these trends produce increasing dissatisfaction and outright disaffection with the performance of existing representative democracies. In his contribution to this volume, Klaus von Beyme shows that the history of representative democracy has been marked by ongoing disgruntlement and outright attacks on its defective forms. But he pays special attention to a new and serious challenge that confronts both consolidated and unconsolidated (and allegedly non-defective) representative democracies: populism. According to von Beyme, the weaknesses of representative democracy provide the ideal soil for the growth of either right-wing ethnopopulism in Europe or left-wing redistributional populism, as in Latin America. While he warns against the false temptation of so-called direct democracy, he shows that the embrace of populism as a governing strategy is a latent 'auto-immune disease' that thrives whenever wide gaps develop between the ideals and the functional reality of representative democracy. If 'the people' are unsatisfied and increasingly angry with their representatives, some leaders or groups are easily tempted to represent themselves as the saviours of the people, and to get their hands on governing institutions to govern in the name of the people, and for the people.

The fossilising of the conventional mechanisms of representative democracy and the practical violation of its core principles are not the only difficulties presently confronting this form of government. There are growing signs as well that representative democracy is now threatened by an inhospitable international situation. The so-called third wave of democratisation has stalled, giving way to the birth of a new type of regime, that of strongly guided, illiberal or defective democracies (Zakaria 1997; Merkel 2004; Keane 2009). The new, non-consolidated democracies in Eastern-Central Europe (e.g., Ukraine and Georgia), in Asia (e.g., Indonesia, Thailand) and in Latin America (e.g., Venezuela, Bolivia) are cases in point. Although they often enjoy a measure of pluralism and sometimes even fair elections, they are marked by corrupted political parties, grave deficiencies in the rule of law, malfunctioning or non-existent integrity systems, media unfreedom and by illiberal governing strategies. Strange as it may seem, representation and accountability are not the weakest parts of these regimes. Typically, these purely electoral democracies are in a sense 'over-representative', or 'pseudo-representative', in that they are excessively responsive to the real or imagined claims of the bulk of the population. The electoral and sometimes demagogic appeals of governments to the majority of the population are a direct response to certain needs of the population: the government of Putin's Russia represents widespread sentiments favouring a strong state and a 'managed democracy', while the left-wing populist policies of Hugo Chávez and Evo Morales are responses to the (self-perceived) interests of the majority of the society for a fair distribution of corporate profits and economic resources. These typically presidential regimes are in a sense responsive to the electorate; but they are undoubtedly less responsive to what is usually called pluralism, open media, the rule of law and other elements of the political common good. Their processes of representation are mixed with plebiscitary elements, with claims that representatives are 'soldiers of the people' (Chávez). Intermediary institutions, such as parties, interest groups and parliaments do not actively represent the will of the people; it is rather the *caudillo*, the president, the leader of the popular 'movement' that claims to represent the nation's will. This form of politics has more than a faint resemblance to the type of popular sovereignty proposed by Carl Schmitt (1923) in his infamous critique of the emerging representative parliamentary democracies of the early twentieth century. Plebiscitary or populist politics constitute pseudo-representation: based on claims that the direct and unfiltered will of the people is both honoured and implemented, such politics leads to the weakening and deinstitutionalisation of representative democracy itself.

The health problems of contemporary representative democracies are further complicated by the emergence of global powers – China and Russia – whose present leaders are clearly not committed to the ideals and institutions of representative democracy (Keane 2009). Contrary to Fukuyama's end of history speculations, these powers increasingly represent an alternative regime to the representative democracies of Asia and elsewhere. Though the contributors to this volume are generally persuaded that there are no normatively acceptable and practically viable alternatives to democratic representation in sight, emerging global realities may not care much for viability or normative considerations. The wider implication of the Chinese and Russian models of authoritarian state capitalism is clear: the so-called third wave of democratisation has failed to spread the model of representative democracy globally. With the striking exception of India, consolidated representative democracies are still geographically particular: very much confined within the OECD world.

The dysfunctions of representative democracy

Among the unusual features of our scholarly investigation of representative democracy is its suggestion that many current problems are intrinsic to the logic of representative democracy itself. In accordance with the already-mentioned disappointment principle, bellyaching against representative democracy is not new; indeed, it could even be said that frustration with democracy based on complaints about parties, parliaments and politicians who favour their own interests and fail to represent the real interests of the people are symptomatic of the widespread confusion in our times about the nature of democracy in representative form. The problem faced by representative democracies is not only that they produce self-interested politicians who neglect or violate their duties as representatives of the people. Representative democracies are also vulnerable to an auto-immune disease: a pathology that stems from the behaviour of politicians who try to correct such defects by representing their constituents too directly, for instance by pandering to the immediate interests of a supposed majority of voters. Representative democracy is currently under attack from two sides: from the twin weakness of being both 'under-responsive' and 'over-responsive' to electors. Under-responsiveness refers to the under-representation of the interests of people with a weak political voice and favouritism towards the rich and powerful who are equipped with the means of organising and articulating their interests, often at the expense of others. Over-responsiveness refers to the way neo-populist democracies in Latin America and elsewhere over-represent the immediate social interests of the majority of the population, and do so by disregarding or clamping down on the core institutions of representative democracy, including independent media and the rule of law.

Dissatisfaction and disaffection with representative democracy are however not just the result of confusion, or of an intellectual misunderstanding of the core principles of representative democracy. The disgruntlement is also the result of a widening gap between the problems linked to the malfunctioning procedures and poor substantive performance of representative democracies and the growing expectations harboured by most people, experts and general publics alike. People expect much more today from representative democracies than they did in the past, say, during the early years of the twentieth century. A century ago, in countries such as the United States, France and Britain, which were among the first to call themselves representative democracies, the range of functions performed by the state was rather limited and rights to vote had still not yet been extended to all adult men and women. Since the rebirth of democracy after World War Two, publics have become increasingly sensitive to the core principles of democracy; not surprisingly, these same publics demand, more strongly and sometimes more vociferously, that representative democracies must live up to the expectations they generate. At some point in its development, as Drude Dahlerup and Philippe Schmitter show below, representative democracy stopped being just a procedure for selecting and rotating elites. The *what* of representation (i.e., which interests are represented) and the *who* of representation (i.e., who participates in the selection of representatives, and who becomes a representative) gained at least as much relevance as the *how* of representation that relied upon freedom of the press, multi-party competition and fair elections.

The growth of *who* questions on the political agenda certainly adds to the pressures on representative democracies to perform well. Many representative democracies are today moving from limited towards more complex and controversial notions of citizenship. According to the standard definitions, Alonso notes, two dominant visions of citizenship have serious implications for the functional legitimacy of representative democracy. According to territorial definitions of citizenship (*ius solis*), the status of being a citizen comes with being born within the territory of the *demos*. By contrast, ethnic visions of citizenship (*ius sanguinis*) require that people be born of citizens who already belong to the *demos*. According to both definitions, people who are residing within a territory temporarily, for instance as tourists or as family visitors or on business, should not be considered citizens with rights of representation and participation in the government of the state. But what about those immigrants who come to live permanently within the borders of a state? Should they be excluded from membership? If they are, who then represents their interests, and how? In a world in which large-scale migration has become a global phenomenon, the conflicting criteria for who rightly belongs to the *demos* have pressing consequences for the quality of representative democracy. It is often pointed out that the 'modern nation-state system has regulated membership in terms of one principal category: national citizenship' (Benhabib 2004: 1) and, as a consequence, that 'citizenship is an immensely powerful instrument of social closure' (Brubaker 2004: 141). But, says Alonso, the fact of being a member of a *demos* has a troubling flipside. What about those who are already formally incorporated within a *demos* but who do not wish any longer to belong to it, preferring to belong to another *demos*? When people are granted a particular membership of a polity by default, that is, by the natural fact of being born into the territory that defines such membership, and when those same people do not feel part of the political community so defined, they will tend to draw the political conclusion that they are not represented by the so-called representative institutions and instead give their support to separatist and irredentist movements.

The tricky and controversial matter of *who* belongs to the category of the represented is compounded by the addition of *what* questions to the agenda of representative democracies. Representative democracies are experiencing a long-term shift from limited state functions toward a very wide range of government policies that include such complex matters as investment and banking; gender equality; the inclusion of cultural, ethnic and religious minorities; the protection of different lifestyles and values; social justice and urban regeneration; global justice, and the protection of the planetary biosphere. The growing number of *what* questions serves to increase greatly the expectations of publics. Amounting to something like a long-term revolution from limited to enhanced enfranchisement, *what* questions propel a dramatic expansion of the scope and power of government administration. By nurturing an ever-wider range of state prerogatives, *what* questions also greatly complicate – and potentially obfuscate – the lines of open and contestable representation between governors and the governed.

The future of representative democracy

What (if anything) can be done about these various dysfunctions of representative democracy? Where can things be done, and by whom? Answers to these questions are not straightforward, but it is clear that civil societies, politicians and governments are not sitting on their hands while watching events unfold before their eyes. Things are happening; the further democratisation of otherwise stable representative democracies is under way, albeit through reforms and policy innovations that are unevenly distributed across time and place. This book documents some of the most pertinent reforms and innovations that are taking place in many representative democracies, in response to their alleged performance and legitimacy difficulties. It reveals that degrees of success vary and that not everyone is in agreement that piecemeal institutional reforms will change things for the better. The contributions of Schmitter, Wessels, Beetham, Dahlerup and Alonso show that many reforms focus either on the core institutions of representative democracy (elections, parliaments and parties) or on the structures of state institutions, and that they have one thing in common: they are all intended to make institutions more inclusive, publicly transparent and accountable – in a phrase often used by their champions, more 'representative' and more 'democratic'.

This volume offers several examples of the efforts that are under way to deal with the dashed expectations and defects of representative democracy. Using the method of comparing the performance and deficits of political representation in existing democracies with both their core principles and voters' evaluations of the institutional mechanisms of democratic representation, across a wide number of countries, Bernhard Wessels draws mainly optimistic conclusions. From the contrasting points of view of elected representatives and voters, he argues, the state of political representation in the democratic world, in aggregate terms, is not as bad as the proponents of the crisis scenario make out. He does however concede that there is one weak link within the institutional mechanisms of representation: elections. There is much empirical evidence that shows that voters do not see elections as serving political representation well; this misgiving, he argues, directly affects the legitimacy of representative democracy. Wessels concludes that there remains room for political manoeuvre, and that the mechanisms of representative democracy are capable of applying their own self-correcting instruments so as to bring about the reform of electoral institutions that would simultaneously increase their representativeness and legitimacy.

David Beetham examines the prospects for the reform of parliaments in contemporary representative democracy, starting with a negative note: citizens place them at the bottom of the list of institutions that deserve their confidence or esteem. Beetham explains why this is so and considers the efforts undertaken by parliaments to address these issues, and to implement innovations. He draws the strong conclusion that although parliaments are dogged by numerous problems, they remain of vital importance for the present and future of democratic representation. A 'competitive executive democracy' without strong and effective parliaments would be an 'unacceptably thin version of democracy', he says; and he therefore concludes that parliaments need to be regenerated in various ways, including the adoption of list proportionality voting arrangements, strengthening parliamentary supervision of foreign policy and experiments with youth and 'virtual' parliaments. Beetham also issues a warning: the experiments that are currently under way, with fostering new extra-parliamentary ways of engaging citizens in politics, may serve in reality to further weaken the power of parliaments and to increase the levels of public alienation from politics that they are designed to reduce.

The systematic under-representation of women is another issue targeted in this volume. In her analysis of the evolution of women's representation since the early days of representative democracy, Drude Dahlerup pays special attention to the mechanisms for engendering democracy that have mushroomed during recent decades. She shows that women are demanding more from representative democracy than they did fifty years ago. To be democratic, representative democracy must be inclusive and, with respect to women, this means a politics of forceful presence and not just the formal recognition of rights. She argues that it is not enough that procedurally representative democracy follows the norms of free and fair periodic elections backed by freedom of communication and the rule of law. Civil societies expect more from representative democracy. Legitimacy does not rest exclusively with procedures. The increased relevance of the issue of women's representation in politics is a reflection of this change of expectations, and no democracy can possibly claim legitimacy today if it does not pay attention to women – and to the problem of 'grey men's clubs' (a phrase used in Norway by the proponents of women's compulsory representation on the boards of public limited companies, enacted in 2003). Empirically, this point is underlined by the sudden growth of quotas and other institutional reforms directed at increasing the visible representation of women in democratic institutions, such as parliaments and political parties, all over the world.

Questions centred on the under-representation of national minorities lie at the heart of the contribution by Sonia Alonso. Against a long tradition of scholarship that has supposed that multinational representative democracies are a contradiction in terms, she shows that minority nationalism is not necessarily an obstacle to the stability of democracy in representative form. Alonso describes how minority nationalism in Europe has grown stronger, not weaker, during recent decades. And although there are still places, such as Northern Ireland and South

Tyrol, where dual national identities continue to be rare, she demonstrates that the growth of plural national identities is moving representative democracy away from its traditional dependence on the nation state into new multinational state forms. She explains that this trend has gathered pace because of representative democracy, and not in spite of it. She goes on to argue that representative democracy is the only system that makes possible the cohabitation, in conditions of equality and freedom, of different national identities within the same state. She urges that the cohabitation of democracy and (minority) nationalism is best guaranteed by the establishment of multiple or compound forms of representation, for instance through the federalisation of state power. Under such conditions, territorial representation becomes as important as the representation of individual citizens; minority nationalists are encouraged to give up their defence of a type of political representation that is ethnically based in favour of representation that is territorially based. As a result, membership of one nation ceases to exclude membership of another. Dual national identities gather strength. Spain is the most obvious example of this, but not the only one. Alonso points out how dual identities are also presently flourishing in Scotland and Wales (Ishiyama and Breuning 1998), in Italy (Tambini 2001) and in Belgium ('the typical Belgian citizen – Walloon or Flemish – holds multiple identities' [Hooghe 2004: 16]). The same trend is evident even in Jacobin France, where 'regional and national identities are not felt as mutually exclusive', so that in places like Brittany and Alsace 'a massive majority feels a sense of belonging to both territorial levels' (Schrijver 2004: 201).

A new ecology of democratic representation?

The reform of electoral mechanisms and parliamentary assemblies, and the strengthened role of women and national minorities within the mechanisms of democratic representation, are evidently important ingredients of the rejuvenation of representative democracy. Discretionary voting, lotteries for electors and vouchers for financing political parties are among other possible reforms suggested by Philippe Schmitter. These suggestions undoubtedly deserve further consideration and practical experimentation, but other contributors to this volume go further: they interpret the various experiments being conducted on representative democracy as symptomatic of its mutation into unfamiliar forms. They suggest that what we are witnessing is not so much a crisis of representative democracy as its transformation into something new. In his chapter, Michael Saward prepares the ground for this rethinking by pointing out that the state-centred model of representative democracy, with its formal reliance upon elections, parties, parliaments, a free press and a written constitution, by no means exhausts the potential of democratic representation. Representative practices are flourishing underneath and beyond states, for instance within the complex institutional networks of civil society. The ecology of democratic representation is rapidly changing; so too are the conventional meanings of constituency and the rhythm of representation, neither of which are still tied exclusively to geographically defined constituencies and periodic election cycles. Plausible claims by leaders and groups that they are representative, despite the fact that they are unelected, are surfacing in a widening set of locations, often on an ad hoc basis, using a richer repertoire of non-state and non-elected criteria, including (for instance) professional expertise, common decency, commitment to human rights, and celebrity. In this sense, Saward concludes, we are 'not so much dealing with a threat to representative democracy', but rather with 'the potential evolution of democracy across the wider canvas of democratic representation'.

Zürn and Walter-Drop reinforce this perspective by highlighting the contemporary flourishing of cross-border mechanisms for representing interests and making and enforcing decisions. They insist that in principle there is no necessary clash between 'effective problem-solving through international institutions' and 'democratic political processes'. Zürn and Walter-Drop admit that global realities are more dismal than textbook descriptions of representative democracy and its principles. The long-distance chains of representation that link citizens to global institutions like the G20, the United Nations and the World Bank are very long indeed. States are the most powerful actors within these institutions; and, not surprisingly, most citizens, far from thinking of themselves as members of a transnational *demos*, feel rather distant from global institutions whose power to shape the lives of hundreds of millions of people is normally unchecked by elections and parliaments, or for that matter by any other form of citizens' input. Zürn and Walter-Drop nevertheless point to important counter-trends, for instance the evident growth of global non-governmental organisations that demand their rights of representation, and new signs that the arguing and bargaining that routinely takes place in global institutions is strengthening a shared sense of solidarity, that is, a mutual willingness among representatives to comply with decisions and (implicitly) to recognise the rights of others who are currently not represented. These counter-trends, they conclude, give hope to the possibility of democratising acts of representation, for instance through public forums, the 'enfranchisement' of NGOs, regional parliaments (such as the European Parliament) and other innovative reforms.

Robyn Eckersley illustrates another important development at the global level, one that has equally radical implications for the inherited understanding of how representation is supposed to work under democratic conditions. She concentrates on the growth of efforts to represent (non-human) nature by persuading citizens and elected representatives that animals, plants and whole landscapes are worthy of human protection and care. She shows that efforts to publicly represent the biosphere are challenging the boundaries of representative democracy, in effect by demanding recognition of hitherto neglected constituencies and unrepresented interests. Eckersley questions the anthropocentrism of standard models of representative democracy: their presumption that it is persons, or their interests, identities or places of residence, that are the only proper object of representation. She works through a wide range of conflicting views on the subject of non-human nature. Eckersley goes on to show just how complicated and fraught is the task of framing convincing accounts of the relationship between human and non-human nature; and she provides a warning that nature advocacy must steer clear of questionable views, such as the idea that nature is a passive substance, or that it can be freely acted upon as a mere resource for human ends. 'Whenever we represent nature,' she concludes, 'we unwittingly or otherwise, also represent ourselves, and the sort of world we wish to inhabit.'

John Keane's contribution attempts to combine these innovative perspectives by proposing a fundamental revision of the way we currently think about democracy and representation. This revision pinpoints an epochal transformation that is taking place in the contours and dynamics of representative democracy in countries otherwise as different as the United States and India, France and Japan. He gives special priority to long-term processes of institutional innovation in the decades since 1945, which have witnessed the invention of approximately one hundred new devices for the public monitoring and control of power. Public interest litigation, participatory budgeting, truth and reconciliation bodies, integrity commissions, carbon councils, workplace co-determination, weblogs, democracy cafés, cross-border open methods of coordination, summits, citizens' assemblies and many other experiments now form part of the political landscape of actually existing democracies. Keane pays attention to the historical novelty of these inventions, which in his view prompt novel questions: might some parts of the world – the European Union is naturally an important test case – be living through an historic transformation of democracy? He calls into question 'end of history' perspectives and maritime metaphors (Huntington's 'third wave' of the sea simile has been the most influential), both of which are seen to be much too bound to the surface of things, too preoccupied with continuities and aggregate data, to notice that political tides have begun to run in entirely new directions. The claim is that from roughly the mid-twentieth century our world has been living through an historic sea change, one that is taking us from the old world of representative democracy in territorial state form towards a form of 'monitory democracy' defined by the multiplication and dispersal of many different power-monitoring and power-contesting mechanisms, both within the 'domestic' fields of government and civil society and beyond, in cross-border settings that were once dominated by empires, states and business organisations. Concentrating on the growth of communicative abundance, the media saturation of societies, Keane raises questions about the causes and causers of this new historical form of democracy, its advantages and disadvantages, and why it has fundamental research implications for how we think and practice representative forms of democracy in the coming decades.

When all is said and done, what does the future hold for representative democracy as we have known it for a generation? Klaus von Beyme tables the possibility that citizens and representatives, elected and unelected alike, may well have to get used to the melancholia induced by the wide gaps that currently exist between the promise and performance of democratic representation. Ankersmit (2008) warns that there are good reasons for being worried about the present predicaments facing representative forms of democracy. Despite their impressive performance in the decades after World War Two, democracies are confronted by new endogenous threats and exogenous troubles that seriously hamper their adequate functioning. He shows that a good case can be made for tackling these threats with new and effective solutions that draw on creative analyses and empirically based discussions of the kind that are presented in this book. Yet he also considers the sobering thought that we are living through times that point towards the obsolescence of representative democracy. He points out that history offers no eternal, time-transcendent certainties. He suggests that it is therefore probable that in a thousand years – roughly the time it took a comprehensive working model of representative democracy to mature – democracy as it came to be described in the textbooks of twentieth-century political science will be a thing of the past, along with other dead forms of political rule that include papal autocracy, royal absolutism, enlightened despotism, Caesarism, fascism and communism.

Pulled in various directions by negative and positive trends, does democracy in representative form have a future? The nineteenth-century American poet and writer Walt Whitman famously noted that the history of democracy could not be written because representative democracy as he and others knew it was not yet properly built. From the standpoint of the early twenty-first century, and the possible emergence of a more complex understanding and practice of democratic representation, the same point is put differently in this volume: we do not know what will become of representative democracy because its fate has not yet been determined.

REFERENCES

Achen, C. and L. Bartels (2004) 'Blind retrospection: Electoral responses to drought, flu and shark attacks', *Working Paper 2004/199*, Madrid: Instituto Juan March.

Ankersmit, F. (2008) 'On the future of representative democracy', available at www.thefutureofrepresentativedemocracy.org

Benhabib, S. (2004) *The rights of others: Aliens, residents and citizens.* New York: Cambridge University Press.

Brubaker, R. (2004) *Ethnicity without groups.* Harvard University Press.

Bühlmann, M., W. Merkel and B. Wessels in collaboration with L. Müller (2008) *The quality of democracy: Democracy barometer for established democracies.* Zürich: National Center of Competence in Research (NCCR Democracy 21), Working Paper No. 10a, revised version March 2008.

Crouch, C. (2004) *Post democracy (themes for the 21st century).* Cambridge: Polity Press.

Dahl, R. A. (1989) *Democracy and its critics.* New Haven, CT: Yale University Press.

(2006) *On political equality.* New Haven, CT: Yale University Press.

Dalton, R. (2004) *Democratic challenges, democratic choices: The erosion of political support in advanced industrial democracies.* New York and Oxford: Oxford University Press.

Fearon, J. (1999) 'Electoral accountability and the control of politicians: Selecting good-types versus sanctioning good performance', in Manin, Przeworski and Stokes (eds.), pp. 55–97.

Fukuyama, F. (2006) *The end of history and the last man.* New York and London: Free Press.

Ginsborg, P. (2005) *The politics of everyday life: Making choices, changing lives.* New Haven, CT and London: Yale University Press.

Hooghe, L. (2004) 'Belgium: Hollowing the center', in U. Amoretti and N. Bermeo (eds.) *Federalism and territorial cleavages.* Baltimore: Johns Hopkins University Press, pp. 55–92.

Ishiyama, J. T. and M. Breuning (1998) *Ethnopolitics in the new Europe.* Boulder, CO and London: Lynne Rienner Publishers.

Katz, R. S. and P. Mair (eds.) (1994) *How parties organize: Change and adaptation in party organizations in western democracies.* London: Sage.

Keane, J. (2008) 'Hypocrisy and democracy', *WZB-Mitteilungen* 120 (June): 30–2.

(2009) *The life and death of democracy.* London: Simon & Schuster.

Manin, B. (1997) *The principles of representative government.* Cambridge University Press.

Manin, B., A. Przeworski and S. Stokes (eds.) (1999) *Democracy, accountability and representation.* Cambridge University Press.

Maravall, J. M. (1999) 'Accountability and manipulation', in Manin, Przeworski and Stokes (eds.), pp. 154–96.

(2008) *La confrontación política.* Madrid: Taurus.

Maravall, J. M. and I. Sánchez-Cuenca (2008) *Controlling governments: Voters, institutions, and accountability.* Cambridge University Press.

Meier, C. (1995) *Athen. Ein neubeginn der weltgeschichte.* München: Goldmann Verlag.

Merkel, W. (2004) 'Embedded and defective democracies', *Democratization* 11(5): 33–58.

Pitkin, H. (1967) *The concept of representation.* Berkeley: University of California Press.

(2004) 'Representation and democracy: An uneasy alliance', *Scandinavian Political Studies* 27(3): 335–42.

Powell, G. B. and G. Whitten (1993) 'A cross-national analysis of economic voting: Taking account of the political context', *American Journal of Political Science* 37(2): 391–414.

Rosanvallon, P. (1998) *Le peuple introuvable: Histoire de la représentation démocratique en France.* Paris: Gallimard.

Schmitt, C. (1923) *Die geistesgeschichtliche lage des heutigen parlamentarismus.* Berlin: Duncker & Humblot (7th edn. 1991).

Schmitter, P. and A. Trechsel (2004) *The future of democracy in Europe: Trends, analyses and reforms.* A Green Paper for the Council of Europe. Strasbourg: Council of Europe Publishing.

Schrijver, F. J. (2004) 'Electoral performance of regionalist parties and perspectives on regional identity in France', *Regional & Federal Studies* 14(2): 187–210.

Stokes, S. (2003) *Mandates and democracy.* New York: Cambridge University Press.

Tambini, D. (2001) *Nationalism in Italian politics: The stories of the Northern League 1980–2000.* London and New York: Routledge.

Wolin, S. S. (2004) *Politics and vision: Continuity and innovation in western political thought.* Expanded edition, Princeton and Oxford: Princeton University Press.

(2008) *Democracy incorporated: Managed democracy and the specter of inverted totalitarianism.* Princeton and Oxford: Princeton University Press.

Zakaria, F. (1997) 'The rise of illiberal democracy', *Foreign Affairs* 76(6), November/December: 22–43.

1 Representative democracy and its critics

Nadia Urbinati

The democracy of the moderns

The term 'representative democracy' conveys the complexity, richness and uniqueness of the political order of the moderns, an original synthesis of two distinct and in certain respects alternative political traditions. 'Democracy', a Greek word with no Latin equivalent, stands for direct rule ('getting things done') by the people. Representation, a Latin word with no Greek equivalent, entails a delegated action on the part of some on behalf of someone else.[1] As a mixture of these two components, in its standard meaning representative democracy has four main features: (a) the sovereignty of the people expressed in the electoral appointment of the representatives; (b) representation as a free mandate relation; (c) electoral mechanisms to ensure some measure of responsiveness to the people by representatives who speak and act in their name; and (d) the universal franchise, which grounds representation on an important element of political equality.[2] The central element of this standard account is that constituencies are formally defined by territory, not economic or corporate interests or cultural identities, an aspect that has belonged to democracy since Cleisthenes' reform of *demes* in Athens during the sixth century BCE: 'in almost every democracy in the world, citizens are represented by where they live' (Rehfeld 2005: 3). This basic formal equality in the distribution of voting power among adult citizens gives the mark of authorisation and legitimacy to a government that relies upon consent, yet not on the direct presence by the people in the lawmaking process.

---

[1] See Ober (2008). The noun *dēmokratia* seems to have a history traceable to its Myceanean invention and the assembly form with which it is associated has older and Eastern origins: John Keane, *The Life and Death of Democracy* (2009). Concerning the lack of the word democracy in the Latin language and the differences between Greek and Roman political traditions and institutions, see Dunn (2005, in particular pp. 23–70).

[2] See Urbinati and Warren (2008: 389). For an historical overview of the evolution of representative government after the French revolution see Klaus von Beyme, Chapter 2 in this book.

Since representative democracy is first and foremost the name of a form of government, reference to people's sovereignty and authorisation is essential, not accessory (Habermas 1996: 462–515). Electoral representation is for this reason crucial in expressing the will of the people, even if the claims of elected officials to act in the name of the people unavoidably become an object of contestation by citizens. This tension is at the core of representation but it also accounts for the complexity of representative democracy. Representation is the locus of the dynamics that keep modern democracy in motion and the political process that activates the communication between state institutions and society. Thus, although political representation starts with elections, because it starts with the equal distribution of voting power, a merely electoral rendering of representative democracy does not exhaust the meaning of representation and democracy. Nor does it exclude the possibility of a different approach and also different institutional solutions. Far from a homogenous category, representative government can be best described as a complex and pluralistic family whose democratic wing is not the exclusive property of those who argue for participation against representation and its representative wing is not the exclusive property of those who identify it with the electoral selection of an elite against popular participation.

Elections simultaneously separate and link citizens and government. They create a gap between state and society at the same time as they allow them to communicate and even conflict, but never fuse. As the only institutional site of popular will and the point of contact between parliament and the extra-parliamentary realm, elections can be seen from different political angles. They can be used to recreate the body of the sovereign at the symbolic and institutional level, thereby dampening social and political conflicts, and periodically restoring the balance between legitimacy and legality. They can also serve as a provisional truce between the institutional powers and the sovereign that keeps the conflict alive yet never creates a stable balance between the two. Or, as the history of European socialist parties shows, they can serve as a substitute for revolution, a legalised battle that, while deradicalising social claims, performs the civic function of educating the formerly excluded to citizenship and making them identify with the nation.

Whatever role elections have played in practice, in theory popular mobilisation is contingent upon the existence of exceptional political circumstances; but the aim of elections is to make people's direct participation inessential to the performance of deliberative institutions. As a matter of fact, the deterrent power of elections lies in their ability to stimulate decisional activism among those who can be held

accountable: the representatives, not the people. To put things paradoxically, elections make apathy, not agency, the main quality of popular sovereignty. A *post factum* strategy of control, they make citizens'
participation during the period between elections superfluous and in
this sense make democracy an accessory to representative government.
Politicians are sufficiently constrained by their concern with polls.[3]
Their ambiguous character explains why elections make representative
government amenable to democratisation but never truly democratic.

The dilemma remains. If elections alone qualify representative government as democratic then it is hard to find good arguments against
the critics of contemporary democracy who, from the left and the right,
set out from time to time to unmask the role of the people as a 'mere
myth'. It would be just as hard to devise criteria to detect and obstruct
the oligarchic degeneration and corrupting practices of representative
institutions. The very proposal to extend the meaning of democratic
deliberation to include the informal discursive character of a pluralistic
public sphere of associations, political movements and opinions, risks
looking like an ideological refurbishment, functional to the new communicative strategies for selecting elites. Indeed, it is a fact that only
the elected have both deliberative and decision-making power, unlike
citizens, whose freedom to discuss and criticise proposals and policies
does not ensure that their opinions will affect the legislative setting.

Yet notwithstanding the fact that the history of representative government resembles a story that has not been substantially edited since
its institutional beginning in the eighteenth century, the adoption of
universal suffrage has produced radical changes that cannot be appre-
ciated unless we review the overall political life generated by the representative process. Democratic society brings to light the limits of a
conception of representation as an individual-to-individual relation
between the candidate and the electors sealed by elections. It reveals,
as we shall see below, the limits of a conception that rests on the for-
malistic element of authorisation and on a juridical interpretation of
representation as an agent/principal relation.

A democratic theory of representation compels us to go beyond the
intermittent and discrete series of electoral instants (sovereign as the
authorising *will*) and investigate the *continuum* of influence and power
created and recreated by political *judgement* and the way this diversi-
fied power relates to representative institutions.[4] As a matter of fact,

---

[3] For a discomforting analysis of the unavoidable limits of political accountability in
contemporary representative democracies see Dunn (1999).
[4] Dahl hinted at this extension of the conception of democracy (1971: 20–1).

'a people of electors by itself is not capable of initiative, but at most of consent'; yet a representative democracy is not a consenting 'crowd of inorganic voters' (Cochin 1979: 80–1). Political parties and movements are the means citizens create to give their political presence an effective and persistent character through time. Their strength and social rootedness signal the strength of democratic representation.

While it is true that the will cannot be represented, as Jean-Jacques Rousseau argued, judgement can be. Political judgement is an essential faculty in a political order based on speech, majority rule and indirect politics. Approaching representation and participation from the perspective of judgement, rather than simply the authorising will, makes us fully appreciate the worth and problems of indirectness in democratic politics. Indirectness (and speech as its highest form) makes room for an informal participation and non-electoral kinds of representation. It also encourages the formation of political associations and parties, which can organise citizens' participation and ensure that their influence is not episodic and scattered. Representative democracy is thus the name of a type of government that starts with elections but develops beyond them. It opens up a domain of participation that, although informal and not authoritative, can deeply influence the political direction of a country.

The democratic *process* of representation is the most original aspect of the form of government of the moderns. As a process, it is permanently open to solutions that may not please us: it may encourage democracy's self-creation and improvement but also forms of elitist pressure by organised interests or the populistic manipulation of the general opinion by private potentates and tycoons. To fully grasp this complexity and confront the problems awaiting the future of representative democracy, democratic theory has to transcend the classical conception of popular sovereignty by which democracy has been identified since the beginning of modernity. It has to reinterpret popular sovereignty as a *diarchy* of will and judgement, and thus the source of an endogenous tension between institutionalised power and extra-institutionalised power, or between state institutions and citizens' participation. Stressing the role of political judgement entails recuperating the *negative power* the sovereign people retains as a power to investigate, influence and censure their lawmakers and laws. This negative power, which Pierre Rosanvallon has recently named 'counter-democracy', undergoes an important transformation in democratic thought and practice that pertains to the understanding of representation as a democratic process and institution rather than a violation of democracy (Pettit 2003: 138–62; Rosanvallon 2006: 21).

As historians have copiously demonstrated, and we shall explain below, representation emerged in the Middle Ages within the juristic tradition. Its genesis accounts for its mix of private (*Vertretung* or legal representation in court) and political (*Repräsentation* or representation in government) elements. Thus, on the one hand, representation conveys the idea of somebody being authorised to act or speak for somebody (the Latin word *re-presentare* means to make something manifest or present). On the other hand, it conveys the idea of the representative forming a unitary will that did not exist before.[5] From this dual nature another duality arises: the fact that representation has both a passive and active character. In the juristic tradition, the representative is unavoidably related to the represented not only because he depends upon the latter's designation or choice but also because he is under the inspection or monitoring surveillance of the represented. Hans-Georg Gadamer has highlighted the surplus of action created by representation:

> The important thing about the legal idea of representation is that the *persona repraesentata* is only the person represented, and yet the representative, who is exercising the former's right, is dependent on him (Gadamer 2004: 141, note 250)

Representation designates a relation of *interdependence* that brings to the fore a novel kind of liberty, one that does not need to be associated with the agent's direct action or presence in the place where decisions are made, as was the case in ancient democracy. The sources of representation's richness and faults rest precisely in its complex relation to political autonomy. No one else was able to render this tension better than Immanuel Kant, who was not only the philosopher who categorically defined the concept of freedom as exit from tutelage or autonomy, but also the political theorist who declared representation an essential condition for constitutional government. Kant was aware that representation made autonomous persons (citizens) trust someone else to act on their behalf, more or less like individuals, such as children, women, servants and aliens, who were declared in need of tutelage by the civil authority.[6] Not surprisingly, as Klaus von Beyme points out in his chapter, critics of representative democracy have turned precisely to direct presence as the unavoidable condition of political autonomy when they wanted to stress the ambiguous nature of this form of government.

---

[5] On the use of representation as a device to create the state's *persona ficta*, see Skinner (2002: 177–208).

[6] Accarino (1999: 17–18). I discuss Kant's conceptualisation of representation and how he opposed it to servile dependence in Urbinati (2006, chap. 3).

In the remainder of this chapter I shall revisit two classical arguments against the idea that democracy can become representative. These arguments pivot around two intertwined issues, one pertaining to the identity of the sovereign and the character of sovereign politics, and the other to the relationship of power that representation establishes. On the one hand, representation has been accused of surreptitiously producing a transfer of power from the principal to the agent. On the other, representative democracy has been seen as oxymoronic precisely because liberty cannot bear indirectness and cannot be disassociated from the will. Although the acquisition of representation to democratic vocabulary is today undisputed, so that we speak interchangeably of democracy and representative democracy, these criticisms are not obsolete. To some, 'democratic theory has little to gain from talking the language of representation'; its main concern should be citizens' 'opportunity' 'to practice direct democracy' in a representative system, rather than representation itself.[7] More recently, and from a very different perspective, Bernard Manin has re-emphasised the undemocratic character of representation and resumed the argument of Carl Schmitt, who in the late 1920s defined representative government as a mixed constitution. With this definition, Schmitt followed Aristotle and, especially, Montesquieu, the theorist of moderate government who made the idea of the incompatibility of democracy and representation an ironclad maxim (Schmitt 1928, § 16: IV, 2, 251; Manin 1997: 236).

Different as they are, both idealist views and realist approaches to democracy rely – whether explicitly or not – on a conception of democracy that is based on a simple idea of political equality and liberty, tailored to the model of a direct sovereignty of the will. Yet the history of modern democracy is characterised by a gradual integration of elements such as representation, political parties and deliberative public opinion that, while not democratic in themselves, work together in a system of government that is permeable to political equality and able to absorb the transformation of politics it engenders.[8] The analysis of these criticisms should prompt us to reclaim the distinctiveness of representative

---

[7] Mayo (1960: 103); Pennock (1983: 5). Even more critical is Barber (1984: 145), who declares representation 'incompatible with political freedom'.

[8] David Stasavage has conducted interesting research on active representative assemblies in European small and large states between 1250 and 1750. The conclusion of his research shows that, although one cannot refer to those representative institutions as democratic, they had important positive effects on financial credit because they served as 'a mechanism by which creditors could monitor and influence state financial decisions' (*The Rise of Political Representation and the Problem of Public Credit in Europe, 1250–1750*, draft manuscript, p. 6).

democracy and interrogate our political institutions from the perspective of their consistency with democratic values and principles.

Representation, pluralism and legitimacy

In an illuminating comparative study of republican forms of government, Scipione Maffei, writing in 1736, maintained that representation's functions of containment and unification could also be found in the Roman Empire (Maffei 1979: 51–5). Maffei relied on Tacitus, who had described the parliamentary gatherings in which the German tribes used to collect their claims before sending them to the Roman Senate. Representation unified the large territory of the Empire by creating a federative system in which communities ruled themselves on issues pertaining to the government of their localities, while submitting to the central power on issues of military defence and taxation. Yet notwithstanding Maffei's perspicacious link between federalism and representation in Ancient Rome, it was in the Middle Ages that the rule of contract (of representation) in public law was fully inscribed (Gierke 1958: 61). Indeed, the sending of ambassadors from local and distant communities to appear before the Senate did not imply any decisions on the part of the ambassadors (Millar 2002: 163).[9]

Representation was born in a confrontational environment, within Christianity and between secular and religious powers. Its origins are to be found in the context of the medieval Church and the relationship of power between localities and the emperor, and between the nobles and the king. As John Keane explains, it was in Spain during the kingship of Alfonso IX that the *cortes* was 'invented' as a place for making decisions by 'representatives of various social interests, drawn from a wide geographic radius' (Keane 2009, chap. 3). The same tension that opposed the king and nobles in Spain was to be found within the Church during the recurrent disputes over whether the pope or the council of bishops represented the unitary body of the Christians.

Representation was born as an institution of power, containment and control, and as a means of unifying a large and diverse population. These two aspects presumed an active involvement of both partners because the representative, who was sometimes called 'procurator' and 'commissary', was supposed to speak or act for a specific group of

[9] As for 'representation' within Rome, the requirement of publicity, 'namely, that a range of public acts should be performed "under the gaze of *populous Romanus*" was the only sense in which representation was in action: in the sense that "whoever was present in the Forum at the relevant moment did 'represent' the Roman people as a whole"' (Millar 2002: 6).

people, who endowed him with the power of representing their interests in front of an authority that was recognised as superior.[10] When a given community delegated some members to be represented before the court of the king or the pope, with powers to bind those who appointed them, there lay the origins of representation. Then the technique was transferred to other contexts and used for other purposes.

In the form of a synthesis, unification (of the multitude) and subjection (to the decisions made by chosen delegates) merged in the institution of representation. These two functions dramatically clashed in eighteenth-century France, when representation became the bone of contention in the struggle for the control of sovereign power between a newly born civil society and the king (Derathé 1970: 290–1). The French monarchy's shift from delegation (with instructions) to representation (without instructions) during the debates that accompanied the convocation of the General Estates is an eloquent illustration of the relationship between the character of sovereignty and the normative statute of representation. Before 1789, the 'parliaments were royal courts. They exercised final appellate jurisdiction in the king's name,' but did not legislate (Doyle 1987: 157–8). Thus the moment *les corps* claimed the authority to bind their representatives with instructions *via elections* they challenged the king's prerogatives head on, and pushed the monarch into the awkward position of defending free mandate and opposing the unity of the nation (the king himself) against '*ses parties*' (Cochin 1979: 81–2; Revel 1987: 225–42; Mounier 1989: 866–7). Binding delegation was functional to state unity as long as the identity of the sovereign was unquestioned, physically visible, personified and its legislative power was undivided and absolute. Free mandate emerged as a function of state unity when the subjects started claiming a share in state power and the body of the sovereign became a collective construction and the result of a process of ideological unification. This casts light on the role of ideology and political parties as important factors in preserving the link between citizens and representatives.[11]

As Thomas Paine eloquently stated in 1792, it is wholly inaccurate to see representation as a mere remedy for the implementation of popular sovereignty in a large territory. In fact, representation *allows* popular

[10] Pitkin (1967) located the transition in the terminological meaning of the word representation from 'standing for' to 'acting for' between the second half of the sixteenth century and the first half of the seventeenth century.

[11] As Kishlansky's analysis of the birth of the electoral process in seventeenth-century England shows, there was a chronological and functional link between the adoption of the electoral method to appoint lawmakers, the transformation of the elected from delegates to political representatives, and the emergence of ideological forms of grouping (Kishlansky 1986: 12–21).

sovereignty to exist and to operate in a legal and social space composed of individuals who have the same rights and who are not defined by their social status or community membership.[12] The size of the geo-political space is not what justifies the need for representation, which is not, for this reason, a mere expedient for coping with a large state. For Paine, Athens proved by default that if Athenian democracy had a turbulent and unstable life, it was because it did not have institutional means to cope with the effects of individual freedom. Without the unifying work of representation, Athenian democracy *lacked* the capacity of transforming the plurality of interests and views held by its free and equal citizens into a unitary process of decision that was able to protect the 'general interest' from direct interference by factions and classes (Paine 1989: 170). Reasoning from these premises, Fisher Ames had argued a few years before Paine that it was incorrect to think of representation in terms of a 'copy' or even an 'image' of society, simply because the representatives did not 'reflect' the opinions of the represented, as if they were a mirror (Bailyn 1992, vol. 1: 892).

In conclusion, the defence of representation and popular sovereignty went hand in hand with the building of representative democracy. Furthermore, it was deeply intertwined with the democratic transform-ation of society; the idea that all the citizens should somehow partici-pate in the formation of the sovereign politics *qua* citizens, with their votes and their judgement (Rosanvallon 1992: 71; Ankersmit 2002: 93). Within this all-inclusive, artificial and egalitarian perspective, polit-ical representation was needed to recreate the link between society and the state previously made by ascriptive communities, feudal estates and the king.

Representation brought to the floor two correlated issues, that of pluralism and that of legitimacy. On the one hand, it forced polit-ical theorists to rethink the meaning of the unity of the sovereign and the place of freedom of speech and association in political life – two basic freedoms without which neither elections nor the representative process could have occurred (it is accurate to say that representation facilitated the encounter of liberalism and democracy). On the other, it forced theorists of sovereignty to rethink the meaning of the sov-ereign will in relation to a mediated and indirect political process of decision making. This process that elections put in motion was centred on the influential role played by judgement, a faculty, as Rousseau acknowledged, that can be represented. In a word, both the nature

---

[12] Despite its small territory, Athenian democracy declined because it had no 'method to consolidate the parts of society' (Paine 1989: 167).

of sovereignty and the statute of representation needed to go through normative and conceptual revisions in order for representation to be rethought along the lines of a democratic process of opinion and will formation that involved both state institutions and society. The issue of pluralism (and the unity of the sovereign) was widely debated in the second half of the eighteenth century; the issue of legitimacy (and the statute of representation) acquired momentum in the early twentieth century. In both cases, discussions of the meaning of representative democracy took place in the midst of revolutionary transformations, a coincidence that speaks for the innovative character of the form of government of the moderns.

The sovereign will against representation

Until the end of the eighteenth century, democracy was defined by adjectives like 'pure' and 'absolute', wherein 'pure' entailed citizens' direct lawmaking and 'absolute' meant 'simple' government as opposite to constitutional checks and the division of powers.[13] This, together with the idea of the incompatibility of democracy and representation, constituted the foster child of the modern conception of sovereignty. They were entrenched in a voluntaristic view of sovereignty that excluded *a priori* indirect forms of political activity because it identified autonomy with the immediacy of presence – immediacy in the time dimension, wherein the political event (decision) and the political actor (the people) coincided (Urbinati 2006, chaps. 2 and 3). This position was equally shared by defenders of monarchical absolutism as well as theorists of moderate or republican government. For instance, in his attack on the representative revolution, Robert Filmer (1991: 56–7) raised a question that was to become central in the ensuing debate on political representation: how can it be claimed that the people retain their 'natural liberty' if they do not give the representatives 'instructions or directions what to say or do in parliament'? Almost a century earlier, Jean Bodin had explained that for the sovereign to preserve its supreme power delegates must not become representatives.[14] Drawing on Bodin, Montesquieu

---

[13] According to Wood (1969, chap. 5) the expression 'representative democracy' appeared in a letter by Alexander Hamilton to Governor Morris in 1777. The word appeared also in 1787–8 in Condorcet's *Lettres d'un bourgeois de New-Haven à un citoyen de Virginie* (now in volume 9 of his *Oeuvres*) even if its usage became more familiar after 1792, with the fall of the monarchy and the election of the new convention to give the country a republican constitution (cf. Rosanvallon 1998: 11). Keane (2009: 162) remarks that the Marquis d'Argenson opposed 'true' (as representative) to 'false' democracy already in 1765.

[14] In ancient Rome – which Bodin, like Rousseau later on, took to be the model of the republic – sovereignty 'remained in the people' even when 'its exercise' was delegated

and Rousseau both reached surprisingly similar conclusions, although they approached the problems of sovereign identity and the sovereign exercise of power differently. Montesquieu, the mentor of liberal representative government, merged self-government (sovereignty) and direct government (democracy) and created a firm opposition between representation and democracy. His formulation has became paradigmatic: a government is democratic if 'the people as a body have sovereign power' and if 'the people alone ... make laws' (Montesquieu 1989, book 2, chap. 2). England was a model of good or moderate government because it was constitutional and electoral, that is to say neither 'absolute' nor 'direct' or 'pure' (wherein it was clear that democracy could be neither of the two).

Rousseau used Montesquieu's argument to define the body politic and to separate the foundation of the state (sovereignty) from the forms of government, one of which was democracy (Rousseau 1987, book 1, chap. 6). He constructed political legitimacy or sovereignty on the principle of direct legislation, and in this way opposed sovereignty to representation. Hence, whereas Montesquieu argued that a state where the people delegated their 'right of sovereignty' could not be democratic and must be classified as a species of mixed government, actually an elected aristocracy, Rousseau saw such a state as illegitimate because the people lost their political liberty along with the power to vote directly on legislation; unless all citizens were lawmakers, there was no such thing as citizenship.

An important factor that brought modern theorists of sovereignty to consider representation illegitimate lay in their criticism of the medieval tradition, to which, as we saw, representation belonged. The rejection of representation was a chapter in the criticism of the theory of the alienation of sovereignty, bequeathed to the moderns by the natural law tradition.[15] In Rousseau's vocabulary, like that of the theorists of absolute monarchy, delegation was a form of direct decision by other means, while representation defined a reallocation of sovereignty. Thus, the contract of alienation defined representation only, but not delegation, which relied upon the imperative mandate. Indeed, representation, not delegation, was for Rousseau the *bête noire* of sovereignty, the

---

to one or more magistrates (Bodin 1992: 2–5). Rousseau considered Roman tribunes to be the only good examples of representation because they did not make decisions (Rousseau 1987: 198–9).

[15] See Derathé (1970: 252–64). The text in which Rousseau expressed a more benign opinion on representation is the *Lettres écrites de la montagne* (letter VIII in particular), in which he stressed his opposition to popular initiative so as to induce Vaughan (1962, vol. 2: 187–8) to argue that he reduced the legislative power of the people to impotence (in *Oeuvres complètes*, Paris: Gallimard, vol. 3, 1964).

remnant of a patrimonial conception of the state.[16] In Rousseau's mind, representation would rekindle the medieval logic of natural law because it claimed, absurdly, that sovereignty can be alienated like any other property and that its alienation would not alter the identity of its owner. Hence his famous definition:

Sovereignty cannot be represented for the same reason that it cannot be alienated. It consists essentially in the general will, and the will cannot be represented. The will is either itself or something else; no middle ground is possible. The deputies of the people, therefore, neither are nor can be its representatives; they are nothing else but its commissaries. They cannot conclude anything definitively. (Rousseau 1987: 198)

Thus, when he wrote in *The Social Contract* that representation was a modern institution, Rousseau referred precisely to the feudal tradition and meant to say not that the ancients were unaware of the distinction between the actor and the function, but that the ancients did not apply the logic of *res privata* to *res publica*. As for representation, Rousseau was a *discontinuist* much like Montesquieu, who also deemed it not an ancient institution but a creation of the Germans.[17] However, unlike Montesquieu, who used the term 'modernity' both descriptively and approvingly, Rousseau gave it essentially a negative connotation. The former saw representation as both modern *and* a sign of progress. The latter saw it as both modern *and* a sign of feudal regression to a privatistic notion of the public.[18] It was part of the natural law tradition against which Rousseau opposed his theory of the social contract as an act of *constituēre* versus *alienare*. A system based on representation was

---

[16] Grotius (1925, vol. 2, chap. 22, sec. 11) had theorised it. Reasoning from the logic of Roman private law, he had argued that the people could alienate their freedom just as a person could legally alienate his property because sovereignty could be held 'either with full property right (*jure pleno proprietas*), or with usufruct only (*jus usufructario*)'.

[17] On the two theses concerning the genesis of representation, one claiming the *continuity* between the ancient and the modern world, and the other claiming *discontinuity*, see Clarke (1964: 278–316).

[18] Rousseau's source was d'Holbach, who derived representation and all forms of delegated institution from the 'old German nations' (d'Holbach 1778–9). D'Holbach's source was Tacitus' *Germania* (§ 11) which described the forms of representation and parliamentary institutions used by the German tribes. Yet Montesquieu was the first to construct the theory of the government of the moderns or non-Roman (representative versus direct government) based on Tacitus (*The Spirit of the Laws*, book 11, chap. 6). A further important source is that of Jean Louis de Lolme (or Delolme), who in 1771 wrote a defence of English representative government against the ancient myth of direct ruling (Jean Louis de Lolme [or Delolme], *Constitution of England, or An Account of the English Government: in which it is compared, both with the republican form of government, and the other monarchies in England*, London: Robinson and Murray, (1771), 1789).

a system in which the 'social man' (bearing partial interests) was the actor, not the citizen (bearing the general interest).

From this perspective, we can understand why Rousseau confined delegation rigorously to the bounds of a principal/agent relation and stripped it of any political role. In legal usage, mandate is a fiduciary contract that allows the principal to temporarily grant an agent her power to take certain specified actions in order better to protect her interests but does not alienate or delegate her will to make decisions. This was Rousseau's substitute for 'representation' in the legislative setting. It was consistent with a voluntarist politics and a juridical notion of sovereignty. It allowed for delegation, but not representation, as the title of chapter 15 of book 3 of his *Social Contract* suggests.

Rousseau's logic has mesmerised supporters of strong democracy as well as its sceptics, who doubt both the possibility of democratising representative government and the feasibility of direct self-government. The question, however, is why Rousseau's premises should go unchallenged and, moreover, whether their outcomes truly foster full participation and curtail the political influence of delegates vis-à-vis the sovereign. Delegates are to the people as ambassadors are to the state they represent: they do the 'dirty' work their sovereign needs to do in order for his or her plans to work, but lack formal power to make decisions in the sovereign's place. However, they have significant discretion to explore the best means of achieving the sovereign's chosen end, and even to suggest which end the sovereign might want to choose. Ambassadors' experience and knowledge enhance the inherent power of their role, so that, depending on their personal abilities, they can accumulate much more power than elected representatives with free mandate, even though *de jure* they have no power at all (Friedrich 1963: 309). Like ambassadors, Rousseau's delegates had very substantial 'power', although they held it informally and behind closed doors. Unlike elected representatives, they had access to a range and degree of influence that could not be easily assessed and formally limited, but was *de facto* largely discretionary. This was why Kant argued that a non-representative form of government cannot be the norm because it cannot guarantee a government of laws, even when all the subjects consent to the laws, as in a direct democracy.[19]

Rousseau denied that the delegates could have a lawmaking function; he did *not* reject delegated politics. Indeed, despite the fact that he thought representative government violated popular sovereignty, he

---

[19] Kant (1991: 125–7) and 'On the Common Saying: This May be True in Theory, but it does not Apply in Practice' (Kant 1991: 74).

neither proposed lottery nor rotation (traditionally associated with democracy) nor rejected elections. Rousseau restated Montesquieu's idea that lottery was democratic and election aristocratic and concluded, with Aristotle, that whereas all positions requiring only good sense and the basic sentiment of justice should be open to all citizens, positions requiring 'special talents' should be filled by election or performed by the few (Rousseau 1987: 198). The former only decide or ratify (by raised hands or direct voting) what the latter propose or deliberate on (preferably *in camera*).

It is thus not by chance that Rousseau rejected both democracy and representation. They were, he thought, both structurally based on discussion and opinion, and therefore fatally inclined to corruption. Indeed, an open deliberative trial would require that all citizens were extremely virtuous in order not to listen to the sirens of interests and not to tailor the general will to their private preferences. Hence, either the sovereign was made only by the virtuous few (but this would violate the legitimating principles of inclusion and equality) or the sovereign body was made by all citizens doing only the minimal work of authorisation: saying yes or no to proposals devised by few (hopefully virtuous) delegates. In the end, only direct ratification by the citizens distinguished Rousseau's mixed-government republic from today's representative government (cf. Fralin 1978: 1–11). His true antithesis of representation was a delegated politics with direct (and silent) ratification, not a full-fledged participatory (and discursive) *polis*. Today's electoral democracy seems to be the belated offspring of Rousseau's model.

The criticism advanced by modern theorists of sovereignty against representative government tells us something important: it is the statutory rendering of the function that elections enact (delegation or representation), rather than election per se, that defines the character of representative government. It is the way representation is implemented that reveals what elections produce or, in other words, how sovereignty is conceived and what the sovereign's responsibilities are. The difference between direct and represented government pertains to what the elected are supposed to do. Rousseau's model of political institutions is consistent with a delegated (as non-deliberative or discursive) democracy, not a representative (as deliberative) democracy. It is based on popular sovereignty as a unitary act of the will, which the citizens perform either by electing law-redactors (lawmakers with instructions) or by voting on the laws directly.[20] Delegation, unlike

---

[20] Rousseau (1985) proposed imperative mandate as a solution to the impossibility of direct lawmaking in *The Government of Poland*.

representation, means that the delegates discuss and deliberate but do not have the last word; they opine but they do not will. They are commissaries of the sovereign. According to Carl Schmitt, this is the only condition under which representation 'can be viewed [...] as a distinctly democratic method' (Schmitt 1928, section 19: III, 1–2, 284–5). But, of course, this is not representation, but delegation, as Rousseau well understood.

Certainly, both Rousseau and Schmitt agreed that deliberation as the dialectics of discussion and ideas must be disassociated from decision and must not occur in the place where the sovereign decision is made. Indeed, when parliament becomes the place of representative politics, it fatally acquires the character of an *agora* or a marketplace of ideas, and this brings dissension to the core of the state. Liberal politics, Schmitt (rightly) concluded, is characterised by representation as the advocacy of interests, the tool that transforms (or, in Schmitt's mind, deforms) politics in a permanent process of mediation and compromise. Once again, however, it is the unity of the sovereign that is at stake in this criticism of representation, not a broader or deeper participation by the citizens.

The paradox of Rousseau's paradigm (and Schmitt's as well) is that divorcing delegated politics from participation (the magistrates, who only discuss/the people, who only vote without talking) results in consequences that Rousseau himself (unlike Schmitt) would have disliked: on the one hand, it stresses the role of state-led professionalised politicians, and on the other (as with Schmitt) it reduces citizenship to voting understood as an act of plebiscitarian unification of society. These outcomes were envisaged by Joseph-Emmanuel Sieyès when he applied the logic of the division of labour to representation and made elections (free competition and remuneration by voting) a strategy for making politics a profession like any other (Sieyès 1985: 262). When citizens are required to do nothing more than give their assent or vote, elections become a means for creating 'two peoples': 'the producers' and 'the auxiliaries', a class of citizens who make the laws for all and a class of citizens who obey them. For Sieyès politics was a realm of competence, not equality; it was not by chance that he kept representative government separate from democracy (Sieyès 1998: 184). It was a *grande machine politique* managed by the active professional few with the confidence of the politically passive many (cf. Bastid 1939).

Pure procedural democracy against representation

Along with the obvious critiques of representation in the name of strong participatory democracy, the voluntaristic conception of sovereignty has indirectly served the cause of the critics of the 'ideology of democracy' and strengthened their case for a *pure procedural interpretation of democracy*. Within this rich and distinctive category, I discuss two groups: the *democratic elitists*, who defended an electoral and minimalist definition of democracy; and the *democratic formalists*, who argued for a definition of representative democracy that located deliberation essentially within the parliamentary setting. Despite their significant differences, both types of proceduralism shared the mythology of formalism and positivism, an approach that has utilised Rousseau's classical view of sovereignty to disprove the very possibility of a democratic theory of representation.[21]

Democratic elitists acquired momentum in the post-World War Two European reconstruction of constitutional democracy. They revamped a realist view of politics that was motivated by the meritorious intention of disassociating democracy from the totalising forms of mass mobilisation, like nationalism and Nazi-fascism, which had plagued the continent in the interwar period. They made Rousseau's conception of sovereignty the 'pure' norm of modern democracy and thus trapped democracy in the cul-de-sac of either the 'unrealistic' 'classic doctrine' of the general will or the 'realist' rendering of the will of the people as the factual will of an elected class of officials (see especially Michels 1962: 75). Joseph Schumpeter adopted the same strategies as the pre-World War One anti-democratic elitists (Michels and Pareto) when he proposed that democracy is either pure utopia or an 'ideological' fiction created by the ruling class to gain consent. Schumpeter concluded that whether or not the government of the moderns is democratic depends only on how elites are selected and the basis of their selectable characteristics. Democracy means simply that these characteristics are not associated with inborn qualities and can *de jure* be acquired by all. The minimal but legally guaranteed equality of the right to vote is what makes inclusion democratic; regular elections and free competition

---

[21] Supporters of a proceduralist definition of democracy belong in the tradition of juridical and logical positivism, whose theoretical foundation was the distinction between facts and values. From David Hume and Jeremy Bentham to H.L.A. Hart and Hans Kelsen, this tradition has tried to oppose the ethical doctrine of the state, which they saw as an attempt to counter the individualist and conventionalist theory of representative government. Since the 1930s, this approach has acquired the obvious merit of providing for the most radical alternative to the triumphant experimentations of ideological and organic models of the ethical state, Nazi-fascism and communism. The dualism between facticity and normativity was their strategy to counter ideology in politics in the name of the fallacy of substitution of the 'ought' for the 'is'. Accordingly, an ideological approach to democracy (indeed 'the ideology of democracy') meant deriving prescriptive or desiderative conclusions from assertive or descriptive theses.

of political programmes is what makes that basic right translate into democratic government. Representation plays no other role besides that of filling the institutional function of lawmaking. Schumpeter's rendering still seems to be the best picture of our system of government. All things considered, what makes it democratic is the equal legal right citizens have to elect and be elected, to dismiss and be dismissed (Schumpeter 1962: 284–5).

Democratic formalists have advanced a rendering of proceduralism that is more subtle and captivating, although their conclusion is not more favourable to representative democracy than that of the elitists. This rendering was done in the first half of the twentieth century along with, and as a defence of, the democratic transformation of continental constitutional states. Its main interpreter and advocate was Hans Kelsen, the pioneer of the science of the juridical norm and, in his early career, an astute supporter of constitutional democracy against the assault on equal liberty from new socio-economic corporate interests and old authoritarian state apparatuses. Kelsen used the weapons of formalism to counter those threats. His strategy was revived after World War Two in order to deflate comprehensive interpretations of democracy sponsored by ideological (Marxists) and religious groups (above all Catholics).[22]

Kelsen tried to disassociate democracy from its ideological and religious appropriations by stressing the formal and procedural aspects of representative democracy. To do so, he redefined the relationship between democracy and representation. First of all, Kelsen disaggregated the principle of political equality from the doctrine of popular sovereignty, which he deemed a 'political fiction', a term that in his vocabulary denoted lack of normative consistency because of an unwarranted mix of 'ought' and 'is' assertions, of descriptive and evaluative arguments.[23] Liberating democracy from ideology (political fiction) and making it an issue of procedural correctness was for him a strategy of supporting democracy against secular or religious attempts to make it a political game in the service of some supposedly superior values, and to make the representative an agent of ideals external to democracy.

Kelsen countered the 'ideology of democracy' with the clever strategy of limiting representation to the legal theory of contract (as Rousseau had implicitly suggested), but reached the anti-Rousseau conclusion

---

[22] See for instance Maritain (1943). For a criticism of Marxists' appropriation of representative democracy see Bobbio (1955).

[23] Kelsen (1999: 297–9) argued that every political regime is involved in the production of norms, and he defined democracy as an institutional and procedural order organised by the ground norm of 'equality of all citizens'.

that representation *was* acceptable. Representative government was formally a violation of both the democratic norm ('equality of all citizens') and the contractual norm (legal dependence of the elected on the electors). Nevertheless, Kelsen argued that representative government could be justified by relying upon exogenous factors (functionalism and organisational division of labour), but not the democratic principle: 'the legislative power is better organised when the democratic principle, according to which the people should be the legislator, is not carried to extremes' (Kelsen 1999: 292).

Revisiting Kelsen's goal, we can derive an important lesson from his argument: representative democracy is an oxymoron *whenever* we extend the rules of juridical representation (the legal theory of contract of delegation) to political representation. Let us follow Kelsen's reasoning.

Kelsen synthesised the 'true relationship of representation' in the following three norms, wherein the last two derive logically from the first: (a) the representative must be appointed or elected by the represented (principle of autonomy); (b) the representative must be 'legally obliged to execute the will of the represented' (imperative mandate); and (c) the fulfillment of the representative's obligation must be 'legally guaranteed' (recall). These three norms do not merely denote the democratic form of representative government. They also denote the institution of representation in the public sphere and imply that for a government to be democratic and representative at the same time it is not enough that elected officials during their tenure 'reflect the will of the electorate' and that elections make them 'responsible' to the electors. Indeed, these are simply 'political' kinds of binding, and in this sense 'fictional' and illusionary, not formally normative.

Simply 'political' binding (or *representativity* and *advocacy*) is fictional or ideological because it rests *merely* on the intention or the voluntary commitment of the actors, without being legally binding. It is an *imperfect* binding, like moral duty is imperfect in relation to legal obligation. Political binding can be subjected to ethical norms – like honesty or prudence on the side of the elected and disinterested participation or civic virtue on the side of the electors – which are, however, only mere instructions and a matter of good will, and in fact fictional, or an object of ideological discourse. Hence Kelsen's conclusion: 'Legal independence of the elected from the electors is incompatible with legal representation', the only non-fictional form of representation. In his view, Rousseau was correct to argue that unless the sovereign employs delegates with instructions it is no longer sovereign. Representation sanctions the death of sovereignty.

The dualism between 'legal norm' and 'political fiction' is the key to the recovery of the role of judgement in the theory of sovereignty. Kelsen used the expression 'political fiction' for critical purposes, in order to denote any formula or judgement that could not be translated into legal language. Political fictions refer to evaluations of merit or demerit, opinions and ideologies – that is to say judgement of values that are the expression of emotions and passions.[24] Rationalism is the subtext of an understanding of representative democracy as oxymoronic. The ontology of the juridical norm – Kelsen's belief in the legal dimension as the only 'real' dimension – leads to the same conclusion as the ontology of presence and the sovereign will. Politics as a process of opinion formation that involves ideological discourse or 'political fiction' (that is to say representation as a process) is the dimension that escapes both (Ankersmit 2002: 93–9).

The mythology of formalism and positivism in its elitist as well as its proceduralist version indicates that the root of the problem is the extension of the paradigm of the will to politics (the source of the juridical model of contract), not the idea of popular sovereignty per se or democracy. Representation as a contract (delegation) is in itself a denial of political representation. A democratic theory of representation cannot benefit from it, and in fact needs to emancipate itself from it.

Beyond the will and the contract: representation as political process

If representative government was a system in which the will of the representative assembly was the will of the people in a juridical sense, Rousseau's sarcastic references to the fictitiously free and de facto enslaved Britons would be justifiable. Equally justifiable would be Kelsen's claim that the mythology of parliamentary sovereignty inaugurated by the English and French revolutions is a sophistry that has done representative democracy a disservice, since it has indirectly justified its critics' indictment of its aristocratic nature. Starting from Rousseau's and Kelsen's premises, in the absence of imperative mandate the idea that representation is a transfer of sovereign power from the people to the assembly would be trivial and mistaken (Kelsen 1999: 290–1). However, Rousseau's and Kelsen's sarcasm amounts to a 'caricature' rather than a description of representative democracy, which is a political process that is not, and cannot be, rendered in juridical terms of

---

[24] Kelsen (1999, 8–9). For a distinction between several meanings and uses of 'ideology' see also Kelsen (1992: 35–6).

a contract – either as an act of transfer or its opposite, delegation with instructions (Bobbio 1999: 417–21).

Rousseau was correct to stress the difference between political and private interests (the general will versus the will of all). Both political representation and contractual or juridical representation are forms of representation of interests, but the nature of those interests is not the same. In the case of a principal/agent relation, the interests to be represented are partial or private; but in the case of political representation, interests are general in the sense that they pertain to the citizen body as a whole and to each as a general subject. However, Rousseau made a 'fatal error' when he identified the sovereignty of the state with its individual members. He glossed over the fact that the exercise of sovereignty depends on coercive power since it expresses itself in the form of a command or a law, not an agreement (Carré de Malberg 1922, vol. 2: 166). The difference between political and private representation is reflected in the difference between law and contract. Contract presupposes a horizontal relation, while law presupposes a vertical one. The representatives (like the citizens in a direct democracy) have the power to make decisions that are collective in the sense that they apply to all the members of the body politic. On this account, unless all decisions are always unanimous, direct government would face the same problem as representative government.

Thus, since representation functions politically (to make laws) in a collective and public setting, and since laws cannot be treated like contractual agreements because they impose their authority on all indiscriminately, not just on those who agree with them or those whose ideas are represented by the majority, it is extremely important that we abandon the logic of the contract implied by the will-based theory of sovereignty.

The fact that representation cannot be regulated and checked like a 'contract' of delegation does not mean, however, that citizens can only check representatives through elections. Rousseau was right to say that representation cannot be a contract. Yet just because political representation can only exist in the juridical form of a non-legally bounded mandate, some other form of 'mandate' is needed to check representatives. That is why it is inappropriate to posit a radical dualism between imperative and free mandate *if* the latter is meant to be both political and legal. The very fact that representatives play an active (legislative) role implies that they are *not* independent of the electors; it implies a political kind of 'mandate'.

To clarify this point it may be useful to see in what sense political representation is unique and why it cannot be understood as an act of mere authorisation or contract.[25] There are at least three reasons why this is the case.[26]

(1) Since representatives make laws that all citizens, not only those who elected them, must obey, political mandate entails that representatives represent the entire nation, not just the constituency that elected them.[27] This not only means that their mandate is non-contractually based, but also that it is based on a flagrant violation of the contractual mandate; this makes the legal ban on imperative mandate *politically* empty although *legally* necessary and in fact enforced in most constitutions (except for the United States). It also means that the representative cannot ignore the perspective of the 'will of the people' and concentrate only on her relationship with her constituency. Critics of popular sovereignty overlook the fact that the traditional idea that representation is a 'defective substitute' for democracy derives from a conception of sovereignty that is both context-specific and tailored to a view of politics as will or simply decision. As an answer to critics of sovereignty (Young 1997: 359), I would say that *this* idea, *not* the 'will of the people' as the general and unifying criterion of political judgement, is the source of the apparent contradiction between representation and democracy.

(2) The juridical mandate makes the representative directly responsible and legally accountable to his client. But the political representative, as Kelsen rightly argued, is neither legally accountable to those who voted for her nor obligated by personal relationships. Free mandate allows representatives to make decisions that do not subvert or displace the general nature of the law because it prevents them from transcribing the particular wills they represent directly into the norms of the state, thereby imposing the will of some onto the entire body of citizens. They are the very democratic norms of political liberty and equality that prohibit legally bound mandate and denote the specificity of political representation.[28]

---

[25] Carré de Malberg (1922, vol. 2: 209–21) provided the best analysis of the differences between private delegation and political representation.

[26] I analysed these three reasons in Urbinati (2005: 194–222).

[27] I am here referring to the nation as a juridical entity, not ethnic or cultural, or as the unity of legal subjects (individuals treating one another according to 'a genuine obligation' rather than as objects of domination) according to a formulation that was originally made by Sieyès (1985: 198).

[28] Mansbridge's (2003: 515) maxim, 'representation is, and is normatively intended to be, something more than a defective substitute for direct democracy', relies on the fact that electoral representation is not a contract but an original and complex form of participation.

(3) A private lawyer has only those powers the client grants him. But electors have no legal power to make their opinions compulsory like instructions. This means that the currency of political representation is promises (with a moral commitment on the part of the elected and, at most, their prudential calculus in seeking re-election or simply the desire to be popular). In a word, the currency of representation is *ideological* in that it is an *interpretative* or *artificially created similarity* between the representative and her electors (not pictorial or mirror-like similarity). It is similarity of ideas, not essential or substantive similarity. The seed of the democratic character of representation germinates from the paradox that although a representative is supposed to deliberate about things that affect *all members* of the polity, she is also supposed to have a sympathetic relation *to a part* (the part that votes for her) (Kelsen 1929, chap. 2). In substance, a relation of *ideological sympathy and communication* between the representative and her electors is necessary and can occur *only because* political representation excludes legal mandate and is not a contract. The sympathetic relation of the representative to the part that voted for her is, and must only be, a matter of opinions or ideas, an informal and thus not authoritative kind of relation. This means, however, that the representative is not *politically* autonomous from her electors although she must be *legally* autonomous (Thompson 1987: 113). From a political perspective, the democratic representative is not like Burke's trustee because she is in a permanent relation to her constituency; but, technically, like Burke's trustee, she is a representative of the entire nation.

In democratic politics, representation is not 'acting in the place of somebody', but being in a *political relation* of ideological sympathy or a relation of attraction between the ideas of the electors and the ideas of those in the place of whom the representatives act in the legislature (from which derives the citizens' quest that representatives' choices should enjoy representativity or be in a reflective adhesion with citizens' opinions; Böckenförde 1991, chaps. 6–7). The assumption of this (idealised or ideological) kind of sympathy (which is the foundation of the advocacy aspect of representation) is reflected in the statute that regulates how representatives vote in the representative assembly. Except in clearly specified cases (which pertain to decrees, not laws), the voting must be public. Electors need to know what the representatives do and say and how they vote in the assembly because they need to compare representatives' judgement to their own judgement.

That a political representative is required to share her ideas *only* with her electors, not with the whole nation *as* a homogeneous body, entails that representation is itself a denial of populist democracy. Indeed, in order to acquire the moral and political legitimacy to make laws for all, representation must articulate pluralism but not superimpose an unreflective unity over an indistinct mass of individuals.[29] It is thus important to make clear that representation is a *process of seeking unity not an act of unification*. As such, it presupposes and fosters pluralism, one that is not a mere social given but a political construction made by free citizens (electors and elected) in their conflicting divisions or sympathetic alliances. Representative democracy is based on political parties and partisanship.

'Political process' is the key term. The process of representation puts an end to the *sovereign* as an ontological collective entity that proclaims its will (by an act of authorisation) and makes room for *sovereignty* as an inherently plural unifying process. Within this scenario, political groups or parties (ideological representations of the social and political reality) are not optional or accidental; they constitute the representative process, which is not and cannot be a personal relationship, like the client-lawyer relationship (cf. Muirhead 2006; Rosenblum 2008). For this to happen, however, partisanship (or the *ideological sympathy and communication* between the representative and her electors) needs to occur within and in relation to an imagined general will; the opposite would be the factional conquering of the public by sectarian or corporate interests, and even through civil war. Political *partisanship* is an articulation of, and concurrence with, the idea of 'the general' that constrains and limits all particular interests that exist in society (Rawls 1993: 165). Political partisanship relies upon an interpretation of sovereignty that links together the will (authoritative power) and judgement (the informal power of opinion), that operates within civil society as a means by which society relates to state institutions.

Epilogue

Elections 'make' representatives but they do not 'make' representation; at a minimum, they make *responsible* and *limited* government, but not *representative* democracy. Representation activates a kind of political unity that can be defined *neither* in terms of a contractual agreement

---

[29] I have analysed the differences between representative democracy and populistic democracy in Urbinati (1998: 110–24).

between electors and elected *nor* resolved into a system of competition to appoint those who are to pronounce the general interest of all. It designates a comprehensive form of political process that is structured in terms of circulation of judgement and influence between institutions and society and has political parties or movements as its indispensable pivoting forces. Representation makes contemporary democracy an uninterrupted dynamic of the reactions of civil political society to the actions by institutional political society.[30] Furthermore, it invites us to explore and regulate the other pole of sovereignty – that of judgement. When judgement is introduced into our understanding of sovereignty, it is clear that a theory of democratic representation must attend to the equal *circumstances of political judgement*. Citizens' rights to an equal share in determining the political will (one person, one vote) must go together with having meaningful opportunities to form their ideas and give them public voice, ultimately to control those who have the material power of disseminating opinions and strongly influence the political game.

This shift in focus from electoral authorisation to these indirect forms of participation should work as an invitation to legislators and citizens to sharpen their institutional imagination and create new legal and institutional means to improve transparency and public scrutiny in the intricate network of interdependency between representatives and the represented; to regulate and limit the use of private and corporate money and social influence in electoral campaigns and the lawmaking process more generally; and even more urgently, to protect the independence of public media from the power of ruling majorities and the pluralism of information from the excessive influence of private potentates. Whereas in ancient direct democracy the oligarchic menace to the rule of the *demos* materialised in the suspension of the equal distribution of the right to vote in the assembly, in representative democracy the oligarchic threat arises from within the domain of judgement, as an unchecked and exorbitant force of shaping opinions that domesticate citizens' critical voices and tame their power of surveillance and control.

REFERENCES

Accarino, B. (1999) *Rappresentanza*. Bologna: Il Mulino.
Ankersmit, F. R. (2002) *Political representation*. Stanford University Press.

---

[30] On democratic representation as a process that relies on multiple sources and forms of influence and communication that citizens activate through media, social movements and political parties, see Urbinati (2006, chap. 1) and Michael Saward's chapter in this volume.

Bailyn, B. (1992) *The debate on the constitution: Federalist and antifederalist speeches, articles, and letters during the struggle over ratification*, 2 vols. New York: The Library of America.

Barber, B. (1984) *Strong democracy: Participatory politics for a new age.* Berkeley: University of California Press.

Bastid, P. (1939) *Les discours de Sieyès dans les débats constitutionnels de l'An III (2 et 18 Thermidor). Édition critique avec une introduction et des notes*, Paris: Hachette, pp. 58–9.

Bobbio, N. (1955) *Politica e cultura*. Turin: Einaudi.

(1999) *Teoria generale della politica*, ed. M. Bovero, Turin: Einaudi.

Böckenförde, E. W. (1991) *State, society and liberty: Studies in political theory and constitutional law*. New York and Oxford: Berg.

Bodin, J. (1992) *On sovereignty: Four chapters from the six books of the Commonwealth*, ed. J. Franklin. Cambridge University Press.

Carré de Malberg, R. (1922) *Contribution à la théorie générale de l'État*, 2 vols. Paris: Librairie Recueil Sirey.

Clarke, M. V. (1964) *Medieval representation and consent: A study of early parliaments in England and Ireland, with special reference to the modus tenendi parliamentum*. New York: Russell & Russell.

Cochin, A. (1979) *L'esprit du jacobinisme. Une interpretation sociologique de la révolution française*. Paris: Presses Universitaires de France.

D'Holbach, P.-H., T. Baron (1778–9) *Représentants*. In *Encyclopédie; ou, Dictionnaire raisonné des sciences, des arts et des métiers, par une société de gens de lettres. Mis en ordre & publié par M. Diderot; & quant à la partie mathématique, par M. D'Alembert*, 36 vols. Lausanne: Sociétés typographiques, 1781–82.

Dahl, R. A. (1971) *Polyarchy: Participation and opposition*. New Haven, CT: Yale University Press.

(2001) *How democratic is the American constitution?* New Haven, CT: Yale University Press.

Derathé, R. (1970) *Jean-Jacques Rousseau et la science politique de son temps*. Paris: Librairie Philosophique Vrin.

Doyle, W. (1987) 'The parlements', in K. M. Baker (ed.) *The French Revolution and the creation of modern political culture: vol. 1, The political culture of the old regime*. Oxford: Pergamon Press, pp. 157–67.

Dunn, J. (1999) 'Situating democratic political accountability', in A. Przeworski, S. C. Stokes and B. Manin (eds.) *Democracy, accountability, and representation*. Cambridge University Press, pp. 329–44.

(2005) *Democracy: A history*. New York: Atlantic Monthly Press.

Filmer, R. (1991) *Patriarcha* (1680), in J. P. Sommerville (ed.) *Patriarcha and other essays*. Cambridge University Press.

Fralin, R. (1978) *Rousseau and representation: A study of the development of his concept of political institutions*. New York: Columbia University Press.

Friedrich, C. J. (1963) *Man and his government: An empirical theory of politics*. New York: McGraw Book Company.

Gadamer, H. G. (2004) *Truth and method*. London, New York: Continuum.

Gierke, O. von (1958) *Political theories of the middle age*. Cambridge University Press.

48   *Nadia Urbinati*

Grotius, H. (1925) *De jure belli ac pacis libri tres* (1625), 2 vols. Oxford: Clarendon.

Habermas, J. (1996) *Between facts and norms: Contributions to a discourse theory of law and democracy.* Cambridge, MA: MIT Press.

Kant, I. (1991) *The metaphysics of morals* (1785). Cambridge University Press.

Keane, J. (2009) *The life and death of democracy.* London: Simon & Schuster.

Kelsen, H. (1929) *Vom Wesen und Wert der Demokratie.* Tübingen: Mohr.

(1992) *Introduction to the problems of legal theory.* Oxford: Clarendon Press.

(1999) *General theory of law and state.* Union, NJ: The Lawbook Exchange.

Kishlansky, M. A. (1986) *Parliamentary selection: Social and political choice in early modern England.* Cambridge University Press.

Maffei, S. (1979) *Il Consiglio politico finora inedito presentato al governo veneto nell'anno 1736.* Venice: Palese.

Manin, B. (1997) *The principles of representative government.* Cambridge University Press.

Mansbridge, J. J. (2003) 'Rethinking representation', *American Political Science Review* 97(4): 515–28.

Maritain, J. (1943) *Christianisme et démocratie.* New York: Éditions de la Maison francaise.

Mayo, H. B. (1960) *An introduction to democratic theory.* New York: Oxford University Press.

Michels, R. (1962) *Political parties: A sociological study of the oligarchical tendencies of modern democracy.* New York: The Free Press.

Millar, F. (2002) *The Roman Republic in political thought: The Menahem Stern Jerusalem Lectures.* Hanover and London: University Press of New England.

Montesquieu C. L. de S., Baron de (1989) *The spirit of the laws* (1748). Cambridge University Press.

Mounier, J.-J. (1989) 'Rapport du comité chargé du travail sur la constitution', in F. Furet and R. Halévie (eds.) *Orateurs de la révolution française*, vol. 1. *Les constituants.* Paris: Pléiade.

Muirhead, R. (2006) 'A defense of party spirit', *Perspectives on Politics* 4: 713–27.

Ober, J. (2008) 'The original meaning of "democracy": Capacity to do things, not majority rule', *Constellations* 15(1): 3–9.

Paine, T. (1989) *The rights of man* (1791–92), in B. Kuklick (ed.) *Political writings.* Cambridge University Press.

Pennock, J. R. (1983) 'Introduction' in J. R. Pennock and J. W. Chapman (eds.), *Liberal democracy. Nomos XXV.* New York: NYU.

Pettit, P. (2003) 'Deliberative democracy, the discursive dilemma, and republican theory', in J. S. Fishkin and P. Laslett (eds.) *Debating deliberative democracy.* Malden: Blackwell, pp. 138–62.

Pitkin, H. (1967) *The concept of representation.* Berkeley: University of California Press.

Rawls, J. (1993) *Political liberalism.* New York: Columbia University Press.

Rehfeld, A. (2005) *The concept of constituency: Political representation, democratic legitimacy and institutional design.* Cambridge University Press.

Revel, J. (1987) 'Les corps et communautés', in K. M. Baker (ed.) *The French revolution and the creation of modern political culture: vol. 1, The political culture of the Old Regime.* Oxford: Pergamon Press, pp. 225–42.

Rosanvallon, P. (1992) *Le sacre du citoyen. Histoire du suffrage universel en France.* Paris: Gallimard.

(1998) *Le peuple introuvable. Histoire de la représentation démocratique en France.* Paris: Gallimard.

(2006) *La contre-démocratie. La politique à l'âge de la défiance.* Paris: Editions du Seuil.

Rosenblum, N. (2008) *On the side of the angels: An appreciation of parties and partisanship.* Princeton University Press.

Rousseau, J.-J. (1985) *The government of Poland* (1772). Indianapolis: Hackett, pp. 36–7.

(1987) *On the social contract or principles of political rights* (1762), in *Basic political writings.* Indianapolis: Hackett, pp. 139–227.

Schmitt, C. (1928) *Constitutional theory* (2008 edn.) Durham and London: Duke University Press.

Schumpeter, J. (1962) *Capitalism, socialism, and democracy* (1942). New York: Harper Torchbook.

Sieyès, E.-J. (1985) *Écrits politiques.* Paris: Editions des archives contemporaines.

(1998) 'Bases de l'ordre social', in P. Pasquino, *Sieyes et l'invention de la constitution en France.* Paris: Odile Jacob.

Skinner, Q. (2002) 'Hobbes and the purely artificial person of the state', in *Visions of Politics.* 3 vols. Vol. 3. Cambridge University Press, pp. 177–208.

Thompson, D. F. (1987) *Political ethics and public office.* Cambridge, MA: Harvard University Press.

Urbinati, N. (1998) 'Democracy and populism', *Constellations* 5(1): 110–24.

(2005) 'Continuity and rupture: Political judgment in democratic representation', *Constellations* 12(1): 194–222.

(2006) *Representative democracy: Principles and genealogy.* University of Chicago Press.

Urbinati, N. and M. Warren (2008) 'The concept of representation in contemporary democracy', *The Annual Review of Political Science* 11: 387–412.

Vaughan, C. E. (1962) *The political writings of Jean-Jacques Rousseau*, 2 vols. New York: Wiley.

Wood, A. G. (1969) *The creation of the American revolution, 1776–1787.* Chapel Hill: University of North Carolina Press.

Young, I. M. (1997) 'Deferring group representation', in I. Shapiro and W. Kymlicka (eds.) *Ethnicity and group rights. Nomos XXXIX.* New York University Press.

2 Representative democracy and the populist temptation

Klaus von Beyme

During the second wave of democratisation that followed World War Two, existing forms of representative democracy proved so superior that few critics thought it necessary to examine and classify them. It is true that during the late 1940s there were debates about whether a parliamentary system should be introduced in the United States (von Beyme 1987: 38 f.), and that even the American Political Science Association (APSA) – which normally refrains from issuing ex-cathedra normative statements – made pronouncements about moving 'toward a more responsible two-party system' and a presidential system with a different form of representative government, an American functional equivalent of British cabinet government (Committee on Political Parties of the APSA 1950). Yet during this period only one established democratic regime was transformed, the French Fourth Republic in 1958. All other new democracies of the period displayed considerable stability.

The term 'defective democracy' (Merkel 2004) was coined only during the so-called third wave of democratisation, which began in the mid 1970s. As we shall see in this chapter, contemporary typologies of representative democracy now regularly include its deficient forms, a move which has heightened awareness of the ways in which today's consolidated representative democracies suffer from defects – just as early representative forms of government suffered defects, and could hardly be called democracies. The mother of parliamentary governments, Britain, was, for instance, a latecomer to democratisation, at least when measured by its achievement of universal suffrage (rather than the male-only suffrage that existed in France well into the twentieth century, and in Switzerland until 1971). Britain took a long time to pass from Samuel Sandy's first moves to establish a more responsible government in 1741, to the year 1835, when it was finally recognised that no prime minister could govern without the confidence of a parliamentary majority. The pattern in Sweden was similar. Representative government existed there in the form of assemblies of estates – until 1866. When the old feudal system was overcome, Sweden still took half a century to implement parliamentary democracy, in 1917 (von Beyme 2000a: 16 ff.). In terms of Braudel's history of *longue durée*, Sweden and other early representative regimes have been dubbed a 'kind of parliamentarism' (Palme 1969; Turkka 2007, 14 ff.). But 'parliamentarism' did not initially include fully responsible parliamentary government – even if parliaments or estates (as in the Swedish 'Frihetstiden' of the late eighteenth century) held sway in the system. These regimes were not only deficient democracies; they were also defective parliamentary systems, even though they were undoubtedly forerunners of contemporary forms of representative democracy.

Apart from traditional parliamentary and presidential democratic representation, there are three different theoretical and ideological interpretations of representative democracy in our times. First, there are those who call for its consolidation by analysing the ways in which present-day regimes suffer various deficiencies. These theories of *defective democracy* no longer classify regimes using formal criteria (whether they are parliamentary or presidential forms of representative democracy, for instance); they examine more deeply the integration of several subsystems or 'partial regimes' within a system of consistent democratic rules of the game in an 'embedded democracy' (Merkel 2004: 33). A second approach is evident in *normative theories* which analyse the deficiencies of representative democracy in order to develop visions of a 'better democracy'; for instance in the spirit of 'republicanism', 'deliberative democracy', 'reflexive democracy' and other concepts that strive for the 'democratisation of democracy'. Here the analysis of representative democracy does not get bogged down in details of existing institutional forms. Different types of representative democracy are envisaged; they serve as a permanent normative challenge for its transformation or reform. A third approach expresses political dissatisfaction with consolidated forms of representative democracy. In some countries, parts of the electorate and small groups of political entrepreneurs show signs of increasing disaffection with the formalist routines of the system. They develop *new populist visions* of a better, more representative and direct democracy – in opposition to the merely procedural democracy of elite competition.

Historical background

'Representative democracy' is a rather vague, catch-all term. In order to make sense of the different interpretations that have appeared today it is important to sketch their historical background, in order to distinguish different forms of the representative system, which (to repeat) was not always seen to be identical with democracy.

In nineteenth-century Europe, representative government was the comprehensive term used when developing typologies of constitutions. Beyond that, there was little agreement among observers. English writers, for instance, noted that in the German language various words for representation coexisted, such as *darstellen, vertreten, repräsentieren*. These writers also had different notions of representation, which was not always used in a political sense (Pitkin 1989: 132; Birch 1993: 71). In some cases, as in the work of Benjamin Constant, 'representative constitution' and 'constitutional monarchy' were frequently used as synonyms. Most interpreters, however, treated constitutional government as a subtype of representative government. It was opposed to absolutist, despotic or bureaucratic forms of government – those which Kant called an *Unform*, a 'non-type' of government. Contrary to Rousseau, Kant (1964, vol. 4: 465) did not identify the republic with direct democracy: 'Every true Republic is – and cannot be otherwise – a representative system of the people.'

After 1789, political theory became increasingly divided into ideological camps. Conservative writers were inclined to identify 'representative government' with 'popular sovereignty', in a negative way. Liberals, on the other hand, used the term representative government in exactly the opposite way, as a synonym for political systems with elections, but not with universal suffrage, which later came to be considered as the minimal criterion of 'democratic popular sovereignty'. Representative democracy was discussed by John Stuart Mill in his book *Representative Government* (1861 [1960]). He saw two kinds of dangers associated with it: a low-grade intelligence of the representative body, controlled by popular opinion, and class legislation by the numerical majority (1861[1960], chap. VII: 256). The common mode of avoiding these dangers was by limiting the democratic character of representation, through a more or less restricted suffrage. This was feasible for a certain transitional period, but Mill's way out of the predicaments of representative democracy was a 'proportional electoral law' that aimed to create a broad representation of different groups and interests. However, pure proportionalism ought to be tamed by double votes for those with university education and the establishment of a Committee on Legislation comprised of appointed electors entrusted with writing the law, or so he thought. Such a committee would turn the representative body into an agenda-setting institution, leaving the proper legislation to the committee itself.

Representative government among liberals proved to be a popular notion because it excluded an imperative mandate, whereby constituencies could impose concrete orders on how their representatives should vote in parliament. Edmund Burke, in his famous 1774 speech to the electors of Bristol (1864: 447), alienated his constituency when he promised 'to live in the strictest union' with his constituents, but then went on to declare that mandates 'are things utterly unknown to the laws of this land'. He was not re-elected. John Stuart Mill (1873 [1958]: 240) even refused to canvass and answer questions concerning religion and representation. Moreover, he advocated electoral rights for women, a position which was not very popular at that time. A 'well known literary man', not named by Mill (1873 [1958]: 239), noted that 'the Almighty himself would have no chance of being elected on such a programme'.

Meanwhile, in France, the term *gouvernement représentatif* was accepted earlier than in Germany. In Germany most writers continued to speak of *Landstände* (estates) – thereby avoiding the modern connotation of the term representation, which meant for many contemporaries the process of election of representatives by the voters of the whole country, but with a limited mandate for legislation. Legislation generally was shared with the Crown. In his early days as a religious conservative, Lamennais (1823: 5) criticised representative government as a 'fashionable notion': 'Ce prétendu gouvernement représentatif ne représente rien.' A pamphlet written by him displayed the typical conservative identification of representative government with constitutional monarchy and, more specifically, with the British system. Some pamphlet writers in the post-1815 era of restoration went even further by calling the term representative government a 'perfidie criminelle', simply because it combined a 'passive principle of government' with an 'active notion of representation' (Réfutation 1816, in Lamennais 1823: 72).

The advocates of representative government, for their part, transformed the notion of representation into a historical ideology by tracing it back to the liberties of old Germanic tribes. Some legal scholars did the same for Spain, for instance by pointing to the role of the Visigoths, who founded an early civilisation on the Iberian peninsula; something similar happened in Russia, where the Varagians, invading from Scandinavia, were said to have founded the first state on Russian soil in Novgorod (von Beyme 1965). The legend of 'gothic government' was challenged by such political thinkers and parliamentarians as Sieyès, Guizot, Comte and Mohl; Sieyès was so thoroughly socialised into the spirit of the principle of popular sovereignty during the French Revolution that he even called the British House of Lords a 'monument of gothic superstition' – so demonstrating that the notion of 'gothic government' was still familiar, though no longer used in a positive way.

'Constitutional monarchy', in the British sense, was seen to be compatible with a form of parliamentary government in which parliament itself was in control. In the German-speaking countries, however, talk of constitutional monarchy was frequently used to resist parliamentary government. From 1815 until 1918, the whole idea of a representative government incorporating a strong monarch was advocated, and conservatives from Sweden to Italy accepted this new form of hypothetical balance of power, developed in a kind of German-Austrian 'Sonderweg', or special path of development. In Britain itself, the principles of parliamentary government were accepted rather late; measured against the doctrine of the 'Crown in parliament', the term was often considered an insult. From Burke to John Stuart Mill, thinkers who favoured a parliamentary system with the legislative branch in control used terms like 'representative government', 'constitutional government', 'responsible government' and 'mixed government'. In 1834/35, the final conflict between king and parliament was decided in favour of parliamentary representation and majority rule, which were from thereon accepted without further interference by the monarch. Parliamentary government developed as a notion during the short period between the two major episodes of parliamentary reform in 1832 and 1867. Parliament was sovereign, but in the absence of a clearly defined party system. In the era of Disraeli, when alternative parties began to grow stronger, new terms appeared, such as 'party government', 'cabinet government' and – following Bagehot – 'prime ministerial government'. Most such terms had ideological connotations that did not always survive the hand of classifications drawn up by scholars.

In the second half of the nineteenth century, representative government was increasingly used as a generic term, one that was subclassified according to the different types of relationship between parliament and the executive. The classifications usually distinguished between the monastic system of *parliamentary government* and dualistic systems such as *presidential government* (USA) and the *directorial type* (Switzerland). Contrary to a widespread misconception, *semi-presidential regimes* (a term coined by Duverger) were subtypes of parliamentary government, simply because within these regimes the popularly elected president is confronted with a prime minister who needs the confidence of the parliamentary majority, while the president has the counter-weapon of the dissolution of parliament in his/her hands (von Beyme 2000b: 12 ff.).

Since the victory of universal male suffrage – in Britain this came later than in France and Germany – the term 'representative government' was mostly substituted by the terms 'democracy' or 'representative democracy'. Within these systems, representatives are rather free agents who refuse mandates from their constituents. The mandates are developed not so much by the constituencies, which are normally quite heterogeneous, but rather by party machines – imposing party discipline with the exception of some moral issues based on strongly held principles. As Hanna Pitkin (1967: 221) pointed out in her seminal book *The Concept of Representation*, 'representative government is in reality just party competition for office'. This was in tune with Schumpeter's conception (1942, chap. 23), which reduced democracy to a 'democratic method' that organises competition among political leaders. In Germany, emphasis was given to 'party democracy' or *parteienstaatliche Massendemokratie*, a system in which representation is reduced to 'meetings of party delegates with a mandate' (Leibholz 1967: 94).

Challenge I: defective democracies

Bitter ideological conflicts about representative government withered away after 1945. In one variant or another, parliamentary government became the preferred model of all political parties. Very few advocated the alternative of a council (free, Soviet-style) system (von Beyme 2000b: 202 ff.). Although left-wing extremism among communists used to be a major challenge to what they called 'liberal bourgeois democracy', this challenge withered away, especially after 1989. In 1992, even Russia witnessed the bizarre spectacle of a former communist, Khasbulatov, lecturing deputies in the Duma (the Russian parliament) about presidential, parliamentary and semi-presidential systems, and in a conventional way, in order to compile guidelines for a future Russian Constitution.

Gradually, however, dysfunctional developments within representative democracies spawned new ideological quarrels about the most appropriate forms of representative government. In several waves, party government in contemporary forms of representative democracy began to be criticised. There were attempts to outline new models, such as the 'parliamentary investigation state' and 'parliamentary control-state' (Küchenhoff 1967: 881). Neologisms flourished. Something like a terminological chaos set in.[1]

---

[1] A more detailed survey of the literature would include the following neologisms: *Räte-Republik*; council system; soviets; post-democracy (Colin Crouch); charismatic media democracy (Korte); anocracy (Gurr); transitional hybrid regimes (Przeworski); defective democracy (Merkel); exclusive democracy; illiberal democracy (Zakaria); delegative democracy (O'Donnell); democracy of enclaves; minimal democracy; façade democracy; participatory democracy (Pateman, Barber); republicanism (Pocock); deliberative democracy (Habermas); dialogic democracy (Giddens); reflexive democracy (Schmalz-Bruns); subpolitical democracy (Ulrich Beck); and cosmopolitan or transnational democracy (Held).

At the beginning of the twenty-first century three major challenges to liberal representative democracies can be observed. First, there are growing numbers of defective variants of liberal representative democracies which emerged in the wake of the third wave of democratisation at the end of the twentieth century. Second, we witness the populist attack against mature and young representative democracies by right- and left-wing populism. Finally, our period is marked by ongoing normative critiques of representative democracy because of their deficient plebiscitary and participatory mechanisms. Let us examine each of these challenges.

Among the prominent approaches to analysing the performance of new representative democracies is the theory of defective democracy (Merkel 2004). Four different species of defective democracies have been identified. The first is *exclusive democracy*, a type of regime that shows an incomplete democratic electoral regime and thus excludes certain layers and groups from effective participation in the polity. The second is *illiberal democracy*: a regime which lacks an effective rule of law to protect individual freedoms. Third, there is *delegative democracy*, a type of defective, plebiscitarian democracy that remains semi-pluralistic and tends to concentrate political power in the executive, thus frequently violating parliamentary and judicial institutions. The fourth type is a *democracy of enclaves*, in which crucial power effectively remains outside the representative system, mostly within the military sphere (Merkel *et al.* 2003: 69, 72 f.).

Among the electoral democracies counted by Freedom House in 2008, almost half can be labelled as defective (Merkel 2010: 494). In all variants of defective democracy, a democratic constitution and elections have survived. But participation (it is said) does not lead to comprehensive, all-inclusive representation. This shortcoming highlights the point that in any liberal representative democracy there is a necessary balance between representation through the participation of all the citizens and the existence of unelected institutions, such as courts and judicial review. Defective democracies are nevertheless representative only in the abstract sense. While in many countries more neutral institutions, such as constitutional courts, have the highest reputation among the citizens, things are different within many defective democracies. As a general rule, within these defective democracies participation and a certain degree of representation are to be found, but elections are not always fair and guarantees of liberal principles of human and social rights are underdeveloped (Collier and Levitsky 1997). But despite such defects, these diminished subtypes of liberal 'embedded democracy' can sometimes be considered as strongly representative while only weakly democratic in a liberal sense. Particularly in 'delegative democracies', charismatic presidents clash with parliamentary assemblies over who is truly representing the people. With the 'mandate of the people' legitimated by referenda, charismatic presidents restrict or circumvent parliaments by direct recourse to the people. As illiberal and sometimes outright authoritarian their mode of governance may be, these presidents mostly rely on stronger support among the represented than do the parliamentary representatives. This is confirmed, for example in Latin America, through many opinion polls (e.g., Latinobarómetro) or electoral analyses. Plebiscitarian appeals for direct representation are more popular than representative and deliberative forms of parliamentary representation in most of the defective democracies.

While some authors do not accept 'grey zones' on the spectrum of political regimes, and consider hybrids as based on a logically inconsistent taxonomy (Przeworski *et al.* 2000: 57), most writers acknowledge that there are hybrids between what is called liberal democracy and authoritarian regimes. There is indeed something linking these regime types, including 'façade democracy', where democratic and representative institutions disguise authoritarianism. Authors who consider democratic elections and vertical accountability as sufficient conditions for democracy often fail to distinguish between Sweden, the United Kingdom and France, on the one hand, and Russia, Indonesia and Bolivia on the other, even though all governments within these countries are democratically elected. The point is that the distinction between liberal and defective democracies is based on a static analysis of the status quo. Considered as hard-and-fast regime types, they fail to integrate a dynamic temporal dimension. Such a time dimension is, however, explicitly included in approaches known as 'consolidology' (Schmitter 1995; Linz and Stepan 1996; Croissant and Merkel 2004). Consolidating regimes have in turn been classified into three types (Beichelt 2001: 143). These include *formally democratic parliamentary systems* (Estonia, Latvia, Slovenia, Czech Republic, Hungary); *transitional regimes as balanced systems* (Bulgaria, Macedonia, Moldova, Rumania); and *minimal democratic regimes* (Slovakia, Russia, Ukraine). These different consolidating regimes in turn can be subdivided into 'parliamentary systems' (Slovakia) and 'regimes dominated by a president' (Russia, Ukraine). The latter type shows just how quickly all taxonomies can become obsolete. Slovakia is an example: within the space of a few years, it adopted a formally democratic system and was the first former communist country after Slovenia to be integrated into the Eurozone. During the same period, in a contrasting case, it became doubtful whether Russia remained a 'minimal democratic' or 'semi-authoritarian' regime.

This dynamic uncertainty helps explain why, within the overall comparative analysis of contemporary forms of representative democracy, consolidating systems mostly play a marginal role – with the possible exceptions of the Czech Republic, Slovenia and Hungary. This neglect of consolidating systems has been reinforced by the ways in which their initial representativeness was crafted through 'electoral engineering', itself a subtype of 'institutional engineering' (Krohn 2003: 61). Such engineering created unstable electoral systems and volatile voting behaviour, which in turn have cast doubt on the 'representative' character of some of the new democracies. The great transformation of dictatorships into democracies during the third wave meanwhile resurrected old debates. Juan Linz (1990) came up with the idea that presidential systems ruined democracy (especially in Latin America). Dieter Nohlen and others (Nohlen and Fernández 1991) were able to show that the degradation of democracy was due not simply to the form of representative government, but that party systems also have to be taken into consideration, and that parliamentary and semi-presidential governments also stagnate and decline under certain social and political circumstances (which was certainly true of the earlier fate of Italy, Austria, and the Weimar Republic between the World Wars). Eastern Europe constituted the great field of experiments with representative government. Again, the empirical results have been classified in different ways: within this region, parliamentary systems fared better than semi-presidential regimes (Lijphart 1992, 1994; Merkel *et al.* 1996: 85), but the causality is in fact the other way around: socio-economically developed societies and politically more mature systems, such as the Czech Republic or Hungary, chose parliamentary government, whereas less developed countries opted for semi-presidentialism, a model, among the mature Western systems, that proved to work efficiently only in France.

Challenge II: populism

Liberal representative forms of government are today confronted not only by analyses of defective democracy; more dangerous are the challenges posed by populist movements, populist parties, politics and policies.

Many consolidated parliamentary party governments in Western Europe have been challenged increasingly by right-wing populist attacks, ranging from the Haider phenomenon in Austria, Le Pen's National Front in France to Berlusconi's Italy. Even in Scandinavia, right-wing populist parties have emerged. Not only have they attacked taxation, welfare and immigration policies; they also criticise the mode of governing by established party cartels, for instance by claiming to represent 'the people' against the 'political class'. Populist movements sometimes pit 'elite-directing forms of politics' against former 'elite-directed politics' (Inglehart 1990: 338). Building on the 'participatory revolution' of the 1970s and 1980s, populists complain about the way electoral competition has changed, in favour of medium range, non-encompassing ideologies, special issues and a growing impact of individual candidates and their profiles (Kaase 1984). In the 'Third World', the left-wing populism of Chávez, Morales and others protests against the social exclusion and ethnic marginalisation of the indigenous population. In Europe, by contrast, right-wing populism protests against the inclusion of immigrants and politically active minorities. With respect to representative democracy (perhaps as a contrast) it should be noted that these right-wing populist movements normally do not challenge democracy as a whole, but only representative institutions such as parliaments, which are said to have been captured by an elitist political class out of touch with the real interests, values and opinions of ordinary people.

Historically speaking, populism began as a kind of mystical union of the people; it was a syndrome rather than an ideology (Wiles 1969: 166). Leaders boasted of their direct communication with the people. While right-wing populists in Europe think more in terms of political parties such as FPÖ (Austria); Forza Italia, Lega Nord (Italy); FN (France); DPP (Denmark); SVP (Switzerland); or VVD (the Netherlands), left-wing populists in Latin America (Venezuela, Bolivia, Ecuador) mobilise their supporters primarily by state-sponsored movements. The basic creeds of both types of populism are:

(1) *Populist propaganda is less programmatic and more moralistic.* Since populists quite frequently pretend to reject science and its inhuman rationalism, they appeal to common prejudices of 'the people' and hardly ever participate in theoretical debates. They prefer conspiracy myths: 'we have been cheated' or 'we have been neglected by the establishment' are popular slogans. 'Virtue' resides in the simple people and their collective traditions. Populists consciously break political taboos in political discourse, in order to give a voice to the ordinary people whose interests were not represented by the established political class.

(2) *Populists fight the 'corruption' of established elites, who are declared to be unrepresentative of the people.* Populists prefer the term 'political class' instead of the positive connotations of the notion 'elite'. In Third World countries, primitivism (such as the mystification of Aztec heritage in Mexico) merges with progressivism, and is often close to socialist ideas. There is rarely a consistent doctrine; sometimes populists begin as a single-issue-movement, which does not create a system of integrated creeds, as in an ideology, but only a stubborn obsession with one issue that is said to be relevant to the whole society.

Populists' ideas of representative government depend on their location in the left–right spectrum. There is a debate as to whether all populist movements are right-wing or are just the more moderate form of right-wing extremism. Recently, left-wing populists have been discovered in Western Europe (or rediscovered, since they already existed in nineteenth-century Russia and the United States). Green movements were falsely considered populist due to their unconventional modes of mobilising people, campaigning and behaving in parliament. Although this new political style was clearly anti-establishment, the Greens never referred to 'the people'. They opposed any kind of charismatic leadership, and they turned out to be representative of considerable parts of the highly educated middle classes. The same was sometimes said of the post-communist parties, such as the PDS/'Die Linke' in Germany, which became an important party for representing East German interests after the post-1989 reunification. However, this suspicious labelling was never convincingly substantiated. Although parties like 'Die Linke' in Germany may propagate some unrealistic distributional demands in their programme, their behaviour in parliament and in regional government does not justify the use of the label 'populist'.

The notion of populism should therefore be distinguished from extremist movements – even though the latter, such as fascists, have many populist features. Today there are neo-fascist parties – such as the NPD in Germany – that in fact display few populist features and behave like fascists in rather bourgeois guise. Populism is however accepted as a kind of honorary title; as Haider (1994: 57) explained in his book *Freiheit, die ich meine* (*The Liberty I Have in Mind*), within a democracy populism is a necessary movement in the fight 'against the commands from the ivory tower of the political class' and its 'contempt for the people'.

Seymour Martin Lipset in his *Political Man* (1960) was the first to write about the 'extremism of the centre'. But he had mostly Third

World countries in mind. In Latin America, left-wing populism is widespread and has enjoyed a remarkable renaissance after the failure of the so-called Washington consensus that flourished during the 1990s. Meanwhile in Europe, itself pressured by European integration and globalisation, populism in the liberal-conservative centre of the party spectrum has become more frequent, as evidenced by Poujade in France and Glistrup in Denmark to Blocher in Switzerland. Recent economic losers also turn toward the populists. They blame a degenerate representative system and its elitist cartels, and within the regime they denounce cooperation with identifiable, standard scapegoat figures: ranging from the European bureaucracy in Brussels to foreign investors 'invading' the country with their neo-liberal ideology, the CIA, or even the United States as a whole. Populists have traditionally fought three principal enemies: big industry; trade unions (especially when they cooperate with big industry in corporatist institutions) and the 'state within a state' of the established elites bent on harmonising their interests. More recently immigration, Europeanisation and globalisation have become the major target of right-wing populists. Populists no longer make the state the target of demands for sustenance; rather, they demand that the state must serve the 'ordinary people', who are usually defined rather vaguely. Enlightened followers of old modernisation theories – such as Przeworski (2000: 187 ff.) – were inclined to correlate the stability of representative democracy with levels of economic or demographic growth. But populism shows that there is another side of the coin: the emergence of groups that are so bored and dissatisfied with democracy that they complain about the fact that high levels of economic performance produce losers, especially during processes of rapid change.

Instead of faith in the traditional party, populists often favour a society of free associations – in the French leftist tradition of Proudhon or British guild socialism, and in the more conservative tradition that is closer to the ideas of Otto von Gierke (Priester 2007: 220). The opposition to 'big corporations' does not mean that all populists fight against capitalism, not even its neo-liberal version. On the contrary, many populists could be called 'anarcho-liberal'; from Glistrup and the Progress Party in Denmark to Haider's (1994: 150 ff.) FPÖ in Austria and Blocher's SVP in Switzerland, one kind of conservative populism (particularly in Scandinavia) is predominantly directed against the welfare state. Many populists have accepted the logic of individualisation. This is another reason why they prefer rather loose networks instead of organised parties. Political entrepreneurs prevail among the leaders of populist movements, such as Poujade, Fortuyn and Haider. Berlusconi is certainly the prototype of these political 'parvenus', who benefited from a degenerating party system in Italy. Only a minority of European populists today identify with right-wing extremism. Initially Le Pen in France did this, but even this most enduring elder statesman of a populist movement tried to move away from the extreme right.

Extremist movements tend to believe in the overthrow (or radical change) of the existing system; they do not recognise constitutional rules. By contrast, most populist movements and parties grudgingly accept the rules and want to change only single elements, such as immigration laws, welfare entitlements for immigrants, internal security and electoral laws. They also demand the direct election of the presidency. This is in accordance with their demand for a strong leader and a strong state. Where this already exists, as in Austria, Haider (1994: 235) complains about the costly duplication of offices. Populist movements and parties are rarely revolutionary. They hope to bring the establishment back on the 'right road' to a strong state with nationalistic elements and proclaim a 'Second Republic', as in Italy; or a 'Third Republic' in Austria (Haider 1994: 189); or a 'Fourth Republic' in Poland under Kaczynski.

(3) *Populism was originally a rural movement. In the era of globalisation it tends to become an urban phenomenon.* Competition from foreign migrants was always a breeding ground for populists in cities of the United States. The new populists also claim that the 'native' people are alienated and doomed to decline. Populists pretend to represent the nation. Only leftist populists sometimes claim to be fundamentally opposed to these right-wing populist ideologies. But even Proudhon, a foe of Napoleon III, proved at one point during his career after 1848 to be ready to cooperate with Bonaparte, only to find himself deeply disappointed when the president of the Second French Republic – and from 1851 on, the Emperor – refused to accept him as a political partner. Today, one issue that separates right- and left-wing populists is immigration. Left-wing populists favour more immigration and a multicultural society, which is abhorred by right-wing populists (Betz 1994: 179 ff.). Neither variant of populism is nationalist in the traditional sense; they typically favour regional autonomy and decentralisation.

(4) *Populism is organised by charismatic leaders, such as Poujade or Le Pen in France, Haider in Austria, or Berlusconi in Italy.* The leader claims the special title of 'representing' the needs of the people. If this charisma fails, or is substituted by bureaucratic leadership, and by what Max Weber called the *Veralltäglichung des Charismas*, the everyday

'routinisation' and decline of the special attraction of the leader, the populist movement quickly disintegrates. In Germany, the downfall of Schönhuber, the founder and leader of the populist Republicans, quickly led to their marginalisation. Similar signs of disintegration troubled Blocher in Switzerland, especially when his movement rejected his policies. When Pim Fortuyn was killed in Holland, his movement found it difficult to find a substitute leader. In many countries, the intellectualisation of populist leadership has not been successful; the masses grow bored by the oft-repeated slogans (Stöss 2000: 178). A lack of professional behaviour in parliaments has also proved detrimental to the long-run growth of populist movements. And when populist styles of policy making are adopted by big non-populist parties, the smaller populist groups lose their advantage. However, the overcoming of succession problems at the top of their parties by Dutch, Austrian and Swiss right-wing populists suggest that those parties do not necessarily 'die' with their leaders, but that they can successfully mobilise political sentiments against global-isation, Europeanisation and immigration.

The routinisation of populist movements sets in as they draw closer to power; this is why many of them prefer to remain in opposition, in order to cling onto the 'purity' of their basic creeds. Nothing is more compromising for populists than being held responsible for bad pol-icies – as Haider found when in government in Austria. The same dynamic weakened Gregor Gysy, a left-wing populist in the Berlin gov-ernment; it also weakened populists who supported bourgeois govern-ments, as in the Benelux and Scandinavian countries. Party coalitions are always shaky, but coalitions of populists are much more likely to be unstable. Some electoral successes have resulted in disaster because the more extreme right-wing populists lacked professional cadres enabling them to act successfully when in parliaments, as the NPD (*National-Demokratische Partei Deutschlands*), the DVU (*Deutsche Volksunion*) and the Republicans, all of whom won temporary representation, showed in the German Länder diets (Holtmann 2002). However, the endur-ing success or survival of the right-wing populist parties in Denmark, Norway, Switzerland and the Netherlands shows that right-wing popu-lism has become an enduring feature in many of the Western European party systems.

A unique case in Western Europe is Berlusconi, who reshuffled the whole Italian party system in the early 1990s. When his 'Second Republic of Italy' proved to be even more corrupt and undemocratic than the former *classe politica*, Berlusconi was toppled. He was able to survive for a while only with the help of a democratised neo-fascist movement and regional populist groups, such as *Lega Lombarda*. The case is unique in European history because Berlusconi – accused of corruption, sex scandals, interference in judicial matters and changing the electoral law in his favour – managed to win re-election in 2008. Berlusconi's style of populist governing displays certain traits which are more typical for Latin American than Western Europe: all the scandals and the disdain for the judiciary, the parliament and traditional parties strengthened his charismatic appeal as a 'true leader' and paid off in the electoral arena.

Since the 1980s, a normative debate about the virtues and failures of populism has been developing. The established parties have tended to regard populist movements as a bad influence. In Germany – a country that invented the constitutional possibility of outlawing a party, an innovation subsequently copied by countries such as Russia – the prohibition of new, unwelcome competitors was considered. But in the age of new social movements, the creative forces of populists have also been discovered, even by formerly leftist authors (Priester 2007: 220). That is why populist leaders are classified according to whether or not they develop representative democracy in seminal ways. De Gaulle and Gandhi are regarded as 'good populists'; militant regional populists, such as Sinn Fein or ETA, or racist and xenophobic parties are said to be 'bad populists', as long as they support terrorism and discriminate on racist grounds.

The populist revolt against representative democracy is characterised by three additional developments:

(1) Populist styles have infected the leadership of established parties and changed the rules of representative government, as was demonstrated by leaders such as Blair in Britain and Schroeder in Germany. Charismatic media democracy has created a populist style in conventional politics (Korte 2003).

(2) In most Western European systems, populism has so far posed no substantial threat to representative democracy. During the first three decades after 1945, populist parties usually won less than 10 per cent of the votes; the notable exception was Glistrup's Progress Party in four elections between 1973 and 1979. Since then, however, an increasing number of populist parties received more than 10 per cent of the popular votes: the Front National in France; the FPÖ in Austria; Berlusconi's Forza Italia, later renamed Popolo della Libertà; Blocher's SVP in Switzerland; the Lijst Pim Fortuyn in the Netherlands; the Danish People's Party; and the Norwegian

Fremskrittspartiet. Italy's Forza Italia and the SVP became the strongest populist parties in Europe. Swiss populists sometimes have enjoyed considerable success, but their victories are extremely volatile. Large fluctuations in their level of support can be rapid (data in Betz 1994: 3), as the withering Poujade movement found in a few years in the Fourth French Republic. Most populist movements were, by contrast, flash-in-the-pan parties. Only populist leaders who turned to authoritarian rule (Perón in Argentina) or (because the alternatives had dried up) successfully occupied the political centre and substituted their populist image for the attitude of 'statesmanship' (Berlusconi in Italy) were able to remain a decisive factor in the representative system of their country.

(3) Two variants of 'inbuilt populism' in contemporary representative democracies have been identified (Decker 2006b: 22, 26). In the first, moderate populists accept the constitutional-representative model of democracy and, paradoxically, strengthen it by emphasising the need for inclusion of more groups, interests and issues. In the second, radical populists favour plebiscitarian democracy; 'decisionism', in the shape of the claimed unitary will of the people, serves as a substitute for deliberation. Plebiscitarian democracy is potentially a danger for representative democracy, but political parties challenging the system – with the exception of Italy – were historically never strong enough to change the system and its institutions. More recently, Germany proved to be well protected against right-wing extremism and populism because of its Nazi past, and because the country's two major parties are moderately welfare-oriented, on two occasions merging their forces in a grand coalition to reform the system.

In sum: the slogans used by catch-all parties are increasingly stolen from populist groups. Populists have remained radical because when they stay in opposition they do not like compromise. Populists pretend to mobilise, but frequently the result has been the manipulation of their supporters through forms of pseudo-participation. As soon as populists become established, they learn to make compromises with other groups. If and when they are accepted, populist parties – whether from the right or left – tend to lose substantial parts of their distinctiveness.

Challenge III: alternative normative models

In the literature on the subject, new notions of the decline and renewal of traditional representative democracy are spreading. New types of

democracy are announced (it seems) every day: 'democracy of negotiation'; 'civil society'; 'cooperation among networks'; 'subpolitics'
(Ulrich Beck); a combination of Habermas and theories of civil society
known as 'cosmopolitan democracy' or 'transnational democracy' (Held
1993); 'reflexive democracy' directed against centralised and homogeneous structures of decision making and in favour of multi-layered
processes of decision making connected by networks (Schmalz-Bruns
1995: 164). Other approaches, such as the analysis of 'post-democracy',
carry negative connotations; still other normative approaches speak
more positively of republicanism, deliberative democracy (Habermas)
and dialogic democracy (Giddens). The latter approach points out that
in the age of 'post-democracy' not only do virtually all of the formal
components of representative democracy survive (a point conceded by
Crouch 2005: 12, 22), but that elites receive ever less deference because
'the secrets of politicians are laid bare to the democratic gaze'.

Some strands of the new normative thinking insist that the integration
of citizens into a democratic society through a common social morality
is more important than institutional integration (Münkler 2006: 22).
Republicanism, an old tradition of political thinking that stretches back
to the Renaissance, has recently been rediscovered. Often contrasted
with liberalism, republicanism is said to have the advantage of being
more democratic than liberalism – and more liberal than traditional
(representative) democracy (Llanque-Kurps 2003: 7). Republicanism
aims at the revitalisation of citizenship through decentralised self-
government; since Hannah Arendt, it has directed its energies against a
state apparatus legitimated through nationalised and state-funded parties, and against the apolitical privatism of a depoliticised population.

Republicanism sees an inevitable connection between citizens' virtues and self-government. Liberalism does not rule out such a combination, but considers it contingent, as a republican communitarian puts
it (Sandel 1995: 57). So how intimate can or should the relationship
between liberalism and republicanism be? Even writers who claim to
have shown that our whole political knowledge is obsolete, especially the
concept of representative democracy, have launched polemics against
all the attempts since John Rawls to revitalise a public ethic in the tradition of Kant. Some liberal-minded thinkers consider that democracy
should be reinvigorated, especially its 'laicist functions of organising
special interests, conflict resolution and guarantees for civil liberties'
(Zolo 1997: 217). Other authors are more firmly opposed to the 'tyr-
anny of common sense' proclaimed by 'communitarian lay priests' and
cast their vote for an 'egoistic society' (Herzinger 1997: 61). So while
some normative thinkers hail the 'return of citizens', others celebrate

the 'true representation of egoistic interests' in a 'realistic model of democracy'. Habermas (1992: 360 f.) has doubted the feasibility of a polemical (liberal) separation of civil society and state since, in his view, the task of balancing interests and powers requires a rule of law framework (*Rechtsstaat*). Some critics (Latour 1995: 68, 188) believe that modern constitutions have become a victim of their own success, and that they are prone to collapse because the mobilisation of collective groups has created so many hybrid forms that the constitutional framework can no longer keep them together. This is surely an exaggeration. Fighting for deliberative democracy, Habermas (1992: 446) has admitted that civil society is always in danger of degenerating, for instance because of movements which defend traditions and identities against capitalist modernisation, or which exceed influence-seeking by trying to transform themselves into power organisations; or by social revolutions driven by historical subjects that see themselves teleologically as torchbearers of progress. But even this realistic view of deliberative democracy has attracted harsh critics, such as Richard Rorty (1989). Although he shared with Habermas a commitment to the principle of the *citoyen engagé*, Habermas, in his view, remains a 'metaphysical thinker' because of his continuing attachment to 'consensus through free communication'.

Discourses based on the model of deliberative democracy have stronger normative components than the liberal state, but weaker components than the republican ideal. Both norms start from a vision of a political 'whole'. There the agreement ends. Liberalism postulates, in a rather abstract way, that the constitution is the point of reference; republicanism, on the other hand, begins from the principle of sovereign citizenship. Along these lines, the model of deliberative democracy sketches a vision of a decentralised society that creates a political public sphere in which deliberation about various social problems and interests becomes possible. Deliberative democracy is a normative hope. Leftist writers complain that it contains hardly any fundamental criticism of capitalism – only the denunciation of abuses by transnational corporations – yet many right-wing movements, such as Blocher's Peoples Party in Switzerland, are also rather capitalist-minded and offer no hope for the fundamental change of the system. If we look at former leftists like Hardt and Negri (2002) in their vision of 'Empire', there seems to be no hope for fundamental change. Foucault's spirit is spreading. Each power structure bears inherently its counter-power.

Torchbearers of 'radical politics', such as Anthony Giddens (1994: 112), have meanwhile developed the idea of 'dialogic democracy'. They hope that this normative concept will be more than an extension of liberal democracy. They expect it to create not just new rights of interest representations, as in representative democracy, but further the aims of cultural cosmopolitism, which is considered decisive for the rebuilding of social solidarity, for instance by new social movements. Identity politics has become a catchword of post-modern democracy and has changed the connotations of representation. According to Colin Crouch (2005: 119), however, the prospects are slim for 'trying to move beyond identity politics to a "Third Way" political appeal which tries to evade the very idea of identity'. Political parties that claim to represent the masses of people need to do so by articulating an identity for those people (Pizzorno 1993). Yet the more these identities are artificially constructed, the more other possible identities are neglected. The established parties not surprisingly have been compared to large corporations: both avoid risks. Corporations dislike risky investments, whereas established catch-all parties try to avoid investing in identity-building for new social movements (Crouch 2005: 120), which can be successful only when they cooperate with established interest groups and parties – as the ecological or the feminist movements have shown.

Post-democracy has not kept 'pace with capitalism's rush to the global' (Crouch 2005: 29). The erosion of large collective organisations left huge segments of the population, at best, under-represented in the political sphere. Corporate elites dominate the public arenas, with the representation of workers thinning out in the post-corporatist age. Increasing social inequality has been translated into a post-democratic inequality of interest representation in parliament and government.

Deliberative versions of democracy are less concerned with this supposedly asymmetrical interest representation; they are more interested in creating arenas for deliberation and 'better argument'. Equal representation becomes secondary to a deliberative discourse for the sake of the public good.

Direct plebiscitarian democracy – an alternative to liberal representative democracy?

Representative democracy – dubbed 'liberal democracy' by both liberals and their enemies – is torn this way and that by utopian demands and functional realities. The rhetoric of democracy grew weaker after 1990, when the system became unchallenged, due to the collapse of authoritarian alternatives. In consequence, representative democracy is said by many populists, including the followers of Haider and Blocher, to be 'minimalistic' and thus not worthy of the enthusiasm of citizens. Even defenders of liberal democracy like Andrew Levine (1981: 7) have admitted that 'the political institutions proper to liberal democratic politics, representative government and the party system, so far from implementing democratic values, may actually betray them'. In this perception, liberal democrats are pretending to be both liberals and democrats. The theory to which they are committed is genuinely liberal but – at least in its practical implementation – not genuinely democratic. At best, representation, which once meant the notion of independent legislators who follow their consciences and instincts, is now guided by changing popular moods in a system of *Stimmungsdemokratie* (democracy based on popular moods).

Direct democracy and popular legislation are frequently demanded, and even accepted by the radical wing of liberal democrats, from Carole Pateman (1970: 111) to Benjamin Barber (1984: 10, 33). They harbour the stubborn belief that there is no question of whether direct democracy should be organised; the question is only how it can be implemented (Decker 2006a: 5). Non-normative scholars try instead to examine things empirically. They ask whether direct democracy and legislation via referenda within a deliberative discourse is really better and more efficient. One survey has examined some 550 popular initiatives and referenda. The result is not encouraging: no Habermasian 'power-free discourse' has been discovered. The results of referenda are mostly middle class and status quo-oriented. Radical groups or even semi-leftist groups, such as trade unions, have normally failed to gain anything from popular legislation. Meanwhile, the growth of the welfare state has been promoted by representative parliamentarians in Northern Europe, rather than by Swiss methods of direct democracy (Freitag and Wagschal 2007: 326 f.; Moser and Obinger in Freitag and Wagschal 2007: 357). More innovative legislation arising from direct or participatory initiatives is not anticipated by most experts (Kranenpohl 2006: 38). As a consequence of the impracticability of direct democracy, the independence of representatives has survived; in many cases, representatives have had to decide things after the failure of popular votes (switching from left-hand traffic to right-hand traffic in Sweden, or lowering the voting age to 18 years in Denmark, for instance). Tellingly, Brown and Sarkozy, leaders in two major countries that face hostile majorities against the EU constitution, admitted that next time around there will be no referendum on this question. Referenda can sometimes serve as a complementary advice mechanism, as in Italy, where consultative referenda have frequently produced rather reasonable results that have served as guidelines for representative decision makers in the pre-Berlusconi era. Sometimes an equal ranking of representative and direct democratic legislation is envisaged. This is very difficult to achieve, especially in two circumstances: in a federalist system, where there is a danger that the federal chamber loses its *raison d'etre*; and in a system with a sovereign constitution and judicial review by a constitutional court, where *ex-ante* judgements of courts have been recommended in order not to violate the 'sovereignty of the people' (Kranenpohl 2003). Such empirical doubts about the efficiency of direct democracy have not convinced normative theorists. The latter emphasise – not without good reason – that direct democracy has positive impacts on political socialisation and learning, which in the long run stabilise representative democracy (Waschkuhn 1998: 514).

All these conflicting trends bring us to a paradox of postmodernism: in 1968, the criticism of liberal democracy took violent forms fuelled by radical normative theory. More than forty years later, normative theory, which has grown more realistic and has learned from the criticisms generated by the 1968 generation, finds itself confronted with the same objections that were posed against representative democracy in 1968: that it represents not much more than a normatively embellished duplication of a dreadful political reality. This goes to show that political science seems to follow 'kitchen-sink art' and other variants of postmodernism: forms of art that do not lead to a higher ideal of normative aesthetics, but backwards, to a miserable everyday life which is begrudgingly accepted.

REFERENCES

Anonymous (1816) *Réfutation de la doctrine de Montesquieu sur la balance des pouvoirs et aperçus divers sur plusieurs questions sur la droit publique.* Paris.

Barber, B. (1984) *Strong democracy.* Berkeley: University of California Press. Translated as *Starke Demokratie. Über die Teilhabe am Politischen.* Hamburg: Rotbuch Verlag.

Beichelt, T. (2001) *Demokratische Konsolidierung im postsozialistischen Europa. Die Rolle der politischen Institutionen.* Opladen: Leske & Budrich.

Betz, H.-G. (1994) *Radical right-wing populism in western Europe.* Houndsmill: Macmillan.

Beyme, K. von (1965) 'Repräsentatives und parlamentarisches Regierungssystem. Eine begriffsgeschichtliche Analyse', *Politische Vierteljahresschrift* 6(2): 145–59.

   (1987) *America as a model: The impact of democracy in the world.* Aldershot: Gower.

   (1988) 'Right-wing extremism in post-war Europe', *West European Politics* 11(2): 1–18.

   (2000a) *Parliamentary democracy: Democratization, destabilization, reconsolidation, 1789–1999.* Houndsmill: Macmillan.

   (2000b) *Parteien im Wandel. Von den Volksparteien zu den professionalisierten Wählerparteien.* Opladen: Westdeutscher Verlag (2nd edn. 2002).

Birch, A. H. (1993) *The concepts and theories of modern democracy.* London: Routledge.

Burke, E. (1864) *To the electors of Bristol (1774)*. In Burke, *Works, vol. 1*. London: Henry G. Bohn, pp. 442–9.

Collier, D. and St. Levitsky (1997) 'Democracy with adjectives: Conceptual innovation in comparative research', *World Politics* 49(3): 430–51.

Committee on Political Parties of the American Political Studies Association (1950) *Toward a more responsible two-party system*. A Report of the APSR, Supplement 88.

Croissant, A. and W. Merkel (eds.) (2004) 'Consolidated or defective democracy? Problems of regime change'. Special issue of *Democratization* 11(5).

Crouch, C. (2005) *Post-democracy*. Cambridge: Polity Press.

Decker, F. (2006a) 'Direkte Demokratie im deutschen "Parteienbundesstaat"', *Aus Politik und Zeitgeschichte* 10: 3–10.

— (ed.) (2006b) *Populismus. Gefahr für die Demokratie oder nützliches Korrektiv?* Wiesbaden: VS Verlag für Sozialwissenschaften.

Faltin, I. (1990) *Norm, Milieu, politische Kultur*. Wiesbaden: DUV.

Forst, R. (2007) *Das Recht der Rechtfertigung*. Frankfurt am Main: Suhrkamp.

Freitag, M. and U. Wagschal (eds.) (2007) *Direkte Demokratie. Bestandsaufnahmen und Wirkungen im internationalen Vergleich*. Münster: LIT.

Giddens, A. (1994) *Beyond left and right: The future of radical politics*. Cambridge: Polity Press.

Gurr, T., T. Robert, K. Jaggers and W. Moore (1991) 'The transformation of the western state: The growth of democracy, autocracy and state power since 1800', in A. Inkeles (ed.) *On measuring democracy*. New Brunswick: Transaction, pp. 69–104.

Habermas, J. (1992) *Faktizität und Geltung*. Frankfurt am Main: Suhrkamp.

Haider, J. (1994) *Die Freiheit, die ich meine*. Frankfurt am Main: Ullstein.

Hardt, M. and A. Negri (2002) *Empire – die neue Weltordnung*. Frankfurt am Main: Campus.

Hartleb, F. (2004) *Rechts- und Linkspopulismus*. Wiesbaden: VS Verlag für Sozialwissenschaften.

Held, D. (1993) *Political theory today*. Oxford: Polity Press.

Herzinger, R. (1997) *Die Tyrannei des Gemeinsinns. Ein Bekenntnis zur egoistischen Gesellschaft*. Berlin: Rowohlt.

Holtmann, E. (2002) *Die angepassten Provokateure. Aufstieg und Niedergang der rechtsextremen DVU als Protestpartei im polarisierten Parteiensystem Sachsen-Anhalts*. Opladen: Westdeutscher Verlag.

Inglehart, R. (1990) *Culture shift in advanced industrial society*. Princeton University Press.

Ionescu, G. and E. Gellner (eds.) (1969) *Populism: Its meanings and national characteristics*. London: Weidenfeld & Nicolson.

Kaase, M. (1984) 'The challenge of the "participatory revolution" in pluralist democracies', *International Political Science Review* 5(3): 299–318.

Kant, I. (1964) *Werke* (ed. Weissschädel). Wiesbaden: Insel-Verlag.

Khasbulatov, R. I. (1993) 'Kakaya vlast' nuzhna Rossii', *Sotsiologicheskie issledovaniya* 11: 18–31.

Korte, K.-R. (2003) 'Populismus als Regierungsstil', in N. Werz (ed.) *Populismus*. Opladen: Leske & Budrich, pp. 209–22.

Kranenpohl, U. (2003) 'Verkürzen Verfassungsrichter Volksrechte?' *Gesellschaft–Wirtschaft – Politik* 52(1): 37–46.

(2006) 'Bewältigung des Reformstaus durch direkte Demokratie?' *Aus Politik und Zeitgeschichte* 10/2006: 32–8.

Krohn, T. (2003) *Die Genese von Wahlsystemen in Transitionsprozessen. Portugal, Spanien, Polen und Tschechien im Vergleich.* Opladen: Leske & Budrich.

Küchenhoff, E. (1967) *Möglichkeiten und Grenzen begrifflicher Klarheit in der Staatsformenlehre.* Berlin: Duncker & Humblot.

Lamennais, F. R. de (1823) *Extraits du drapeau blanc. Plan d'un libre intitulé: Observations sur le gouvernment de l'Angleterre, dit gouvernement représentatif constitutionnel.* Paris.

Laski, H. (1944) 'The parliamentary and presidential systems', *Public Administration Review*, Autumn: 347–59. See also D. K. Price, 'A response to Mr. Laski', *Public Administration Review*, Autumn: 360–3.

Latour, B. (1991) *Nous n'avons jamais été modernes.* Paris: La Découverte.

(1995) *Wir sind nie modern gewesen: Versuch einer symmetrischen Anthropologie.* Berlin: Akademie Verlag.

Leibholz, G. (1967) *Strukturprobleme der modernen Demokratie.* Karlsruhe: C. F. Müller.

Levine, A. (1981) *Liberal democracy: A critique of its theory.* New York: Columbia University Press.

Lijphart, A. (ed.) (1992) *Parliamentary versus presidential government.* Oxford University Press.

(1994) *Electoral systems and party systems: A study of twenty-seven democracies.* Oxford University Press.

Linz, J. (1990) 'The perils of presidentialism', *Journal of Democracy* 1(1): 51–69.

Linz, J. and A. Stepan (1996) *Problems of democratic transition and consolidation: Southern Europe, South America, and post-communist Europe.* Baltimore: Johns Hopkins University Press.

Lipset, S. M. (1960) *Political man.* London: Mercury Books.

Llanque-Kurps, M. (2003) *Klassischer Republikanismus und moderner Verfassungsstaat.* HU Berlin: Habilitationsschrift.

Mair, P. (2002) 'Populist democracy vs party democracy', in Y. Mény and Y. Surel (eds.) *Democracies and the populist challenge.* Houndsmill: Macmillan, pp. 139–54.

Merkel, W. (2004) 'Embedded and defective democracies', in Croissant and Merkel (eds.), pp. 33–58.

(2010) *Systemtransformation. Eine Einführung in die Theorie und Empirie der Transformationsforschung.* Wiesbaden: VS Verlag für Sozialwissenschaften, 2nd rev. and exp. edition.

Merkel, W., E. Sandschneider and D. Segert (eds.) (1996) *Systemwechsel 2. Die Institutionalisierung der Demokratie.* Opladen: Leske & Budrich.

Merkel, W., H.-J. Puhle and A. Croissant (eds.) (2003) *Defekte Demokratien. Bd.1, Theorien und Probleme.* Wiesbaden: Vs Verlag für Sozialwissenschaften.

Mill, J. S. (1861). *Representative government.* London: Dent (1910, 1960).

(1873) *Autobiography.* London: Oxford University Press (1928, 1958).

Mulgan, G. (1994) *Politics in an antipolitical age.* Cambridge: Polity Press.

Münkler, H. (2006) 'Der Wettbewerb der Sinnproduzenten', *Merkur* 60(1): 15–22.

Nohlen, D. and M. Fernández (eds.) (1991) *Presidencialismo versus parlamentarismo*. Caracas: Nueva Sociedad.

Palme, S. U. (1969) 'Vom Absolutismus zum Parlamentarismus in Schweden', in D. Gerhard (ed.) *Stände-Vertretungen in Europa im 17. und 18. Jahrhundert*. Göttingen: Vandenhoeck & Ruprecht, pp. 368–97.

Pateman, C. (1970) *Participation and democratic theory*. Cambridge University Press.

Pitkin, H. F. (1967) *The concept of representation*. Berkeley: University of California Press.

——— (1989) 'Representation' in T. Ball, J. Fare and R. L. Hansen (eds.), *Political innovation and conceptual change*. Cambridge University Press, pp. 132–54.

Pizzorno, A. (1993) *Le radici della politica assoluta e altri saggi*. Milan: Feltrinelli.

Priester, K. (2007) *Populismus. Historische und aktuelle Erscheinungsformen*. Frankfurt am Main: Campus.

Przeworski, A., M. Alvarez, J. Cheibub and F. Limongi (2000) *Democracy and development: Political institutions and well-being in the world, 1950–1990*. Cambridge University Press.

Rorty, R. (1989) *Contingency, irony, and solidarity*. Cambridge University Press.

Sandel, M. J. (1995) *Liberalismus und Republikanismus: von der Notwendigkeit der Bürgertugend*. Vienna: Passagen.

Schmalz-Bruns, R. (1995) *Reflexive Demokratie. Die demokratische Transformation moderner Politik*. Baden-Baden: Nomos.

Schmitter, P. (1995) 'The consolidation of political democracies', in G. Pridham (ed.) *Transitions to democracy: Comparative perspectives from southern Europe, Latin America and eastern Europe*. Dartmouth: Aldershot, pp. 535–69.

Schumpeter, J. A. (1942) *Capitalism, socialism and democracy*. New York: Harper.

Stöss, R. (2000) *Rechtsextremismus im vereinten Deutschland*. Berlin: Friedrich Ebert Stiftung (3rd edn.).

Taggart, P. (1995) 'New populist parties in western Europe', *West European Politics* 18(1): 34–51.

Turkka, T. (2007) *The origins of parliamentarism: A study of Sandy's Motion*. Baden-Baden: Nomos.

Vorländer, H. (2003) *Demokratie*. München: Beck.

Walzer, M. (1992) *Zivile Gesellschaft und amerikanische Demokratie*. Berlin: Rotbuch Verlag.

Waschkuhn, A. (1998) *Demokratietheorien*. München: Oldenbourg.

Werz, N. (ed.) (2003) *Populismus*. Opladen: Leske & Budrich.

Wiles, P. (1969) 'A syndrome, not a doctrine: Some elementary theses on populism', in G. Ionescu and E. Gellner (eds.) *Populism: Its meanings and national characteristics*. London: Weidenfeld & Nicolson, pp. 166–79.

Zolo, D. (1997) *Die demokratische Fürstenherrschaft. Für eine realistische Theorie der Politik*. Göttingen: Steil.

3 The wider canvas: representation and democracy in state and society

Michael Saward

The future of democracy will hinge in part on what practices we think of as representative, and how they might be, or become, democratic. Claims and practices of diverse actors, from NGOs to celebrity activists to spiritual leaders, and new devices of governance such as participatory budgets and citizens' juries, are challenging received ideas of democratic representation. Elected national legislatures remain vital parts of this picture, as the contributions of Wessels and Beetham in this volume (Chapters 4 and 5) make clear. But there is a practical broadening and diversifying of representative claims and practices that has an impact on our very ideas of democratic representation. The core task of this chapter is to scan and interrogate key issues and tensions that extending the idea of representation brings into focus.

The key argument I offer here is built around the following points:

1. *Representative democracy* as we know it is (presented as) state-based, or 'statal';
2. But it does not exhaust *democratic representation* which is found, unevenly, through civil society;
3. A key factor behind points 1 and 2 is that concepts which dominant approaches to democratic representation tie to the state – not least legitimate authority – are not in fact confined to statal institutions and practices;
4. The comparatively *settled* world of representative practices in the state, and the comparatively *unsettled* world of representative practices in civil society, are linked through various parallels, dependencies, continuities, exchanges and mergings;
5. Critics and advocates may stipulate that representative democracy is solely concerned with the narrow canvas – statal representative democracy. But material and theoretical developments now push us to recognise that this stipulative choice can only be made from *within* a

74

wider canvas of practices denoted by the idea of societal democratic representation.[1]

Figure 3.1 is an attempt to capture the sense that political representation is increasingly a broad and highly diverse phenomenon in terms of form, scope and quality.[2] At this level of abstraction, democratic representation is depicted as one type of political representation, and representative democracy as one (familiar, persistent and crucial) type of democratic representation. Distinctions are drawn between the three nested fields in order to stress their deep interdependence. Democratic representation is a diffuse, uneven and often unsettled field of political practices. Representative democracy, as a centralised state system, is both continuous with and altered by developments in the wider unsettled field of democratic and political representation in which it is located. The key point is that representative democracy does not exhaust democratic representation. Democratic representation ought not to be understood as confined to a set of statal institutions, but rather understood more broadly (and indeed more complexly) as a quality which may be more or less present in a wider set of diffuse locations and (especially) practices.

To help us fix our thoughts around these categories – democratic representation, and within that representative democracy – let me offer some brief initial examples (I discuss further examples in the course of the chapter). Non-state democratic representation may occur, for example, in and around various interest and pressure groups, the workplace or the corporation, social movements both old and new, and in clubs, societies and advocacy groups in local communities. A number of prominent observers, working in different traditions of democratic theory, have discussed these and other examples (e.g., Bachrach 1967; Barber 1984; Hirst 1994 and 1997; and Pateman 1970). Statal representative democracy concerns the familiar institutions of the state: legislatures, executives, judiciaries and an array of other public bodies.

Figure 3.1 includes four nodes of variation across the three nested domains. These four nodes consist of topics in which both key differences and continuities between the domains of representative democracy and democratic representation are expressed. These four nodes are (1) institutional presence, (2) modes of exit and voice, (3) location and

---

[1] I borrow some of this terminology from a brief discussion of different conceptions of liberalism by Michael Walzer (1992).

[2] A version of Figure 3.1 appeared in Saward (2010). It is used here with the kind permission of Oxford University Press.

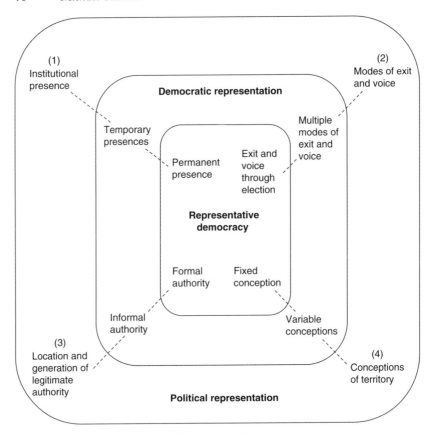

Figure 3.1. Domains of representation

generation of legitimate authority, and (4) conceptions of territory. For each of these four nodes, Figure 3.1 includes summary terms for conventional understandings of representation. So, for example, for node 1 (institutional presence), the wider domain of democratic representation is normally understood to involve temporary and shifting modes of representation, while the narrower statal domain involves the more permanent presence of representative state institutions. It is worth emphasising that these are not the only points of variation across the three nested domains that we might have examined, but they are key ones.

Taking on board this idea of nested domains makes a difference to our understanding of representative democracy and its possible futures when compared to more conventional approaches to representation and democracy – as I hope to show. I will develop these comments further, focusing in turn on the four nodes of variation expressed in Figure 3.1, later in the chapter. But I first focus on work that is especially germane to the crucial third node of variation, the one that is concerned with the location and generation of modes of legitimate authority, through a reading of key aspects of legitimacy and authority in the writings of Max Weber and David Easton.[3] This issue is especially critical in that we need to see how political authority has misleadingly, though influentially, been confined to statal institutions and processes. I seek to build on selected influential insights of Weber and Easton, in part by taking up threads which they introduce but do not themselves pursue, in order to help us to recognise the credibility of disparate claims to political authority beyond the state itself, and what this can mean for our views of democratic representation.

Successful claims?

In 'Politics as a Vocation', Max Weber famously defined the modern state as 'a human community that (successfully) claims the monopoly of the legitimate use of physical force within a given territory' (Weber 1991 [1921]). Normally this is taken to mean that the modern state *possesses* such a monopoly, both by definition and in fact. But the 'successfully' in Weber's definition is highly suggestive, in ways that Weber himself arguably did not fully pursue. He implies strongly that such claims just *are* successful, or fulfilled:

At the present time, the right to use physical force *is ascribed* to other institutions or to individuals only to the extent to which the state permits it. The state *is* considered the sole source of the right to use violence. (1991 [1921]: 78, emphasis added)

It is clear, however, that *claims*, *ascriptions* and *considerations* are open-ended in terms of their consequences. We can usefully retrieve a sense of the dynamics of the claim – the performance and the generation of the view that such a monopoly exists, the generation of images and narratives that foster the ascriptions and the considerations (cf. Barker 2001). Part of what needs to be generated is a sense of legitimacy (which Weber makes clear means 'considered to be legitimate'). We need to draw out the instability of the claim, the importance of practices which can convince

---

[3] I recognise that of course both Weber and Easton had much more to say on these topics than I indicate here, and that there is a significant critical literature on both writers. My intervention is partial and targeted; I do not claim to be offering a comprehensive critique.

audiences of the claim's reasonableness or veracity, and what this may imply about the character and locale of claims to legitimate authority.

It is some degree of success in the practice of *claiming* rather than the *possession* of the attribute of legitimate authority that distinguishes the statal, in the Weberian view. There is a tight link between claiming legitimacy, on the one hand, and claiming to be a (democratic) representative, on the other. However, such practices of claiming are much more widespread than statal forms (Saward 2009). In claiming authority over others, one claims the right to speak for, or to stand for, those others, for some set of interests. Such claims can be highly varied and ubiquitous throughout and across societies. The range of broader societal claims is not exhausted in reactive counter-claims to the state's; they may be partial claims over some areas of policy, or some issues, or some smaller part of the territory, for example. In short, the representative claim is a claim and not necessarily a fact fully established through the existence of specific formal institutions (such as parliaments or town councils); it is societal as well as statal, and invokes some degree or domain of legitimate authority or spokesmanship (Saward 2006). Arguably, Weber was too quick to say that such claiming is part of the political dynamic of the state only.

There are threads in 'Politics as a Vocation' which indicate Weber's recognition of this alternative view. He notes that there are many kinds of 'political associations', and that the concept of politics 'is extremely broad and comprises any kind of independent leadership in action'. He goes on to mention banks, unions, town councils and voluntary associations. He then says, 'our reflections are of course not based upon such a broad concept. We wish to understand by politics only the leadership or influencing of the leadership of a *political* association, hence today, of a *state*' (Weber 1991 [1921]). This is familiar and influential reasoning. But we can justifiably ask: why 'of course'? Why 'hence'? Weber simply stipulates (though it is presented in the impersonal locution 'are designated' [1991 (1921): 77]) that only the state can be a political association.

Let me turn to the *performance* of claims to extend the point. Weber argues that there are three sources of perceived legitimacy: tradition, charisma and legal-rationality. But 'charisma' for example is not a self-evident quality; it does not arrive fully formed within any given context. The perception that this quality is present depends on a culturally specific understanding of charisma. Particular qualities may be perceived as adding up to 'charisma' through processes of performative *iteration* of norms and practices which form this concept's condition of possibility (Butler 1997; Derrida 1998). Charisma is a performatively produced, culturally specific artifact, a construct of a dynamic process of acting-out and claiming. And one key aspect of that quality is that what grants credibility to claims to legitimate authority (based on 'charisma' or other-wise) belongs culturally and socially to the wider, uneven and unsettled, societal canvas. If legitimate for Weber means 'considered to be legitim-ate', then who is doing the consider*ing*? Where is the time dimension, the dialogical dimension, the contingency, and perhaps above all the necessity of *continuous* iteration of the claim if it is to succeed? In short, where are all the dimensions which press us to situate policies, represen-tation, claim making and leadership in the uneven and unsettled wider canvas of civil society, and not solely in the state? Charisma's above-the-fray quality in Weber, its definitive presence, depends on its singu-lar location in a state which always already possesses legitimate author-ity. If we question the latter, we also question the Weberian stipulations about the sources of claims to legitimate authority. Civil society contains originators of claims, not just their recipients.

Charisma and tradition are not state properties, or solely available as strategies to state actors. To be culturally available as types, they must be culturally produced across society. State actors could not claim (charismatic and other types of) authority unless similar claim-mak-ing resources were present, however unevenly, throughout the relevant society as well. The 'marks' of authority are not state monopolies, how-ever important they are within and for the state. Weber does say that 'charismatic domination' can be achieved or perceived with respect to prophets, heroes and demagogues as well as party leaders (1991 [1921]: 79). These need not be state actors, a point that sits in tension with his earlier claims that political leadership is exhausted within the narrow canvas of the state.[4]

No claim to a monopoly in Weber's terms can ever be complete; alter-native and additional claims will occur in society too. And again, in all of this claims to a monopoly of legitimate violence are also claims to representation – 'I or it stand(s) for an ideal of authority such that I have the right to speak or stand for you.' Claims to representation pervade the comparatively unsettled domain of civil society – and some of them

---

[4] Much of this can also be gleaned from exploring Beetham's (1991) full and effect-ive critique of Weber's three-part typology of legitimate authority. Legality requires legal demonstration or paradigmatic performance. Acceptability of rules in context requires performances of claims about the character of that cultural context, and of the consequent appropriateness of the rules (there will and can never be self-evident presence or absence of assent to rules). And acceptability of 'express' consent is not just (a) evidence that it happened, but (b) most importantly, a *claim* that (e.g.) voting statistics stand for assent, or symbolise consent. Express means, straightforwardly, express*ed*: claimed, performed, demonstrated.

will experience degrees of success, and thereby confer a sense of legitimate authority in Weberian terms.

Weber powerfully set up the terms in which the discussion of representative democracy came to be framed. But analysis of Weber's key concepts in fact leads us away from representative democracy as a centralised set of (state) institutions and towards a wider canvas of democratic representation within which that set is located. What comes into focus is an alternative view of democracy as in part a process of claim making and claim reception in a variety of shifting spaces and practices. The wider canvas includes a wider range of claims to representation, a greater sense of contingency and political unsettledness, and also a greater potentiality (I put it no stronger than that at this point) for practices of democratic representation.

Allocating values?

David Easton, in his classic account of the 'political system' (1965), famously and influentially defined politics as the 'authoritative allocation of values'. Although keen to avoid the concept of the state, hence replacing it with 'the political system', Easton locates the mechanisms and processes of this authoritative allocation within the structures we would conventionally associate with the state. Alongside Weber, this is a highly influential analysis that leads to the location of 'representative democracy' entirely within the state. But it, too, does so by assuming that the state is the only set of mechanisms by which 'values' are 'authoritatively allocated'. Against this view, but also working with the grain of Easton's underlying analysis, I argue that many other actors, through varied practices, allocate values within and across societies. Politics is not so much the authoritative allocation of values as the *contest* over the sites, styles and bases of allocation, values and authority. I will pick up on selected aspects of Easton's themes in order to illustrate my basic point.

First, Easton is clear that there is only one set of authorities, and they are state authorities. If this is the case, then on the grounds that democracy ought to be applied where decisions are made by the few for the many, we would only be concerned about achieving representative democracy in the state. My point in response is that the formal/state versus informal/non-state distinction is overplayed; for instance there are elements of the formal in the supposed non-state domain of the informal (e.g., in the formally constituted and to some degree binding rulings of groups like trade unions or professional associations).

Second, Easton speaks of 'the exclusive role of authorities in producing outputs' (1965: 349). To be sure, stable states tend to be highly effective output producers. But to say that they are so exclusively would be to argue that no non-state actor or association could produce or generate social outputs with any degree of authority. Easton does consider cases where 'Other members of a system engage in political activities that may flow into the environment' (1965: 349), and offers an account of how unions can hold strikes that damage the economy. Elsewhere he notes that authorities are 'ranged on a continuum' (1965: 213) from primary and most inclusive to a secondary and narrower range. It is not always clear, but it is likely that Easton here refers only to actors within state structures, from legislative representatives through to more 'informal' interest representation in state bureaucracies. But the narrow range – issues such as housing or charity or working conditions – can be highly significant from 'lived' and other perspectives, depending on the circumstances of the people on the receiving end of the value allocations. Further, such allocations can and have occurred through agencies outside state structures, including relatively permanent or established ones. In the case of union decision making, though, Easton writes that unions 'are not to be considered as producing political outputs in my sense of the term' (1965: 349). Why? In the end, the substance of his argument can be seen as driven by his methodology. Easton's overall task in his work in systems theory has been to build a social scientific theory of politics. As a core part of this ambition, definitions of concepts must apply to specific parts of the system if they are to foster empirical investigation. Thus, the trade union's strike cannot be considered an output because then 'the study of outputs would be no further ahead than when we began our analysis' (1965: 350). In short – putting the point too bluntly, especially for an admirer of Easton's work – operationalisability comes before nuance.

Third, Easton writes of 'binding decisions' by governments – as so many other political scientists do. If we unpack this notion, it carries both the sense that (a) decisions made by a legitimate government in accordance with constitutional provisions are factually binding, and (b) a more normative sense that a single source of bindingness itself is vital if society is to avoid social chaos. Another important sense of binding decisions is less commonly discussed, however: the plural, lived experiences of bindingness. Through civil associations many citizens (and resident non-citizens, and denizens, and refugees, and illegals – the plurality of categories helps to make the point) experience complex and shifting degrees of bindingness of decisions taken by others who are not necessarily state actors. Bindingness is *abstractly* general and statal; it is *concretely* partial and differential and may be societal as well as statal. Relatedly, one might question the strong assumption that the effectiveness of bindingness depends on its emanation from a single source.

Finally, a point in favour of Easton's analysis is that he recognises the importance of states *working on* their legitimacy. The claiming of legitimacy is an active and constant task (1965: 308). State actors engaged in this task need to use legitimising ideologies creatively, up to and including the deployment of a 'fabricated public image'. But again, and by the same logic, a variety of civil actors fabricate images, modify and deploy ideologies, gather supporters, organise formally, and generate a sense of authority.

In short, with Easton some key stipulative definitions and assertions are pursued to the point where we are led to cast aside notions that representative or democratic politics can occur outside the state. Putting the point bluntly, for Easton (and Weber), the political realm *is* the state, which in turn is the sole location of political legitimacy and authority. Easton does write that political representation can operate 'without foreseeable limit' (1965: 253), but proceeds to limit its scope to state structures. Scholars influenced by Weberian or Eastonian approaches have little reason to study democracy and representation in any other spatial or institutional context. But if we treat the stipulations with scepticism, picking up other rich implications in Weber's and Easton's work, the path opens up for different sorts of questions. Perhaps politics always was of/in society as well as the state, and perhaps each is a potential field of democratic representation?

One objection to this line of critique might be that authority is indeed a property found in and outside state structures, but that different types of authority are prevalent in the different spheres. The objection would be that state authorities are 'in' authority, in that their authority derives primarily from the position they occupy, and not from their own expertise. Similarly, a non-state actor with authority is 'an' authority; his or her authority derives primarily from specialist knowledge, experience and/or expertise. In the first case, it is the source of the authoritative judgement that counts; in the latter, it is the content. I would argue, however, that the In/An authority distinction is blurred, and that that blurring is significant for how we ought to view democratic representation. Varied locales and situations can generate senses and degrees of In-ness. Occupying a key position within a major professional association, or being chief executive of a major corporation, or head of a faith-based organisation that formulates and delivers welfare policies, for example, can generate degrees of In-ness. Note further that the effectiveness of In can depend in part on the supportive presence of An – for example specialist support for government rulings.

Importantly and more generally, note also that all In claims are in part an historical sedimentation of an earlier, and in some sense persistent, An claim: positional authority cannot be claimed before positions are established largely on the authority of An claimants. So, if In and An display such attributes of mutual dependence, then both the source and the content of the claims matter (*contra* Friedman 1990: 81).

Sketching on the wider canvas

Building on these brief critiques, I move on now to indicate some key features of the wider canvas of practices of democratic representation, and within it of 'representative democracy'. My overall point is to underline the theoretical and empirical importance of the wider canvas of democratic representation. Doing this comprehensively would require a much fuller analysis; here, I restrict myself to key illustrative arguments. In so doing I refer to the four nodes of variation across the nested domains of democratic representation/representative democracy introduced in Figure 3.1.

For each of the nodes 1–4 in Figure 3.1, it is true that 'representative democracy', as conventionally discussed, is distinct from many practices in the wider field of democratic representation. For node 1, there is a common perception that representative democracy in the state involves permanent institutional presences (parliament, departments of state, and so on), whereas the wider societal domain consists of representative relationships – if they are conceived that way at all – which are more temporary or fleeting. For node 2, citizen exit and voice as means of political expression are, for representative democracy, conventionally seen as operating through exit mechanisms via voting in elections, while in the wider societal domain they are seen as operating primarily through voice in more informal settings. For node 3, as we have seen in the discussion above, formal and legitimate representative authority is conventionally seen as located more or less exclusively within the state. For node 4, statal representative democracy is conventionally seen as contained within and ruling over a nation state, and representation on the wider societal canvas as offering a more mixed set of conceptions of political territory.

The key points, however, arise from many and varied *interruptions* of the apparently clear or sharp conventional distinctions between practices of representation in the two nested domains – interruptions that take us further down some of the underexplored paths noted in the critiques of Weber and Easton. In that context, the following brief discussions and illustrations focus on selected interruptions within the four nodes of variation respectively. These interruptions are expressed variously in terms of: (a) continuities in practices, (b) mutual influences, (c) overlaps, (d) mergings, (e) parallels, (f) dependencies and (g) exchanges between the two nested domains. Clearly this is a huge topic that calls for more extensive analysis; these notions comprise an illustrative selection, rather than a definitive set.

1.   *Institutional presence*

How is democracy rendered or registered as present, in institutional terms? In essence, 'representative democracy' is widely perceived as a complex system and structure of government which has a *permanent and tangible presence*, not least in the institutions such as parliament, judiciary and civil service. That permanence and tangibility is contrasted with political phenomena outside the state structure, which are institutions and practices which may be conceived as *temporary, fleeting or mutating presences*.

But on closer view a kind of analytical merging between the two domains is evident. The routine institutional 'tangibility' of the state is often assumed in an everyday sense, but interestingly questioned by scholars who have struggled to define the state, which has proven to be 'elusive' (Caporaso 1989). Painter argues that efforts to emphasise or define the state in terms of its being a tangible 'thing' at all are serving to reify the concept. Preferring to analyse the state in terms of its practices, he writes:

Reification presents the state as a thing; a more or less unified entity that can be the subject of actions such as deciding, ruling, punishing, regulating, intervening and waging war. Understanding states in terms of prosaic practices reveals their heterogeneous, constructed, porous, uneven, processual and relational character. (Painter 2006: 754)

Ironically, practices of political representation outside the state may be *more* 'tangible' because they will often more readily be locatable within specific organisations or movements. For example, the 'representativeness' of a local pressure group focused on immediate questions of town development may be highly if fleetingly apparent, where parliament's representation of the people as a whole may not.

The question of permanence is clearly one where interruption of the distinctions between the two domains is evident. Certain core state structures may well have highly enduring configurations, but (1) a great many functions, and styles of institutions charged with them, have moved in and out of state structures, ownership or regulatory control over the years; (2) renaming, reconfiguring and repositioning of organ-isations and practices within state bureaucracies is regular and common across a range of states; and (3) the dissolution and creation of newly constituted states is – of course – familiar from the years since the great transformations in eastern Europe in particular. Institutions and prac-tices of representation outside state structures are capable of generating a sense of 'permanence' too. Consider the role of major stakeholders in global sustainable development processes including the Johannesburg World Summit on Sustainable Development in 2002 (Hemmati 2002). In these respects we have an interruption in the apparent distinctive-ness of statal and societal representation; there are stronger elements of continuity between the two than it is commonly thought.

A further interruption centred on the idea of the 'exchange' of func-tions between the two domains may also be evident. Since the begin-nings of the Thatcher/Reagan era of privatisation and contracting out in the UK and the USA in the 1980s, many states have divested them-selves of (at least direct responsibility for) a range of functions which for decades had widely been regarded as core state functions. The global banking and wider economic crisis that started in 2007 has sparked a counter trend. As Rosenau (2000: 185) has written:

a pervasive tendency can be identified in which major shifts in the location of authority and the site of control mechanisms are underway on every contin-ent and in every country, shifts that are as pronounced in economic and social systems as they are in political systems. Indeed, in some cases the shifts have transferred authority away from the political realm and into the economic and social realms even as in still other instances the shift occurs in the opposite direction.

Stakeholder participation and modes of 'co-governance' signal shifts from the societal to the statal; privatised public functions, up to and including military and security functions (Barley 2007), signal shifts in the other direction. And it is evident that complex evolutions and decisions can bring about the state or state-like institutionalisation of initially 'private' practices and institutions (Rosenau 2000: 187–8).

In short, these interruptions call into question overly stark distinc-tions between spheres of 'representative democracy' and democratic representation with respect to the nature of institutional presence. In part, they do so by questioning the similarity of one set of statal insti-tutions to another, a key part of the conventional sense of permanent institutional presence in the narrower domain. The political world looked at through the eyes of statists who see democratic representation as exhausted within 'representative democracy' is flat, with units called nation states or countries repeating across virtually every bit of land on the globe. However, as Clifford Geertz (2000: 229) has written, the 'illusion of a world paved from end to end with repeating units that is produced by the pictorial conventions of our political atlases, polygon cutouts in a fitted jigsaw, is just that – an illusion'.

A look at the wider canvas of democratic representation brings into view a much more variable and non-repeating topography. Different countries differ radically in terms of culture, legitimating narratives, power and resources. Some will have thriving, fast-changing and dynamic realms of democratic representation, while others may tend to be stifled by overbearing states. Here, in short, the unsettled world of democratic representation does the work of *unsettling* myths about the essential similarity of the modes and cultures of representative democracy around the world. The work of political scientists with an anthropological and interpretive bent – Schaffer (1998) and Chabal and Daloz (2006) for example – has gone a long way towards in-depth illustration of Geertz's basic point.

2.   *Modes of exit and voice*

Modes of exit and voice are vital underpinnings of democratic politics in a quite general sense.[5] In democratic contexts, broadly speaking, citizens normally have opportunities and rights to select parliamentary or council representatives through elections, and to voice their concerns and preferences freely. For the narrower domain of statal representative democracy, exit in the form of voting in elections is conventionally understood to be the formal and dominant mode. For the wider domain of societal democratic representation, voice in varied informal settings is conventionally understood as the dominant mode. Elections matter hugely to democratic representation, of course. Indeed, in democratic terms the state is often equated with the use of elections, and the societal with their near absence. Also familiar is the use of a closely aligned distinction between formal and informal representation, which is often read in terms of an elective/non-elective distinction. Such distinctions crucially serve to reinforce the idea that democratic representation is a practice located (and locatable only) within state structures.

But these apparently sharp and clear distinctions can be interrupted, too, not least in the form of continuities of practice across the (porous) boundary between the two domains. Specifically, representative democracy in the state follows the logic of election, but so do many institutions in civil society. The latter might be differently elective at

---

[5] The notions of exit and voice are derived from the classic work by Hirschman (1970).

a different level, but like elections to a local school board they can be more or less settled practices. Representation in civil society tends generally to be more unsettled – uneven and sporadic – but we can still say that it follows a logic of exit (in addition to voice) even where in some cases that logic is not pursued through elections as such. Election is one mode of the logic of exit. Others may include no longer attending meetings, or no longer funding an organisation or movement, or changing consumption habits, as a result perhaps of decisions about leadership, goals or even public image.

A further important point of continuity between the two domains is the common basis of representation in claim making (Saward 2006). A variety of non-elected actors claim to be representatives, explicitly or implicitly, and sometimes their claims have particular resonance with their audiences because they can do things that conventional elective claimants (e.g., parliamentarians) cannot do (or cannot do so readily). For example, in comparison to a range of unelected representatives unelected claimants can have more scope to claim to represent partial interests; can claim to stand for evolving interests aside from electoral constraints and distortions; can claim to be temporary representatives with respect to pressing but passing issues; can often claim to speak for interests (or would-be constituencies) that span different national or other political boundaries with a greater freedom than elected actors; can make comparatively explicit claims, because they need more clearly to alert and to build the constituency for their claims; and can open up new patterns of representation that are alternative to statal elective patterns (for example, one-to-many or one-to-some rather than the blanket one-to-all).[6] Opportunities for representative claim making may differ markedly from one domain to another, but the basis of representation in processes of claim making is itself a key point of continuity across domains.

Further, although on one level in conventional elections we choose specific elected representatives, we cannot choose not to be represented by statal elected representatives on a more general level. States are (in principle) compulsory entities. We do not choose non-elected representatives in such a clear way, but neither are we *fated* to have them or follow them in the same way. 'Choice' works differently in the case of unelected representatives. Often it is a choice in the mode of representation rather than a choice of a specific representative,

---

[6] Consider Paul Hirst's associative democracy model, where the exit principle is put to work in a proposal for a major disaggregation of the state along radically pluralist lines, a design appropriate where major forms of governance no longer have 'a single authoritative centre' (1997: 34).

though the 'exit' mechanism will often be highly relevant for the latter cases.

It is true that we are accustomed to seeing democratic legitimacy in 'representative democracy' as the product of free and fair elections (setting aside debates about the democratic credentials of different systems of election). Where such electoral procedures are stable, considered a deep part of the political culture, as thoroughly 'settled', they are often seen as providing in themselves a full measure of democratic legitimacy. But by applying insights about alternative mechanisms of exit and voice we can begin to assess representative claims in comparatively unsettled societal practices. There are varied and mixed mechanisms of accountability of civil society claimants to legitimacy which can be, and have been, more or less effective. One could list for example elections within bodies such as trade unions; and professional norms and associations whose role it is to publicise and even punish norm transgression. Many such mechanisms can be seen today as operating and evolving in a highly dynamic, global-scale 'constitutionalisation' (in terms of the nation state) of non-political space (Thompson 2008). I pick up this issue of assessment in the following section.

3.   *Location and generation of legitimate authority*

The earlier comments on aspects of classic works by Weber and Easton provide resources, first, for arguing that legitimate authority is not a product that exists in a certain secure quality, quantity or persistence; it is more sporadic, uneven and unpredictable than that. And second, it provides grounds for arguing that its potential locations are both statal and societal. Manifestations of legitimate authority may be more settled within state structures and more unsettled outside them, but the picture is uneven; there is a continuum of practices rather than a hard-and-fast divide.

The assertion that legitimate authority is not a given or natural feature of any part of the political landscape, let alone given for the institutions of 'representative democracy' alone, helps to highlight the fact that individuals and institutions actively foster a sense of their own legitimacy and authority. In this respect, the influence of our thinking about representation outside state structures, where (as noted) actors must work harder and be more explicit about the basis of their representative claims, interrupts received wisdom about the givenness of legitimacy and authority in the state. If legitimate authority is a construct, which needs constant building or repair, then the activity of building and repairing is no less essential within as well as outside of the state.

It is, in short, the assertion, the demonstration, the advertising, the claiming – the performing – of 'legitimate authority' which does the work (successfully or otherwise) of establishing its presence, in and for the state no less than outside of it. The often necessarily more visible performing of legitimate authority outside the state is also reflected in performative practices within state structures. In this respect, again, there are interruptions of the presumed distinctiveness of representation in the two nested domains, in terms of continuities and overlaps.

It might be objected that states/governments still decide issues exclusively, in that they authoritatively allocate values not in the sense that they monopolise the authority to do so, but rather that their version of authority is the one that matters (the decisive one). In response, however, one can note the proliferation of more or less effective decision points and practices beyond and across states. Examples include: devolved decision making (for example through integrity bodies) that gives powers to non-elective regulators as representatives of the public interest (see Keane's discussion of the growth of 'monitory democracy' in Chapter 9); formal 'stakeholder' participation, as at the World Summit on Sustainable Development; the representative roles of varied UN agencies; modes and practices of professional self-regulation in the public interest. Other examples include: the second set of rulers in a polyarchy, i.e., corporate leaders in the terms of Dahl (1985); think tanks and interest groups and lobbies who draft legislation and regulations; and assorted modes of network governance, as in the European Union (see Majone 1994 and Schmitter in Chapter 8). Again, we see interruptions in terms of continuities and overlaps between practices on the narrower and the wider canvasses.

These considerations leave aside a key issue, however. In Figure 3.1, the 'inner' boundary is expressed as lying between 'representative democracy' and 'democratic representation'. My comments so far have focused on how the boundary between these two domains can be challenged. But to think about the location and generation of legitimate authority, the topic of this section of the chapter, we need to consider also the boundary between 'democratic representation' and the wider, most encompassing domain, 'political representation'. My argument is that among the many manifestations of political representation across civil society there are examples of democratic and non-democratic representation. What distinguishes the democratic and the non-democratic? The question is challenging, not least because (as we have seen) we are dealing with many cases of representative claims which do not belong to the statal 'representative democracy' domain and which often are not straightforwardly elective, and do not correspond to fixed territorial constituencies. Relevant examples might include claims from leaders or members of trade unions, business associations, interest groups, social movements, religious or cultural minority communities, or local protest organisations.

In essence, what distinguishes democratic claims is that they demonstrate a sufficient degree of 'chosenness' in the context of a reasonably open society. In other words, there is reasonable evidence that constituents of a given representative claim do accept that claimant as speaking for, or acting for, them with regard to a certain set of purposes. Chosenness is, admittedly, not an elegant concept; it is meant to encompass both literal choices by constituencies (of representatives through formal voting) and wider means by which groups or communities can be said to choose those who claim to speak for them.

In a complex and pluralistic civil society, clear and paradigmatic moments of *choice* may not be evident – although many civic associations, for example, do hold democratic votes for their representatives – but *chosenness* is a wider category which can encompass a wider set of phenomena. A representative claimant might be voted into office or position democratically. Or, he or she might demonstrate chosenness through acclamation in an appropriate way (Schwartzberg 2010), or by being greeted by silence in a key moment where silence clearly equates to acceptance (Bachrach and Baratz 1970), or by not being objected to when opportunities for objection by appropriate constituents arise (cf. Runciman 2007). Clearly the context from which observers might reasonably infer chosenness matters; an open society is one which demonstrates high levels of freedom of speech, association and information. The operation and protection of such freedoms at a high level can lead us to take seriously potential sites and moments of chosenness for representative claimants in civil society.[7] As these comments suggest, there is an unavoidable element of contingent judgement in assessing the democratic character of representative claims on the wider canvas.

Crucially, there is no such thing as total, permanent democratic legitimacy of representative claims across the wider canvas. Democratic legitimation is an attribute of certain claims (where sufficient evidence of chosenness is present), but it is an attribute both limited and buffeted by time. Chosenness may not need constant renewal, but it does need regular renewal. In civil society, a number of representative claims may be deliberately time-limited by claimants themselves – for example,

---

[7] Difficult issues such as defining the appropriate constituency and specifying elements of an open society are discussed in more detail in Saward (2010).

the leader of the local community group seeking to save the local park from housing development plans may claim to be representative of a specific group for this specific purpose and only for the time that it takes to achieve the desired outcome (or indeed to fail and perhaps disband). Elected parliamentarians of course face time limits – their electoral terms are limited. But how strongly representative of their constituencies they may claim to be (or be perceived to be) may wax and wane over time also *within* their electoral terms, depending on their skills, their stance on key issues, and so on. In this respect, the position of elected representatives is comparable, for example, to that of a local community group leader. Certainly, given the over-time quality of democratic representation, for civil society actors in particular we need to accept that democratic legitimacy for representative claims is always provisional.

Does the degree of internal democracy in (say) a local community group contribute to the chosenness of its leader's or spokesperson's claims? Yes, but it is not the only or even the most important factor, as my comments above suggest. Community groups, or business associations, claim to represent constituencies beyond the boundaries of their formal membership (if indeed they have the latter). It is their chosenness in the eyes of such wider constituencies that are most critical in assessing the democratic legitimacy of claims. Overall, it is not hard to claim to represent a community of people. It can be very hard to communicate one's claims to that community effectively, and to convince its members that one really does speak for them for some specific purpose. A great many representative claims fail. But some succeed, to a degree and for limited and fluctuating periods of time. Given the contingency involved in the judgements, it would be churlish of observers to deny that such representative claims bear a degree of democratic legitimacy.

One fact that distinguishes many representative claims on the wider canvas is that they have no formal or clear connections to parliament, MPs, or the executive branch of government. There are varied forms of non-departmental public bodies (NDPBs) which are variously established by, formally linked with, or accountable to parliaments or core executives. Members of such bodies – many of which may play monitory roles, in Keane's terms (see Chapter 9) – may claim a degree of democratic legitimacy for their representation by virtue of the formality of their connection to (perhaps reliance on) legislative or executive authorities. This potential route to democratic legitimacy – formal connection – is quite different to that of a range of civil society actors, for whom contingent judgements of chosenness are the clearest claim to democratic legitimacy.

4.   *Conceptions of territory*

I noted above, for statal representative democracy, how political legitimacy is linked to a tightly fixed, national sense of territory, as in the
Weberian tradition. Democratic representation, on the wider canvas,
contains additional claims and practices, often involving perceptions of
democratically legitimate representation based, for example, on notions
of connection or confirmation, which do not have such a fixed conception. Here, the different perspectives available may for example lead to
(a) a challenge to the idea that interests within the nation state are best
characterised or formalised as having a territorial basis, and (b) a challenge to ideas of the primary significance of national boundaries for key
political issues.

Often, such styles and claims of representation that are less identified
with or dependent upon given national borders will be discussed under
the heading of 'functional representation', the presumed opposite to
territorial representation. But functional representation is too restrict-
ive a label for the huge range of organisations, actors and practices who
claim (or for which is claimed) a degree of legitimate authority for their
representative claims outside state structures, sometimes successfully.
'Functional' carries the implication that there was (always) a function
to be fulfilled that a territorially based entity could not by its nature
fulfil, at least not adequately. In some respects, in an age of extensive
cross-border exchanges and international coalitions and networks in a
number of policy areas, the term might be coming into its own. But it
sets aside too readily the extent to which the 'function' in a given case
is often *generated* by the explicit or implicit representative claims that
groups or networks may make.

This characteristic of the broader idea of democratic representation
stems from major and complex shifts in material conditions which are
often – if not always accurately – discussed under the heading of 'globalisation'. Developments in ICT in particular have facilitated huge
transformations in financial and other global information flows which
have effectively de-territorialised significant areas of political authority,
contestation and regulation. I will not go into these issues here – the
stories are well told in a number of outlets spanning several years (see
Held and McGrew 2000 for one reasonably comprehensive account of
the arguments).

A perception of democratic legitimacy for non-state actors within the
broader domain of political representation will often be linked to variable rather than fixed or national conceptions of territory. Transnational

non-governmental organisations (NGOs), from Greenpeace to Amnesty International to Oxfam and Band Aid, claim degrees and styles of (democratic) representation that are complexly spatial rather than fixedly territorial. Transnational corporations, especially when propounding public interest motives (often today under the broad heading of 'corporate social responsibility'), make a range of representative claims on behalf of (for example) stakeholders, or the business community, or consumers, rather than simply shareholders. There are many other such examples.

In short, there is a world of (democratic) representation which, among other things, generates and operates with different senses of spatiality from the more limited category of territorial state-based representative democracy.

Stepping back: democratic representation

On the wider canvas, political representation occurs at many and shifting points within and across the political units (bounded nation states) which are the foundation for 'representative democracy'. Many manifestations of non-statal political representation can plausibly be seen as instances of democratic representation. Within *that* broad field, unsettled and uneven as it is, we can locate the specific, more settled, institutions and practices of 'representative democracy'. The crux of my argument is that the present and future of representation should be explored within the field of the wider referent, democratic representation, rather than confined by unreasonable stipulation to state institutions. Perhaps its past would also have been explored more in this way were it not for powerful stipulations in the theories and definitions of crucially influential figures such as Weber and Easton.

In making these points, I have discussed briefly a range of others: the importance of practices and performances of claiming as projections of authority and legitimacy; the potential multiple sites and styles of democratic representation (e.g., permanent and temporary, territorial and non-territorial); the range of actors who, to widely varying degrees, may successfully claim requisite degrees of representativeness, legitimacy and authority; and varied ways in which political actors might come to be seen as 'representatives' (election matters, but varied other modes of confirmation and connectedness can also underpin successful representative claims). Democratic representation emerges from this analysis as a diffuse quality of political practices across and between societies, rather than a specific set of institutions.

REFERENCES

Bachrach, P. (1967) *The theory of democratic elitism*. Boston: Little, Brown.

Bachrach, P. and M. Baratz (1970) *Power and poverty*. Oxford University Press.

Barber, B. (1984) *Strong democracy*. Berkeley: University of California Press.

Barker, R. (2001) *Legitimating identities*. Cambridge University Press.

Barley, S. R. (2007) 'Corporations, democracy, and the public good', *Journal of Management Inquiry* 16(3): 201–15.

Beetham, D. (1991) *The legitimation of power*. Basingstoke: Palgrave Macmillan.

Butler, J. (1997) *Excitable speech: Politics of the performative*. London and New York: Routledge.

Caporaso, J. A. (ed.) (1989) *The elusive state*. London: Sage.

Chabal, P. and J.-P. Daloz (2006) *Culture troubles: Politics and the interpretation of meaning*. London: Hurst & Co.

Dahl, R. A. (1985) *A preface to economic democracy*. Cambridge: Polity Press.

Derrida, J. (1998) *Limited Inc*. Evanston, IL: Northwestern University Press.

Easton, D. (1965) *A systems analysis of political life*. New York and London: John Wiley & Sons.

Friedman, R. B. (1990) 'On the concept of authority in political philosophy', in J. Raz (ed.) *Authority*. Oxford: Basil Blackwell, pp. 56–91.

Geertz, C. (2000) *Available light: Anthropological reflections on philosophical topics*. Princeton University Press.

Held, D. and A. McGrew (eds.) (2000) *The global transformations reader: An introduction to the globalization debate*. Malden, MA: Polity Press.

Hemmati, M. (2002) *Multi-stakeholder processes for governance and sustainability*. London: Earthscan.

Hirschman, A. O. (1970) *Exit, voice, and loyalty*. Cambridge, MA and London: Harvard University Press.

Hirst, P. (1994) *Associative democracy*. Cambridge: Polity Press.

  (1997) *From statism to pluralism*. University College London Press.

Majone, G. (1994) 'Independence versus accountability? Non-majoritarian institutions and democratic governance in Europe', in J. J. Hesse and T. A. J. Toonen (eds.), *The European yearbook of comparative government and public administration*, vol. 1. Baden-Baden and Boulder, CO: Nomos/ Westview Press.

Painter, J. (2006) 'Prosaic geographies of stateness', *Political Geography* 25(7): 752–74.

Pateman, C. (1970) *Participation and democratic theory*. Cambridge University Press.

Rosenau, J. N. (2000) 'Governance in a globalising world', in D. Held and A. McGrew (eds.) *The global transformations reader*. Cambridge: Polity Press, pp. 181–90.

Runciman, D. (2007) 'The paradox of political representation', *Journal of Political Philosophy* 15(1): 93–114.

Saward, M. (2006) 'The representative claim', *Contemporary Political Theory* 5(3): 297–318.

(2009) 'Authorisation and authenticity: Representation and the unelected', *Journal of Political Philosophy* 17(1): 1–22.

(2010) *The representative claim*. Oxford University Press.

Schaffer, F. (1998) *Democracy in translation*. Ithaca, NY: Cornell University Press.

Schwartzberg, M. (2010) 'Shouts, murmurs and votes: Acclamation and aggregation in ancient Greece', *Journal of Political Philosophy*, published online 3 March.

Thompson, G. (2008) *International quasi-constitutionalism and corporate citizenship: Language, troubles, dilemmas*. Milton Keynes: The Open University.

Walzer, M. (1992) 'Comment', in C. Taylor, *Multiculturalism and the 'politics of recognition'*. Princeton University Press.

Weber, M. (1991 [1921]) *From Max Weber: essays in sociology*, eds. H. H. Gerth and C. Wright Mills (new edition). London: Routledge.

4   Performance and deficits of present-day representation

Bernhard Wessels

The problem

Many observers of democracy insist that political representation is in crisis; even books have been entitled accordingly (Köchler 1985; Hayward 1996). The debate and diagnosis is probably as old as democratic political representation itself (Pitkin 1967), but the more recent debate was stimulated by an increase of participatory demands, the so-called participatory revolution of the 1970s that led Habermas to conclude that 'the grammar of politics is at stake' (Habermas 1987). The demand side is one aspect of this alleged crisis. The other aspect is whether politics still has the capacity to deliver public goods and to solve problems in the face of economic globalisation. Some have concluded that representation is in crisis from two sides, and that their interaction is reinforcing the crisis: higher demands for participation and effective state control coincide with the decreasing capacity of representative institutions to deliver.

If this pessimistic claim is true, both input and output legitimacy are in danger, and democracy itself is in question. In this chapter, I shall bring some empirical evidence to bear on the question of the degree to which the grammar of politics is out of step with the demands and wishes of people. Many studies start at the very end of the political process evaluating the question of representation, namely by comparing outcomes with demands. However, it seems worthwhile evaluating the process of representation itself. If the translation of preferences into policies is a problem, outcomes may not systematically reflect demands just because the political process shows deficits, irrespective of the factors that constrain the steering capacity of politics. What Habermas has highlighted as the problem of politics is just this point: that (the) people are not satisfied with the limited opportunities institutional representative politics offer. Thus, this chapter deals with citizens' evaluations of the contribution of elections, parties and politicians to political representation. Secondly, the chapter deals with the quality of political representation in a very specific way, relying on findings from the literature and empirical analysis. To determine quality a yardstick has first to be defined. There are many visions of representation and as many potential yardsticks (Pitkin 1967). The range runs from the match of demands and policies (where preferences are mirrored) to good leadership and measures of the public good character of outcomes (what democracy is good for). Most measures rest on normative assumptions the researchers make about good representation and democracy. Here, no claim will be made as to what is good and bad representation. Rather, the normative assumptions of different visions of democracy, their 'blueprints', will be taken as starting points for evaluating to what degree particular patterns of representation are suited to the mode of representation the institutions aim at. Thus, a claim will be made that different visions of democracy aim at different types of representation. This claim has consequences, because it binds political representation to democratic procedures and political competition.

After clarifying the starting point for the evaluation of political representation in liberal democracies, this chapter goes on to investigate elections and citizen representation in more than thirty countries. The analysis of the quality of the political process from the perspective of those who are represented is followed by an examination of the degree to which varieties of democratic 'blueprints' are embedded in political institutions and shape political representation. The comparative analysis of voters' and representatives' policy positions and preferences will be used for this purpose. The analysis begins from the observation that there are two basic visions of representative democracy: the majoritarian and the proportional vision of representation (Huber and Powell 1994; Powell 2000). These visions are institutionalised in different ways. The most important is the type of electoral system that is chosen. The question is to what degree do institutions effectively provide incentives for political actors to implement the specific vision of representation? Here I shall look at the process of representation from the perspective of political representatives, their roles and their quality of policy representation. Final sections of this chapter ask where the feeling of being represented or not comes from and whether it matters – and whether it can be improved.

Political representation – which model?

The evaluation of the performance and deficits of present-day representation needs a yardstick. Since we are dealing with democratic representation, the crucial question is whether given institutions work in a proper way to induce satisfactory political representation. The claim here is that liberal democracy has only one established model of representation: party democracy. It should come as no surprise that all empirical studies of political representation refer in one way or another to *responsible party government*. What does this model exactly imply? It is a simple model with the following simple assumptions, which however have far-reaching consequences:

- there must be competitive elections;
- elections must offer alternatives, i.e., voters must have the chance of selecting between at least two parties which offer different policies; elections must be meaningful;
- voters must have preferences;
- voters are aware of the differences between parties and vote accordingly;
- parties must be cohesive enough to enable them to implement their policy programme; and
- institutions must offer incentives for representatives to act according to the preferences that are expressed in elections.

To put things simply: there must be choices, and they must have effects that translate into representation (Thomassen and Schmitt 1999). The institution central to this process is the body of public elected representatives, the parliament. The supremacy of parliament – at least in parliamentary systems – is of crucial importance for representation. David Beetham, in Chapter 5 of this volume, stresses that if voters want to hold governments accountable, they have to rely on parliaments. The responsible party model implies collective representation. Theoretically, there is an alternative, dyadic representation, a direct relation between electors and elected, that allows for the greater independence of elected representatives from political parties. However, it is hard to conceive of controls over the process of representation without political parties. Philippe Schmitter, in Chapter 8 of this volume, questions this claim. He regards the functional capacity of political parties as nowadays so limited that he hardly sees any use for them. David Beetham takes an intermediate position. He regards political parties as too selective in favour of the rich and party donors, and too dominant in the political process to perform the necessary functions well. Nonetheless, he does not doubt that these kinds of collective and organised actors are necessary for ensuring the accountability of governments.

This is only one part of the issue. For democracies also differ in their approach to representation. The institutionalisation of a particular type of democracy is in effect a decision for a particular blueprint of representation, either a 'majority-control vision' or a 'proportionate influence vision'. Thus, whether the conditions for representation are (considered as) good or bad depends largely on (a) the way institutions are built, and (b) whether they are effective. The implementation of elections alone is not a sufficient condition for democratic representation – even though it is a necessary condition (Merkel 2004). Elections must encourage the elected to act according to the preferences expressed by voters, but things are never that simple. The two different visions of democracy aim at different forms of representation. To put it simply, the proportional vision of democracy focuses on the representation of as many voters as possible; the majority-control vision on the representation of a majority of voters.

The institutional preconditions for both forms differ. The proportional vision requires a proportional electoral system, which allows some electoral success even when the share of votes is small. In a situation of full proportionality, the minimum number of votes required for gaining a seat is the number of electors divided by the number of elected. This implies multi-member districts, or perhaps even one national district. Candidates run on party lists and the selection of candidates is normally fully in the hands of political parties. The usual outcome is a multi-party system in which candidates are offered the incentive to win the necessary number of votes in a particular area of the political space where their party is located. This implies that candidates must target the median voter of their party.

The vision of a majoritarian model is institutionalised through a majoritarian electoral system, normally with single-member districts. In contrast to the proportional model, it implies centripetal instead of centrifugal political competition. Candidates must win the majority (or plurality) of votes. In a full majoritarian system, this means winning 50 per cent plus one vote of the electors. In single-member districts, this is defined as the number of electors divided by the number of seats/ constituencies multiplied by one half, plus one.

Obviously, in the majoritarian model candidates have to target the median voter of any constituency. As Cox has shown, only two candidates are normally viable candidates; in general, the number of candidates who have a chance of winning a seat is district magnitude (number of seats distributed in the district) plus one (Cox 1999). In a single-member district, the result is mostly a competition between two candidates. This does not necessarily result in a two-party system. Logically, it is possible that candidates in every district run for a different party. In strongly regionally divided societies, single-member district majority systems commonly produce a multi-party system. However, in most countries single-member districts result in a system of two-party competition.

What does this all imply for representation? Obviously, electoral institutions provide incentives for candidates to develop a particular understanding of whom they want to represent. In single-member districts, the median voter is the focus of attention, while in list systems it is the median party voter. The question is whether in fact these different visions of democracy and their institutionalisation translate into different forms of representation? To highlight the implications again: if the two visions of democracy are measured against a common yardstick, then they would necessarily lead to the conclusion that their democratic quality is different. If the yardstick of proportionality is used, multi-party representation is evaluated positively. If the yardstick of majoritarianism is used, then two big parties, one of which is dominant, is judged as good representation. Thus, measured against their own respective yardstick, they both may perform well but differently. Whether these differences in the character of political representation are significant will be explored with empirical data later in this chapter.

Meaningful elections?

The basic claim of democratic theory and its responsible party model is that elections are meaningful. They are presumed to be the starting point of political representation; without them democratic representation is virtually inconceivable. Through elections, representatives win a mandate to act on behalf of the represented. The people are sovereign, hence representatives are their agents. However, this principle of democratic representation can only work to legitimate a political system and the actions of its representatives if the basic institution of elections is perceived as effective enough to hold the elected accountable.

The debate about the 'meaningfulness of "democratic elections"' (Merkel 2004) shows that it is neither self-evident nor sufficient to conclude straightforwardly that free elections imply meaningful elections and good representation. This point is made in new approaches for measuring democracy (Hadenius and Teorell 2005) and empirical analyses of democratisation processes (Lindberg 2006).

The key question is how do voters perceive elections and how do their perceptions translate into a feeling of representation? In the Comparative Study of Electoral Systems (CSES), Module 2, I and other colleagues asked the following question in some thirty-seven countries by drawing on post-election surveys of the voting-age population:

Thinking about how elections in [country] work in practice, how well do elections ensure that the views of voters are represented: very well, quite well, not very well, or not well at all?

The results (Figure 4.1) show that there is huge variation in the perception of elections as conducive to representation, with a minimum of 25 and a maximum of 75 per cent of the respondents answering 'very well' or 'quite well'. Proportions are as low as 25 and 35 per cent for such established democracies as Japan and Germany; and as high as 71 and 79 per cent for the USA and Denmark. For new democracies, the range is between 28 per cent (Slovenia, Czech Republic), and 58 per cent in the Philippines and even 60 per cent for the limited democracy of Hong Kong. However, on average across all the countries, only 49 per cent of voters view elections as serving their political representation either quite well or very well.

This finding does not necessarily imply that the 51 per cent not regarding elections as ensuring representation do not feel themselves to be represented. It indicates only that for many voters in many countries elections are not working in the ideal way. If we turn to those actors who are supposed to represent, parties and politicians, the figures are higher and show a similar degree of variation. In CSES, we asked the voters to answer the following two questions with 'yes' or 'no':

Would you say that any of the parties in [country] represent your views reasonably well?

and

Regardless of how you feel about the parties, would you say that any of the individual party leaders/presidential candidates at the last election represent your views reasonably well?

For parties, the range is between 24 (Kyrgyzstan) and 87 per cent of voters (Switzerland). For candidates, the range is 22 (Kyrgyzstan) to 83 per cent (New Zealand); for one and/or the other the range is 24 in Korea to 91 per cent in Switzerland (Figure 4.2). The cross-country mean for party representation is 57 per cent; for leader representation, 58 per cent. On average, 68 per cent of voters feel either represented by a party or by a leader (or both).

From comparisons of the data on feelings of representation by elections, parties and leaders a simple conclusion can be drawn: voters can indeed feel represented by parties or leaders even if they regard elections as a poor instrument of representation. Further elaboration of this

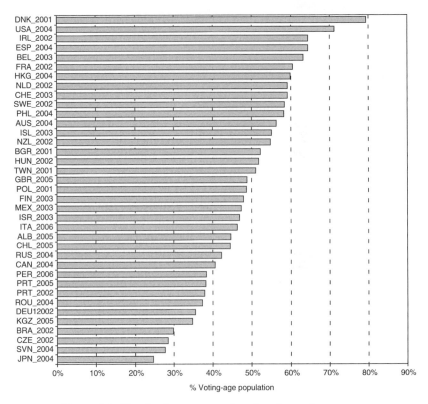

Figure 4.1. Do elections ensure that the views of voters are represented? Proportion of positive answers of voting-age population
Source: Own calculations; The Comparative Study of Electoral Systems, Module 2, 2001–6 (www.cses.org); post-election surveys, representative of the voting-age population.
Key: ALB_2005, Albania; AUS_2004, Australia; BEL_2003, Belgium; BRA_2002, Brazil; BGR_2001, Bulgaria; CAN_2004, Canada; CHL_2005, Chile; CZE_2002, Czech Republic; DNK_2001, Denmark; FIN_2003, Finland; FRA_2002, France; DEU12002, Germany; GBR_2005, Great Britain; HKG_2004, Hong Kong; HUN_2002, Hungary; ISL_2003, Iceland; IRL_2002, Ireland; ISR_2003, Israel; ITA_2006, Italy; JPN_2004, Japan; KOR_2004, Korea; KGZ_2005, Kyrgyzstan; MEX_2003, Mexico; NLD_2002, Netherlands; NZL_2002, New Zealand; NOR_2001, Norway; PER_2006, Peru; PHL_2004, Philippines; POL_2001, Poland; PRT_2002, Portugal; PRT_2005, Portugal; ROU_2004, Romania; RUS_2004, Russia; SVN_2004, Slovenia; ESP_2004, Spain; SWE_2002, Sweden; CHE_2003, Switzerland; TWN_2001, Taiwan; TWN_2004, Taiwan; USA_2004, United States of America.

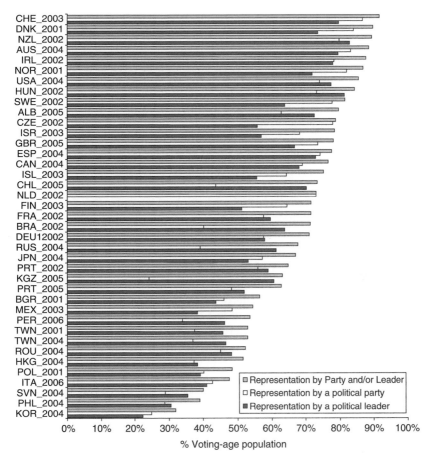

Figure 4.2. Feelings of being represented by a political party or/and a political leader (rank ordered by representation by a party and/or a leader)

Source: Own calculations; The Comparative Study of Electoral Systems, Module 2, 2001–6 (www.cses.org). Post-election surveys, representative of the voting-age population.

Key: ALB_2005, Albania; AUS_2004, Australia; BEL_2003, Belgium; BRA_2002, Brazil; BGR_2001, Bulgaria; CAN_2004, Canada; CHL_2005, Chile; CZE_2002, Czech Republic; DNK_2001, Denmark; FIN_2003, Finland; FRA_2002, France; DEU12002, Germany; GBR_2005, Great Britain; HKG_2004, Hong Kong; HUN_2002, Hungary; ISL_2003, Iceland; IRL_2002, Ireland; ISR_2003, Israel; ITA_2006, Italy; JPN_2004, Japan; KOR_2004, Korea; KGZ_2005, Kyrgyzstan; MEX_2003, Mexico; NLD_2002, Netherlands; NZL_2002, New Zealand; NOR_2001, Norway; PER_2006, Peru; PHL_2004, Philippines; POL_2001, Poland; PRT_2002, Portugal; PRT_2005, Portugal; ROU_2004, Romania; RUS_2004, Russia; SVN_2004, Slovenia; ESP_2004, Spain; SWE_2002, Sweden; CHE_2003, Switzerland; TWN_2001, Taiwan; TWN_2004, Taiwan; USA_2004, United States of America.

issue is needed. One point concerns the static quality of cross-section data and its limited ability to say something about processes. A second point concerns the question of how these results fit with the debates about declining trust in parties, politicians and politics in general.

Regarding the first point, there is only an indirect way of assessing the dynamics of political representation and the role of elections, since no time-series data exists for a comparative perspective. Yet one indication of whether elections and political representation are in decline could be that younger age cohorts compared to the older ones show even less positive evaluations of elections, parties and leaders. A comparison of the youngest cohort (16–25) with four older ones (26–35, 36–50, 51–65, 65+) on the question of whether elections serve representation shows that there is no statistically significant difference between the cohorts; the greatest difference between cohorts is only 2.9 percentage points. However, feelings of being represented by a party or a leader show statistically significant differences between the younger and the older cohorts. Those feelings increase linearly with age. The difference between the youngest and the oldest cohort is 15.5 percentage points, with regard to parties, and 14 percentage points with regard to leaders. Thus, younger voters are not less satisfied with elections as a means of political representation, but they feel much less represented by parties and leaders. Interestingly, levels of education show exactly the opposite tendency: the better educated citizens are, the more they both regard elections as a means of representation and feel represented by parties and leaders. Percentage point differences between those having reached formal education up to the primary level and those having achieved post-secondary education are not as large as for age cohorts, but are consistently between 5 (for elections) and 8 percentage points (for party and leader representation). Given the fact that younger age cohorts tend to be better educated than their predecessors, this result reveals a complex balancing influence of countervailing factors. In the two youngest cohorts, 42 per cent have achieved post-secondary education; in the 36–50 years age cohort the figure is 39, in the next older one 31, while in the oldest cohort the figure is only 20 per cent.

Concerning the widely reported distrust in political parties and other political actors: trust in political parties is tricky because parties are partisan organisations. Political competition and choice in elections are based on the fact that there is a party which some of the voters like, which implies that these voters rather dislike their competitors. In terms of trust, this means that trust in the selected party may be high, but not in other parties. Parties are not institutions but actors. This is why a comparison of figures on trust in institutions and actors, like parties, politicians or governments, is tricky. In-group/out-group mechanisms, and sometimes outright hostility, form part of the game of democratic choice, as can be demonstrated by empirical findings. A comparison of the wide range of countries and party systems considered here shows that every person who identifies with at least one party on average dislikes 1.9 other parties. Like-dislike is indicated by the respondents on an eleven-point scale, stretching between 'like' and 'dislike'. The four best scores, and the four worst, have been used here to differentiate between 'like' and 'dislike' respectively: the three middle scores have not been used.

Concerning the state of political representation, two messages can be drawn from the data. First, younger voters are obviously more sceptical than older ones as far as the capacity of parties and leaders to represent is concerned. However, the young are not more sceptical about elections as a means of representation. At the same time, the better educated – the younger cohorts are on average better educated than the older – are more positive about the performance of parties and politicians. Taking this finding together with the knowledge that has existed now for roughly fifty years – that electoral experience matters a lot for political integration and attachment to parties – the scepticism of the young is not necessarily a generation effect, but a life-cycle effect. This implies that in future the evaluation of political representation will not necessarily be more negative than today. However, this statement has to be handled with care. Without time-series data, no clear conclusions are possible.

The second message is that feelings of being represented in a democracy also entail feelings about oppositional interests, groups or parties. The frequently observed distrust in parties and politicians is a normal element of the democratic struggle. Why should one trust the enemy, the opposing party? Parties are not institutions but partisan organisations, representing particular interests, in opposition to others. This point is validated by the finding that among those who identify with at least one party, but dislike no party, the proportion of those who feel represented either by a party or a leader is smaller than among those who dislike at least one party. Among the former, 64 per cent feel represented by a party, and 63 per cent by a leader. Among those who like and dislike parties, the proportion who feel represented by parties and by leaders is seven percentage points higher, 71 and 70 per cent. This shows that disliking other parties contributes to a feeling of being represented by one's own party.

As a means of representation, elections are obviously meaningful to voters if they really lead to the representation of their views by parties

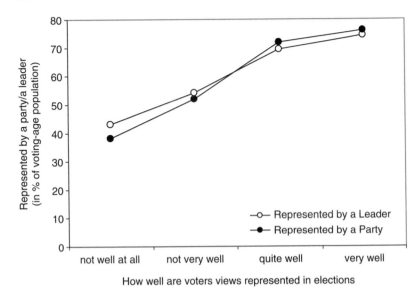

Figure 4.3. The quality of elections and feelings of being represented by a party or a leader
Source: Own calculations; The Comparative Study of Electoral Systems, Module 2, 2001–6 (www.cses.org); equal sample weights for thirty-eight countries. Post-election surveys, representative of the voting-age population.

or leaders. Where this is not the case, elections are not regarded as conducive for representing voters' views. Thus, one of the reasons for the poor evaluation of elections in some countries is that they do not represent voters' views. Figure 4.3 illustrates this very clearly. If elections are regarded as conducive to representing voters' views, then three-quarters of those surveyed feel represented by parties and leaders.

Does it matter which vision of democracy and representation is institutionalised? Specifically, does the difference between majoritarian electoral systems and proportional electoral systems account for differences in the feeling of being represented? Results in fact do not depend on the electoral system. On average, for all countries, there are no clear differences between majoritarian, mixed or proportional systems. Fifty three per cent of voters in majoritarian systems regard elections as conducive to political representation; in mixed systems, the percentage is 47, while in proportional systems the figure is 49 per cent. On the question concerning by whom voters in these different systems of representation feel represented, the common expectation would be that

Table 4.1. *Party and leader representation in systems structured by different visions of representation*

	Electoral System		
	Majoritarian	Mixed	Proportional
Represented by ...	%*	%*	%*
*Parliamentary and presidential systems***			
- a leader only	17.6	23.9	15.4
- a party only	11.6	14.3	15.5
- party and leader	70.8	61.9	69.1
*Only parliamentary systems***			
- a leader only	7.1	15.6	11.0
- a party only	12.0	13.8	18.2
- party and leader	81.0	70.6	70.8

* Base: all of the voting-age population that feels represented = 100%;
** Ten out of thirty-eight studies under investigation represent presidential or semi-presidential systems; the remainder are parliamentary systems.
Source: Own calculations: The Comparative Study of Electoral Systems, Module 2, 2001–6. Post-election surveys, representative of the voting-age population.

in majoritarian systems political representation is more personalised, while in proportional systems it is more party-defined.

However, the empirical findings suggest that there is not much difference between majoritarian and proportional systems when it comes to people feeling represented by either parties or leaders. For the political systems under investigation, the difference is merely two percentage points between majoritarian and proportional systems (Table 4.1). With regard only to party representation, the difference is four percentage points. This is somewhat higher, but not significant.

Turning to parliamentary systems, leader representation is a little higher in proportional systems than in majoritarian systems. The overarching result is that in both systems the vast majority of people feel represented by both a party and a leader. Thus, the two visions of democracy and representation do not significantly shape feelings of representation. Even if a more differentiated measure of the characteristics of a political system is used – the World Bank's Good Governance Index of Accountability, for example – differences reflected in these scores do not account for the differences in the levels of evaluation of elections, parties and leaders.

What might be the reasons for this finding? An answer can best be formulated by making use of the principal/agent approach. What are principal/agent relations in matters of political representation? Leaving aside presidential systems, the chain of delegation in parliamentary democracies is assumed to run from voters to elected representatives, that is, parliamentarians; from legislators to the executive branch; and from there to the heads of executive departments. Parliamentary democracy is based on the supremacy of parliament. In terms of principal/agent theory, accountability is simple, following the singularity principle, that is, 'single or non-competing agents for each principal; a single principal for each agent'. Parliament is accountable to voters; government is accountable to the parliament (Strom 2000).

The findings indicate that even in single-member district systems (SMD), as well as in proportional systems, accountability is organised differently, and can be best conceptualised in terms of the responsible party model. The responsible party model produces a system of accountability that is not necessarily implemented constitutionally. In such a system of accountability, political parties implicitly offer a contract between voters and those who are elected. Voters vote for a programme offered by one of the parties; parties commit their MPs to this programme, and because of this commitment 'parties are essential for making the democratic accountability of MPs meaningful' (Müller 2000). In terms of the principal/agent approach, delegation runs from voters to parties, from parties to MPs and government officials; accountability consequently extends from government officials and MPs to political parties, and from political parties to voters.

What is rational – and normatively positive – about this system? Voters can rely on the programming of politics by political parties, which claim the capacity to implement these policies. Individuals never can. Representation is collective, not dyadic, as in the personalised model. The security of expectations for voters is much higher with regard to expected outcomes. Thus, the security that representatives act in accordance with the wishes of people, instead of substituting elites' private desires for promised public policy goals is much higher – even though Laver (1997) has highlighted that it is an open question whether the institutional mechanisms really serve democracy through processes of delegation and accountability in the way they should, a point that will now be dealt with in the following section.

Institutional incentives and political representation

We have so far dealt with the question of whether elections are meaningful and how much they contribute to the sense of political representation among voters. This input perspective now has to be complemented with details of what happens in the process of representation itself, that is, whether the alternative visions of democracy affect the role of representatives itself and policy representation. In order to judge this aspect of the process of representation, hypotheses about the relationship between incentives and roles, and roles and policy representation are needed. A full-blown analysis would try to determine to what degree the relationships among incentives, roles and representation shape the feeling of being represented among electors. However, data for such a full-fledged model is still unavailable.

The history of empirical research on political representation is now quite long, having started with the famous 1957 study of Miller and Stokes (Miller and Stokes 1963). Warren Miller brought his design to Europe and it was established in a number of studies of representation in France, Germany, the Netherlands and Sweden. Meanwhile, the Nordic countries developed a common research design, and in 1996 a study of political representation with survey among members of national parliaments and the European parliament was conducted by Jacques Thomassen and Bernhard Wessels (Katz and Wessels 1999, Schmitt and Thomassen 1999). While this last-mentioned study comes close to providing the required design, the voters' surveys that have so far been conducted do not allow the question of levels of satisfaction with representation to be properly addressed.

Here, findings from two different sources are therefore used to ascertain to what degree electoral system incentives (a) induce the proper role orientation towards representation; and (b) produce the expected representation outcome. For (a) results are drawn from the European Representation Study, which conducted surveys among members of national parliaments in eleven European countries, and among the members of the European Parliament in 1996 (Schmitt and Thomassen 1999; Katz and Wessels 1999) and in particular a book chapter on role orientations (Wessels 1999b). For question (b), findings derive from the project on 'Policy representation in Western democracies', a collaborative effort by a group of principal investigators of national representation studies and their comparative reanalysis of these country-specific data (Miller et al. 1999).

Electoral incentives and representational roles

Why are roles so relevant? From a sociological perspective, roles can be defined as a set of expectations connected with a particular social position in a society (Dahrendorf 1968). The role of legislator consists of the rights, duties and obligations that are connected with the position of being a representative. His/her role orientations are shaped by expectations about representatives' position, rights, duties and the like. That is, 'the chief utility of the role-theory model of the legislative actor is that, unlike other models, it pinpoints those aspects of legislators' behavior, which make the legislature an institution' (Wahlke *et al.* 1962: 20).

The general concept of representational roles and their style and focus dimension became prominent in American legislative research during the last several decades (Miller and Stokes 1963; Miller 1988). In Western Europe, the analysis of style proved less useful, mainly because it overlooks the role of parties, which is highly important in European political systems (Holmberg 1989; Thomassen 1991). However, the focus dimension of representation does matter in Europe. Evidence from Sweden, for example, shows that personal characteristics have a moderate impact on the role of being a representative. This impact becomes higher as the focus of representatives becomes more specific; conversely, the more specific is the focus of representation, the higher is the effect on policy representation (Esaiasson and Holmberg 1996: 67, 73). The evidence from the Swedish study nevertheless suggests that one shortcoming of prior research is that the definition and measurement of representational roles were not specific enough, mainly because most research concentrates on the trustee–delegate approach, i.e., the style dimension. Thus, here I shall concentrate on the *focus* of representation.

The focus of representation can be group specific or regionally defined. A simple hypothesis can be put forward: the more electoral law is personalised, the more representation works in a personalised way. In the extreme case, single-member districts encourage the representation of the whole constituency, and a single national district, if it is a majority system, would represent the nation. For obvious mathematical reasons, such single districts are not feasible, and that is why the larger the district, the more proportional is the system, which implies that parties are competing and the focus of representation is the median party voter.

This can be elaborated a little further with reference to the literature. Legislators in smaller districts are more visible and more accessible to their constituents, whereas members of larger delegations may be better able to escape the pressure of constituents (Jewell 1970). Cox (1997) has demonstrated that electoral systems shape the structure and character of political competition by having an influence on *strategic voting* as well as on *strategic entry*, i.e., the decision of political actors to enter the political competition or not. He found that district magnitude is the most important factor for strategic behaviour, both of electors and elites. This is due to the degree to which elections are *personalised* or *partisan*. In electoral districts in which only one or a very small number of representatives are elected, the individual candidate is more visible and more subject to competition than in large districts.

Thus, the basic hypothesis here is that the more personalised an electoral system (the smaller the district in terms of mandates to be filled), the narrower regionally will be the representational focus chosen by a representative. However, in systems where parties define the success of the candidates, because their list placement is decisive, the focus is more broadly defined in either regional or group terms: either the nation or the party voters will be the chosen reference point. This leads directly to another hypothesis: the smaller the district and the more personalised is electoral competition among candidates, the more the focus of representation is defined in terms of the constituency.

The *average district magnitude* is a rough estimate of how strongly an electoral competition is personalised or partisan. Thus, the simple test is to explore whether there is a relationship between district size and the focus of representation. Figure 4.4 shows the result. Although the scatter plot illustrates that the statistical relationship is far from perfect, the clear pattern is that the larger the district magnitude the less MPs adopt a representational role linked to the constituency. More importantly, the smaller the district, the more local is the representational focus. The implication is clear: electoral incentives based on alternative visions of democracy have effects in the expected direction.

Electoral incentives and policy representation

The question is whether electoral incentives produce good political representation. In tackling this question, I rely on national studies from France, Germany, the Netherlands, Sweden and the USA. The studies include Miller and Stokes's 'classic' work on the United States in 1957 (Miller and Stokes 1963); Converse and Pierce's study of France in 1967 (Converse and Pierce 1986); Holmberg *et al*'s. studies of Sweden in 1968, 1985 and 1988 (Esaiasson and Holmberg 1996; Miller 1999); Thomassen *et al.*'s studies of the Netherlands in 1971, 1977 and 1989 (Andeweg *et al.* 1989); Herrera *et al.*'s study of the USA in 1986–7 (Herrera *et al.* 1992); and Herzog and Wessels' study for Germany in 1988–9 (Herzog *et al.* 1990, 1993).

My suggestion is that two different mechanisms of electoral law affect representation and thereby the outcome of policy representation in a specific way. Representatives in majoritarian systems are more

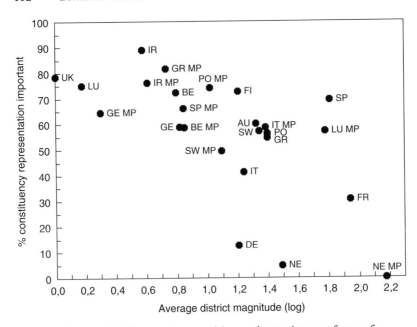

Figure 4.4. Electoral competition and constituency focus of representatives in Europe (percentage of MPs and MEPs who regard constituency representation as important)

Country abbreviation + 'MP': members of national parliaments; country abbreviation only: members of the European Parliament.

Aggregate correlation = −.63, sign. .001, n = 25.

Individual-level correlation = −.24, sign. .000, n = 1681.

Source: Wessels (1999b). Surveys among the members of national parliaments and the European Parliament, research project 'Political Representation in Europe'.

oriented towards the median voter, whereas representatives in proportional systems are more strongly oriented toward the representation of their party's voters. But there is no 'black and white' in representation; as demonstrated in the last section, in systems of majority-control democracy, party representation is as important as in proportional systems.

Since my main objective in this part of the chapter is to investigate the degree to which representatives in different systems are oriented toward the representation of party voters rather than the median voter, a score has been calculated that compares the absolute mean distance between representatives of a particular party and their party voters with the absolute mean distance to the 'median voter'. The measure, which is based on the comparison of collectivities (MPs and voters), subtracts from the absolute mean distance to party voters the absolute mean distance to the 'median voter'. The distance to the 'median voter' position is calculated as the absolute mean difference between the mean position of MPs of a particular party on any issue and the mean position of all voters on that same issue.

Luckily for this analysis, each of the five political systems under investigation is structured by a specific type of electoral system. The systems fit nicely on a majoritarian–proportional continuum. At the majoritarian pole, France has an absolute-majority rule in single-member districts. On the first ballot, a majority of votes is required for election; if no candidate wins a majority, a plurality suffices in the second ballot. This procedure has been called the 'Romance majority rule' (Nohlen 1978); Lijphart (1984) calls such systems 'mixed majority–plurality systems'. The United States has a relative-majority rule in single-member districts, in which a plurality of votes is required for election (Nohlen 1978). The German electoral system stands in between the majoritarian and proportional systems; it is often referred to as 'personalised proportional vote' (Nohlen 1978). In Germany, voters cast two ballots simultaneously, one for a candidate to be chosen by the plurality rule in single-member districts, and the other for a party list to be awarded seats by proportional representation in a state-wide multi-member district. 'Each party then gets its plurality-won seats plus the number of seats won by the proportional rule less the number of plurality-won seats' (Riker 1986). Sweden and the Netherlands have a list-proportional representation but differ with respect to proportional corrections. In Sweden, a special formula allows small parties to gain additional mandates from a larger party in order to make representation fairer (Nohlen 1978). The most purely proportional system can be found in the Netherlands. There the voter has one vote, which is cast for the leader of the list of the preferred party. Yet there is also the possibility of preference voting for a candidate different from the first one on the list, although *de facto* this preference voting has hardly any effect, since the first-placed candidate gains on average about 90 per cent of the vote.

This favourable continuum from majority to proportional rule can also be seen as a continuum stretching from a system of personalised politics to a system with party-centred politics. Electoral laws in majoritarian systems promote the candidates; in proportional systems, they promote parties. For (re-)election in majoritarian systems, candidates depend mainly on the electorate. This is not to say that party support does not matter, but in proportional systems it is imperative that the candidate gain a favourable position on the party list. According to the majority-control vision of democracy, the presence of 'a party or candidate located at or very near the median voter' implies that 'strategic incentives for the parties and the rational choices of the voters act together to provide victories for the party that is closest to the median' (Huber and Powell 1994). In contrast to this centre-driven electoral competition, the 'proportionate influence vision' of democracy suggests that 'the parties do not – must not – converge to the center unless virtually all the voters are located very close to it' (Huber and Powell 1994). This view is emphasised in the literature on the structure of party systems and party competition (Downs 1957; Sartori 1976). From each of these considerations, a straightforward hypothesis can be deduced: candidates in majority systems are more concerned with the majority of the electorate (in the constituency), whereas candidates on party lists are more concerned with the (median) *party* voter. Thus, in majoritarian systems, candidates focus relatively more on the 'median voter'; in proportional systems, relatively more on the (median) party voter.

Results confirm the hypothesis (Figure 4.5). The rank order of countries with respect to the magnitude of change in Y (the distance to party voters) matches the electoral system order described above almost perfectly. The two majoritarian systems rank highest, followed by Germany with its mixed system of one vote for a candidate and one vote for a party list. Then comes Sweden; the Netherlands rank lowest as it is the most proportional system, with the exception of 1971, when it was close to Sweden. The results force the conclusion that the normative standards embedded in the electoral institutions produce the desired representative effects. Representation works. The results also fortify the claim of the responsible party model since in both majoritarian and plurality systems the representation of party voters is what MPs do – with the qualification that there is a trade-off between median voter and party voter representation. In short, results indicate that while present-day representation does not work perfectly, at least not with regard to voters' evaluation of elections, it works reasonably well. The two general visions of democracy, with their particular focus on representation, operate in the expected direction, which implies that institutions not only matter, but they matter as intended by their designers.

Feelings of being represented or not – where do they come from and does it matter?

There are two remaining questions. First: when and why are elections regarded as poor instruments of political representation and, if they are

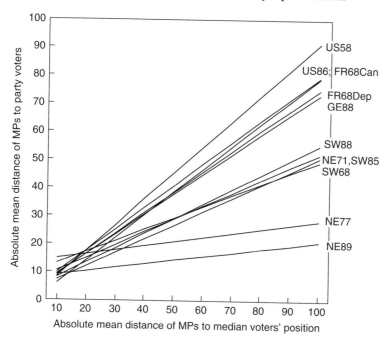

Figure 4.5. Party- vs. median-voter effect on policy representation*
Source: Wessels (1999a). National representation studies (voter and MP surveys) in the USA, France, Germany, Sweden and the Netherlands. Numbers after country abbreviation indicate year of the studies.
* Absolute mean distances: measure of issue congruency over a number of political attitudes of MPs and voters.

seen as poor instruments, can we draw conclusions about the possible improvement or reform of political representation from our explanations? Second: do the findings at all matter for the future of democracy and representation? More specifically: does the evaluation of representation by people have any effect on the need of democracy for acceptance, legitimacy and support?

Turning to the first question, the reasons why voters regard elections as good or poor means for getting their views represented are manifold. Institutions may be too badly designed to translate votes into effects. Political actors – parties or politicians – may perform poorly. With regard to institutions and their effectiveness, a crucial point is that who one votes for and who governs make a difference. If there is no difference in political supply, or the existing differences in political supply are not translated into different policies and outcomes, the act of choice in elections becomes meaningless, as do elections. Concerning the performance of political actors, it is more difficult to judge. The reason is that the evaluation of the performance of politicians and governments is widely influenced by partisanship. What is therefore needed is not a partisan yardstick, but a measure that tells us something about the degree to which politicians perform according to their general role of serving the public good. Corruption violates this criterion. Very simply put: if who one votes for does not matter, who governs also does not matter and that if politicians are corrupt, elections become meaningless.

This point is visible in the attitudes of people. If voting and who is in power make a difference, and if there is no corruption, the proportion of those who regard elections as meaningful is much higher than for the opposite case (Figure 4.6). The data suggests that both institutional weaknesses and the malperformance of politicians contribute to a poor evaluation of elections as a means of representation.

We can go a step further by relating institutional performance and representation by parties and politicians to the evaluation of elections. This makes possible a comparison of the impact of institutional and actors' performance on the evaluation of elections. If neither voting nor who is in power makes a difference, so that people do not feel represented by either a leader and/or a party, only 26 per cent regard elections as meaningful. By contrast, if institutions are regarded as effective and both parties and leaders are seen to perform their role as representatives, 64 per cent regard elections as meaningful channels for expressing the wishes of voters (Table 4.2). Furthermore, if institutions are regarded as effective but their results are nevertheless not seen as representative – implying that parties and politicians perform poorly – 38 per cent regard elections as meaningful. If there is no institutional effectiveness, but people nonetheless feel represented by a party and a leader, 54 per cent regard elections as meaningful. The implication is that while institutions matter, actors matter more. Whatever the level of institutional performance, if actors perform, elections are evaluated more positively than in the opposite case (see Table 4.2).

Does it matter for democracy whether people regard their institutions as proper and feel themselves to be represented? Democracy is a fragile public good and needs support; its capacity to successfully implement collective binding decisions would vanish if support declines. The majority principle would no longer be accepted, and the interplay of government and opposition would come into question. Classical theorists like Max Weber and modern theorists of political support, especially

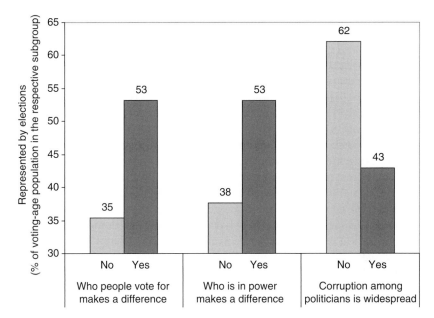

Figure 4.6. Institutional effectiveness of elections and government, political corruption and the evaluation of elections
Cross-country averages (country samples equally weighted).
Source: Own calculations: The Comparative Study of Electoral Systems, Module 2, 2001–6. Post-election surveys, representative of the voting-age population.

Table 4.2. *Institutional efficacy, political representation and the evaluation of elections*

Institutional Efficacy	Per cent of voting-age population in the respective subgroup who regard themselves as represented by elections *Representation by ...*			
	none	Leaders	Parties	Parties + Leaders
None	26%	29%	38%	54%
Power makes a difference	33%	34%	44%	55%
Voting makes a difference	34%	40%	51%	58%
Power and voting make a difference	38%	40%	53%	64%

Cross-country averages (country samples equally weighted).
Source: Own calculations: The Comparative Study of Electoral Systems, Module 2, 2001–6. Post-election surveys, representative of the voting-age population.

David Easton, have made it clear that every political order, and democracy in particular, needs legitimacy. What is less clear is how much legitimacy and political support a democracy needs in order to survive. This is the reason why it is so difficult to talk of a crisis of legitimacy. However, there is certainly a consensus that the more support democracy has, the better. Looking at the relationship between institutional effectiveness, representation through elections, parties and leaders, on the one hand, and support for democracy on the other, it is clear that it matters for democracy how institutions and representation are evaluated. Among those who see little or no institutional effectiveness and do not feel represented, satisfaction with democracy is as low as one-third. Among those who judge institutions to be effective, see that elections serve representation, and feel represented by parties and leaders, more than three-quarters are satisfied with the working of democracy. As for the evaluation of elections, there is an interesting relationship between the evaluation of institutions and representation by actors, this time in favour of institutions. Of those who see that it makes a difference whom the people vote for, who is in government, and who also regard elections as meaningful, but who do not feel represented by either a party or a leader, 60 per cent are satisfied with the working of democracy. Of those who feel represented by a party and a leader but regard institutions and elections as poor, only 51 per cent are satisfied with the working of democracy (Table 4.3).

The figures show that meaningful elections make all the difference. If they guarantee representation, levels of satisfaction with democracy jump. If, in addition, voters identify with parties or a party and a leader, satisfaction increases almost to the maximal point. Thus, in the evaluation of elections, it matters more whether there are political actors who perform well as representatives. For the evaluation of democracy, it matters more whether the institution, elections in the first instance, perform well. While political representation and judgements about it continue to be a complex issue, institutional designs matter: for the feeling of being represented, and the interplay of institutions with the performance of political actors are vital for the legitimacy and support of democracy and, thus, the system of democratic representation itself.

Conclusion

This analysis has looked at the evaluations of representation by voters across more than thirty countries, the effects of electoral institutions upon elected representatives, and their effects on policy representation. The results suggest a rather undramatic picture of the state of

Table 4.3. *Institutional effectiveness, political representation and satisfaction with the working of democracy*

	Per cent of voting-age population in the respective subgroup satisfied with the working of democracy *Representation by ...*			
Institutional Efficacy	none	Leaders	Parties	Parties + Leaders
None	33%	40%	46%	51%
Power makes a difference	33%	35%	41%	52%
Voting makes a difference	40%	34%	47%	53%
Power and voting make a difference	39%	40%	51%	52%
Represented by elections	57%	57%	69%	76%
Power and voting make a difference to feeling represented by elections	60%	57%	75%	77%

Cross-country averages (country samples equally weighted).
Source: Own calculations: The Comparative Study of Electoral Systems, Module 2, 2001–6. Post-election surveys, representative of the voting-age population.

political representation. Based on data drawn from these countries, 68 per cent of citizens feel either represented by a party or a leader or both. Certainly, this is not close to what is normatively desirable. That one-third do not feel represented is a sizeable proportion. On the other hand, by empirical standards 68 per cent is quite a high level of satisfaction with the working of democracy. Furthermore, the claim made here that representation in liberal democracy is party democracy based on responsible party government is not contradicted by the results. People obviously rely more on parties than on persons to mandate representatives. There is a difference between majoritarian and proportional systems, in that in the trade-off between party voter- and median voter-representation, median voters are relatively better off under majoritarian conditions. However, despite these positive findings, there is one serious shortcoming of representation in the countries under investigation. This concerns elections as an institution. On average across all countries, only 49 per cent of voters regard elections as serving political representation either quite well or very well. In quite a number of countries, twenty out of thirty-seven, the performance of elections is regarded as poor, with less than half the voters convinced that they serve the representation of interests.

What are the implications of this finding? The consequences for democracy should neither be underestimated nor exaggerated. However, it is clear from the results presented here that the legitimacy of democracy comes into question whenever elections do not perform well. The sense of satisfaction with the working of democracy drops below 40 per cent if elections do not work satisfactorily. If the performance of elections is satisfactory, then the minimum level of satisfaction with democracy is 57 per cent, and this increases up to 77 per cent on average across countries when people also feel represented by a party and a leader. Thus, the legitimacy of democracy depends to a large extent on whether elections are meaningful, in the sense that they induce processes of representation. No theory and no empirical analysis have yet shown what threshold of support is minimally required to avert the breakdown of democracy. However, there is no doubt that democracy is fragile and vulnerable to a decline in support, at least in the long run. Thus, the relevance of the performance of elections for representation and legitimacy cannot be overestimated.

The analysis presented here shows that there are three factors which partly explain why elections are regarded as satisfying or not. The first is whether voting is perceived to make a difference. Regardless of other factors, whenever this perception is absent, only one-third of people are satisfied with elections; when the opposite is true, the proportion increases to more than 50 per cent. The second factor is whether those in power are perceived to make a difference. Here, the proportions are very much the same as for perceptions that voting makes a difference. Thirdly, when voting and those in power make a difference, and people feel represented by a party and/or a leader, close to two-thirds regard elections as satisfactory. What is the implication? Only when elections make a difference and produce feelings of representation, does a majority of people regard them as proper. Thus, the existence of alternatives, alternatives that allow people to feel represented, are crucial. This means that elections must be based on real and substantive competition, and that competition is not 'artificial' but instead has a tangible link with the interests of people, who can therefore identify with the political offers made to them. Thus, only if the supply-side of politics is sufficiently differentiated and these differences are seen to matter, do elections as institutions gain support. This seems to be a trivial observation if only because the choice among alternatives is the whole purpose of elections. However, empirically speaking, it seems not so trivial, since in the majority of countries either political supply is not differentiated enough or it makes no difference in policy terms.

The burden for improving the situation is initially with political actors. Competitors must substantially differ. The race to the centre, toward the median voter, may be the best way for parties to gain office, but they may also destroy belief in elections and in democracy itself. Parties and politicians should thus be policy seekers instead of vote seekers. On the other hand, political institutions also bear a burden. This is indicated by the finding that many more people feel represented by a party or a leader than those who evaluate elections positively. This gap may indicate that voters find something on offer but also find elections do not really translate offers into policy differences. In this case, elections and election results do not fully translate into feelings of representation.

Improving democracy from this viewpoint means making elections more meaningful in the sense that political actors provide differentiated, alternative policy proposals, and that institutions translate election results into those desired policies. For political representation in liberal democracies all this implies that there is still a lot more room for improvement. Improvement is a challenge, but it may also be a good solution for some of the problems representative democracy faces, at least according to those who have diagnosed a crisis of representation. The results of the research summarised here imply that elections as the major and the only democratically legitimated way of popular government have not yet reached their limits. Improvement of elections means stretching their limits. From this perspective, electoral democracy still has a long way to go, but a long future, so long as it can be improved.

REFERENCES

Achen, C. H. (1978) 'Measuring representation', *American Journal of Political Science* 22(3): 475–510.

Andeweg, R. B., R. Hillebrand, R. van Schendelen, J. Thomassen and M. L. Zielonka-Goei (1989) *Dutch parliamentary study 1990, manuskript für das symposium on parliamentary research.* Leiden, pp. 13–16.

Converse, P. E. and R. Pierce (1986) *Political representation in France.* Cambridge and London: Belknap Press.

Cox, G. W. (1997) *Making votes count: Strategic coordination in the world's electoral systems.* Cambridge University Press.

(1999) 'Electoral rules and the calculus of mobilization', *Legislative Studies Quarterly* 24(3): 387–419.

Dahrendorf, R. (1968) *Homo sociologicus.* Köln, Opladen: Westdeutscher Verlag.

Downs, A. (1957) *An economic theory of democracy.* New York: Harper and Row.

Esaiasson, P. and S. Holmberg (1996) *Representation from above: Members of parliament and representative democracy in Sweden.* Aldershot: Dartmouth.

Habermas, J. (1987) *Theorie des kommunikativen Handelns (Vol. 2): zur kritik der funktionalistischen Vernunft*. Frankfurt am Main: Suhrkamp.

Hadenius, A. and J. Teorell (2005) 'Assessing alternative indices of democracy', *Political concepts: IPSA Committee on Concepts and Methods Working Paper Series* (6), Mexico City.

Hayward, J. (ed.) (1996) *The crisis of representation in Europe*. Abingdon, Oxon: Routledge.

Herrera, C. L., R. Herrera and E. R. A. N. Smith (1992) 'Public opinion and congressional representation', *Public Opinion Quarterly* 56(2): 185–205.

Herzog, D., H. Rebenstorf, C. Werner and B. Wessels (1990) *Abgeordnete und Bürger*. Opladen: Westdeutscher Verlag.

Herzog, D., H. Rebenstorf and B. Wessels (eds.) (1993) *Parlament und Gesellschaft: eine Funktionsanalyse der repräsentativen Demokratie*. Opladen: Westdeutscher Verlag.

Holmberg, S. (1989) 'Political representation in Sweden', *Scandinavian Political Studies* 12: 1–36.

Huber, J. D. and G. B. Powell Jr. (1994) 'Congruence between citizens and policymakers in two visions of liberal democracy', *World Politics* 46(3): 291–326.

Jewell, M. E. (1970) 'Attitudinal determinants of legislative behaviour: The utility of role analysis', in A. Kornberg and L. D. Musolf (eds.), *Legislators in developmental perspective*. Kingsport: Kingsport Press, pp. 460–500.

Katz, R. S. and B. Wessels (eds.) (1999) *The European parliament, national parliaments, and European integration*. Oxford University Press.

Köchler, H. (ed.) (1985) *The crisis of representative democracy*. Frankfurt/M., Bern, New York: Lang.

Laver, M. (1997) *Private desires, political action*. London: Sage.

Lijphart, A. (1984) *Democracies: Patterns of majoritarian and consensus government*. New Haven, CT: Yale University Press.

Lindberg, S. I. (2006) 'The surprising significance of African elections', *Journal of Democracy* 17(1): 139–51.

Merkel, W. (2004) 'Embedded and defective democracies', *Democratization* 11(5): 33–58.

Miller, W. E. (1988) *Without consent: Mass-elite linkages in presidential politics*. Lexington: University Press of Kentucky.

(1999) 'Elite-mass linkages in representative democracies: Introduction', in Miller, Pierce, Thomassen *et al.*, pp. 1–8.

Miller, W. E. and D. E. Stokes (1963) 'Constituency influence in Congress', *American Political Science Review* 57(1): 45–56.

Miller, W. E., R. Pierce, J. Thomassen *et al.* (1999) *Policy representation in Western democracies*. Oxford University Press.

Müller, W. C. (2000) 'Political parties in parliamentary democracies: Making delegation and accountability work', *European Journal of Political Research* I 37(3): 309–33.

Nohlen, D. (1978) *Wahlsysteme der Welt. daten und analysen*. München: Piper.

Pitkin, H. F. (1967) *The concept of representation*. Berkeley: University of California Press.

Powell, G. B. (2000) *Elections as instruments of democracy: Majoritarian and proportional visions.* New Haven, CT and London: Yale University Press.

Riker, W. H. (1986) '"Duverger's law" revisited', in B. Grofman and A. Lijphart (eds.) *Electoral laws and their political consequences.* New York: Agathon Press, pp. 19–42.

Sartori, G. (1976) *Parties and party systems.* Cambridge University Press.

Schmitt, H. and J. Thomassen (eds.) (1999) *Political representation and legitimacy in the European Union.* Oxford University Press.

Strom, K. (2000) 'Delegation and accountability in parliamentary democracies', *European Journal of Political Research* 37(3): 261–90.

Sullivan, J. L. and R. E. O'Connor (1972) 'Electoral choice and popular control of public policy', *American Political Science Review* 66: 1256–68.

Thomassen, J. (1991) 'Empirical research into political representation: A critical reappraisal', in H.-D. Klingemann, R. Stöss and B. Wessels (eds.). *Politische Klasse und politische Institutionen: Probleme und Perspektiven der Elitenforschung.* Opladen: Westdeutscher Verlag, pp. 259–74.

Thomassen, J. and H. Schmitt (1999) 'Introduction: Political representation and legitimacy in the European Union', in H. Schmitt and J. Thomassen (eds.), *Political representation and legitimacy in the European Union.* Oxford University Press, pp. 3–24.

Wahlke, J. C., H. Eulau, W. Buchanan *et al.* (1962) *The legislative system: Explorations in legislative behavior.* New York, London: John Wiley & Sons.

Wessels, B. (1991) 'Abgeordnete und Bürger: Parteien und Wahlkreiskommunikation als Paktoren politischer Repräsentation', in H.-D. Klingemann, R. Stöss and B. Wessels (eds.), *Politische klasse und Politische Institutionen.* Opladen: Westdeutscher Verlag, pp. 325–56.

(1993) 'Politische Repräsentation als Prozeß gesellschaftlich-parlamentarischer kommunikation', in Herzog, Rebenstorf and Wessels (eds.), pp. 99–137.

(1999a) 'System characteristics matter: Empirical evidence from ten representation studies', in Miller, Pierce, Thomassen *et al.*, pp. 137–61.

(1999b) 'Whom to represent? Role orientations of legislators in Europe', in Schmitt and Thomassen (eds.), pp. 209–34.

5   Do parliaments have a future?

David Beetham

Parliaments and legislatures are supposedly the central institution of representative democracy. Yet across all continents they come near the bottom of the list of institutions, public or private, in their level of citizen confidence or esteem.[1] By way of illustration, here is what the Clerk to the Australian House of Representatives told colleagues in the Association of Secretaries General of Parliament in 2000:

> During the last year the advertising industry, the news journalists and the used car salesmen of Australia had cause for rejoicing. Previously, they had been at the bottom of a list of professions ranked according to the public's perception of their trustworthiness. Members of Parliament were ranked just above them. However, a survey was released in July, altering the ranking … the survey placed the nation's legislators last in perception of trustworthiness in a list of professional groups. (Beetham 2006a: 98–9)

Or, to take an example from Europe, I read in a recent number of the *Journal of Democracy* that 'only a fifth of Poles think that their parliament is useful' (Rupnik 2007: 20). Such views are not isolated, but typical of consistent survey data across all continents. Is this anything new? Does it matter?

Let me begin by addressing the first question. There are perfectly understandable reasons why parliaments collectively as institutions have rarely enjoyed a particularly high or positive public profile. Let me mention just two. First, what most citizens expect from the democratic process is the delivery of outcomes – economic well-being, personal and collective security, health, education, a functioning transport system, and so on. These are the responsibility of elected governments or executives, whether elected through parliaments or separately. Of course the work of parliaments is necessary to secure the delivery of these public goods, through facilitative legislation, approval of revenue, oversight of public expenditure, and so on. But it is governments, not

---

[1] See the table in Beetham (2006a: 110).

parliaments that take and expect the public credit for their delivery, and the responsibility for failure.

A second reason is more subtle, but was well put to me by Tony Wright MP, Chair of the Public Administration Select Committee of the UK House of Commons. A parliament has no collective identity, he observed, and no person or body to speak for it as an institution. There are only individual parliamentarians, working separately or as members of a party, who occupy a common space to engage in a variety of different purposes. Parliament is simply a building, in which a multitude of activities is carried on, but without any corporate identity. Governments, by contrast, have a clear collective identity and a recognisable public profile, which they work hard to promote.[2]

These features have always been there. Yet there are other factors we can point to which have recently become more pronounced, and which have contributed to a decline in public confidence or esteem. Let me emphasise that I am not saying that the work of parliaments is any less necessary or important than in the past. At issue is their relationship with the public, and how they are perceived by them. A plausible hypothesis is that the decline in public esteem is related, on the one hand, to the erosion of representative and accountability functions with a high public salience; on the other, to parliaments' association with aspects of politics that have become increasingly unpopular, not to say discreditable, in the public mind. These are also significant issues in their own right.

Representation

A traditional function of a parliament has been to represent the views of the public to government, through members who are in close touch with their respective electorates. Yet from the standpoint of *government*, this is now far too crude and imprecise a method for assessing public opinion. This can be done much more accurately through targeted opinion surveys, focus groups, market research and the whole battery of instruments for assessing the fluctuating state of electoral opinion. From the standpoint of the *citizen*, a much more effective way of channelling opinion to government is through membership of a relevant association or single issue campaign, which can bring a weight of opinion and influence to bear on government directly, through collective rather than individual voice. From both sides parliament is bypassed as a representative channel. An extreme, though not untypical, recent

---

[2] Interview with Tony Wright (15 December 2004).

example of this, was the Poverty Reduction Strategy Papers (PRSP) process, whereby recipient governments in sub-Saharan Africa were required by the international agencies to consult domestic NGOs on their strategies, though not parliaments, even though it was parliaments that were going to have to approve the legislation and financial arrangements to implement the resulting policies (Beetham 2006a: 161–3).

Accountability

Here I am referring to a parliament's function of holding the government to account. As far as the individual citizen is concerned, a traditional recourse for complaint or redress in the event of maladministration or malfunctioning of some public service, at least in constituency-based systems, has been through the individual member of parliament. This is a role in which members have been able to achieve considerable visibility. Now, however, with the outsourcing of government services on the one hand, and the development of a consumer culture on the other, complaints and redress procedures have become both more service-specific and highly professionalised. So there are formal complaints procedures attached to every public service, and ombudsmen, public defenders, regulatory commissions, etc., both in general and specific to each service. There is also (as John Keane points out in Chapter 9) increasing use of the courts, both for redress, and for upholding basic citizen rights which are guaranteed in the constitution.

No doubt this professionalisation of citizen defence is to be welcomed. And of course parliaments have a crucial role in legislating the framework within which these watchdog bodies operate, and maybe also in providing for their oversight. Yet in so doing parliaments are becoming removed from the front line of a process which has a high public salience, so that it is hardly surprising to find, say, in Latin America, that the role of public defender stands so much higher in public esteem than that of parliamentarian. Indeed, in respect of the protection of citizen rights, parliaments nowadays seem to take on the logic of executives rather than of individual citizens.

On the one hand, then, has come the erosion of representative and accountability functions which give parliaments and parliamentarians public visibility and support. On the other, parliaments are associated with features of the political process that are increasingly held in disrepute, of which political parties and 'money politics' are the most obvious.

Political parties

If parliaments typically come second to last in public esteem, political parties occupy the very bottom place, and of course parliaments are closely linked with them.[3] To be sure, political parties have always been associated with an aspect of the democratic process with which many people feel uncomfortable: competition, division, opposition, argument, emphasis on difference. Again, however, we can trace recent changes which have further eroded public support, of which the following are perhaps the most significant:

(1) The disintegration of traditional social bases combined with the reduction of ideological differences under the pressure of economic neo-liberalism has made mainstream parties increasingly indistinguishable from each other, and less vote-worthy as a consequence. While there are obvious exceptions – Left parties in Latin America, ultra-nationalist parties in Europe, which increase voter turnout by supporters and opponents alike – argument between parties seems increasingly formal rather than substantive. Insofar as this is so, then a key criterion identified by Bernhard Wessels (in Chapter 4) as crucial to meaningful elections – that parties should differ in the policies they offer – is not met.

(2) Political parties have withered as active membership organisations and become largely 'cadre' or 'cartel' parties for those seeking public office, and for coordinating them behind a leadership once office is obtained. Whatever popular implantation they once had has now largely been lost, while at the same time there has been an increasing interpenetration of parties and the state. Paradoxically, as Peter Mair writes, we see 'an apparent weakening of the role of parties as representative agencies on the one hand, and an apparent strengthening of their role as public office-holders on the other ... a contradiction between the legitimacy (or its absence) of parties on the one hand, and their privileged position on the other' (Mair 1994; 1997: 127).

(3) Internal party disciplines are now so tight that those who step out of line risk forfeiting career prospects, if not their party membership or seat. From the standpoint of parliaments, executive control of a parliamentary or legislative majority means that a parliament's oversight and scrutiny capacity may be disabled as a consequence, whatever parliament's formal powers. From the standpoint of the

---

[3] See the table mentioned in note 1 above. For evidence of growing popular disenchantment with political parties see Mair 1997.

public, witnessing representatives regurgitating or voting the party line regardless of what they actually think hardly encourages respect among thoughtful electorates.

In the light of these negative features, and the low standing of political parties more generally, I am not convinced that Bernhard Wessels' data about the extent to which people feel represented by a political party can be viewed as grounds for confidence that all is well with party democracy. Perhaps more clarification is needed about what exactly lies behind 'feelings of being represented' by a political party. It is striking, for example, that the EU member states included in Wessels' Figure 4.2, with the exception of Italy, score highly on his scale of assumed party representativeness, whereas the EU average for the percentage of citizens expressing trust in political parties is exceptionally low, at around 15 per cent.[4]

'Money politics'

Most though not all of the issues that come under this heading relate to the electoral 'arms race' and the increasingly burdensome cost of getting elected to a national parliament. *Either* this falls as a personal cost on candidates, so that only the already wealthy are likely to achieve elected office; *or* the financing of elections for candidates or parties has to be sought from wealthy donors or corporations, whose interests may come to take priority over those of constituents; *or* both of these things happen simultaneously, as in the USA. In a recent survey of elected members in twenty-two developing countries, the authors observed:

> More than four out of five respondents state that they supply the majority of funds for their campaigns, often at the risk of personal bankruptcy ... As a result, many resort to relationships with individual donors who expect preferential treatment once the candidate is elected, while many reformers choose not to run at all, leaving the field to candidates who are independently wealthy. (Baer and Bryan 2005: 4)

In this context it is significant that the Inter-Parliamentary Union, while keeping the latest global data on the gender and ethnic composition of parliaments, has no usable data at all on the occupation, class position or wealth of parliamentarians prior to election, since these are simply not recorded by parliaments.

---

[4] See EU Commission (2004: 10) and Figure 4.2 in Chapter 4 of this volume, by Bernhard Wessels.

A different issue in many developing countries is the huge gap between parliamentary salaries and lifestyle and those of the average constituent, so that even those members without prior wealth come to constitute a quite separate class. This causes particular resentment when parliamentarians are seen to vote themselves huge salary increases. Rare are the countries, such as Ecuador, where parliamentary salaries are fixed at the average national wage, or St. Kitts, where salary increases are decided only after extensive public consultation and debate, or Vietnam, where half the elected parliamentarians are part-timers, pursuing everyday jobs in their constituency.[5] Although so large an economic gap does not exist in developed economies, the professionalisation of politics there has produced its own construction of parliamentarians as a separate and remote political caste.[6]

The conclusion from the evidence presented so far – about the erosion of representative and accountability functions with a significant public salience, and the association of parliaments with features of the political process that are becoming increasingly discredited – is not that parliaments are no longer important. Rather it is that we have been witnessing a level of public alienation from parliaments that is new and also perfectly explicable once these considerations are taken into account. And declining public support in turn diminishes a parliament's confidence in the face of the executive and weakens its position in the competition for the funds needed to improve its work.

Does this matter? Suppose for argument's sake that we are moving or have moved to a system of 'competitive executive democracy', with executives employing refined instruments of public opinion testing, and accountable to professionalised commissions and mechanisms of individual complaint and redress, with elite parliaments in a predominantly supportive and subordinate role to executives – would much have been lost, particularly if the system delivered outcomes that corresponded and were sensitive to people's preferences? Such a system might be termed 'neo- Schumpeterian' or 'neo-Weberian', remembering Weber's developed concept of competitive leadership democracy, with leaders appealing to the people directly over the heads of parliament and party (though it is also worth remembering that Weber assigned important functions to parliament, for example as the forum for testing potential leadership claims, and as the guarantor of essential citizen rights; Weber 1994; see also Beetham 2006b).

---

[5] Evidence provided in returns from member parliaments of the Inter-Parliamentary Union.
[6] See the 'second revolution' in democratic politics discussed by Philippe Schmitter in Chapter 5 of this volume.

We would surely conclude that this was an unacceptably thin version of democracy, in which the citizen was constructed largely as an individual consumer of public services, not as a potentially active partner in a collective democratic process, and in which there was no continuous or vigorous public debate and contestation about key collective choices facing the society. The question then follows: can and should parliaments act as an important (though not the only) mediating point for citizen participation and influence, and as the key locus for national debate about key collective decisions? Or should we accept that these are taking place in a parallel public sphere outside parliaments and largely bypassing them? If so, is there a price to pay for that?

Reforms being undertaken by parliaments

I propose to approach these questions crabwise, so to say, by first reporting on a working programme I led for the Inter-Parliamentary Union (IPU) in collaboration with its member parliaments, to find out what parliaments themselves were doing to address these issues – which resulted in a book entitled *Parliament and Democracy in the Twenty-first Century: A Guide to Good Practice*.[7] I should say that the recognition of a serious problem of public credibility on the part of parliaments was only one of the motivations for the programme. Another (hence the choice of title) was pressure from the IPU council to encourage those member parliaments in less-than-democratic countries to move further into the democratic age.

We decided at the outset that the wrong way to proceed would be to set out a highly prescriptive list of what a parliament had to do to be counted as 'democratic'. Instead we invited the member parliaments to submit their own examples of democratic reforms or good working practice which they thought worth sharing with others, and which would form the core of a published volume. However, we had to give them a 'steer' in the form of a brief explanatory text and a template or framework of what we understood to be 'the parliamentary contribution to democracy', which is reproduced as an appendix to this chapter.

The returns from member parliaments proved 'lumpy', in terms of who replied, the quality of the replies, and the range of issues covered in the framework. They were sufficient to show, however, that there was an enormous amount of effort being undertaken by parliaments across all continents to re-engage with their publics. At the risk of overhasty

---

[7] Reference in footnote 1 above.

generalisation I will simply itemise some of the main areas of current reform, as they touch on the issues already mentioned.

- Many parliaments are taking steps to make their composition more representative, both in terms of electoral opinion and the population's social composition. As to the first of these, a number of parliaments with single-member constituency plurality systems are incorporating an element of list proportionality into their voting arrangements, to a greater or lesser degree. As to the second, measures to improve ethnic and gender representation are in train almost everywhere, though the latter (see Drude Dahlerup's contribution to this volume) have been much more successful in new parliaments where there are not large numbers of men to be displaced.

- Most parliaments are making great efforts to communicate more effectively with their electorates. Committee meetings have been opened up to the media, parliamentary proceedings are broadcast in real time on dedicated channels, websites carry extensive information and the opportunity for constituents to interact with their members, and so on.

- Special efforts are being made to reach out to young people and educate them in the work of parliament. These go beyond the traditional school visits to parliament, to include the establishment of youth parliaments on a national and regional basis, the creation of virtual parliaments where students can engage in a variety of role playing, board games for younger children who have to surmount a range of hurdles to get a legislative bill enacted, and so on. Perhaps the most developed programme is in Denmark, where all pupils from a given school year across the country prepare bills on their chosen topics in school, the best ones of which are then selected to be debated by their proponents in a televised session at the national parliament.

- Many parliaments now have arrangements for interested individuals and groups to present evidence to legislative committees or committees of enquiry, the best of them offering user-friendly advice on how to make the most impact. Women's groups presenting evidence on gender budgeting to finance committees have provided a frequently cited example.

- In a number of democratic countries constituency members are being given a new role, and greater visibility, through deciding on development projects for their constituency up to a certain value of the relevant government budget. This is a more formalised version of the traditional constituency member's concern to win government contracts for the locality, albeit perhaps at the risk of increasing dependency on the executive.

Much other evidence was provided in the returns about the streamlining of parliamentary business, including the online tracking of legislative proceedings, and improving oversight of government international policy, though these are not directly relevant to the issues being considered here. If we concentrate simply on parliaments' efforts to re-engage with their publics, the examples given above constitute a substantial programme of reform and innovation, though naturally not uniform across all parliaments.

However, if we compare the above list of reforms with the problems outlined in the first part of the paper, it is evident that, however praiseworthy, the former still remain some way off the pace. If the issue is that parliaments have lost representative *functions*, then making their composition more representative will not address this particular deficit. If the problem is that parliaments don't have the capacity or will to hold executives to account when it matters, then more effectively communicating information about their work will hardly restore public confidence in their usefulness. Nor do the reform measures listed do anything to address the discredit attached to political parties and 'money politics', with which parliaments are inexorably associated. It is not surprising, therefore, that many of the proposals which have recently been canvassed to re-engage citizens with politics, to extend their opportunities for contributing to the policy process, and to experiment with new forms of representation and deliberative democracy, should ignore parliaments altogether. I shall survey these proposals briefly in the next section, and then consider how they might be adapted to improve the public salience of parliaments, rather than bypass them.

New forms of citizen participation and representation

Systems of representative democracy have traditionally allowed plentiful opportunity for direct citizen engagement with the decision-making process, whether informally, through single-issue campaigns, protests and demonstrations, or more formally, through consultative mechanisms and service on public bodies of all kinds, national or local. Recently there has been a lot of experimentation in many countries with new forms of citizen engagement with governmental decision making, or in some cases the revival and extension of old forms of such engagement. I reviewed a number of these in a recent book and assessed them against criteria such as their representativeness, the quality of engagement and deliberation, degree of influence on decisional outcomes, and so on (Beetham 2005, chap. 6). And there is now a huge academic literature devoted to describing and assessing these different forms of citizen engagement (Fung and Wright 2003; Gastil and Levine 2005; Smith 2008). There is only space here to give the barest summary of four of these, which will however be important for the last section of the chapter.

Consultative mechanisms

Governments have always consulted with relevant publics over their policy and legislative proposals, but now many do this more systematically and extensively, and in new ways. We should distinguish consultations which are public (and therefore potentially involving a wider range of people, even if only as 'audience', and the opportunity for public debate) from focus groups and other private forms of ascertaining public opinion. The former may comprise public meetings and workshops which are open to anyone interested (and therefore not necessarily representative), or to those whose membership is selected to reflect given characteristics of the population. The latter may be constituted as standing panels for particular areas of policy, or be assembled for a single issue. National consultation exercises may be replicated in many different regional and local centres, so as to involve larger numbers and generate local media attention and public interest. And of course the Internet greatly expands the numbers accessible in any consultation process, and makes devices such as e-petitions relatively simple to introduce.

Citizens' juries, consensus conferences

Whereas consultative mechanisms allow citizens simply to present their views, these deliberative forums, meeting over a few days on a given policy issue, are distinguished by the quality of their deliberation and by the fact that they conclude with a decision or recommendation, albeit one that is rarely binding on the relevant public authority. Their membership is typically selected by stratified sampling so as to be broadly representative of the population. In most respects they conform to the ideal of a representative assembly, in which deliberation is not distorted by ambition, party influence, or the pressure of sectional or financial interests.

Co-governance innovations

As their name implies, these give citizens a guaranteed degree of influence on policy or budgetary outcomes, and typically involve a much wider proportion of the relevant population than the forums mentioned above. As such, they are found only at the level of local or, at most, regional government. Classic examples are the participatory budgeting assemblies in Porto Alegre and the people's planning meetings in Kerala, though smaller-scale examples are to be found in many countries in matters such as community policing, urban regeneration, local environmental improvement, and so on.

Referenda and citizen initiatives

These can be binding on government and involve the whole of a given electorate, though only after a relatively high threshold of supporting signatures has been attained. Examples from Switzerland and US states are increasingly appealed to as successful ways of involving the population directly in the policy process. However, experience from these countries shows that they also suffer from some of the drawbacks of the electoral process, in that success may depend on the size of budgets and the slickness of organisation.

What is noticeable about most of these initiatives, and the discussion of them in the academic literature, is that they completely ignore or bypass parliaments. While at first glance they might seem to be complementary to the formal representative process, there is a danger that they only serve further to diminish its significance and public legitimacy. At the same time they are not unproblematic themselves. Mostly they comprise one-off initiatives, rather than continuous citizen engagement. While these might be appropriate for discrete policy issues which can be considered in isolation, they are unsuitable where decisions require relating one policy or budgetary issue to others. If membership of the consultative forum or whatever is open to any citizen, it will be skewed towards the already engaged and vocal. If it is selective, only small numbers are likely to be involved. In contrast with these experiments, the formal representative process, based as it is on election by the whole electorate acting as equals, on continuity of deliberation and decision by elected assemblies with law-making and tax-raising powers, and on their responsiveness and accountability to a range of publics, has potentially much greater legitimacy and effectiveness and, at national level, provides a clear focal point for public engagement and debate on major issues of concern.

For these reasons we must conclude that the formal representative process still carries much greater weight and potential than the other modes of representation considered by Michael Saward (Chapter 3 in this volume), however valuable his extension of the concept of representation may be. Moreover, if we consider more recently established democracies, the evidence suggests that the presence of a strong and effective legislature is the key to successful democratic consolidation (Fish 2006).

Given the continuing centrality of parliaments, then, we should seriously consider, first, what measures might be needed to restore public confidence in the integrity of the parliamentary process and remove some of its negative associations; secondly, we should explore whether some of the participatory innovations outlined above could be incorporated into the functioning of parliaments, rather than bypassing them, so as to increase the level of public engagement and ownership in what remains a core democratic institution. This will form the subject of the last main part of this chapter.

Restoring public confidence in parties, elections and the integrity of parliamentarians

In Chapter 4 of this volume Bernhard Wessels argues that representative democracy can only be *party* democracy. I broadly agree with this conclusion, except that political parties need substantial reform to give them greater popular implantation, less dependence on wealthy and powerful interests and less rigid top-down control over their representatives in parliament. After all, if they were abolished, they would have to be reinvented in some form, since they still give electors some measure of predictability that their policy choices will be followed in parliament, and governments some predictability that the programmes endorsed by the electorate can be implemented through the legislative process. Even the arch-individualist Edmund Burke acknowledged the necessity of party: 'When bad men combine', he wrote, 'the good must associate.' But he added that you should not 'blindly follow the opinions of party, when in direct opposition to your own clear ideas: a degree of servitude that no worthy man could bear the thought of submitting to' (Burke 1834: 151).

At the core of present concerns lies the issue of party and election financing. In my view the income of political parties should be restricted to only two sources. One would be subscriptions and donations from members and registered supporters, with a very low ceiling per individual (say $1000), to encourage wide rather than narrow recruitment. The US Democratic Party campaigns of Howard Dean in 2004 and Barack Obama in 2008 have shown how democratic renewal is possible through the mobilisation of huge numbers of supporters, and their contribution not only to the election itself, but to the political process on a more continuous basis. A second source, outlined by Philippe Schmitter in this volume, would be public funding, allocated according to electoral votes or through an annual voter choice linked to a voter registration process, which would allow a more regular citizen assessment of the respective parties' agendas and performance. No other sources of income or benefits in kind should be allowed for parties and candidates, other than those from public sources equally available to all.

The principle at issue here should be clear: only citizens treated as equals may be a source of party and candidate funding, whether indirectly, through specifically approved public funds, or directly, as registered members and supporters. Anything else produces a distortion of the representative process, and compromises the supposed equality of the ballot. Such a principle would in practice also offer the public a minimum sense of ownership of political parties and their activities. In return for the receipt of public funds, parties could be required to meet specified criteria for the process of candidate selection, including local balloting of the membership as well as ensuring gender balance. Parties in parliament could be debarred from expelling members who spoke or voted against the party line (though sanctions are desirable to prevent members from changing party allegiance altogether). This, together with the local selection of candidates, could go some way to loosening the stranglehold of party leaderships over their parliamentary followers.

Modes of enhancing citizen engagement with parliaments

If one side to reforming the representative process of parliaments is to deal with the deficiencies of political parties, the other is to link parliaments with some of the new forms of citizen engagement advocated in the recent literature on participation, and summarised earlier. The following are some of the ways in which these might be integrated into the parliamentary process, so as to give citizens a greater involvement in, and sense of ownership of, the representative system which acts in their name:

Deliberative forums

The key here is the democratic principle of selection by lot, where everyone has an equal chance to be selected, and a process of deliberation which is not distorted by party or sectional and financial interests. The most effective way of integrating this method into parliament would be to make it the principle of selection for the second, revising chamber of the legislature, subject to control for social and regional balance. Members could serve for a single, six-year term, with a third being replaced every second year. Induction and training procedures would have to be thorough, as would retraining schemes for enabling the return to previous employment, which would have to be guaranteed. Other practical difficulties to be ironed out need not detain us here. In principle any citizen could be called on, as with jury service, and the process of selection and training could be given substantial publicity, as well as attention in the school curriculum.

Selection by lot is highly democratic, in treating citizens equally, and in not assuming that representatives possess superior qualities from the rest of us, as in the aristocratic view of representation (Manin 1997, chap. 5). Unlike the deliberative forums espoused in the literature on participation, however, this second chamber would be permanent, could involve significant numbers of citizens over time, and would exercise substantial decisional powers. As such it could act as an effective check on a party-controlled lower house, and a counter-weight to a conception of politics as a wholly separate profession.

Citizen initiatives

The disadvantages often mentioned in connection with citizen legislative initiatives which lead to a binding referendum are that they may produce incoherence where policies are inter-related, and that they diminish the standing of the representative process more than they complement it. A simple way of integrating them at the parliamentary level would be to require that citizen initiatives which met a given signature threshold should be formally introduced and debated in parliament, with decisions being reached through the normal parliamentary process. In this way the integrity of the representative system would be preserved, while citizens would have the opportunity to contribute to the legislative agenda directly, if an issue of general concern could gather sufficient public support.

Consultative mechanisms

Most of the methods of consultation with the public developed by governments have also been employed at some time or other by parliaments, and there is no reason why these methods might not be used more systematically, for example in pre-legislative hearings or budget committee proceedings, as well as special commissions of enquiry.

While new media and IT applications can greatly expand the scope of public access, there is at the same time considerable danger of overload, and also of overlooking the continuing importance of physical or geographical space and location. Parliamentary committees or even a whole chamber (as in South Africa) could 'go to the country' to take soundings and receive submissions in different regional centres, and generate considerable positive publicity and public attention in the process. 'Your listening parliament comes to town' is not a bad slogan for re-engaging with the electorate.

Co-governance innovations

All the co-governance innovations discussed in the literature can work only at the local, not the national level, so they could not be replicated in a parliamentary context. In any case, parliament itself is in theory the archetypal co-governance institution, working on behalf of citizens at the national level. For a parliament to be so in practice requires effective, not just nominal, autonomy from the executive. The parliaments that come nearest to achieving this are those which, besides having sufficient resources and expertise under their own independent control, are not regularly subject to a single party majority where the same party also controls the executive. That is a matter for the electoral system as much as for the organisation of parliament itself.

Conclusion: political agency

This chapter's argument can be simply summarised. It is that representative assemblies with lawmaking and tax-raising powers remain indispensable elements of a democratic polity. National parliaments continue to be essential, even, or perhaps especially, in a globalised world. The erosion of public support and respect for them is therefore a serious matter. Proposals for re-engaging citizens in politics through new forms of participation are likely to further this erosion if ways cannot be found to incorporate them into the established representative process. Only a reinvention of parliaments that goes further than anything currently envisaged will meet the demands of the situation.

The argument naturally raises the question of who are the potential agents who might initiate a reinvention on this scale, and what incentive they might have for doing so. Governing executives, it could be said, are rarely in the business of surrendering power, and are perfectly content with compliant legislatures. Parliamentarians, for their part, are quickly socialised into established ways of working, and look to progress in a parliamentary or governmental career within predictable parameters. And political parties remain happy to engage in the 'arms race' of electoral and pre-electoral spending, provided they have a chance of outdoing their competitors. All of the key 'change agents', in sum, seem naturally disposed to sustain the status quo.

However, a number of considerations should be set against this rather complacent, not to say pessimistic view:

(1) Over the last fifteen years parliaments have shown themselves capable of initiating quite substantial reforms, examples of which were listed earlier in this chapter. They have done so in response to a number of different pressures. There has been recognition of lost public confidence, due to finance scandals, declining voter turnouts and political apathy among the young. There has been strong pressure for more effective representation of women and ethnic minorities. There have been technological changes which have encouraged more effective communication with constituents. And there has been peer-group influence, as parliaments have increasingly looked to see how other parliaments are addressing problems which they have in common. It is too soon to say that these processes have come to an end, or to define their limits.

(2) Over the same period, electorates have become more educated, more demanding and more vocal. Although this has coincided with a turn away from involvement in formal representative politics, it has been reflected in increased participation in civil society organisations, campaigning groups, protest movements, and so on, from the local to the global. Governments and parliaments have found it increasingly important to engage with such groups, if only to pre-empt disruptive protests which can hinder the implementation of chosen policies. As far as parliaments are concerned, this trend partly explains the readiness of the most progressive ones to involve concerned publics in pre-legislative scrutiny, select committee hearings and major enquiries into aspects of government policy. Hence, more radical or inclusive ways of engaging with the public could be seen as an extension of a process which is already under way.

(3) The era of individualistic consumerism, characteristic of the past two decades, in which 'individual choice' has been promoted as the panacea for all problems, private or public, and 'politics' have been readily dismissed as irrelevant to people's lives, is already undergoing transformation in the face of the financial and economic crises. The importance of the public sphere is being rediscovered. Even

more significant in this transformation are the pressures from a rapidly escalating environmental crisis. These pressures can only be addressed by *collective* choices and decisions, often controversial ones, which impact directly on lifestyles, local environments, consumer preferences or sheer survivability. Some have argued that we will see a reversion to authoritarian modes of government in the face of these pressures. However, this is unlikely given the character of electorates in established democracies. Much more likely, seeing that difficult collective choices will depend on public support for their implementation, is more direct and continuous engagement by government at all levels with their electorates, who in turn will have a strong incentive to become much more engaged themselves. The precise forms of such engagement are impossible to predict, but that the combined forces of social, technological and above all environmental change will open up the existing processes of representative democracy to radical change is a plausible assumption. And with every new scientific review of the environmental evidence, the timescale for such changes becomes rapidly foreshortened.

REFERENCES

Baer, D. and S. Bryan (2005) *Money in politics*. Washington DC: National Democratic Institute.

Beetham, D. (2005) *Democracy: A beginner's guide*. Oxford: Oneworld Publications.

(2006a) *Parliament and democracy in the twenty-first century: A guide to good practice*. Geneva: Inter-Parliamentary Union.

(2006b) 'Weber and Anglo-American democracy', in K.-L. Ay and K. Borchardt (eds.) *Das Faszinosum Max Weber*. Konstanz: UVK Verlagsgesellschaft, pp. 343–51.

Burke, E. (1834) 'Thoughts on the cause of the present discontents', in *The works of Edmund Burke*. London: Holdsworth and Ball, vol. I, pp. 124–53.

EU Commission (2004) *Eurobarometer 61*. Brussels: EU Commission.

Fish, M. S. (2006) 'Stronger legislatures, stronger democracies', *Journal of Democracy* 17(1): 5–20.

Fung, A. and E. O. Wright (eds.) (2003) *Deepening democracy: Institutional innovations in empowered participatory governance*. London and New York: Verso.

Gastil, J. and P. Levine (eds.) (2005) *The deliberative democracy handbook: Strategies for effective civic engagement in the 21st century*. San Francisco: Jossey-Bass.

Mair, P. (1994) 'Party organizations: From civil society to the state', in R. S. Katz and P. Mair (eds.) *How parties organize*. London: Sage, pp. 1–22.

(1997) *Party system change*. Oxford University Press, pp. 125–36.

Manin, B. (1997) *The principles of representative government*. Cambridge University Press.

Rupnik, J. (2007) 'From democracy fatigue to populist backlash', *Journal of Democracy* 18(4): 17–25.

Smith, G. (2008) *Democratic innovations: Designing institutions for citizen participation.* Cambridge University Press.

Weber, M. (1994) 'Parliament and government in Germany in a new political order', part IV. In *Political writings.* Cambridge University Press, pp. 209–33.

Appendix 1. *The parliamentary contribution to democracy: a framework*

Basic objectives or values. A parliament that is:	Requirements	Possible procedural and institutional means for the realisation of these objectives or values
Representative	An elected parliament that is socially and politically representative, and committed to equal opportunities for its members so that they can carry out their mandates	Free and fair electoral system; means of ensuring representation of/by all sectors of society with a view to reflecting national and gender diversity, for example by special procedures to ensure representation of marginalised or excluded groups Open and democratic party procedures, organisations and systems Mechanisms to ensure the rights of the opposition and other political groups, and to allow all members to exercise their mandate freely and without being subjected to undue influence and pressure Freedom of speech and association; parliamentary rights and immunities, including the integrity of the Presiding Officers and other office holders Equal opportunities, policies and procedures; non-discriminatory hours and conditions of work; language facilities for all members
Transparent	Parliament that is open to the people and transparent in the conduct of its business	Proceedings open to the public; due notice of business; documentation available in relevant languages; availability of user-friendly tools, for example using varied media, such as the world wide web; own public relations officers and facilities Legislation on freedom of/access to information

Appendix 1 *(cont.)*

Basic objectives or values. A parliament that is:	Requirements	Possible procedural and institutional means for the realisation of these objectives or values
Accessible	Involvement of the public, including civil-society and other peoples' movements in the work of parliament	Effective modes of public participation in pre-legislative scrutiny; right of open consultation for interested parties; public right of petition; systematic grievance procedures Various means for constituents to have access to their elected representatives Possibility for lobbying within the limits of agreed legal provisions that ensure transparency
Accountable	Members of parliament who are accountable to the electorate for their performance in office and for the integrity of their conduct	Effective electoral sanction and monitoring processes; reporting procedures to inform constituents; ethical standards and enforceable code of conduct Adequate salary for members; register of outside interests and income; enforceable limits on election expenditure
Effective *At all levels*	Effective organisation of business in accordance with the above democratic norms and values	Mechanisms and resources to ensure the independence and autonomy of parliament, including parliament's control of its own budget and own business committee Availability of non-partisan professional staff separate from main civil service Adequate unbiased research and information facilities for members; procedures for effective planning and timetabling of business; systems for monitoring parliamentary performance; opinion surveys on perceptions of performance among relevant publics

Basic objectives or values. A parliament that is:	Requirements	Possible procedural and institutional means for the realisation of these objectives or values
a) in relation to the national level	Effective performance of legislative and oversight functions, and as national forum for issues of common concern	Systematic procedures for executive accountability; adequate powers and resources for committees; accountability to parliament of non-governmental public bodies and commissions Mechanisms to ensure effective parliamentary engagement in the national budget process in all its stages, including the subsequent auditing of accounts Ability to address issues of major concern to society; to mediate in the event of tension and prevent violent conflict; to shape public institutions that cater for the needs of the entire population For parliaments that approve senior ranking appointments and/or perform judicial functions: mechanisms to ensure a fair, equitable and non-partisan process
b) in relation to the international level	Active involvement of parliament in international affairs	Procedures for parliamentary monitoring of and input into international negotiations; mechanisms that allow for parliamentary scrutiny of activities of international organisations and input into their deliberations; mechanisms for ensuring national compliance with international norms and the rule of law; inter-parliamentary cooperation and parliamentary diplomacy
c) in relation to the local level	Cooperative relationship with state, provincial and local legislatures	Mechanisms for regular consultations between the presiding officer of the national and subnational parliaments on national policy issues in order to ensure that decisions are informed by local needs

Source: Beetham (2006a: 10–11).

6   Engendering representative democracy

Drude Dahlerup

Introduction

Fifty years ago politics was totally male dominated. In any political institution, a woman was an exception, a stranger. Since then, a process of engendering has taken place in politics, even if women are still vastly under-represented.[1] It has been a slow process with great variations in time and space, and not without backlashes. But in terms of gender composition, the political arena will never look the same as it did in the 1930s and 1950s.

The recent adoption of *gender quotas* for public elections by countries all over the world represents an attempt to change traditional male dominance in politics and speed up the process of engendering. Although highly controversial, electoral gender quotas have during the last two decades been adopted in constitutions or in legislation in almost fifty countries, while in about fifty additional countries one or more of the political parties represented in parliament have introduced quotas for their own election lists (Dahlerup 2006; www.quotaproject.org).

This trend points to a new understanding of representative democracy – an understanding that is very far from James Mill's argument that a husband can represent the interest of his wife.[2] But also far from the suffragists' demand for formal rights for women to vote and to stand for public election. Today, the global demand is for nothing short of gender balance in representation, or 'parity democracy', i.e., 50 per cent women and men in all political decision making.

In relation to the crucial question of 'how' in democratic theory, feminist theory and women's movements have pointed to the importance of

---

[1] One may argue that all political decision making is gendered, even purely male-dominated assemblies. However, following the new international terminology, the term 'engendering' is used here to refer to the process of deliberately adopting a gender-equality perspective as well as to actual increases in women's representation.

[2] It was his son, John Stuart Mill, who said that even though his father and his father's circles had a great influence on him, he disapproved of his father's position on women's suffrage – and Bentham, he added, was 'wholly on our side' (Mill 1873: 87–8).

adding the question of 'who'. It is argued that democratic theory cannot merely be concerned with democratic procedures, the how, be it in the city state of Athens or in modern deliberative governance structures, if by so doing it neglects the crucial question of who participates in the decision making, and who has influence.

This chapter will discuss how a new *discourse of exclusion* is challenging male dominance in political institutions, shifting the focus from women's alleged lack of resources to the lack of inclusiveness of the political institutions themselves. This new focus is about the descriptive, e.g., social representation. It will be argued that this approach opens up for broader coalitions of women's organisations, who in spite of their political differences and in spite of other diversities among women may work together against exclusion on account of gender. An example is the 50:50 campaign launched in September 2008 by the European Women's Lobby under the slogan 'No Modern European Democracy without Gender Equality'. The campaign spotlights the current under-representation of women in most elected assemblies in Europe, including in the European Parliament, and sees this under-representation as a serious democratic deficit threatening the legitimacy of European institutions and political parties.[3]

A hundred years ago, indeed just fifty years ago, it was considered improper to label a political system undemocratic 'merely' because women were excluded. There was no UN boycott of Switzerland even though women there did not get the right to vote until 1971. Today, a link is being made between equal representation of women and men and the status of representative democracy, as illustrated in the previous slogan as well as in the following quotations, the first from the 'Platform for Action', adopted by the world's governments at the UN Fourth World Conference for Women in Beijing 1995, and the second from a document issued by the Southern African Development Community (SADC), which is well known for its elaborate gender equality programmes. Achieving the goal of equal participation of women and men in decision making is seen as desirable because it provides a balance that more accurately reflects the composition of society and is needed in order to strengthen democracy and promote its proper functioning:

States parties shall endeavour that, by 2015, at least fifty percent of decision-making positions in the public and private sectors are held by women, including the use of affirmative action measures as provided for in Article 5. States parties shall endure that all legislative and other measures are accompanied

---

[3] www.womenslobby.org (accessed 7 February 2009).

by public awareness campaigns which demonstrate the vital link between the equal representation and participation of women and men in decision making processes, democracy, good governance and citizen participation.

(Southern African Development Community [SADC] 2008, art. 12)[4]

It is interesting to note that the SADC document establishes the need to develop public awareness about the link between the inclusion of women, and democracy and good governance. The assumption that there is such a link is relatively new, although it is often phrased somewhat vaguely. This chapter will look at this link at *the abstract, theoretical level*. But, as in several other contributions to this book, discussions of the de facto functioning of democracy also compel us to look into the norms and practices of political institutions, *the meso-level of politics*. The adoption of electoral gender quotas directs our attention to this level. Pushed to extremes, one may ask whether the widespread adoption of electoral gender quotas represents a threat to the principles of democracy, as some quota opponents argue (Offe 2001), or whether the inclusion of women (and other under-represented groups) in parliaments and local councils rather provides an opportunity to revitalise a representative democracy in crisis, as some quota advocates argue (Squires 2007). The fact that electoral gender quotas have been adopted in democratic countries, as well as in semi- and non-democratic countries, renders this issue even more complex.

In the language of contemporary international organisations, 'engendering' entails the inclusion of a heretofore missing gender perspective into a subject, correcting a gender-blind approach, as in 'Engendering Development' (World Bank 2008), 'Engendering all Programmes' (African Union 2003), 'Engendering Legislation/Budgets' (iKNOW-Politics), 'Engendering the Global Agenda' (Pietilä 2002). Engendering representative democracy is used here in relation both to changing discourses and theories of democracy and to the actual entrance of women into previously male-dominated political decision-making bodies. 'Feminising' is another term used, as in Joni Lovenduski's (2005) *Feminizing Politics*. Both terms imply a process perspective, however 'engendering' is preferred here, since 'feminisation' connotes a process in which women are becoming the majority, as in the 'feminisation of poverty'. The public elected assemblies, which are the focus here, are very far from a state of female dominance.

---

[4] The African Union (AU) and the European Union (EU) also have explicit goals with regard to 'full participation', 'equal partners' and 'gender parity', including recommendations for positive measures.

This chapter will place the issue of gender quotas in the broader perspective of engendering representative democracy in theory as well as in practice. It will first look more closely at the concepts of the 'how', the 'who' and the 'what' of representative democracy. This is followed by a discussion of theories of exclusion/inclusion of women in male-dominated politics. The following three empirical sections present an overview of variations over time and space in women's political representation as well as the recent global adoption of electoral gender quotas. There follows a discussion of the importance of the nomination processes, an often neglected level in theories of democracy. Against this background, the final section offers some conclusions concerning the complex equation of the inclusion of women and the development of representative democracy.

The 'how', the 'who' and the 'what' of representation

Unpacking the meaning of representation, Yvonne Galligan defines three distinct but interrelated dimensions: *who* represents, *what* is represented and *how* it is represented (Galligan 2007: 557). This chapter will discuss how the arguments for a more inclusive representative democracy are constructed. It will be shown that the issue of gender quotas in politics – so controversial and yet so popular – sheds new light on the link between the 'how' and the 'who' of representative democracy. Does the inclusion of women on an equal footing with men require and, in itself, lead to changes in the structure and functioning of political institutions, which in many countries were created before women had access to the precincts of politics? The question of 'what' is to be represented is no less complex:

Women's equal participation in decision-making is not only a demand for simple justice or democracy but can also be seen as a necessary condition for women's interests to be taken into account. Without the active participation of women and the incorporation of women's perspective at all levels of decision-making, the goals of equality, development and peace cannot be achieved. (from Article 183, United Nations Fourth World Conference on Women 1995)

Women's Environment & Development Organisation (We-Do), a New York based, global NGO, uses the following formulation in its campaign:

When women are represented in a critical mass in policy-making bodies their perspectives and experiences are more likely to be taken into account, their concerns given higher priority, and action becomes possible.[5]

---

[5] From the We-Do 50:50 Campaign, 'Getting the Balance Right in National Parliaments', www.wedo.org (accessed 8 June 2008).

The question of the 'what' (whose interests are to be represented) is central to most campaigns for increasing women's representation, as in the quotations above. However, the link between *descriptive* (social representation) and *substantive* representation (action for), to use Hanna Pitkin's terms (1967), is contested in contemporary research on politics and gender. While most empirical studies have concluded that it is women politicians that have placed gender equality on the formal political agenda, it is also evident that women politicians do not constitute a single political group (Goetz and Hassim 2003; Franceshet and Piscopo 2008; Wängnerud 2009). This chapter argues that the troublesome link between the 'who' and the 'what' – should women prove that they will make a difference in politics in order to claim equal representation? – is not a significant concern within the new discourse of exclusion.

Feminist theories of exclusion and inclusion of women

When liberal democracy was established, according to political theorist Carole Pateman, a constitutive element was the division between a public and a private sphere and the exclusion of women from the public sphere. Women were not considered real citizens. When women began to press for access to the new public arena, they were faced with what Pateman has labelled 'Wollstonecraft's dilemma': it was taken for granted 'that for women to be active, full citizens they must become [like] men'. If, on the other hand, women were to retain their experiences and qualities, so that they were an integral part of their citizenship, they would remain marginalised. Consequently, the very notion of citizenship needs to be expanded (Pateman 1989: 14). This dilemma has haunted feminist movements for centuries, often expressed as the choice between equality and difference.

The arguments used in campaigns for women's suffrage reflected this dilemma. Interestingly, one can find virtually the same considerations in modern public discussions of why it is important to increase women's political representation, perhaps by introducing gender quotas. According to *the justice argument*, women should be granted suffrage as a natural right, today expressed in terms of human rights. Women, thus, do not have to prove whether they are similar or different or whether they will make a difference.

Demands for suffrage and, later, for equal representation have also been based on the need for representation of women's life experiences, *the experience argument*. In a third type of argument, *the interest argument*, a conflict of interests between men and women is emphasised and, consequently, men cannot represent women, contrary to what James Mill argued. In the suffrage campaign the obvious male bias of the marriage laws of that time was often mentioned, for example the 'Code Napoléon' from 1804 in Title VII, chap. 3, on illegitimate children: 'Scrutiny as to paternity is forbidden. Scrutiny as to maternity is admissible'!

As can be seen, both the experience argument and the interest argument involve suffrage/representation as a means of changing policies, not just as a goal in itself. Research into the actual use of these arguments reveals ambivalences and strategic considerations: in feminist movements, all three arguments have sometimes been used at the same time, even by the same people, depending on the context (Kraditor 1965; Evans 1977; Dahlerup 1978). Later, feminist scholars adopted these three types of arguments for women's representation in their theoretical work (Hernes 1982; Phillips 1995).

More recent political theory has argued that we are dealing with a false dichotomy, since the opposite of equality is not difference but inequality. The deconstruction of this dichotomy opens the way for an equality policy based on difference, not necessarily sameness (Bacchi 1990). Moving away from the dilemmas imposed on women, new arguments in the theoretical as well as the public debate focus on *the exclusion of women*.

Arguments for inclusive democracy

Feminist theory has strongly criticised liberal democratic theory for its 'false universalism'. It is not the case that all citizens or all inhabitants of a country have the same possibilities of influencing political decision making, even if formal rights to participate have been granted. Consequently, the feminist critique adds the concerns of women to the point, expressed ever since the birth of liberal democracy, that the formal, individual equality cannot be viewed independently of social inequalities in society at large.[6]

What are the arguments? 'No democracy without the full inclusion of women', is a normative standpoint, as is the opposite, traditional point of view, that one can speak of democracy even if women are de jure or de facto excluded. Iris Marion Young argues for the inclusion of women from the perspective of *democratic legitimacy*: 'The normative legitimacy of a democratic decision depends on the degree to which those affected by it have been included in the decision-making processes and have had the opportunity to influence the outcomes ... on

---

[6] Classic Marxism rejected the very concept of liberal equality: 'Dies *gleiche* Recht is ungleiches Recht für ungleiche Arbeit' (Marx 1875 vol. 19: 21).

equal terms' (Young 2000: 5–6, 23). Based on her model of deliberative democracy, Young argues against seeing the notion of inclusiveness as a kind of interest representation. Rather, her model 'emphasises
the ideals of inclusion, political equality, reasonableness, and publicity'
(2000: 17). According to Young, the arguments against such inclusiveness, for instance through the use of quotas for women and for other
groups, derive from a misunderstanding of the nature of representation
more generally. Representation is not about a relation of substitution or
identification but a 'differentiated relationship' among political actors
(2000: 123). In Chapter 1 of this volume, Nadia Urbinati also argues
for seeing representation in this way, as a process.

But post-structuralist feminist theorists have objected to such
demands which, in their view, tend to construct women as belonging
to a single group. Hasn't feminism fought hard to abolish this categor-
isation (Butler 1990)? The answer to this criticism, in my view, is that
when women are excluded as a category, it is vital to speak about the
category 'women' and to make strategic moves as women – even if the
ultimate goal is that in the future gender should not play any role in politics. This strategy does not imply essentialising women as a group with
intrinsic characteristics. Based on the justice argument, quotas may
even be seen as merely creating opportunities for individual women to
compete for political seats.

The widespread use of the concept of 'identity', in my opinion, constitutes a major problem in the intense discussions about women as
a group. The present-day fashion of speaking of social movements in
terms of 'identity movements' is unfortunate; it downplays the political aspect of these movements, their fight against oppression and discrimination. Should we similarly refer to the working-class movement
as an 'identity movement'? Obviously, that would be wrong. From a
social movement perspective, a common ideology and solidarity within
a group – be it workers, blacks, women, immigrants or homosexuals –
is clearly a result of organisational effort, not something instinctive or
inherent (Dahlerup 2004). In general, a discourse of exclusion seems
to open up opportunities for broader coalitions of women's organisations and for the inclusion of women of various political positions, back-
grounds and preferences, even of feminist men, to a greater extent than
a discourse of common identity does.

Theoretical quota arguments

Most quota proponents and quota opponents do not argue theoretically, and within feminist theory, with a few exceptions, most theoretical
arguments relate to women's representation in general.

Anne Phillips could have taken her argument about 'the politics of presence' one step further. She argues that the liberal notion of representation as *representation of ideas* is 'an inadequate vehicle for dealing with political exclusion', and she argues for the importance of a *politics of presence*, advocating, among other things, quotas for women (Phillips 1995: 24–5). Even if Phillips maintains that the politics of presence should not replace the politics of ideas but rather that the two should be combined, she does not herself provide guidance as to how to combine the two. However, the introduction of electoral gender quotas into a party system based on a variety of party programmes in fact provides this combination of ideas and presence.

Quota opponents, such as Claus Offe, argue that 'gender is clearly not the only divide that generates distorted elite composition' (Offe 2001: 49). Should we then have quotas also for ethnic minorities, religious groups, social classes and an endless number of other under-represented groups? Firstly, many countries do have quotas for religious and/or ethnic groups or extended self-government schemes for indigenous peoples. And most individual political parties in list systems have for a long time employed formal or informal candidate quotas in order to include candidates representing (for example) trade unions, business, geographical locations, young people and today, increasingly, immigrants. Secondly, a *discourse of exclusion* does not focus on women or other statistically excluded groups but on the *de facto special treatment favouring males*. So, theoretically, the new question posed is how the continuous privileged position of men in leadership can be justified.

Two contrasting modern discourses on women's under-representation have been identified (Dahlerup and Freidenvall 2005). They are presented in the form of two ideal types – the *incremental* and *fast-track* discourses – that are based on different perceptions of historical change, different goals, different diagnoses and different strategies, summarised as follows:

The incremental track discourse
1. General perception: equality will come about in due time.
2. The goal: more women in politics.
3. Diagnosis of why there are so few women in politics: women's lack of resources and public commitment.
4. Strategy: either no action at all or policies to increase women's resources.

The fast-track discourse
1. General perception: equality does not come about through historical necessity. Backlashes may occur.

2. The goal: gender balance, parity democracy.
3. Diagnosis of why there are so few women in politics: discrimination and various mechanisms of exclusion.
4. Strategy: active measures, such as setting up targets and adopting quotas.

These two tracks are based on different logics. The incremental track discourse draws on the perception that equality – which is the stated goal – will come about in due time. It is based on the *time-lack thesis*, according to which women's under-representation is primarily an effect of women's lack of resources and of old prejudices, which will disappear in due course, as society develops. Consequently, affirmative action measures, such as gender quotas, are seen as unnatural interferences in normal political practices, distorting the principles of liberal democracy.

The Scandinavian countries and the Western world in general have until recently been characterised by the incremental track model. Even women's organisations have previously adhered to this model to a large extent, pushing primarily for women's education, labour market participation and larger commitments in the public sphere as preconditions for political representation. Today, however, women in many parts of the world are as educated as men; women are to a large extent in the labour market and women participate as much as men in social movements and civic life. And yet women's political representation is so much lower than that of men. Hence there is a need for new understandings.

In contrast, the fast-track discourse focuses on men as a gender. It draws on the understanding that male-dominated societies and organisations have an embedded tendency to reproduce male dominance. Open discrimination and structural mechanisms of exclusion are institutionalised in the norms and practices of political life and, consequently, active measures to break with these structures are needed in order to make political life more inclusive for women.

Fast-track policies

The extent to which actual chains of argument follow the inner logic of the two models is an empirical question. The growing body of research on the many new cases of gender quotas in post-conflict countries as well as in countries in the process of (re-)democratisation reveals, not surprisingly, a lot of mixed motives and muddled compromises behind the adoption of gender quotas in politics, as has been the case in Afghanistan, Iraq, Pakistan and Uganda (Rai *et al.* 2006; Tripp *et al.* 2006; Norris 2007).

The 'Platform for Action', adopted in Beijing in 1995, comes close to the fast-track model. Firstly, there is a new diagnosis of women's under-representation, focusing not on women's (lack of) resources but on 'discriminatory attitudes and practices' and 'unequal power relations'. It notes that 'traditional working patterns of many political parties and government structures continue to be barriers to women's participation in public life' (United Nations Fourth World Conference on Women 1995, Art. 182 and 185). Secondly, it states a more radical goal, that of 'equal participation' and 'the equitable distribution of power and decision-making at all levels' (Art. 189). Thirdly, in terms of strategy, affirmative actions are recommended, even if the controversial word 'quotas' is not mentioned.

Sometimes the French concept of 'parité', translated into English as a demand for 'parity democracy', is contrasted with the demand for equal representation through gender quotas. Based on a republican concept of citizenship, the French parité movement, with its radical demand for 50 per cent women and 50 per cent men in all decision making, has stressed that this is not a matter of group or interest representation. Every component of society is made up of two sexes – men and women – and 'parité' represents this duality of humankind, a unity in difference. Accordingly, French-speaking parity advocates refuse to use the word 'quotas' in relation to parity. Mercedes Mateo Diaz argues that this rationale behind parity overcomes Kymlicka's argument against group representation. However, it is, as Diaz rightly states, not possible to distinguish between the two approaches in their practical implementation, even if the rationales behind parity and gender quotas may be different (Mateo Diaz 2005: 21–3). Moreover, on the basis of Young's interpretation of inclusive democracy, the underlying philosophies of quotas and parity might not be so different after all.

The Australian political scientist Carol Bacchi warns against locating affirmative action in the realm of an exemption within anti-discrimination legislation. If gender quotas are characterised as 'preferential treatment', those disadvantaged – in this case, women – may be stigmatised as people in need of special help. If, however, the problem is located within the realm of practices and norms of political institutions, including those of political parties, affirmative action is not reverse discrimination but rather involves attempts to redress entrenched privilege. However, if everything in society were fair, quotas would, of course, be discrimination and would not be needed, as Bacchi argues (1990, 2006).

The long march into institutions

It is significant that in contemporary society, the strong critique of male-dominated political institutions is combined with increased interest by a broad spectrum of women's organisations in participation in formal political institutions. In contrast, the vehement critique of 'the patriarchal and capitalist state' put forward by the radical and leftist Women's Liberation Movement from the 1960s to the 1980s – in line with the overall position of the New Left – implied a rejection of parliamentary politics in favour of outside or anti-parliamentary actions and direct democracy.

A closer look reveals that during the 1980s and 1990s, declarations adopted by the UN increasingly used the language of the Women's Liberation Movement of the 1960s to the 1980s, although in modified form. 'Discrimination' became common in the international vocabulary as well as the concepts of 'exclusion' and 'lack of inclusiveness' (though not 'oppression'!). These concepts then worked their way into documents adopted by the governments of the world. The strong feminist mobilisation of the 1960s to the 1980s no doubt indirectly paved the way for later demands for affirmative action and gender equality policies in general (McBride and Mazur 1995). Devaki Jain writes about the spirit of the 1995 Beijing conference:

There was an almost universal or palpable desire to be in power, to be in leadership, to change the terms of the relationship with the great globe; the mode of operation shifted from one of stating demands and needs to one of seeking control over the decision-making process. There was optimism about this strategy, a belief that women would bring new values to public decision-making. (Jain 2005: 145)

Even if many of the gains of the Beijing conference were later threatened by the growth of fundamentalism and conservatism on the world scene, recommendations for positive action are common in most contemporary international declarations. The introduction of gender quotas in public elections has brought new countries to the top of the world rank order in terms of women's representation.

The actual development of women's political representation

In 2010, women constituted only 19 per cent of the members of the world's parliaments (both houses); men constitute 81 per cent. In 2000, the figure was 13 per cent women. There is surprisingly little variation in the parliamentary representation of women in the major regions of the world, though the Pacific region and the Arab states are at the bottom. An increase has happened in all regions, with the biggest relative increase in the Arab region. Variation within each region is considerable, as between Germany's 33 and France's 19 per cent of women members of parliament, or Argentina's 39 per cent and Chile's 24 per cent. Within countries, large variations may also be found between the political parties. For a very long time the Nordic countries were alone at the top of the world rank order in terms of women's representation, with an average of 37 per cent in 1998 and 42 per cent in 2010. Only the Netherlands came close to the Nordic countries.

Table 6.1 shows that the Nordic countries are being challenged today by other countries, many of which are situated in the global south – with Rwanda, the first country to pass the 50 per cent threshold, at the top of the list.[7] Table 6.1 also shows that most of the newcomers to the top-of-the-world rank order use some type of electoral gender quota. However, the table also reveals that a high level of female representation can emerge without quotas, as the cases of Denmark and Finland illustrate. The new world rank order constitutes a challenge to previous research results, which correlate the level of women's political representation with various structural factors, such as socio-economic development, secularisation and early suffrage. Challenging these more static approaches, Melanie M. Hughes and Pamela Paxton conceptualise stagnation or growth in women's political representation as a result of the balance between forces of change and forces of resistance. They identify 'critical periods' and 'continuous forces' as well as 'episodic forces', for instance the introduction of gender quotas, as being behind the changes (Hughes and Paxton 2008).

Most top countries base their elections on proportional representation systems (PR), and in general women's representation is higher in PR systems than in single-member district systems (Norris 2006). The very low position of the United Kingdom and the USA in the world rank order of women's parliamentary representation, numbers 51 and 72, can be explained in part by their use of single-member constituency systems. The difficulties in combining a single-member constituency system with any type of gender quota are likely to widen the gap between the two electoral systems in terms of women's representation in the future.

The inclusion of women in institutions in crisis?

In public debate, it is often heard that women are merely gaining access to institutions that are losing power, which corresponds to the arguments put forward in several of the chapters in this book that parliaments and

---

[7] Rwanda is listed as a semi-democratic country by www.freedomhouse.org

Table 6.1. *The top of the world rank order of percentage of women in parliament (35 per cent or more)*

Country	Women in national parliament (%)	Quota type	Electoral system
1. Rwanda	56.3 (2008)	Legal Quotas	PR
2. Sweden	45.0 (2010)	Party Quotas	PR
3. South Africa	44.5 (2009)	Party Quotas	PR
4. Cuba	43.2 (2008)	NA	Plurality/maj
5. Iceland	42.9 (2009)	No Quotas	PR
6. Finland	42.0 (2007)	No Quotas	PR
7. Netherlands	40.7 (2010)	Party Quotas	PR
8. Norway	39.6 (2009)	Party Quotas	PR
9. Belgium	39.3 (2010)	Legal Quotas	PR
10. Mozambique	39.2 (2009)	Party Quotas	PR
11. Costa Rica	38.6 (2010)	Legal Quotas	PR
12. Argentina	40.0 (2007)	Legal Quotas	PR
13. Denmark	37.4 (2007)	No Quotas	PR
14. Angola	37.3 (2008)	Legal Quotas	PR
15. Spain	36.3 (2008)	Legal Quotas	PR

Election day figures
Key to electoral system: *PR*: Proportional Representation system with party lists including several candidates: *Plu/major*: Plurality/majority system, often with single-member constituencies.
Key to quota types: *Legal or legislated quotas* are written into the constitution and the electoral law/party law. *Party quotas* are voluntary measures adopted by individual political parties.
Source: Inter-Parliamentary Union (2010): www.ipu.org; International IDEA and Stockholm University (2010): www.quotaproject.org; official statistics. Single or lower houses. Election day figures. December 2010.

party systems are in crisis. Back in the 1970s and 1980s, the radical and socialist feminists argued that institutions of male dominance constantly reproduce themselves – sometimes by moving power to new institutions when women have gained access to others. Does research on women in politics support this rather pessimistic perspective?

The theory of shrinking institutions

The 'theory of shrinking institutions' is inconsistent, and must be rejected. One can only agree with Skjeie that the theory is too vague to allow for testing (1992). What is the causal link supposed to be? Are parliaments losing power and, if so, is this caused by the entrance of more women ('women in, power out')? Or is the idea that women are entering because the power has already left ('power out, women in')? Is there any evidence that male candidates are withdrawing from competition over safe seats? Is the question of majority versus minority governments not more central to the power of parliament than the percentage of women? In a comparative perspective, should parliaments with the highest representation of women, as for instance in the Nordic countries, consequently be the weakest ones?

One should remember that the theory of shrinking institutions emerged in the 1980s, when political scientists were discussing the 'decline of legislatures' due to the rise of corporatism, which is not the main perspective today. Nowadays we talk more about Europeanisation and globalisation, and no doubt it is highly relevant to discuss women's increased presence in national parliaments from this perspective. However, rather than a causal link between the entrance of women and the diminishing power of national institutions, we see here parallel historical developments, I would argue.

The law of increasing disproportions

In contrast, research on politics and gender has confirmed common knowledge that the higher up we go in the system, the fewer women there are, also called the law of increasing disproportion. Farida Jalalzai (2008) found that during the period 1960–2007 only thirty-seven women had been prime ministers and only twenty-five had been presidents in the entire world.

The recent media celebration of the first women to reach high positions in their countries, such as Angela Merkel as the first woman chancellor in Germany and Michelle Barchelet, Ellen Johnson-Sirleaf and Cristina Fernández de Kirchner, the first women presidents in Chile, Liberia and Argentina respectively, seems to conceal the fact that there were more women presidents and prime ministers at the start of the 1990s than at present (Women World Leaders database). However, *the first-time factor* seems important. The very first woman to reach a high position has, no doubt, strong symbolic importance.

It would be wrong to formulate recent developments as a law of an ever-increasing proportion of women in politics. The considerable variation in women's representation in parliaments between neighbouring countries, and even between political parties within the same country, with the left parties typically having the largest share of women representatives, shows that the inclusion of women does not occur 'by itself', for instance through changes in civil society. Rather, the saliency of the issue and the demand for positive action are constructed through public debate and internal party debates about election results – which then spill over into the nomination processes in the following election. Pressure by women's organisations is an important factor, but neither this pressure nor its effects are a constant.

The stronger contemporary claim for the inclusion of women and other under-represented groups may be seen as part of the new 'monitory democracy', as discussed by John Keane in this book, even if the claim itself is old. Whenever the inclusion of women and of other groups is seen as a novelty factor, this inclusion may contribute to a revitalising of old political institutions, and to increasing the legitimacy of representative democracy in countries under democratisation. Women are, however, not well represented in the new structures of global and regional deliberation. The representativeness of these structures is being increasingly questioned today, but research on their gender composition is scarce.

It can be hypothesised that claims for equal representation are more likely to be heard in relation to transparent and elected positions and that informality and network structures favour those already in positions of power. At the same time, some new structures have shown themselves to be more open to the inclusion of women than old structures which often favour the incumbent. Examples of such new structures are Green parties and the new parliament in Scotland, which has by and large surpassed Westminster. In most of these cases, at some point, gender quotas have been adopted.

The worldwide adoption of electoral gender quotas

Within just the last two decades, electoral gender quotas have been adopted all over the world. Even though resistance to electoral gender quotas is strongest in the Western world, established democracies are also today introducing electoral gender quotas by law, most recently in Spain and Portugal.

Electoral gender quotas, quotas for public elections for instance, come in many forms. *Legislated gender quotas* are adopted in constitutions or in electoral law and are now in use in around fifty countries all over the world – in settings as diverse as Argentina (1991), Belgium (1994), Costa Rica (1996), Taiwan (1997), France (1999), Rwanda (2003), Iraq (2004), Uzbekistan (2004), the Palestine Territories (2005), Spain (2007) and Egypt (2009).

In about fifty additional countries, one or more of the political parties represented in parliament have introduced *voluntary party quotas* for their own election lists. This development means that in almost half of the countries of the world some type of electoral gender quota is in use (Dahlerup 2006; Krook 2009; www.quotaproject.org). A more precise taxonomy of quota systems for public elections, however, has to be based on a combination of two dimensions: (1) the above-mentioned distinction between legislated or voluntary quotas; and (2) the level of the electoral process that the quota regulations target – either the pool of potential candidates (aspirant quotas, for instance in shortlists or primaries), the candidates who stand for election (candidate quotas) or those elected (reserved seats). The most common types of quotas are then *reserved seats*, common in Asia and sub-Saharan Africa, *legislated candidate quotas*, the preferred type in Latin America, and *voluntary candidate quotas* in political parties, the preferred quota type in Europe and in Southern Africa.

Gender quotas may be constructed so as to require a minimum representation of women, for instance 20, 30 or 40 per cent, or a maximum-minimum representation of both sexes, for instance no more than 60 per cent and no less than 40 per cent of either sex. In the case of gender-neutral regulations, quota provisions set a maximum for both sexes, which quotas for women do not.

Constitutional rebuilding after civil war or transition from dictatorship to democracy has opened windows of opportunity for quota proponents. The lobbying activities in support of more women in elected positions by women's movements are also finding more resonance today, since the international reputation of countries is becoming increasingly important for political elites. It is exceptionally new from an historical point of view that a high level of women's representation is today seen as an indicator of progress and democratic development.

The effectiveness of gender quotas

A growing body of quota research has revealed that the quota type chosen is an important determinant of the effectiveness of quotas (Norris 2006; Dahlerup 2006; Larserud and Taphorn 2007; Krook 2009). A quota rule that is not designed in a way that is compatible with the existing electoral system, and that does not include rank order rules and sanctions for non-compliance, will have little effect. When France introduced a radical law of 'parité' (50 per cent female and 50 per cent male candidates), the result was a disappointing 12 per cent women elected to the National Assembly in 2002 and 19 per cent in 2007. In Costa Rica, which like France has introduced candidate quotas by law (40 per cent), the quota system resulted in an historic leap in women's representation because of radical rank order rules and rejection of lists that do not comply with the rules by the electoral authorities. Evaluated in purely numerical terms, electoral gender quotas can result in historic leaps in the number of women candidates and/or the number of women elected, as occurred in Argentina, Belgium, Costa Rica and Rwanda (legislated quotas), and in South Africa, Norway and Germany (voluntary party quotas).

With the adoption of quotas, attention is directed towards the selection and nomination processes, key aspects of representative democracy, which are, however, often neglected by democratic theorists.

The procedural link between the how and the who

Shifting the focus from women's lack of resources and from political differences among women, the target under the *discourse of exclusion* is political institutions and their practices. To the normative link, we add at *the meso-level* a new link between the 'who' and the 'how', that is, a link between the lack of representativeness and established norms and procedures.

If the actual outcome of traditional procedures is male dominance, then the institutional procedures are to be scrutinised for inherent gender bias. The feminists' critique is not a critique of the principles of free and competitive elections, freedom of speech, freedom of the press, representative democracy and other fundamental principles of liberal democracy. Today, the opposite of representative democracy is not direct democracy but exclusion, as Michael Saward rightly argues in Chapter 3 of this volume.

We can now turn to the question of whether electoral gender quotas violate the principles of representative democracy, for instance the free choice of the voters, or whether, on the contrary, quotas may contribute to its strengthening. Focus on the process of inclusion and exclusion leads to scrutiny of what has been called *the secret garden of nominations*. Many voters and even some political scientists believe that voters decide who gets elected. However, one may argue that it is the political parties, and within them often a rather small group of people, who are the real gatekeepers to elected offices.

Feminist research has found that actual nomination processes are far from meeting the liberal ideal of free and open competition among individuals based on the qualifications of the potential candidates. Rather, these processes are guided by a complex pattern of deals and of formal and informal quotas. In PR systems, not only the relatively safe seats but even the non-safe positions on the electoral lists are distributed on the basis of deals between different stakeholders: economic interests, organisational interests, ideological fractions, geographical affiliations, and so on. Incumbency is a strong factor that clearly discourages newcomers to the political scene. Another problem has been that women historically were not supposed to be able to represent, for instance, the northern part of the district or the trade unions. Today, in countries and parties with a high level of representation of women, this exclusion mechanism has changed, since women candidates are no longer supposed to represent only the group women (Lovenduski 2005; Freidenvall 2006; Freidenvall *et al.* 2006).

Elin Bjarnegård has taken this research one step further. Arguing that studies of male dominance are much rarer than studies of female under-representation, she proceeds to study the rationale underlying male dominance in politics. With Thailand as her empirical case, Bjarnegård examines how clientelism favours men. In Thailand, as in many other parts of the world, women's position in education and business has improved considerably, while male dominance in politics has remained almost the same. Interviewing MPs about their mentors and how they were selected, Bjarnegård finds that the exclusion of women is based on male clientelist networks and 'homosocial capital' (Bjarnegård 2009; see also Lovenduski 2005). In such a system, as in fact in most others as well, gender quotas are not discrimination against men but, rather, compensation for the present and future discrimination against women.

Nomination for public office is at the heart of representative democracy, and quota advocates may argue that the adoption of electoral gender quotas at best opens up this secret garden, challenges old boys' networks, and makes nominations more transparent and formalised. The recent trend of using primary elections points in the same direction of greater openness, even if primaries do create new problems, such as those related to campaign financing.

Equality of opportunity or equality of result?

The liberal opposition to any kind of quota rests on the preference for equality of opportunity over equality of result, the latter being primarily associated with social democracy or state socialism. But do quotas actually imply equality of result? Why is women's parliamentary representation only 19 per cent worldwide when some kind of electoral gender quota is in use in almost half of the countries of the world? Closer scrutiny of the function of different quota systems will illuminate this question (see Figure 6.1).

	Target group representation guaranteed	Competition between individual candidates
Aspirant quotas	NO	YES
Candidate quotas	NO	YES
Reserved seat quotas	YES	Varies
RS, with election	*YES*	*Only between women*
RS, appointment	*YES*	*NO*

Figure 6.1. Guaranteed seats and competition under different quota regimes
Source: Dahlerup (2007), table 5, p. 83.

Neither *aspirant quotas,* which target the gender composition of the pool of potential candidates for primaries and for shortlists presented to the parties' nominating bodies, nor *candidate quotas* for the lists at elections, be they legislated or voluntary, guarantee the election of a certain number of women.[8] Further, under aspirant and candidate quota systems no individual woman will get her seat without competition. Consequently, rather than restricting the choice of voters, such gender quotas force the political parties to start recruiting women candidates more seriously, thus giving voters a choice between both female and male candidates or, in closed list systems, a choice between lists with different gender compositions. It is not the voters but the prerogatives of the nominating bodies that are being restricted by quota rules.

Only in cases of *reserved seats* do quota regulations target the number of women elected. In Rwanda, for instance, two women per district are elected by a special electorate, making a total of twenty-four women. In Morocco, an additional 'national list' with thirty seats is elected in nationwide competition between women candidates only. In Jordan,

---

[8] There are some exceptions to this rule. The all-women shortlists practised by the British Labour Party in the early 1990s did guarantee the nomination of a woman in half of the vacant seats, which was why it was challenged by the Industrial Tribunal (Lovenduski 2005). In closed-list systems, candidate quotas combined with strong rank order rules, for instance one of alternation between men and women throughout the list, usually guarantee the election of some women, though not in small parties.

twelve seats are allocated to those women candidates that lose an election even though they receive the highest percentage of all votes cast in their respective constituencies but without getting elected ('best loser' system). In Rwanda, several women candidates have also been elected to the so-called 'free' seats, whereas in many other countries reserved seats have become a glass ceiling in terms of an additional number of women being elected.

Increasingly, reserved seats are based on election, not appointment. It would not be correct to say that women parliamentarians who receive their seats by means of reservation do so without competition, but it is competition among women candidates only. Men are *de jure* excluded. That is new. However, it should be noted that the most common feature of contemporary elections is that men – de facto – compete only against men. In strong patriarchal regimes it seems almost impossible for women candidates to compete against men at elections, especially in the countryside.

In conclusion, it can be said that whether gender quotas provide equality of opportunity or equality of result – or no equality at all – depends on the design of the quota system and the electoral system, as well as on the process of implementation.

Quotas in semi- and non-democratic countries

Electoral gender quotas have today been adopted by established democracies as well as by semi- and non-democratic countries, as research by Richard Matland (2006) and Drude Dahlerup (2007) on the diffusion of quotas has shown.[9] Does the fact that Rwanda, number one in the world rank order with 56.3 per cent women in its parliament, is not listed among democratic countries make its quota achievements irrelevant and meaningless? This question must be answered in the negative. As systems of representation predated democracy, so do gender quotas. Legislation is discussed and passed and coalitions are formed in semi-democratic countries and even in many of the non-democratic countries of the world (Gandhi 2008). Elections take place under various degrees of freedom all over the world.

Also in countries like Jordan, Morocco, Rwanda, Sierra Leone, Uganda and Pakistan, women's organisations are working hard to get more women elected, and they would not accept that this is a meaningless endeavour, even if the conditions for women politicians might

---

[9] Based on Freedom House's classifications into democratic, semi-democratic and non-democratic countries.

be very harsh. Research has shown that women politicians can make a difference, even in less democratic states, for instance in relation to the important legislation on combating violence against women and land reforms for the benefit of women passed by the Rwandan parliament (Devlin and Elgie 2008; Powley 2008). When fighting for increasing women's political representation, perhaps by gender quotas, these women's organisations often express the hope that this may contribute to the democratisation of their country.

Conclusion

From the birth of the first political assemblies, political institutions occupied exclusively by men have been the norm. An Aldermen's Council, a parliament or a government comprising elderly men was, until at least the 1960s, not considered illegitimate on the grounds of its high average age or its exclusive maleness. Such assemblies radiated confidence. Previously, even most women did not refer to the political system as undemocratic 'merely' because women were almost totally absent or amounted to only one woman, the 'obligatory woman', who was supposed to represent all women.

Today, all male governments, assemblies or public committees are met with immediate and strong public criticism. Increasingly, there is a global demand for gender balance in political decision making. This chapter has shown that among feminists, but also reflected in formal international declarations, the normative legitimacy of a democratic decision depends on the inclusion in decision making of those affected.

This analysis has identified the link between the inclusion of women in political decision making and the status of representative democracy at two levels of analyses. A *normative link* is being made in feminist theory as well as in actual global discourses: 'no (true) democracy without the full inclusion of women'. But, it has been shown, the link can also be made at *the procedural level*. The *discourse of exclusion* points to the importance of scrutinising representative democracy and representation generally at the meso-level of norms and procedures of political institutions. Feminist research has demonstrated how gender-biased results have been the outcome of seemingly gender-neutral principles and procedures of liberal democracy, including in countries where women today are as well educated and as involved in civic organisations as men.

The link between the inclusion of women and other underrepresented groups and the status of representative democracy is no longer just made within feminist circles but has become a salient political issue. This is evident from the seriousness with which political elites, even though sometimes just rhetorically, respond to the demands for 'more women' or 'equal' representation. The inclusion of women is an issue that few political and party leaders dare ignore in any country where elections take place. Further, international declarations, among them commitments written into UN documents and signed by the governments of the world, affirm the goal of gender balance in politics, if necessary by the use of special measures or gender quotas.

Marian Sawer and others have categorised the legitimacy argument as merely a 'symbolic argument' for increasing women's representation, alongside the argument for the significance of role models (Sawer *et al.* 2006: 17–19). But this chapter argues that today these normative arguments – no democracy without gender balance – have provided a strong impetus to worldwide quota advocacy. Translated into demands for changing established procedures of representation at the procedural level, these normative arguments become much more than just symbolic.

The link between equal representation and democracy/democratisation seems to be more easily made in post-conflict countries and countries in transition to democracy. Many new constitutions represent a kind of starting from scratch and, as in Argentina, Uganda, Rwanda, Bosnia-Herzegovina and Afghanistan, include quotas for women. This may not just be a matter of giving in to pressure from women's organisations and from donors, or perhaps of purely opportunistic motives on the part of the male leadership, but may in fact also involve the recognition that women represent a needed new force. In Peru, one of the arguments in favour of gender quotas was that male-dominated politics had developed in ways so as to have become extremely corrupt. Thus, reconstruction periods may represent an opening for women.

A radical stand on this point was taken in the Human Development Report for the Arab Region, issued by the United Nations' Development Programme (UNDP). In the report, the exclusion of women from the public sphere in many Arab countries is described as one of the three main obstacles to development in the region (UNDP 2003). This statement would seem reasonable to most people familiar with the Arab world. In the Western world until recently, however, the prevailing discourse has been that democracy and gender equality are not intimately or not at all connected.

But things are changing. History textbooks in schools have recently been changed from the unconditional celebration of the birth of 'democracy' at a time when only a minority of citizens had access to representation. The new discourse of exclusion has also established a close link between the 'who' and the 'how' of representative democracy. Because the focus is on the mechanisms of exclusion, and consequently disputes over the 'what' are postponed until later, broader and stronger coalitions of feminists have emerged, including feminist men, for the purpose of increasing women's representation in political decision making.

REFERENCES

African Union Convention on Preventing and Combating Corruption (2003) www.africa-union.org/root/au/Documents/Treaties/treaties.htm

Bacchi, C. (1990) *Same difference: Feminism and sexual difference*. London: Allen & Unwin.

(2006) 'Arguing for and against quotas: Theoretical issues', in Dahlerup (ed.), pp. 32–51.

Bjarnegård, E. (2009) *Men in politics: Revisiting patterns of gendered parliamentary representation in Thailand and beyond*. PhD thesis, Uppsala Universitet: Department of Government.

Butler, J. (1990) *Gender trouble: Feminism and the subversion of identity*. New York: Routledge.

Dahlerup, D. (1978) 'Women's entry into politics: The experience of the Danish local and general elections 1908–20', *Scandinavian Political Studies* 1(2–3): 139–62.

(2004) 'Continuity and waves in the feminist movement', in H. R. Christensen, B. Halsaa and A. Saarinen (eds.), *Crossing borders: Re-mapping women's movements at the turn of the 21st century*. Odense: The University Press of Southern Denmark, pp. 59–75.

(ed.) (2006) *Women, quotas and politics*. New York/London: Routledge.

(2007) 'Electoral gender quotas: Between equality of opportunity and equality of results', *Representation* 43(2): 73–92.

Dahlerup, D. and L. Freidenvall (2005) 'Quotas as a "fast track" to equal representation of women: Why Scandinavia is no longer the model', *International Feminist Journal of Politics* 7(1): 26–48.

Devlin, C. and R. Elgie (2008) 'The effect of increased women's representation in parliament: The case of Rwanda', *Parliamentary Affairs* 61(2): 237–54.

Evans, R. (1977) *The feminists: Women's emancipation movements in Europe, America and Australasia, 1840–1920*. London: Croom Helm.

Franceshet, S. and J. M. Piscopo (2008) 'Gender quotas and women's substantive representation: Lessons from Argentina', *Politics & Gender* 4(3): 393–425.

Freidenvall, L. (2006) *Vägen till Varannan Damernas: Om kvinnorepresentation, kvotering och kandidaturval i svensk politik 1970–2002*. PhD thesis, Department of Political Science, Stockholm University.

Freidenvall, L., D. Dahlerup and H. Skjeie (2006) 'The Nordic countries: An incremental model', in Dahlerup (ed.), pp. 55–82.

Galligan, Y. (2007) 'Gender and political representation: Current empirical perspectives', *International Political Science Review* 28(5): 557–70.

Gandhi, J. (2008) *Political institutions under dictatorship*. Cambridge University Press.

Goetz, A. M. and S. Hassim (eds.) (2003) *No shortcuts to power: African women in politics and policy making*. London: Zed Books.

Hernes, H. (1982) *Staten – kvinner ingen adgang?* Oslo: Universitetsforlaget.

Hughes, M. M. and P. Paxton (2008) 'Continuous change, episodes, and critical periods: A framework for understanding women's political representation over time', *Politics and Gender* 4(2): 233–64.

Inter-Parliamentary Union (2010) *Women in National Parliaments* (website: www.ipu.org/wmn-e/classif-arc.htm).

International IDEA and Stockholm University (2010) *Electoral Quotas for Women* (website: www.idea.int/gender/quotas.cfm).

Jain, D. (2005) *Women, development, and the UN: The sixty-year quest for equality and justice*. Bloomington and Indianapolis: Indiana University Press.

Jalalzai, F. (2008) 'Women rule: Shattering the executive glass ceiling', *Politics and Gender* 4(2): 205–31.

Kraditor, A. S. (1965) *The ideas of the woman suffrage movement 1890–1920*. New York: Doubleday.

Krook, M. L. (2009) *Quotas for women in politics: Gender and candidate selection reform worldwide*. New York: Oxford University Press.

Larserud, S. and R. Taphorn (2007) *Designing for equality: Best-fit, medium-fit and non-favourable combinations of electoral systems and gender quotas*. Stockholm: IDEA (The International Institute for Democracy and Electoral Assistance).

Lovenduski, J. (2005) *Feminizing politics*. Cambridge: Polity Press.

Marx, K. (1875) *Randglossen zum programm der deutschen Arbeiterpartei*, in *Marx-Engels Werke*, vol. 19. Berlin: Institut für Marxismus-Leninismus beim ZK der SED.

Mateo Diaz, M. (2005) *Representing women? Female legislators in West European parliaments*. University of Essex, European Consortium for Political Research Monographs.

Matland, R. (2006) 'Electoral quotas: Frequency and effectiveness', in Dahlerup (ed.) pp. 275–92.

McBride, D. and A. Mazur (1995) *Comparative state feminism*. New York: Routledge.

Mill, J. S. (1873 [1949]) *Autobiography*. Oxford University Press.

Norris, P. (2006) 'The impact of electoral reform on women's representation', *Acta Politica* 41(2): 197–213.

(2007) 'Opening the door: Women leaders and constitution building in Iran and Afghanistan', in B. Kellerman and D. L. Rohde, *Women and leadership*. San Francisco: Jossey-Bass, pp. 197–225.

Offe, C. (2001) 'The politics of parity: Can legal intervention neutralize the gender divide?', in J. Klausen and C. S. Maier, *Has liberalism failed women?* New York: Palgrave, pp. 39–54.

Pateman, C. (1989) *The disorder of women*. London: Polity Press.

Phillips, A. (1995) *The politics of presence*. Oxford: Clarendon Press.

Pietilä, H. (2002) *Engendering the global agenda: The story of women in the United Nations*. Geneva: P. Imprinta.

Pitkin, H. (1967) *The concept of representation*. Los Angeles: University of California.

Powley, E. (2008) 'Defending children's rights: The legislative priorities of Rwandan women parliamentarians'. *The Initiative for Inclusive Security. A Program of Hunt Alternatives Fund*. www.huntalternatives.org

Rai, S. M., F. Bari, N. Mahtab and B. Mohanty (2006) 'South Asia: Gender quotas and the politics of empowerment – a comparative study', in Dahlerup (ed.), pp. 222–45.

Sawer, M., M. Tremblay and L. Trimble (2006) *Representing women in Parliament: A comparative study*. New York: Routledge.

Skjeie, H. (1992) *Den politiske betydningen af kjønn: En studie av norsk topp-politikk*. Oslo: Institut for Samfunnsforskning.

Southern African Development Community (SADC) (2008) *Protocol on gender and development*.

Squires, J. (2007) *The new politics of gender equality*. New York: Palgrave Macmillan.

Tripp, A., D. Konaté and C. Lowe-Morna (2006) 'On the fast track to women's political representation', in Dahlerup (ed.), pp. 112–37.

United Nations Development Programme (UNDP) (2003) *Human development report for the Arab region*. New York: UNDP.

United Nations Fourth World Conference on Women (1995) *Beijing declaration and platform for action*.

Wängnerud, L. (2009) 'Women in parliaments: Descriptive and substantive representation', *Annual Review of Political Science* 12: 51–69.

World Bank (2008) 'Report on engendering development'. Washington DC: The World Bank Group.

Young, I. M. (2000) *Inclusion and democracy*. Oxford University Press.

WEBSITES

www.iKNOWPolitics.org (International Knowledge Network of Women in Politics).

www.ipu.org The Inter-Parliamentary Union's website shows the world rank order in terms of women's representation in parliament.

www.quotaproject.org A website showing every country with gender quotas for parliament, by IDEA, The International Institute for Democracy and Electoral Assistance and Stockholm University.

www.terra.es/personal2/monolith/00women.htm Database on Women World Leaders.

www.wedo.org Women's Environmental and Development Organization.

www.womenslobby.org European Women's Lobby.

7 Representative democracy and the multinational *demos*

Sonia Alonso

This chapter discusses the relationship between representative democracy and minority nationalism. Mobilised national minorities and nationalist unrest are a challenge that most representative democracies manage with success. Representative democracies, in the process of accommodating minority nationalist demands, are transforming themselves into something that was viewed, until recently, as a contradiction in terms: a *multinational demos*, also called by some authors multinational democracy (Tully and Gagnon 2001). I shall argue that it is precisely the emergence of representative democracy and its interconnected logics of competitive elections, majority formation and constitutional amendment that have together given incentives to minority nationalists to defend their claims of national self-determination through democratic means. In turn, the participation of minority nationalists in democratic politics has given state elites incentives to negotiate the demands that nationalists put forward, and to grant them some of their claims. In this manner, minority nationalist unrest has been a trigger for innovative mechanisms of democratic representation in multinational countries.

I use the case of Spain as an empirical illustration of the positive feedback that exists between representative democracy and minority nationalism. The selection of Spain does not imply that Spain is unique. Other multinational countries are going through similar, if not identical, processes of accommodation of minority nationalist claims (Alonso 2010). Spain was chosen because, in contrast to other multinational democracies with a long pedigree, such as Belgium or the UK, it is a young democracy. In 1977, Spain lacked most of the conditions established by Dahl (1971) as essential if a country with considerable subcultural pluralism is to maintain its conflicts at a low enough level to sustain polyarchy. Thus Spain is the best example for showing the viability of democracy *and democratisation* in multinational countries.

Representative democracy and national diversity

Until the American Revolution, the consensus had been that democracies had to be small and homogeneous. If the general will and the common good were the ultimate targets of politics, the political community had to be homogeneous enough to share the same or similar beliefs about what constitutes the common good. This view shifted with the American Founders, who saw representation as a tool to transcend the underlying diversity of human societies. Direct democracy presumed the homogeneity of the sovereign people. Representative democracy, by contrast, requires the abandonment of the Greek ideal of a *demos* that is in agreement because it is homogeneous, the abandonment of the ideal of a general will, and its substitution by the acceptance that there is only a plurality of wills and judgements that can be contested and contestable through the process of political representation.

The consensus nevertheless remained that such plurality could not be extended to the most basic constitutive elements of a human community: a sense of belonging, of sharing language, customs and traditions, the past and the future. A precondition for the successful establishment of representative democracy was still thought to be the existence of one *demos*, understood as one *nation* and one national character.[1]

John Stuart Mill, in his *Considerations on Representative Government*, argued that 'free institutions are next to impossible in a country made up of different nationalities. Among a people without fellow-feeling, especially if they read and speak different languages, the united public opinion, necessary to the working of representative government, cannot exist' (1861 [1958]: 230). Mill was convinced that the existence of a multinational population would invite authoritarianism 'by lending

---

[1] The terms nation and nationalism are highly controversial among political scientists and historians. Most authors agree that a nation is a community of individuals living in and sharing the same territory and united by a common past, a common identity and the expectation of a common future. This is as far as the agreement goes. When it comes to define what this common identity is based upon, disagreement begins to emerge. In real life, the definition of the nation is provided, and very often imposed, by those who believe in its existence. It is nationalists, through their organisations (political parties, social movements, cultural organisations), who define the nation that they claim to belong to, in their own terms. This is why, very often, claims to nationhood contradict each other. Nationalists, on the other hand, are not naïve politicians. They know that the nation will only exist physically if it manages to fuse with a state or a state-like political organisation. This is why *nationalism* is a political ideology that, besides defining the nation, claims the right of a nation to self-determination; that is, the right of the nation to have its own state. A nationalist party is therefore a political party that mobilises the electorate around a nationalist ideology in the name of a particular nation. A *multinational* state is one in which society is divided by competing claims to nationhood.

itself to a divide-and-rule technique' (as quoted by Connor 1967: 32). Writing some decades later, Ernest Barker supported Mill's position and contended that 'in a multinational State the government either pits each nation against the rest to secure its own absolutism, or allows itself to become the organ of one of the nations for the suppression or oppression of others' (as quoted by Connor 1967: 33). The result for an emerging democratic polity was that, in order to escape authoritarianism, it tended to dissolve into as many democracies as there were nations within. Decades later this conclusion was shared by Dahl: 'the price of polyarchy may be a breakup of the country. And the price of territorial unity may be a hegemonic regime' (1971: 121).

This diagnosis of the consequences of establishing a representative democracy in a multinational state remained unchanged until well into the twentieth century. It was reproduced, along the same lines, by scholars of transitions to democracy during the 1970s. Rustow thus warned that 'the only precondition for the establishment of a democratic state is that the great majority of the citizens of the future democracy have no doubt or mental reservation about the political community to which they belong' (1970: 350). Analysts of the transitions to democracy in Eastern Europe and the former Soviet Union in the 1980s and 1990s arrived at similar conclusions (Leff 1999; Roeder 1999; Hughes and Sasse 2001). Some even declared that 'without the right of national self-determination, neither democracy nor the democratic peace is likely to flourish in this part of the world' (Roeder 1999: 854).

A shared idea among all these – in many other ways disparate – authors is that representative democracy is highly unstable and prone to collapse in a multinational polity because the actors in conflict are likely to use authoritarian or violent methods to impose their respective claims. State elites representing the majority's cultural group will be tempted to subvert democratic procedures in order to defend the state's territorial integrity from the secessionist pressures of minority nationalists. In turn, minority nationalists with a secessionist agenda will be tempted to use violence as a way to pressure the state. Thus, the presence of minority nationalism will threaten the territorial integrity of the state and endanger the stability of the democratic regime. When conflicting parties try to impose their will, rather than negotiate to resolve their differing claims, the argument runs, only state break-up can save democracy. In short, what these authors are saying is that national self-determination might be a necessary previous step if democracy is to emerge or survive in a particular territory. Minority nationalists cannot but agree with this conclusion.

The argument about the negative effects of national diversity on the emergence and endurance of democracy is of course applicable to any other source of diversity in society, such as religion, socio-economic status and ethnicity. In theory, the presence of national minorities inside the state is no more detrimental to representative democracy than religious or class heterogeneity. However, and particularly among our western post-industrial secularised democracies of the twenty-first century, this national diversity is singled out as the main remaining source of pluralism with potentially disruptive effects for representative democracy. A likely reason for this perception is that national diversity, unlike religious, class or ethnic diversity, poses a threat to the territorial integrity of the state.

Representative democracies' response to minority nationalism

Much western political thought is based on the idea that a multinational *demos* is an oxymoron. As Tully has put it, 'multinational democracy appears to run against the prevailing norms of legitimacy for a single-nation democracy and it is condemned as unreasonable or abnormal by both the defenders of the status quo and the proponents of secession' (Tully 2001: 2). If by nation we understand a political community of citizens blind to cultural differences of all sorts then a multinational *demos* would certainly be an oxymoron. However, the nation has developed historically as much more than a political community blind to cultural differences:

As for the modern nation, it may, from one angle, be regarded as an outgrowth and specialized political development of the *ethnie*; but from another angle, we may view it as a particular kind of territorial political community whose ideological ancestry can be traced to the classical Greek and Italian city-state. In the uneasy combination of these ethnocultural and ideological lines of descent lies the origin and much of the power of the modern concept of the nation, as well as of its various formulations. (Smith 2000: 66)

The fact that a purely civic understanding of the nation has never really existed belies the oxymoronic view of a multinational *demos*. Not only dictatorial monarchies of the past but also modern representative democracies have made extensive use of cultural assimilation policies (Kymlicka 2003) in order to implement in real life the idea of the nation as a culturally homogeneous group of citizens.[2] With respect to

---

[2] The literature on nationalism, at least since the influential dichotomy elaborated by Hans Kohn in *The Idea of Nationalism* (1944), has usually depicted it as a Janus-faced

territorially concentrated cultural minorities (self-defined as national minorities), the expectation always was, until recently, that they would become anachronistic and isolated and would eventually fade away. Minority nationalist movements, however, did not fade away. The first wave of mobilisation of minority nationalists, dating from the period of formation of the European nation states and of the democratic and industrial revolutions (Rokkan and Urwin 1983), gave way to a second wave during the interwar period (Hebbert 1987; Newman 1996), and to a third wave during the 1960s and 1970s (Urwin 1983; Mair 1990; Tiryakian 1994; Newman 2000). Some authors argue that the period from the end of the 1980s into the early 1990s were years of 'ethnic revival' in western democracies (Türsan 1998; De Winter *et al.* 2006).

In the face of such recurrent waves of minority nationalist mobilisations, and despite their assimilationist tendencies, representative democracies have always been better at accommodating the claims for cultural autonomy and self-rule than any other type of regime. A great majority of present-day democracies with autochthonous territorially concentrated cultural minorities have recognised them as nations, or at a minimum as national minorities or nationalities, and have designed institutional arrangements of political devolution that provide these national groups with different levels of self-rule (Urwin 1983; Lane *et al.* 1991; Tiryakian 1994; De Winter and Türsan 1998; De Winter *et al.* 2006).

Although some forms of political devolution date back to the nineteenth century, the devolution of political power to national minorities under conditions of universal suffrage is a relatively new phenomenon. An early example of political devolution initiated by a representative government under universal suffrage is the 1936 Second Spanish Republic. All other processes of devolution have been implemented after World War Two.

Today, there are many instances of consolidated representative democracies in multinational countries. Belgium, Canada, Denmark, Finland, India, Italy, Spain, Switzerland, South Africa and the United Kingdom are examples and not all are located in the northern hemisphere.

---

phenomenon: civic versus ethnic nationalism; western versus eastern nationalism; liberal versus illiberal nationalism. These typologies rest on 'thinly disguised normative criteria' (Hechter 2000: 6) about 'good' and 'bad' nationalism. 'Good' nationalism is civic, liberal, rational, inclusive and has developed mainly in the West, being inextricably linked with the development of representative democracy. 'Bad' nationalism is based on ethnicity and is therefore deemed ascriptive, exclusive, illiberal and irrational, with a high potential for xenophobia and violent conflict. It has developed mainly in the East, endangering, and even preventing, the establishment and subsequent stability of democracies.

Politicians in these countries, which are so different in terms of levels of economic development, longevity of the regime, geographical location and size, and the level of ethnic heterogeneity and political culture, have managed to establish a stable representative democracy despite the presence of moderate to severe political unrest, and in some cases of secessionist terrorism, by mobilised national minorities claiming their right to national self-determination.

In the following section I shall argue that it is precisely the emergence of representative democracy and of its central institutions – mass parties, elections and parliaments – that has made it possible for minority nationalist movements to thrive. In so doing, representative democracy has minimised minority nationalism's extreme forms (i.e., secessionist violence) and has made the centre-periphery conflict amenable to debate and negotiation.

Representative democracy and minority nationalism: a self-reinforcing relationship

Representative democracy and minority nationalism are connected through a positive feedback loop by which '[i]nitial steps in a particular direction may encourage further movement along the same path' (Pierson 2004: 64).

The combination of representative government and democratic rule, which did not take place until the great democratic revolutions of the late eighteenth century and the extension of suffrage rights during the past two centuries (Pitkin 1967, 2004; Dahl 1989), provided the necessary framework for minority nationalist claims to emerge, and to endure. Their emergence was facilitated by the increasing recognition of the rights of free expression and organisation by democratising regimes. This in turn reduced the risks of political mobilisation to potential nationalist movements and parties, which could organise with less fear of repression. Their energy was the result of nationalist politicians' decision to participate in elections instead of fighting for their cause (national self-determination) from outside the system. This decision in turn depended on the confidence that nationalist politicians had about the degree of fairness and freedom of the electoral process, and about the absence of state repression.

The logic of electoral competition and its impact on nationalist politicians' definition of group membership

Minority nationalist parties that decide to enter electoral politics face the short-term imperative of maximising popular support. Their constitutive 'mission' of fighting for national self-determination would remain utopian without access to political power. The logic of electoral competition has two main consequences for the unfolding relationship between representative democracy and minority nationalism. On the one hand, it structures the choices of nationalist leaders in the future so that membership in the self-defined minority nation becomes voluntary rather than blood-determined. On the other hand, it structures the choices of state politicians, giving them incentives to devolve power to the territory occupied by the national minority.

One perpetual dilemma facing the parties that organise a cultural minority is how to define the members of the self-proclaimed minority nation. This definition is not inconsequential since it determines how large is the pool of voters to which the party directs its electoral appeal. A definition of the nation as an ethnic group reduces the appeal to a smaller pool of voters than a more civic definition. An ethnic group is 'any major collectivity that is socially defined in terms of common descent' (Francis 1976: 6; Horowitz 1985: 56–57). Ethnic membership is not chosen but given. By contrast, a definition of the nation combining civic and cultural components (where the nation comprises all those individuals who share the same cultural features, whether they have obtained them by birth or by assimilation, and/or by all those who live in the same territory) will appeal to a larger pool of voters. Since a nationalist party with governing aspirations cannot expect to win a majority, or even a plurality, of the vote by restricting its appeal to those born into the minority ethnic nation, and since not all of those born into the minority ethnic nation identify themselves with the nation defined in ethnic terms, the party faces almost insurmountable incentives to define the nation in cultural and/or civic terms, thereby expanding its *representative claim* (see Saward's chapter in this volume) to all the voters of the territory occupied by the cultural minority. The more the electoral process is free, fair and truly competitive, the more nationalist party elites will have incentives to appeal to a larger pool of voters and to behave as vote-maximising political organisations.

The logic of electoral competition has a second positive effect upon the unfolding relationship between representative democracy and minority nationalism: it gives incentives to central elites to decentralise power. If minority nationalist parties establish themselves successfully in the electoral arena, state-wide parties will not sit idly watching nationalist parties' success. The response of state-wide parties to the electoral growth of minority nationalism is eventually to include the partial (sometimes total, as in Belgium) adoption of the nationalist parties' agenda of cultural and territorial autonomy (Esman 1977; Rudolf 1977; McAllister 1981; Levi and Hechter 1985; Rudolf and

Thompson 1985; Pulzer 1988; Newman 1994; Olivesi 1998; Tambini 2001; Hooghe 2004; De Winter *et al.* 2006; Thorlakson 2006; Van Haute and Pilet 2006; Meguid 2008; Alonso 2011). The expectation behind this move is that it brings back to state-wide parties the support of voters sensitive to nationalist claims that they have lost to minority nationalist parties. This will be more likely the larger is the electoral threat that minority nationalist parties pose to state-wide parties. Political devolution is, in this context, an electoral strategy of state-wide parties that, by adopting part of the minority nationalist agenda, aims to neutralise the electoral threat coming from growing minority nationalist parties (Meguid 2009; Alonso 2011).

Political devolution, once implemented, facilitates the political representation of the plurality of national identities of state citizens and adds complexity to the issue of group membership. Substate institutions endow individuals 'with multiple group memberships' since these individuals are simultaneously citizens of the state and of its substate territories (Tuschhoff 1999: 18). This reinforces the definition of group membership as a voluntary, and not a birth-determined, act.

Fortunately for democracy, membership in groups is less destabilising to the whole polity when it is voluntary rather than birth-determined. The former gives flexibility and permeability to group borders and identities and allows for the formation of different electoral majorities, depending on time and place. The negotiability and flexibility of cultural-territorial demands that results from this has been widely demonstrated by scholars of ethno-territorial conflicts (Brass 1997; Fearon and Laitin 2000; Brubaker 2004; Chandra 2004).

The logic of constitutional change and its effect on nationalist politicians' allegiance to the democratic regime

The main characteristic of a free democratic society is that it is involved in a continuous process of discussion about constitutional rules. As Schwartzberg has put it, 'the ability to modify law is a quintessential and attractive democratic trait, … a fundamental act of popular sovereignty' (2007: 2). Democracy's ability to repair mistakes, as Tocqueville put it, is based on the ability to modify the law and this, in turn, is based on the principle of human fallibility, adopted by the fathers of the US Constitution during their deliberations on constitutional amendment. The adoption of the principle of fallibility is, in fact, 'the only thing that may induce an outvoted minority to accept the decisions of the majority' (Schwartzberg 2007: 202).

The complexity of a multinational polity based on a multi-level system of government makes unavoidable the permanent deliberation and negotiation of institutions, rules, competencies and claims of all kinds by different majorities constituted at different levels of government. The political actors with competing claims to nationhood and national recognition will always have incentives to change the status quo in their favour, to strike a better deal.[3] This is why competing nationalist claims will never be solved. And yet this is not a threat for the stability of representative democracy, so long as the sovereign people's ability to change the law is respected and protected:

> [T]he language of constitutionalism and struggles for recognition disposes us to presume that there is some definitive and permanent system of rules of mutual recognition, some definitive configuration ... But this is false ... What is definitive and permanent is the democratic discussion and alteration of the rules over time. (Tully 2001: 14)

The constitutional entrenchment[4] of the definition of the state nation works against the peaceful coexistence of representative democracy and minority nationalism. Not only does it signal to national minorities the futility of their fight for national self-determination but it also restricts the sovereignty of the people, passing it on to the judges of the constitutional court. As Schwartzberg has put it, '[e]ntrenchment, rather than restricting the possibility of amendment, shifts the locus of this change away from legislatures and toward the judiciary' (Schwartzberg 2007: 5; see also Maravall and Przeworski 2003). For this reason, the less constitutional entrenchment representative democracy allows for, the stronger will be the allegiance of national minorities to the democratic regime. When the principle of the fallibility of the law is recognised, the representatives of the people with competing national claims and agendas will stick to democratic procedures to defend them. A bad rule (from the point of view of the representative's minority nationalist claim) by one majority can be changed today into a good rule tomorrow by a different majority. Thus, a virtuous circle emerges between representative democracy and nationalist conflict. The more democratic procedures are sustained, the more the minority nationalist claims are amenable to negotiation and the

---

[3] As Beetham admits in his contribution to this volume, this is precisely what 'many people find uncomfortable about the democratic process – competition, division, opposition, argument, emphasis on difference'.

[4] Legal entrenchment refers to any norm that is procedurally difficult to amend. It usually entails textual irrevocability, but it can also take other forms. Entrenchment may be temporally limited or unlimited; it may be formally specified or not; it may occur implicitly, on behalf of normative or positive claims, or *de facto*, when a law is so procedurally difficult to change that amendment is unattainable (Schartzberg 2007).

more stable the democratic regime becomes. When the ability to modify the constitution is recognised and protected, political debate and deliberation substitute for legal imposition and government by judges.

The logic of multiple majority formation in a decentralised democracy and its impact on minority nationalist politicians' political influence

The likelihood that national minorities become permanent political minorities is greatly reduced by the regionalisation or federalisation of the state. Political devolution establishes institutions of self-government at the substate level. As a result, a substate system of party competition emerges. Substate institutions offer voters numerous, overlapping, and sometimes competing arenas of representation (Hamann 1999); they offer citizens a wider choice of representatives, since party systems are multi-dimensional and territorialised.

Minority mationalist parties, by definition, are organised exclusively at the substate level, given that their *raison d'être* is the defence of territorial and cultural interests of a cultural minority which is territorially concentrated. The creation of substate parliaments and executives benefits minority nationalist parties, since their chances of winning a majority of the vote are maximised in substate elections (Brancati 2007; Meguid 2009). Thus, different electoral majorities may emerge at different levels of government.

Moreover, the existence of substate institutions of representation allows minority nationalist parties to trade '(national) policy for (regional) authority' (Heller 2002: 658). The minority nationalist party is in an advantageous position to press for further decentralisation whenever the state party at the national government does not have a sufficient majority to govern (Field 2009). Thus, the minority nationalist party will offer its parliamentary support to the state-wide party, so that the latter can see its policies implemented, in exchange for further authority devolved to the substate institutions.

To sum up, minority nationalist parties, despite representing a minority cultural group, may become the majority in their territories and may be the key to governability at the state level. They thus become an integrated, even 'functional', part of the democratic machinery.

Critics of political devolution argue that it strengthens minority nationalist parties and it sets in train a spiral of secessionist demands. These critics fail to see the relationship between representative democracy and minority nationalism in terms of path-dependency. Increased complexity reduces the incentives of minority nationalist parties to be rigid in their agendas and alliances. The competitors of today may be the allies of tomorrow and the use of political tactics and strategy to achieve the minority nationalist party's aims is preferred over the inflexible loyalty to the party's original 'mission'. As long as minority nationalist parties have a policy issue that they can monopolise, and which allows them to continue to make electoral gains, they will have no serious incentive to transit from the risky and uncertain path of secessionism.[5] The last factor that limits a spiral of minority nationalist radicalisation is the distribution of preferences in the electorate. Minority nationalist parties with an openly short-term secessionist agenda must convince voters that the secessionist agenda is more important than any other problem that exists in the polity, even more important than any other problem in their lives, such that independence will contribute to improve their welfare and the welfare of the society as a whole. This is not an easy task. The more the rights of national minorities are recognised and guaranteed by the democratic state and the more the regional authorities increase their powers, the less the people see necessary – or even legitimate – a secessionist agenda.

Representative democracy and minority nationalism: illustrations from Spain

Spain provides an illustrative case of the positive feedback established between representative democracy and minority nationalism, though by no means the only one. Among Western representative democracies, similar processes are taking place in Belgium, Italy, the United Kingdom and Canada (Alonso 2011).

The 1978 Spanish Constitution was a compromise between two different and traditionally opposed conceptions of Spain. Although Spain is defined as one single nation, the Constitution also recognises the existence of several 'historical nationalities' and 'regions', without mentioning explicitly any one in particular. Thus the definition of which territories within Spain are to be considered 'historical nationalities' and which are to be considered 'regions' was left open by the constitutional fathers (Aja 2003). This 'incomplete articulation of a federal system' (Lancaster 1999: 65) is not untypical of other federal or federalising democracies, such as Belgium and Italy.

---

[5] Minority nationalist parties will often resort to secessionist declarations and to calls for referenda of independence/national self-determination. These acts, however, are less a serious attempt to secede than they are a way of radicalising their discourse in order to mobilise their constituencies, to make the centre-periphery dimension the most salient in voters' minds when they cast their vote.

The Constitution established two main types of regional autonomy. The highest level of autonomy was granted to the 'historical nationalities', those regions that enjoyed a Statute of Autonomy during the Second Republic (Basque Country, Catalonia and Galicia). These regions were offered a 'fast-track' to autonomy. The remaining regions, called Autonomous Communities (AACC), would enjoy a comparatively lower level of autonomy, although the Constitution offered the possibility that after a minimum of five years, they could acquire the same competencies as the Basques, Catalans and Galicians. These Autonomous Communities are the so-called 'slow-track' regions (Moreno 2001; Aja 2003).

The development of civic forms of minority nationalism

All minority nationalist parties in Spain agree that membership of a minority nation is determined by choice, and not by birth. This means that all people who live and work within the territory of a minority nation are considered members of the nation. Even Basque nationalists, who are usually depicted as representing an ethnic type of nationalism, participate in this rhetoric (Conversi 1997). It is a civic-cultural conception of the nation and, both in constitutional and institutional terms, nationalist parties abide by it. Membership in the Basque nation, as in all other nations of Spain, is open to those who are not born into the ethnic group. Minority nationalists are clear on this point:

[T]he opinion of all those who live and work here [Basque Country], no matter where we were born, no matter whether we vote for the Popular Party, the Socialist Party, Batasuna, the Basque Nationalist Party, Eusko Alkartasuna, Ezker Batua or Unidad Alavesa, this has to be our [common] ground. (Ibarretxe, Prime Minister of the Basque Country, *Basque Nationalist Party*, 'Diario de Sesiones del Parlamento Vasco', 30 December 2004: 24)

Catalonia is a nation under construction, a nation that is built day by day with the contributions of many men and women of different origins and cultures. (Puigcercós, *Esquerra Republicana de Catalunya*, 'Diario de Sesiones del Congreso de los Diputados', 23 May 2006: 8947)

The combination of complex national identities and dual citizenship (state and region) makes the defence of an ethnic conception of the nation an almost suicidal strategy for nationalist parties.[6] In a globalised

---

[6] According to a 1996 CIS survey, 7 per cent of Basques, 4 per cent of Galicians and a mere 1 per cent of Catalans contend that the most important factor defining a nation is the ethnic or racial composition of its members. A majority of the respondents in the three regions mention language and history as the defining characteristics of a nation. In Spain as a whole, only 4 per cent of respondents have an ethnic understanding of the nation.

world, in which not only domestic migration but also immigration into the regions from outside Spain is increasing at a fast pace, such a strategy makes even less sense in the medium and long term. Minority nationalists recognise that citizens have multiple positions with respect to territorial self-determination, and also multiple national identities. 'For us, Catalonia is a nation', noted one representative, 'but we know, and we respect, that ... for hundreds of thousands of Catalans, Spain is their nation. If we renounce exclusiveness, these are the two sentiments that we will have to reconcile' (Durán i Lleida, *Convergència i Unió*, 'Diario de Sesiones del Congreso de los Diputados', 2 November 2005: 6186).

Undoubtedly, Basque and Catalan nationalist parties, when in office at the regional level of government, invest a sizeable part of their policy efforts in building a national community. Anyone can be Basque or Catalan but, in order to do so, they have to assimilate into the national cultures, mainly through the learning and use of the vernacular language. The fact of defending assimilationist policies, however, does not make minority nationalists less civic than state nationalists. The evolution towards civic forms of minority nationalism in Spain seems to confirm the conclusion of Nicole Gallant's analysis of minority nationalisms in Canada:

In order to develop a civic narrative about itself, a national minority needs the capacity to build this narrative in a legitimate context ... [I]f the states' goal is to achieve more civic-ness in the identities of the people of the country, then this can be best achieved by granting more autonomy to national minorities (even when they are initially ethnic). (Gallant 2008: 15)

The development of dual identities and dual voting behaviour among the citizenry

The existence of substate levels of government enables individuals to have multiple sources of identification: with the substate territory (i.e., the minority nation), with the state (i.e., the state nation), or with both. This is simultaneously combined with other identities – such as class and religion – that are also potent determinants of political behaviour.

The substate branches of state-wide parties are the main defenders of the dual identity of citizens, although some regionalist parties also participate in this discourse. The defenders of dual identities constantly claim that it is possible to feel Spanish and any other regional/national identity at the same time. 'The Catalan nation does not deny the Spanish nation,' claims one representative, 'it enriches it, because Spain is a nation of nations. We want the [new] Statute [of Autonomy] in order

Table 7.1. *National identities in Spain (percentage of total respondents)*

Region	Spanish identity: 'Only Spanish/ More Spanish than [Region]'		Dual state-and- regional identity: 'As Spanish as [Region]'		Regional identity: 'Only [Region]/ More [Region] than Spanish'	
	1996	2005	1996	2005	1996	2005
Andalucía	15	13	68	69	16	16
Aragón	19	13	63	71	18	13
Asturias	8	9	53	69	39	16
Baleares	23	17	51	52	24	24
Canarias	8	4	46	57	45	37
Cantabria	21	17	68	68	12	10
Castilla-M	46	31	51	63	2	3
Castilla-L	50	38	43	55	5	2
Cataluña	24	17	37	45	37	38
C.Valenciana	34	33	54	56	11	9
Extremadura	27	7	60	81	13	10
Galicia	13	13	44	61	43	25
Madrid	52	33	44	52	2	4
Murcia	37	27	55	65	8	5
Navarra	12	7	49	43	29	37
País Vasco	9	12	36	33	51	46
Rioja	6	15	82	70	12	11
España	22	20	49	57	26	19

Source: Centre for Sociological Research (CIS) no. 2228 (1996) and CIS no. 2610 (2005).

to defy the logic of one state-one nation. We are not a nation without a state, no. We are a nation that already has a state, the Spanish state, which is also ours' (De Madre, Socialist Party of Catalonia, 'Diario de Sesiones del Congreso de los Diputados', 2 November 2005: 6168).

In places where minority nationalism has a strong cultural orientation, such as the Basque Country, exclusive Spanish identity not only has not disappeared but has grown stronger. In 1996, in the Basque Country, 9 per cent of Basques claimed to feel only Spanish; in 2005, this figure had grown to 12 per cent (see Table 7.1). This happened at the expense of dual state-and-Basque identity and exclusive Basque identity, which was lower than in 1996. Surprisingly for some, this happened despite the policies of nation-building implemented by the Basque government, which was in the hands of Basque nationalists between 1980 and 2009.

With the federalisation of Spain, dual identities have been on the rise in almost every region, while exclusive regional or state identities have followed variable paths among the regions, and across time. This is evidence against the argument that the growth of minority nationalism and nationalist parties necessarily strengthens ethnic exclusive identities while weakening democratic values.

Further evidence against this line of thought comes from voting behaviour. The combination of multiple identities and a decentralised institutional structure results in a type of electoral behaviour known as differential voting. Differential voting occurs when voters split their vote between regional and state elections. It usually takes the form of a vote for regional parties (nationalist or regionalist) at the regional level and for state-wide parties at state elections (Montero *et al.* 1991; Pérez-Nievas and Fraile 2000; Orriols and Richards 2005). Differential voting is typical of regionalised and federal countries, as a vast literature on the subject shows (Pallarés and Font 1994; Brown *et al.* 1999; Riba 2000; Hough and Jeffery 2006). All minority nationalist parties in Spain, without exception, achieve better electoral results at regional than at state elections. Movements of votes occur between minority nationalist and state-wide parties. The existence of differential voting suggests that the electorates of the Spanish regions are not segregated into minority nationalist and state 'camps'. For the same reason, no electoral majority has a permanent character.

The recognition that constitutional agreements are fallible and should be temporary

The Spanish *Estado de las Autonomías* is under construction and, very likely, it will always be. The everyday plebiscite of which Renan talked is typical of multinational democracies. In Spain it is practised continuously; by some, to ratify the Spanish nation-state; by others, to demand the recognition of other minority nations; and yet by others to defend the *nation of nations*. As the Prime Minister Rodríguez Zapatero once put it, Spain is 'a union that is not imposed, and a union that is convened on a daily basis' (Rodríguez Zapatero, Prime Minister of Spain, *Spanish Socialist Party*), 'Diario de Sesiones del Congreso', 1 February 2005: 3095).

The provisionality of agreements such as the new Statutes of Autonomy (regional constitutions) passed by the Spanish parliament between 2006 and 2009 was implicitly admitted by a regional MP in Andalusia: '[T]he Statute', she noted, 'will serve as a framework for all Andalusians during, very likely, the next 25 years' (Caballero, *Izquierda Unida*, 'Diario de Sesiones del Parlamento de Andalucía', 16 February 2006: 4620). This representative was not saying that the new Statute of Autonomy of Andalusia is definitive; she was in fact recognising that it has a life cycle, probably of one generation, after which it will be necessary to reconsider it again, and perhaps change it. The Basque Prime Minister, Juan José Ibarretxe, also recognised this when defending the proposed Statute of Autonomy of the Basque Country in the Spanish parliament:

Do you know what Thomas Jefferson used to say? He said that each generation should approve its own constitution. In the Basque Country, all those who are less than forty three years old, men and women, did not have the possibility at the time to vote for the Statute of Gernika [the name of the Statute of Autonomy of the Basque Country]. (Ibarretxe, Basque Prime Minister, *Basque Nationalist Party*, 'Diario de Sesiones del Congreso de los Diputados', 1 February 2005: 3133)

According to nationalist politicians, however, Spain still has a long way to go to reduce the levels of constitutional entrenchment that protect the definition of the Spanish nation. Minority nationalists see Spanish constitutionalism as rigidly fixing the limits of the *demos* in a way that does not correspond to the plural realities of Spain. Some parliamentarians refer to this rigidity as 'constitutional talibanism'. One Basque parliamentarian at the Spanish parliament defended democratic change against rigid constitutionalism as follows:

The border that separates a democracy from an authoritarian system is not the observance of the law. All political systems need to rely on a coercive force and to impose, to demand, the observance of the law in order to survive as political systems. This happens in both democracies and dictatorships ... *The ultimate and fundamental boundary that truly separates democratic from totalitarian systems is not so much the observance of the law but the fact that the law is the reflection of the general will*, that it is the reflection of the will of the majority [emphasis added]. (Erkoreka, *Basque Nationalist Party*, 'Diario de Sesiones del Congreso de los Diputados', 1 February 2005: 3142)

The provisionality of constitutional arrangements, far from creating instability, is in fact a way of engaging national minorities in democratic processes of discussion, of winning their loyalty to the institutions that in turn enable such constant discussion and renegotiation to take place. There is admittedly a downside to this: the amount of time and effort that political leaders dedicate to the issues of centre-periphery conflict may at times prevent them from dedicating more time and effort to other pressing issues. Minority nationalists nevertheless are more amenable to accommodation with a multinational state form when this state form is flexible and changeable. Eventually, this will lead them to break with the ideas of the past and to go beyond the old principle that every nation is entitled to its own state:

This Statute gives concrete form to the slogan about a plural Spain. This Statute defends a federalist culture and it defies the idea according to which a nation must inexorably become a state. Our proposal does not choose between two identities; our proposal juxtaposes different identities. (Herrera, *Iniciativa per Catalunya-Verds*, 'Diario de Sesiones del Congreso de los Diputados', 2 November 2005: 6202)

The increased legitimacy of Spanish democracy

The history of Spanish democracy during the last thirty years cannot be understood independently of the history of the *Estado de las Autonomías*. Democracy and autonomy in Spain have developed simultaneously, and in a constant feedback relationship. Spanish democracy would not have consolidated itself without the federalisation of the state and the federalisation of the state could only have worked under democratic conditions.

Undoubtedly, the rationale guiding the process of political decentralisation has been different for state-wide parties and for minority nationalist parties, as shown by their different institutional preferences, but there is wide agreement that the *Estado de las Autonomías* has contributed to the democratisation of Spain, to the welfare of its citizens, and to the empowerment of its cultural minorities. Political decentralisation began as a means of accommodating nationalist separatism but it has become, with time, an end in itself. Nationalist parties recognise this:

[I]n the recent history of the Spanish autonomic development the same dynamic always repeats itself: that which a few years ago was presented as a grave danger ... for the integrity and even the existence of the State reveals itself, with time, a great formula for the distribution of political power and for the consolidation of a complex system that is enriched by its own plurality, a system that provides instruments of self-government, never privileges, and that recognises and treats differently different realities. (Xuclá, *Convergència i Unió*, 'Diario de Sesiones del Congreso de los Diputados', 20 September 2005: 5570; see also Lagasabaster, *Eusko Alkartasuna*, 'Diario de Sesiones del Congreso de los Diputados', 12 September 2006: 9938)

State-wide parties in favour of decentralisation argue that to decentralise is good in itself, because it brings politics closer to the people, makes politics more democratic, even more efficient. Spaniards agree with this. In a 1998 CIS Survey (no. 2280), 54 per cent of respondents agreed that the *Estado de las Autonomías* had brought politics closer to the people (only 15 per cent disagreed). Nationalist parties use the same rhetoric, implicitly admitting that the right of nations to territorial self-determination alone is not the sole source of democratic legitimacy. Minority nationalists raise the banner of democratic values to legitimise their desire for territorial self-determination. Thus, the discourses of state-wide parties and minority nationalist parties overlap. During the discussions in parliament to reform the Statutes of Autonomy of several Spanish regions, for example, the incumbent Socialist Party proclaimed that:

the reforms of the Statutes of Autonomy ... are moved by one objective: to improve the capacity of institutions to respond to the needs of the citizens, to be more effective ... more receptive to [their] demands. (Fernández de la Vega, vice-president, *Spanish Socialist Party*, 'Diario de Sesiones del Congreso de los Diputados', 21 December 2006: 11475)

Nationalist and regionalist parties have argued along similar lines. 'To give more self-government to the Autonomous Communities is to bring the government closer to the citizen' (Herrera, *Iniciativa per Catalunya Verds*, 'Diario de Sesiones del Congreso de los Diputados', 12 September 2006: 9931). 'The main *raison d'être* of Aragonese nationalism', ran another, 'is to continue our fight for self-government. And this self-government must not be understood as an end in itself but as a method, as a way of improving democracy' (Bernal, *Chunta Aragonesista*, 'Diario de Sesiones de las Cortes de Aragón', 17 May 2006: 5118).

Spanish citizens also have a positive vision of the *Estado de las Autonomías*. According to a 1998 CIS survey (no. 2286), 64 per cent of respondents think that the creation and development of the Autonomous Communities has been a positive event. Spaniards have even developed a taste for decentralisation. In a 2005 CIS survey (no. 2610), 57 per cent of respondents were in favour of further increases of the level of competencies of the regional governments, with only 16 per cent against.

The increased legitimacy of representative democracy in Spain comes from the fact that the groups with competing national claims are certain that their grievances can be institutionally channelled, that laws are not immutable across time and place and that mutual agreement is the only way to give decisions a certain degree of permanence. In the words of the Spanish Prime Minister, Rodríguez Zapatero:

The ballot in democracy puts an end to the debate, but does not resolve it. The debate, in those cases where it revolves around a fundamental norm for our life together, is only resolved through agreement. (Rodríguez Zapatero, Prime Minister of Spain, *Spanish Socialist Party*, 'Diario de Sesiones del Congreso de los Diputados', 1 February 2005: 3095)

Conclusion

In this chapter it has been argued that representative democracy and minority nationalism are mutually reinforcing. Minority nationalism triggers a series of institutional and political adaptations inside the democratic regime aimed to accommodate the demands put forward by minority nationalist parties and, by so doing, the capacity of representative democracies to deal with plural and competing claims increases and deepens. The more democratic the procedures, the larger the chances are of a positive feedback between democracy and minority nationalism. This positive feedback is not to be understood as a deterministic relationship. Democracies will have more trouble dealing with their national minorities during particular periods and some democracies will have more trouble than others. It depends on the institutional structures, the social cleavages, the political conjuncture and, very importantly, the political leadership that are present in each particular democracy at each particular moment. The positive feedback relationship is instead to be interpreted as a general thesis about why the logic of representative democracy is not only compatible with the logic of minority nationalism but also why it is the only form of government that can pull minority nationalisms away from maximalist agendas of state secession.

Spain is a particular illustration of this general thesis. The chapter has shown that nationalist conflict in Spain has become a normal part of democratic politics, despite stirring up debate about the territorial integrity of the state. It could even be claimed that the organisation of Spain's multinational democracy institutionalises permanent conflict about national identity. Political devolution in Spain has encouraged the presence of minority nationalisms and regionalisms. At the same time, however, the complexity of national and regional identities and the wide scope for strategic electoral behaviour make it unlikely that minority nationalists will reject democracy, or that they will pose a threat to the stability of democratic institutions. Before minority nationalists can 'go radical', they must convince their voters that this radicalisation is important and that it will contribute to their welfare. This is not an easy task when the rights of national minorities are recognised and guaranteed by the democratic state.

REFERENCES

Aja, E. (2003) *El estado autonómico. Federalismo y hechos diferenciales.* Madrid: Alianza Editorial.

Alonso, S. (2011) *Challenging the State: Devolution and the Battle for Partisan Credibility.* Oxford University Press.

Brancati, D. (2007) 'The origins and strengths of regional parties', *British Journal of Political Science* 38: 135–59.

Brass, P. (1997) *Theft of an idol: Text and context in the representation of collective violence.* Princeton University Press.

Brown, A., D. McCrone, L. Paterson and P. Surridge (1999) *The Scottish electorate: The 1997 General Elections and beyond.* London: Macmillan.

Brubaker, R. (2004) *Ethnicity without groups.* Cambridge, MA and London: Harvard University Press.

Chandra, K. (2004) *Why ethnic parties succeed.* Cambridge University Press.

Connor, W. (1967) 'Self-determination: The new phase', *World Politics* 20(1): 30–53.

Conversi, D. (1997) *The Basques, the Catalans and Spain.* London: Hurst & Company.

Dahl, R. (1971) *Polyarchy.* New Haven, CT and London: Yale University Press.

De Winter, L. and H. Türsan (1998) *Regionalist parties in western Europe.* London and New York: Routledge.

De Winter, L., M. Gómez-Reino and P. Lynch (eds.) (2006) *Autonomist parties in Europe: Identity politics and the revival of the territorial cleavage.* Barcelona: Institut de Ciènces Polítiques i Socials.

Esman, M. (1977) *Ethnic conflict in the western world.* Ithaca, NY: Cornell University Press.

Fearon, J. and D. Laitin (2000) 'Violence and the social construction of ethnic identity', *International Organization* 54(4): 845–77.

Field, B. (2011) 'Minority government and legislative politics in Spain, 2004–2008' in B. Field (ed.), *Spain's 'Second Transition'? The Socialist Government of José Luis Rodríguez Zapatero.* New York: Routledge.

Francis, E. K. (1976) *Interethnic relations: An essay in sociological theory.* New York: Elsevier.

Gallant, N. (2008) 'Under what conditions can national minorities develop civic conceptions of nationhood?', paper presented at the 18th Annual Association for the Study of Ethnicity and Nationalism Conference, London School of Economics, 15–16 April.

Hamann, K. (1999) 'Federalist institutions, voting behaviour and party systems in Spain', *Publius: The Journal of Federalism* 29(1): 111–38.

Hebbert, M. (1987) 'Regionalism: A reform concept and its application to Spain', *Environment and Planning C: Government and Policy* 5: 239–50.

Hechter, M. (2000) *Containing nationalism.* Oxford University Press.

Heller, W. (2002) 'Regional parties and national politics in Europe: Spain's Estado de las Autonomías, 1993 to 2002', *Comparative Political Studies* 35(6): 657–85.

Horowitz, D. (1985) *Ethnic groups in conflict.* Berkeley: University of California Press.

Hough, D. and C. Jeffery (2006) *Devolution and electoral politics.* Manchester and New York: Manchester University Press.

Hughes, J. and G. Sasse (2001) *Ethnicity and territory in the former Soviet Union.* London: Frank Cass Publishers.

Informe sobre la Democracia en España (2007) Madrid: Fundación Alternativas.

Kohn, H. (1944) *The idea of nationalism.* New York: Macmillan.

Kymlicka, W. (2003) 'Identity politics in multi-nation states', in Venice Commission (2005), *State consolidation and national identity.* Strasbourg: Council of Europe Publishing, Science and Technique of Democracy Series #38, 45–53.

Lancaster, T. D. (1999) 'Complex self-identification and compounded representation in federal systems', *West European Politics* 22(2): 59–89.

Lane, J.-E., D. H. McKay and K. Newton (1991) *Political data handbook: OECD countries*. Oxford University Press.

Leff, C. S. (1999) 'Democratization and disintegration in multinational states: The breakup of the communist federations', *World Politics* 51(2): 205–35.

Levi, M. and M. Hechter (1985) 'A rational choice approach to the rise and decline of ethnoregional political parties', in E. Tiryakian and R. Rogowski (eds.) *New nationalisms of the developed west*. Boston: Allen & Unwin.

Mair, P. (1990) *The West European party system*. Oxford and New York: Oxford University Press.

Maravall, J. M. and A. Przeworski (2003) *Democracy and the rule of law*. New York: Cambridge University Press.

McAllister, I. (1981) 'Party organization and minority nationalism: A comparative study in the United Kingdom', *European Journal of Political Research* 9: 237–55.

Meguid, B. (2008) *Party competition between unequals*. New York: Cambridge University Press.

(2009) 'Institutional change as strategy: The role of decentralization in party competition', paper prepared for presentation at the APSA 2009 Annual Meeting, Toronto, 3–6 September.

Mill, J. S. (1861 [1958]) *Considerations on representative government*. New York: Liberal Arts Press.

Montero, J., J. Ramón and J. Font (1991) 'El voto dual: Lealtad y transferencia de votos en las elecciones autonómicas', *Estudis Electorals* 10: 183–211.

Moreno, L. (2001) 'Ethnoterritorial concurrence in multinational societies: The Spanish comunidades autónomas', in Tully and Gagnon (eds.), pp. 201–21.

Newman, S. (1994) 'Ethnoregional parties: A comparative perspective', *Regional Politics & Policy* 4(2): 28–66.

(1996) *Ethnoregional conflict in democracies: Mostly ballots, rarely bullets*. Westport and London: Greenwood Press.

(2000) 'Nationalism in postindustrial societies: Why states still matter', *Comparative Politics* 33(1): 21–41.

Núñez Seixas, X. M. (2005) 'De la región a la nacionalidad: Los neoregionalismos en la España de la transición y consolidación democrática', in C. H. Waisman, R. Rein and A. Gurruchaga (eds.) *Transiciones de la dictadura a la democracia: Los casos de España y América Latina*. Bilbao: Universidad del País Vasco, pp. 101–39.

Olivesi, C. (1998) 'The failure of regionalist party formation in Corsica', in De Winter and Türsan (eds.).

Orriols, L. and A. Richards (2005) *Nationalism and the Labour Party: differential voting in Scotland and Wales since 1997*. Estudio/Working Paper 213. Madrid: Instituto Juan March de Estudios e Investigaciones.

Pallarés, F. and J. Font (1994) 'Las elecciones autonómicas en Cataluña 1980–1992', in P. del Castillo (ed.) *Comportamiento Político y Electoral*. Madrid: Centro de Investigaciones Sociológicas.

Pérez-Nievas, S. and M. Fraile (2000) *Is the nationalist vote really nationalist? Dual voting in Catalonia, 1980–1999*. Estudio/Working Paper 147. Madrid: Instituto Juan March de Estudios e Investigaciones.

Pierson, P. (2004) *History, institutions, and social analysis*. Princeton and Oxford: Princeton University Press.

Przeworski, A. (ed.) (1996) *Sustainable democracy*. Cambridge University Press.

Pulzer, P. (1988) 'When parties fail: Ethnic protest in Britain in the 1970s', in K. Lawson and P. Merkl (eds.) *When parties fail: Emerging alternative organizations*. Princeton University Press.

Riba, C. (2000) 'Voto dual y abstención diferencial. Un estudio sobre el comportamiento electoral en Cataluña', *Revista Española de Investigaciones Sociológicas* 91: 59–88.

Roeder, P. G. (1999) 'Peoples and states after 1989: The political costs of incomplete national revolutions', *Slavic Review* 58(4): 854–882.

Rokkan, S. and D. Urwin (1983). *Economy, territory, identity*. London and Beverly Hills: Sage.

Roller, E. and P. van Houten (2003) 'National parties in regional party systems: The PSC-PSOE in Catalonia', *Regional and Federal Studies* 13(3): 1–22.

Rudolf, J. (1977) 'Ethnic sub-states and the emergent politics of tri-level interaction in Western Europe', *The Western Political Quarterly* 30(4): 537–57.

Rudolf, J. and R. Thompson (1985) 'Ethnoterritorial movements and the policy process: Accommodating nationalist demands in the developed world', *Comparative Politics* 17(3): 291–311.

Rustow, D. (1970) 'Transitions to democracy: Toward a dynamic model', *Comparative Politics* 2(3): 337–63.

Schwartzberg, M. (2007) *Democracy and legal change*. New York: Cambridge University Press.

Smith, A. (2000) *The nation in history*. Hanover: University Press of New England.

Tambini, D. (2001) *Nationalism in Italian politics: The stories of the Northern League, 1980–2000*. London and New York: Routledge.

Thorlakson, L. (2006) 'Party systems in multilevel contexts', in Hough and Jeffery (eds.).

Tiryakian, E. (1994) 'Nationalist movements in advanced societies: Some methodological reflections', in J. Beramendi, R. Maiz and X. Núñez (eds.) *Nationalism in Europe: Past and present*. Universidad de Santiago de Compostela.

Tully, J. (2001) 'Introduction', in Tully and Gagnon (eds.), pp. 1–35.

Tully, J. and A. G. Gagnon (eds.) (2001) *Multinational democracies*. Cambridge University Press.

Türsan, H. (1998) 'Ethnoregionalist parties as ethnic entrepreneurs', in De Winter and Türsan (eds.).

Tuschhoff, C. (1999) 'The compounding effect: The impact of federalism on the concept of representation', *West European Politics* 22(2): 16–33.

Urwin, D. (1983) 'Harbinger, fossil or fleabite? "Regionalism" and the west European party mosaic', in H. Daalder and P. Mair (eds.) *Western European party systems*. London: Sage, pp. 221–56.

Van Haute, E. and J.-P. Pilet (2006) 'Regionalist parties in Belgium (VU, RW, FDF): Victims of their own success?', *Regional and Federal Studies* 16(3): 297–314.

8   Diagnosing and designing democracy in Europe

Philippe Schmitter

Robert Dahl is famous for the observation that democracy has radically transformed itself – redesigned itself, if you will – over the centuries (Dahl 1996; see also Dahl 1970; 1983; 1989; 2000). The same word, democracy, has prevailed while its rules and practices have changed greatly. In other words – those of de Lampedusa – only by changing has it remained the same. And Dahl does not even hesitate to label these changes as 'revolutionary' – even if most of them came about without widespread violence or institutional discontinuity.

Dahl identifies three such revolutions:

The first revolution was one of *size*. Initially, it was believed that democracy was only suitable for very small polities, such as Greek city states or Swiss cantons. The American constitution redesigned the practice of democracy by making extensive use of territorial representation and introducing federalism – thereby, breaking the size barrier. This set a major precedent in that 'democratic' representation became irrevocably tied to competitive elections in spatially defined constituencies at multiple levels of aggregation. Subsequently, this was followed by a juridical decision asserting the supremacy of the most inclusive ('federal') level and a political process that privileged stable political organisations ('parties') within it.

The second revolution was one of *scale*. Early experiments with democracy were based on a limited conception of citizenship – severely restricting it to those men who were free from slavery or servitude, mature in age, literate or well educated, paid sufficient taxes and so forth. Over time – sometimes gradually, at other times tumultuously – these restrictions were redesigned until the criteria have become almost standard and include all adult nationals, regardless of their gender or other qualifications. No polity today can claim to be 'democratically' representative that does not – at least, formally – respect these criteria, even though the actual practice of the mass franchise virtually everywhere is systematically skewed in terms of turnout and the participation of particular social groups. Moreover, the sheer increase in the scale of the electorate has had a major impact on both the internal organisation of the political parties that competed for votes and the type of politicians who won these elections.

The third Dahlian revolution was in *scope*. Democracies began with a very restricted range of government policies and state functions – mostly, external defence and internal order. Again over time, democratic regimes became responsible for governing a vast range of regulatory, distributive and redistributive issues – so much so that a substantial proportion of gross domestic product is either consumed by these regimes or is handled through their administrative procedures. The impact of this revolution upon democratic representation was more gradual and less obtrusive than with the previous two. It took the form of the expansion of a variety of arrangements for consulting and negotiating with organised interests outside the electoral/territorial constituencies. These 'functional' representatives of classes, sectors and professions – rarely elected and more often selected – were incorporated within the process of public decision making, most often in the drafting and implementing stages, but they also became important in lobbying elected officials in legislative and executive bodies.

Dahl makes a second important general observation about these revolutions. *Most of them occurred without those involved being aware that they were acting as 'revolutionaries'.* Democratic politicians most often responded to popular pressures, externally imposed circumstances or just everyday dilemmas with incremental reforms and experimental modifications of existing policies. These changes accumulated over time until citizens and rulers eventually found themselves in a differently designed polity – while still using the same label to identify it. Indeed, one could claim that this is the most distinctive and valuable characteristic of democracy: its ability to redesign itself consensually, without violence or discontinuity, even sometimes without explicitly diagnosing the need for such a 'radical' change in formal institutions and informal practices.

Diagnosing subsequent democratic revolutions

It is the task of political scientists studying democratic polities to make diagnoses such as Dahl's, and to propose reforms that might sustain or even improve the quality of democracy – whether or not their analyses are accepted by the general public, or by ruling elites. This is my self-assigned task in this chapter, for I am convinced that we are (again) in the midst of a democratic revolution – in fact, in the midst of several simultaneous democratic revolutions. Two of them seem to have exhausted their radical potential and already become well-entrenched features of 'modern, representative, liberal, political democracy', at least, in Europe and North America. Two others, and a possible third, are still very active in their capacity to generate new challenges and opportunities and have still to work their way through the process of redesigning democracy. As predicted by Dahl, politicians seem aware of their existence and political scientists have described them, but neither have grasped their 'revolutionary' implications.

The first of these 'post-Dahlian' revolutions concerns *the displacement of individuals by organisations as the effective citizens of democracy*. Beginning more or less in the latter third of the nineteenth century, new forms of collective action emerged to represent the interests and passions of individual citizens (Schmitter and Lehmbruch 1979). James Madison and Alexis de Tocqueville had earlier observed the importance of a multiplicity of factions or associations within the American polity, but neither could possibly have imagined the extent to which these would become large, permanently organised and professionally run entities, continuously monitoring and intervening in the process of public decision making. Moreover, whether or not these class, sectoral and professional associations or diverse social movements are configured in a pluralist or a corporatist manner, the interests and passions they represent cannot be reduced to a simple aggregation of the individuals who join or support them. They have massively introduced their own distinctive organisational interests and passions into the practice of 'real existing democracies' (REDs) and have become their most effective citizens.

From the perspective of liberal democratic theory, this revolution poses two very important normative challenges. First, the entrepreneurs/leaders of these organisations have rarely been elected to their positions through a competitive process. At best, they can be said to have been 'selected' by members who can (presumably) exercise voice and complain about the actions of their leaders, or who can withdraw their support by exiting and even by joining some other organisation. At worst, these members have been made to contribute involuntarily and/or have no alternative organisation to turn to. Second, to the extent that legitimacy in REDs ultimately rests on the political equality of individual citizens, these organisations are manifestly unequal in their resources and capacities. Indeed, virtually all research demonstrates that small, compact and privileged minorities are much easier to organise and that large, diffuse and under-privileged groups are systematically under-represented in these 'functional' channels.

The second 'post-Dahlian' revolution has to do with *the profession-alisation of the role of politicians.* Liberal democratic theory has always presumed that elected representatives and rulers were persons who might have been somewhat more affected by civic motives, but who were otherwise not different from ordinary citizens. They would (reluctantly) agree to perform 'public service' for a limited period of time and then return to their normal private lives and occupations. While it is difficult to place a date on it, at some time during the twentieth century ever more democratic politicians began to live *from* politics, not *for* politics. They not only entered the role with the expectation of making it their life's work, but they also surrounded themselves with other professionals – campaign consultants, fund-raisers, public relations specialists, media experts and (to use the latest term) 'spin-doctors'. Whether as cause or effect, this change in personnel has been accompanied by an astronomical increase in the cost of getting elected and of remaining in the public eye if one is so unfortunate as to become unelected.

Again, this development is normatively challenging. Professionalisation has not just affected party politicians, but also the representatives of functional interests. Both need more and different resources to occupy their positions; and both find it difficult to resist the temptation of obtaining these resources by shifting to public funding and/or involuntary contributions (not to mention corruption), thereby depriving ordinary citizens of one of their most elementary sanctioning capacities. Both will undoubtedly invoke the 'complexity' of contemporary policy making (not to mention the need for 'secrecy' when it comes to security issues) in order to claim that only they can understand the ramifications of taking decisions on a variety of matters.

In my view, these two revolutions seem to have run their course and there are signs of a reaction against them settling in among mass publics. The usual permanent organisational representatives of class, sectoral and professional interests – especially trade unions – have declined in membership and even in some cases in number and political influence. New social movements have emerged that proclaim less bureaucratic structures and a greater role for individual members – even some enhanced mechanisms for practicing internal democracy. Candidates for elected public office now frequently proclaim that they are not professional or partisan politicians and pretend, as far as possible, to be ordinary citizens. Movements have emerged in some countries, especially the USA, to limit the number of terms in office that a politician can serve. Whether these trends will be sufficient to stop or even invert these two 'post-Dahlian' revolutions is dubious (to me), but they do signal an awareness of the existence of these trends and of their (negative) impact upon the quality of REDs.

Let us now turn to a diagnosis of the two and, perhaps, a third more recent – contemporary and simultaneous – revolutions going on within REDs. The first concerns not so much the scope as the very process of decision making in democracies. Over the past twenty or more years – indeed, much longer in the case of the United States – REDs have ceded authority to what Dahl has called *guardian institutions*. The expression is taken from Plato and refers to specialised institutions – usually regulatory bodies – that have been assigned responsibility for making policy in areas which politicians have decided are too controversial or complex to be left to the vicissitudes of electoral competition or inter-party legislative struggle. Initially, the *locus classicus* was the creation of independent institutions for judicial review of political decisions taken by popularly elected legislative or executive bodies. These 'Supreme' or 'Constitutional' courts have proliferated and become virtually indispensible if a polity is to be recognised as a member of the RED club. A more recent addition to these institutions of 'horizontal accountability' is the independent Central Bank, but earlier examples include general staffs of the military, anti-trust authorities, regulatory agencies and civil service commissions. In each case, it was feared that the intrusion of 'politics' would prevent the institution from producing some generally desired public good. Only experts acting on the basis of (allegedly) neutral and scientific knowledge could be entrusted with such responsibilities. A more cynical view would stress that these are often policy areas where the party in power has reason to fear that if they have to hand over office in the future to their opponents, the latter would use these institutions to punish the former or to reward themselves. Whatever the motives for their creation, the variety, scope and authority of these 'guardians' have greatly increased in recent decades and show no signs of abating.

Their net effect upon REDs has become rather obvious. Although usually well concealed behind a rhetorical veil of ignorance about the potential discriminatory impact of their decisions, contemporary democracies have been increasingly deprived of discretionary action over issues that have a major impact upon their citizens. 'Democracies without choice' is the expression that has emerged, especially in neo-democracies, to describe and decry this situation. Even more potentially alienating is the fact that some of these guardians are not even national, but instead operate at the regional or global level.

This brings me to the second contemporary revolution within REDs or, more accurately, with particular intensity within European

REDs: *multi-level government*. During the post-World War Two period, initially in large measure due to a shared desire to avoid any possible repetition of that experience, European polities began experimenting with the scale or, better, level of aggregation at which collectively binding decisions would be made. The most visible manifestation of this trend has been the EEC, the EC and now the European Union (EU) (Schmitter 2000). But paralleling this macro-experiment, there emerged a widespread micro-level experiment, namely, the devolution of various political responsibilities to subnational units – *provinces, regioni, Länder* or *estados autonómicos*. As a result, virtually all Europeans find themselves surrounded by a very complex set of authorities, each with vaguely defined or concurrently exercised policy *compétences*. The oft-repeated assurance that only national states can be democratic is no longer true in Europe, even though in practice it is often difficult to separate the various levels and determine which rulers should be held accountable for making specific policies. European politicians have become quite adept at passing the buck, especially at blaming the European Union (or the Euro) for unpopular decisions. New political parties and movements that blame the EU for policies over which it has little or no control – for example, over the influx of migrants from non-EU countries – have even emerged, as Klaus von Beyme points out in this volume.

It is here tempting to return to Dahl's original revolution, the radical change in the size of democracy that happened with the foundation of the United States of America. This size problem was resolved by creating a set of local, state and national territorial constituencies nested within a hierarchy that assigned distinctive legitimate authority and relative autonomy to each level. The difference with contemporary multi-level governance in Europe is not only that the component units have historically had much greater autonomy and stronger identities but, more importantly, that the sheer size and heterogeneity of the European citizenry has made it much more difficult to form political parties at the EU level out of pre-existing national party systems. This difficulty, combined with the ambiguous commitment to granting the European Parliament full parliamentary status, has greatly undermined the Parliament's status as a representative body, as evidenced by the almost monotonic decline in turnout for European elections. If that were not enough, the assignment of legal competences to the various levels of the EU is very ambiguous and embedded in treaties that are often contradictory. Even the EU's draft constitution and the subsequent Lisbon version failed to resolve this problem of *Kompetenz-Kompetenz* in a context where many policy issues have been declared 'overlapping'. The only way such a complex polity can function is by almost continuous negotiations among the levels – which make effective representation almost impossible.

Multi-level government could, of course, be converted into something much more familiar, namely, a federal state with clearly delineated competences. Yet resistance to this outcome is likely to remain quite strong for the foreseeable future, as shown by the public rejection of the Draft Constitutional Treaty by France and the Netherlands and (initially) the Lisbon Treaty by Ireland. Even the subsequent ratification of the Treaty is unlikely to dissipate confusion about policy *compétences* and persistent ambiguities about which political institutions are appropriate for each of these multiple levels. And, when it comes to the design question, there seems to be a general awareness that the rules and practices of democracy at each of these levels cannot and should not be identical. Especially when it comes to ensuring the accountability of a polity of the size, scale, scope and diversity of the European Union, what is demanded is a literal reinvention of democracy, a task that was not even attempted by the Convention that drafted the unsuccessful Constitutional Treaty.

There may well be a third contemporary revolution stalking the future of REDs, that of *good governance*. It is too soon to judge whether the extraordinarily rapid and broad diffusion of this concept among practitioners and scholars is merely a reflection of fashionable discourse (and their mutual desire to avoid mentioning *bad government*); or whether it actually signifies and contributes to a profound modification of how decisions are being made in REDs.

If such modification happened then this would have (at least) seven major implications: (1) 'stakeholders' determined by functional effect would replace citizens grouped in territorial constituencies as the principal agents of participation; (2) political parties would have no recognised (and certainly no privileged) access to participation in governance arrangements and would be replaced by individual or collective stakeholders; (3) consensus formation among representatives with unequal functional capacities would replace various forms of voting by individuals or deputies with equal political rights as the usual decision-making mechanism; (4) executive or administrative authorities would routinely take over the role of 'chartering' such arrangements – delegating their scope and determining their composition – so replacing the competitively and popularly elected representatives of legislatures; (5) the 'liberal' distinction between public and private actors would be deliberately blurred in matters of responsibility for both making and implementing publicly binding decisions; (6) the substantive compromises that underlie the process of consensus formation would have to be reached confidentially through opaque combinations of negotiation and deliberation among stakeholders, whose decisions subsequently would be legitimated publicly in terms of their (presumably beneficial) functional impact; and (7) elections would increasingly become 'civic rituals' with less and less impact upon the substance of public policy and, presumably, less and less popular participation.

Needless to say, a good governance revolution defined by all of these features could pose serious challenges to the legitimating principles of contemporary REDs.

The causes of our present democratic revolutions and discontents

We do not have to look far for the root causes of the simultaneous revolutions outlined above: revolutions defined by profound changes of organisational citizenship, professionalisation, guardianship, multi-level government and (perhaps) governance. These changes are exceptionally diverse and strong. The rate, the scale and the scope of changes in the broader context in which REDs are 'condemned' to operate seem to be unprecedented and, most important, beyond the reach of the traditional units of authority that have heretofore dominated the political landscape of these democracies. Most of today's problems are either too small or too large for yesterday's sovereign national states and, hence, as we have just seen, within Europe there has been a vast amount of experimentation with devolution to smaller political units and integration into larger ones. Interestingly, both of these experiments in scale have affected almost all European polities in some way or another, with the exception of the mini-states of Andorra, Lichtenstein, Monaco and San Marino. Cyprus, Luxembourg and Malta have formally joined the EU and the others are informally members of it. For the first time, the level of aggregation at which reforms should be designed and implemented has become almost as important a question as knowing their substance. The old question, that concerning *Que faire?*, now has to be supplemented by a much less frequently asked question: *Où faire?*

Since they are living for the first time in a relatively 'pacified environment', without the prospect of either war or revolution, European democracies will find it difficult to resort to 'emergency' measures or 'temporary' suspensions in order to implement designed reforms against strong opposition. The key problem will be finding the will to reform existing rules among the very rulers who have benefited by them and who usually cannot be compelled to reform by an overriding external threat to their security, or their tenure in office.

One generic issue dominates all speculation about the future design of democracy: *how well do its existing and well-established formal institutions and informal practices 'fit' with the much more rapidly changing social, economic, cultural and technological environment upon which democracy depends, both materially and normatively?*

In the Green Paper that Alexandre Trechsel and I wrote for the Council of Europe we identified the following ten generic sources of change in the complex environment currently surrounding European democracies (Schmitter and Treschel 2004). Each of them presents a *challenge* in the sense that it threatens the viability of the existing rules and practices of REDs; but each also represents an *opportunity* that opens up the possibility of creative and imaginative reforms that could actually improve the performance of these very same 'real existing' liberal democracies. In other words, their impact is theoretically ambivalent which, in turn, generates plausible rival hypotheses whose validity will depend on whether subsequent reforms are enacted and implemented.

1.   Globalisation

Definition: an array of recent transformations at the macro-level that tend to cluster together, reinforce each other and produce an ever-accelerating cumulative impact. All these changes have something to do with encouraging the number and variety of exchanges among individuals and social groups across national borders by compressing their interactions in time and space, lowering their costs and overcoming previous barriers, some of them technical, some geographical, but most of them political. By all accounts, the driving forces behind globalisation are economic. However, behind the formidable power of increased market competition and technological innovation in goods and services lies a myriad of decisions by national political authorities to tolerate, encourage and, sometimes, to subsidise these exchanges, often by removing policy-related obstacles that existed previously. Hence the association of the concept of globalisation with that of liberalisation, whose day-to-day manifestations involve stricter competition, more complex systems of production, greater consumer choice, expanded occupational, educational and geographic mobility and more diverse location of innovations. All these trends appear to be so natural and inevitable that we often forget they are the product of deliberate decisions by governments that presumably understand the consequences of what they have decided to *laisser passer* and *laisser faire*.

Globalisation certainly induces rival research hypotheses. According to some observers, it narrows the potential range of policy responses, undermines the capacity of (no longer) sovereign national states to respond autonomously to the demands of their citizenry and, thereby, undermines established channels of partisan representation and weakens the legitimacy of traditional political intermediaries and state authorities. According to other observers, globalisation widens the resources available to non-state actors acting across national borders and shifts policy responsibility upward to transnational quasi-state actors, both of which undermine established oligarchic and collusive arrangements between political parties and promote the diffusion of transnational norms of human rights, democracy and 'good governance' that find expression through new social movements.

2.   European integration

Definition: the direct impact of EU directives and regulations upon member, candidate and adjacent states and the indirect effect of continuous and varied interaction of politically relevant European actors, both of which tend to produce a gradual convergence toward common norms and practices and, hence, a reduction in the persistent diversity of norms and practices that have historically characterised national states within Europe.

Rival research hypotheses about its impact upon REDs: (1) European integration tends to undermine established national practices of partisan representation and democratic participation without replacing them with supranational practices of comparable nature and importance; (2) European integration, through the 'conditionality' that it imposes on candidate member states and the legal supremacy of European law over member-state laws, tends to promote higher and more uniform standards of democratic performance at the national and subnational levels and encourages associations and movements to shift their attention to the supranational level.

3.   Intercultural migration and cohabitation

Definition: the voluntary and involuntary movement of persons across previously more closed and secured national borders and the permanent residence of increasing numbers of foreigners, especially of non-European origin, within European societies.

Rival hypotheses: (1) migration and the cohabitation of cultures previously separated from each other tend to generate a negative reaction on the part of 'native' inhabitants of more culturally homogeneous European countries, and this finds its expression in xenophobic social movements, ultra-nationalist political parties and racially motivated incidents that undermine the authority of established political organisations and agencies, and force existing national (and, eventually, supranational) governments to adopt policies restricting further in-migration. This in turn has a secondary impact on the rights of national citizens and the stability of existing political competition; (2) migration and the cohabitation of natives and foreigners have a positive impact upon the practice of democracy at several levels of aggregation, especially since migration and cohabitation diversify the bases of recruitment by political parties, shift the existing lines of partisan competition, compel politicians to pay attention to previously ignored issues and, in the longer run, as Sonia Alonso suggests, contribute to the formation of more diverse ('layered') collective identities and greater tolerance by both rulers and citizens.

4.   Demographic trends

Definition: changes in the demographic profile of European societies in the direction of lower birth rates and higher proportions of elderly people.

Rival hypotheses: (1) aged people are more likely to vote and to do so consistently for the same political party, to continue to be members of the same interest associations and, hence, to acquire greater relative influence over the policy process. This influence allows them to appropriate for themselves an increasing share of public funds and selective benefits and leads in turn to youth disaffection with political parties, on the grounds that their leaders are (accurately) perceived as paying increasing attention to the aged (and may themselves be getting older and older); (2) demographic shifts, especially in their territorial impact, and when combined with compensating foreign immigration, are bringing about long-overdue redistributions in political representation and public policy that will enhance regime legitimacy and economic performance – provided that politically disaffected youth eventually become engaged citizens and stable members of parties and associations.

5.   *Economic performance*

Definition: the combined effect of several persistently negative economic components – at a minimum, of lower growth rates, higher levels of unemployment, and more unequal distributions of income and wealth – upon citizens' perception of their individual and collective well-being.

Rival hypotheses: (1) decline in economic performance in Europe, especially relative to the United States, leads to a perception among citizens that their democratic institutions are serving them badly and that they should be reformed in a more liberal 'American' direction, which includes a rejection of traditionally more 'ideological' European political parties; (2) decline in relative and even absolute economic performance is not perceived as a corresponding decline in the quality of life and, therefore, leads to a reaffirmation of the distinctiveness and value of the 'less liberal' political institutions of (continental) Europe, which include those traditional parties and class associations that are seen as responsible for the 'European social model'.

6.   *Technological change*

Definition: the rapid, unpredictable and uncontrollable diffusion of changes in technology across political borders – whether through shared knowledge or commercial competition – and their impact upon the way in which citizens, representatives and rulers exchange information and communicate among themselves, and with each other.

Rival hypotheses: (1) the acceleration of technological change, especially in information and communication technologies, reduces the absolute cost of exchanges, protects the autonomy of users and lowers relative disparities in access between and among citizens, their representatives and their rulers. Technological change therefore both increases political equality and makes it more possible to hold the rulers accountable – provided that existing parties and associations adopt these changes; (2) accelerated technological change only reduces transaction costs for a privileged segment of persons ('the digital divide') and opens up wider disparities between those who can and those who cannot exploit it. These disparities add new elements of discrimination and bias to the political process, but also further divide existing parties and associations along generational lines.

7.   State capacity

Definition: the ability of existing permanent governing institutions, especially at the national level, to carry out effectively and autonomously (in a sovereign manner) the tasks that have been assigned to them by rulers and are expected of them by citizens.

Rival hypotheses: (1) in the present international/interstate context (as captured by items 1, 2, 6 and 10 in this list of challenges), the governing institutions of previously sovereign national states find it increasingly difficult to extract sufficient resources, to regulate internal behaviour and, hence, to satisfy effectively and efficiently the expectations of their citizens within existing borders; this causes a decline of trust in nationally bounded representatives and a reduction of the prestige and legitimacy of rulers; (2) while the above-noted changes in the external context do restrict the autonomy of national states, they also contain incentives for shifting governing tasks to both the sub- and supranational levels of aggregation. These institutions 'beyond and below' the nation state are becoming increasingly (if gradually) capable of satisfying citizen expectations and generating political legitimacy, so that citizens may (eventually) shift their expectations to representative organisations at these levels.

8.   Individuation

Definition: the shift, due to changes in working conditions, living contexts, personal mobility and family structure, in the locus of identity and collective action from historically generated, socio-political encompassing categories such as class, race, religion, ideology and nationality, towards much more fragmented and personalised conceptions of self-interest and collective passion.

Rival hypotheses: (1) individuation at the level of interests and passions undermines the tendency for citizens to support, join and act in conjunction with more encompassing political organisations such as parties, trade unions and nationalist movements. It also produces a structure of intermediary associations that is more specialised in purpose and less connected in action than in the past, leading to a decline in the ability of polities to pursue overriding 'general' or 'public' interests and, ultimately, to a decline in the legitimacy of democracy; (2) individuation may undermine traditional forms of collective action, but it contributes to the legitimacy of new forms of democracy by providing powerful incentives for creating new intermediaries that are more flexible in their structure, participatory in their decision making and capable of forming (and re-forming) networks for the production of public goods of overriding general interest.

9.   *Mediatisation*

Definition: the tendency to acquire information about politics and to receive political messages exclusively from a plurality of sources in the mass media, but especially from television and internet sources that are in commercial competition with each other for the attention of consumers and the profit of owners.

Rival hypotheses: (1) mediatisation destroys previously well-established mechanisms whereby citizens discussed politics directly with each other (and their children) and obtained their information and proximate identity through distinctively public and political intermediaries such as parties, associations and unions. Mediatisation replaces these mechanisms with a commercial nexus that trivialises information about politicians and exploits their personal rather than political actions; (2) the growing plurality of sources, the privatisation of ownership and the competition between firms for consumer attention liberate the media from control by rulers and insulates them from partisan manipulation. This in turn creates a more diverse and accessible 'public sphere' from which citizens can more easily extract information and in which they can participate virtually, at much lower cost and effort.

10.   *Sense of insecurity*

Definition: an increase in the perception, by vulnerable individuals and groups, of having to face avoidable risks and an increase in the magnitude of their probable consequences, due either to threats external to their own society, or to damaging behaviour from their own co-citizens.

Rival hypotheses: (1) the manipulation by rulers of this growing sense of insecurity, especially that due to foreign non-state actors (such as terrorists), reduces basic freedoms and promotes aggressive ('preemptive') behaviour that undermines the accountability of institutions and rulers to citizens and distorts the competition and cooperation of democratic representatives; (2) efforts by rulers to exploit insecurity in order to avoid accountability will generate a reaction among previously apathetic groups of citizens that will resuscitate pre-existing parties, associations and (especially) movements in defence of threatened freedoms and provide a basis for the foundation of new intermediary organisations.

Three tentative conclusions can be drawn from these unprecedented trends:

First, established democracies will find it increasingly difficult to legitimate themselves by comparing their performance with that of some alternative mode of domination, whether real or imagined. Now that liberal democracy has become the norm in so many world regions and overt autocracy persists only in countries with markedly different cultures and social structures, the standards for evaluating what governments do (and how they do what they do) will become increasingly internal to the discourse of normative democratic theory, that is, internal to what differing conceptions of democracy have promised over time, and for which citizens have struggled so hard in the past. This should in turn lead to a convergence in formal institutions and informal practices due to the diffusion of these standards across national borders and, in the case of Europe, to the 'political conditionality' promoted by the EU, the Council of Europe and their respective supranational courts.

Second, new democracies in Central and Eastern Europe and the western parts of the former Soviet Union will find it increasingly difficult to legitimate themselves simply by arguing that they are so burdened by their respective autocratic heritages that they cannot possibly respect the norms of behaviour and attain the levels of performance set by established democracies. The standards that their recently liberated citizens will apply in evaluating their rulers will rapidly converge with those already in use in the rest of Europe. Polities failing to meet these standards will experience more frequent electoral turnover in power and may even be threatened by popular rebellion, unless their newly empowered rulers respect the rules established by the REDs to their west.

Third, in both Western and Eastern cases polities will usually only be able to redesign and improve the quality of their respective democratic institutions and practices by means of partial and gradual reforms. Moreover, these reforms will have to be drafted, approved and implemented according to pre-existing norms. Rarely, if ever, will there be opportunities for more thoroughgoing, large-scale or 'abnormal' changes. After all, how much change in the rules of democracy can one expect from rulers who themselves have benefited from these very same rules? The usual rotation of parties and party alliances in and out of power will, at best, open up only modest opportunities for change.

My primary hypothesis about political design is that *the future of democracy in Europe is to be found less in fortifying, and thereby trying to perpetuate, existing formal institutions and informal practices than in redesigning and changing them.* 'Whatever form it takes, the democracy of our successors will not and cannot be the democracy of our predecessors' (Dahl 1989). As we have seen, thanks to Robert Dahl, there is nothing new about this rule. REDs have undergone several major transformations in the past in order to reaffirm their two central principles: the sovereignty of equal citizens; and the accountability of unequal rulers. Within the framework of these principles, I can see no reason why democracy cannot redesign itself again.

From generic definition to specific reforms

Terry Karl and I have tried to produce the most 'generic' working definition of democracy. We came up with the following: *modern political democracy is a regime or system of governance in which rulers are held accountable for their actions in the public realm by citizens acting indirectly through the competition and cooperation of their representatives* (Schmitter and Karl 1991). Using it as a guideline for designing new institutions and practices does not 'pre-commit' the analyst to any specific model, institutional format or set of decision rules. It leaves open the key issues of how citizens choose their representatives, what the most effective mechanisms of accountability are, and how collective binding decisions are taken. But the definition does provide the three types of actors who are expected to combine through a variety of processes to produce the *summum bonum* of political democracy, namely, accountability constituted by *citizens, representatives and rulers.*

I am convinced that REDs are currently experiencing crises in all three of these dimensions. So far, however, citizens, representatives and rulers have neither agreed on the magnitude of these crises nor on the design of a concerted response to them. With some exceptions, they have responded either weakly or by attempting to reinforce existing rules and practices. There have been some very innovative efforts to transform challenges into opportunities at the local level, but these have failed to prevent a decline in the quality of their respective national institutions. Citizens have become increasingly aware of this 'design problem' and have focused much of their discontent upon representatives, that is, upon politicians as individuals and parties as organisations.

The above-mentioned Green Paper for the Council of Europe responded to these crises by making specific (and relatively modest) recommendations for reform – twenty-eight of them in all. Some proposed reforms were inspired by the dispersed efforts that European democracies are already making; others are novel and have never been tried before in practice.

For reasons of space, all of these proposed reforms cannot be described here in detail, so I will focus briefly on just a few examples in relation to three types of actors: citizens, representatives and rulers.

Citizens

These are the 'principals' upon whom the entire edifice of RED rests. Most of the literature assumes that they are individual persons, whereas here I have argued that the most effective actors are organisations operating as 'agents' by representing diverse categories of citizens. The core normative issues have become, first, the extent to which these increasingly professionalised agents can be controlled by their voters, members, contributors or followers; second, the degree to which the intrinsic equality of individual citizens can be displaced by the intrinsic inequality of their collective representatives; and, third, the capacity of increasingly individualised persons to recognise and trust those who claim to speak for the various (and often conflicting) social categories to which they belong.

Innovations are needed to ensure the greater accountability of agents, to diminish the gap between professional and amateur skills; to increase the range of choice among candidates and associations; and to encourage participation by voters and members. Possible examples include:

Universal citizenship: its aim is to grant voting rights to all legally entitled citizens from the moment of birth, with one parent exercising these rights until the age of political maturity;

Discretionary voting: to allow citizens to spread their vote across candidates according to their intensity of preference and to vote for 'none of the above' (NOTA) when no candidates are preferred; and

Lotteries for electors: to award each voter with a ticket to one of three lotteries (one for first-time voters, one for consistent voters, one for all others) with prizes to distribute funds for public policies.

Representatives

Considered as collective 'agents', representatives have become so omnipresent, embedded and protected in the political process that they are capable of acting as 'principals' independently of the citizens they are supposed to represent. Elections are less able to ensure their accountability – even as competitiveness and rotation in power has increased – thanks to partisan collusion and the absence of credible alternative programmes. 'Selected' or 'self-appointed' agents do not usually have to worry about such obstacles to their tenure, especially if they are acting in the name of such principals as whales, trees or future generations.

Reforms should focus on making elections more competitive; on permitting a wider range of citizens to become representatives; and tying the funding of parties (and other intermediary organisations) to citizen preferences. Possible reforms include:

Shared mandates: these would allow parties to nominate two candidates for each elected position, one to serve as the 'senior' representative, the other as his/her deputy with the distribution of tasks to be determined by parties or candidates;

Variable thresholds for election: to make it progressively more difficult for incumbent representatives to be re-elected by raising the necessary threshold for election; and

Vouchers for financing political parties: these would finance all registered parties through the distribution of vouchers for a fixed sum by citizens when voting. Such vouchers could be combined with NOTA voting to provide an accumulating fund for financing new parties.

Rulers

REDs are not anarchies. They have persons and organisations that exercise authority and that can wield legitimate coercion if necessary. Most of these rulers are elected under competing party labels and have previously played some role as representatives of territorial constituencies – which is not to say that 'selected' and 'self-selected' representatives of other constituencies do not also form part of the ruling elite. What is supposedly distinctive about democratic rulers is their *pro tempore* status and their contingent tenure in office. All REDs are presumed to have regular and predictable mechanisms for holding them accountable for their actions in the public realm – whether this involves citizens directly acting in periodic elections, as in a presidential regime, or indirectly through their representatives, as in a parliamentary regime. Unfortunately, from a democratic perspective, the proliferation of independent guardian agencies has produced a subset of rulers that are not controlled by either of these mechanisms.

What is needed are changes in the rules and incentives that will give amateur citizens some form of collective expression to counter the effect of their increasingly professionalised rulers. These changes will need to address the growing information gap between citizens, their representatives and their rulers; they will also need to improve the system of checks and balances between not just the three classic 'powers' but between all of them and the increased role played by undemocratic 'guardian' institutions and media agents. Possible changes include:

Citizens' assemblies: these would establish an annual assembly composed of randomly selected citizens to review (and perhaps to reject) a limited number of legislative drafts referred to it by a minority of regularly elected deputies;

Electronic monitoring and online deliberation systems: to provide a publicly organised and funded system for monitoring the legislative performance of all elected representatives and for communicating with these representatives;

Guardians to watch the guardians: these would empower the parliament to employ specialists who would have open access to all 'guardian' institutions and who would be responsible for reporting regularly on their performance.

Conclusion

Liberal representative democracy, as presently practised in Europe, is not 'the end of history'. Not only can it be redesigned; it must be redesigned if it is to retain the legitimate respect of its citizens. It has done this several times in the past in response to emerging challenges and opportunities, and there is no reason to believe that it cannot be done again in the present.

The major generic problem of contemporary European democracy concerns declining citizen trust in the institutions of partisan representation, and declining participation in electoral processes. Those reforms that promise to increase voter turnout, to stimulate membership in political parties, associations and movements, and to improve citizen confidence in the role of politicians as representatives and legislators, therefore deserve prior consideration – especially in those cases where they might also make politics more entertaining and appealing to youth. The second most important problem concerns the increasing number of foreign residents and the political status of denizens in almost all European democracies. Measures to incorporate these non-citizens within the political process should also be given a high priority.

As I have already noted, the 'events' that have triggered major reforms in the past, revolutions, wars and economic depression, are no longer available to contemporary REDs. Ironically, the 'Great Recession' that they are currently suffering (2007–10) seems to have dampened rather than enhanced the likelihood of such experiments. Perhaps this is because the 'agent' that previously contributed the most to the redesign of democratic rules, political parties, is precisely the agent that has been most negatively affected by several of the challenges described above. Parties have either lost too many members or too much credibility with citizens, or they have become too internally divided or too dependent upon state support to play the crucial role of putting together a winning coalition capable of promoting alternative institutions. Theorists of 'deepening' or 'strengthening' democracy tend to stress the potential for grass-roots mobilisation and radical decentralisation of power, often in conjunction with the reliance on new communications technologies that facilitate the creation and coordination of 'virtual groups'. However appealing this scenario may be on normative grounds, it fails to explain how such efforts can be coordinated to produce change in large-scale and multi-layered polities; it thus tends to be over-optimistic about the likelihood of reaching agreement within more heterogeneous societies. Such mobilisations from below may be necessary in order to capture the attention of elites and to weaken their prevailing alliances, but in my opinion attaining sufficient motivation to experiment even with such modest reforms as proposed above will depend on reaching novel intra-elite agreements. Who these elites will be and who they will claim to represent is much less obvious than in the past when class cleavages, regional disparities and religious differences were more clearly linked to benefits from reform measures. The interests (and passions) involved in prospective changes of today's rules are less polarised – they include sectoral clashes, generational distributions, lifestyle preferences, eco-logical concerns – and, hopefully, they are therefore more amenable to reasoned debate by better-educated publics and embedded in an over-arching context of regional and global interdependence.

But even if intra-elite compromises on specific reforms do prove to be feasible and acceptable to broader publics, they have rarely been efficacious on their own. In the past, it has usually been 'packages' of interrelated reforms that have been most successful in improving demo-cratic performance and legitimacy. Sometimes this was the result of an explicit and rational calculation of the interdependencies involved; most often, however, it was the product of the political process itself with its inevitable need for legislative alliances, compromises among competing forces and side payments to recalcitrant groups. In other words, in 'real-existing' democracies, the design of reform measures is almost always imperfect, all the more so when the intent is to change the future rules of competition and cooperation between key political actors who owe their power and status to the successful manipulation of the existing ones.

REFERENCES

Dahl, R. A. (1970) *After the revolution? Authority in a good society.* New Haven, CT and London: Yale University Press.
   (1983) *Dilemmas of pluralist democracy: Autonomy vs. control.* New Haven, CT and London: Yale University Press.
   (1989) *Democracy and its critics.* New Haven, CT and London: Yale University Press.

(1996) 'The future of democratic theory', *Estudios*. Working Papers 90. Madrid.

(2000) *On democracy*. New Haven, CT and London: Yale University Press.

Schmitter, P. (2000) *How to democratize the European Union – and why bother?* Lanham, MD: Rowman and Littlefield.

Schmitter, P. and T. Karl (1991) 'What *democracy* is ... and is not', *Journal of Democracy* 2 (Summer), 75–88.

Schmitter, P. and G. Lehmbruch (eds.) (1979) *Trends toward corporatist intermediation*. London: Sage.

Schmitter, P. and A. Trechsel (2004) *The future of democracy in Europe: Trends, analyses and reforms*. A Green Paper for the Council of Europe. Strasbourg: Council of Europe Publishing.

John Keane

This chapter proposes a fundamental revision of the way we think about representation and democracy in our times. It pinpoints an epochal transformation of the contours and dynamics of representative democracy. It tables the claim that from roughly the mid-twentieth century representative democracy began to morph into a new historical form of 'post-parliamentary' democracy, and it explores some of the reasons why this change happened. It proposes that 'end of history' perspectives and maritime metaphors (Huntington's 'third wave' of the sea simile has been the most influential) are too limited to grasp the epochal change – too bound to the surface of things, too preoccupied with continuities and aggregate data – to notice that political tides have begun to run in entirely new directions. My conjecture is that the world of actually existing democracy is experiencing an historic sea change, one that is taking us away from the assembly-based and representative democracy of past times towards a form of democracy with entirely different contours and dynamics of representation.

It is hard to find an elegant name for the new form of democracy, let alone to describe in a few words its workings and political implications; at stake is the tricky task of crafting a plausible 'wild category', a creative neologism that descriptively sums up and makes good analytic sense of novel developments that cannot otherwise be grasped through 'tame' prevailing categories (Eco 1999: 232 ff.). The strange-sounding term *monitory democracy* is the most exact for describing the big transformation that is taking hold in regions like Europe and South Asia and in countries otherwise as different as the United States, Japan, Argentina and New Zealand. Monitory democracy is a new historical form of democracy, a variety of 'post-parliamentary' politics defined by the rapid growth of many different kinds of extra-parliamentary, power-scrutinising mechanisms. These monitory bodies take root within the domestic fields of government and civil society, as well as in cross-border settings once controlled by empires, states and business organisations. In consequence, the whole architecture of self-government is changing. The central grip of elections, political parties and parliaments on citizens' lives is weakening. Democracy is coming to mean much more than free and fair elections, although nothing less. Within and outside states, independent monitors of power begin to have tangible effects. By putting politicians, parties and elected governments permanently on their toes, these monitors complicate their lives, question their authority and force them to change their agendas – and sometimes smother them in disgrace.

Whether or not the trend towards this new kind of democracy is a sustainable, historically irreversible development remains to be seen: like its previous historical antecedents, monitory democracy is not inevitable. It did not have to happen, but it happened; whether it will live or fade away or die remains untreated in this essay (the subject of counter-trends and dysfunctions of monitory democracy is taken up in my *The Life and Death of Democracy* [Keane 2009a]). Certainly when judged by its institutional contours and inner dynamics, monitory democracy is the most complex form of democracy yet. Those with a taste for Latin would say that it is the *tertium quid*, the not fully formed successor of the earlier historical experiments with assembly-based and representative forms of democracy. In the name of 'people', 'the public', 'public accountability', 'the people' or 'citizens' – the terms are normally used interchangeably in the age of monitory democracy – power-scrutinising institutions spring up all over the place. Elections, political parties and legislatures neither disappear, nor necessarily decline in importance; but they most definitely lose their pivotal position in politics. Democracy is no longer simply a way of handling the power of elected governments by electoral and parliamentary and constitutional means, and no longer a matter confined to territorial states. Gone are the days when democracy could be described (and in the next breath attacked) as 'government by the unrestricted will of the majority' (Friedrich von Hayek 1979: 39). Whether in the field of local, national or supranational government, or in the power-ridden world of non-governmental organisations and networks – some of them stretching down into the roots of everyday life and outwards, towards the four corners of the earth – people and organisations that exercise power are now routinely subject to public monitoring and public contestation by an assortment of extra-parliamentary bodies.

Here is one striking clue for understanding what is happening: the age of monitory democracy that began in 1945 has witnessed the birth of nearly one hundred new types of power-scrutinising institutions, unknown to previous democrats. As we shall see, defenders of these inventions often speak of their importance in solving a basic problem facing contemporary democracies, namely how to promote their unfinished business of finding new ways of democratic living for little people in big and complex societies: societies in which substantial numbers of citizens believe that politicians are not easily to be trusted, and in which governments are often accused of abusing their power or being out of touch with citizens, or simply unwilling to deal with their concerns and problems. By addressing such concerns, the new power-scrutinising inventions break the grip of the majority rule principle – the worship of numbers – associated with representative democracy. Freed, as well, from the measured caution and double speak of political parties, some inventions give a voice to the strongly felt concerns of minorities that feel left out of official politics. Some monitors – electoral commissions and consumer protection agencies for instance – use their claimed 'neutrality' to protect the rules of the democratic game from predators and enemies. Other monitors publicise long-term issues that are neglected, or dealt with badly, by the short-term mentality encouraged by election cycles. Still other monitory groups are remarkable for their evanescence; in a fast-changing world, they come on the scene, stir the pot, then move on like nomads, or dissolve into thin air.

By making room for opinions and ways of life that people feel strongly about, despite their neglect or suppression by parties, parliaments and governments, these inventions have the combined effect of raising the level and quality of public monitoring of power, often for the first time in many areas of life, including power relationships 'beneath' and 'beyond' the institutions of territorial states. It is little wonder that the new power-monitoring inventions have triggered outcries against their alleged cultivation of political confusion and general 'distrust and suspicion' of power (Dunn 2010); or that they are remoulding the language of contemporary politics. They prompt much talk of 'empowerment', 'high energy democracy', 'stakeholders', 'participatory governance', 'communicative democracy' and 'deliberative democracy'; and they help spread, often for the first time, a culture of voting and representation into many walks of life. Monitory democracy is the age of surveys, focus groups, deliberative polling, online petitions and audience and customer voting. Whether intended or not, the spreading culture of voting, backed by the new mechanisms for monitoring power, has the effect of interrupting and often silencing the soliloquies of parties, politicians and parliaments. The new power-scrutinising innovations tend to enfranchise many more citizens' voices, sometimes by means of *unelected representatives* skilled at using what Americans sometimes call 'bully pulpits'. The number and range of monitory institutions have so greatly increased that they point to a world where the old rule of 'one person, one vote, one representative' – the central demand in the struggle for representative democracy – is replaced with the new principle of monitory democracy: 'one person, many interests, many voices, multiple votes, multiple representatives'.

Caution must be exercised when trying to understand the new methods of restraining unaccountable power; they are not cut from the same cloth and therefore need careful examination. The new monitory inventions are not exclusively 'American' or 'European' or 'OECD' or 'Western' products. Among their more remarkable features is the way they have rapidly diffused around the globe, from all points on the globe. They mushroom in a wide variety of different settings and there are even signs, for the first time in the history of democracy, of mounting awareness of the added value of the art of invention – as if the democratic ability to invent is itself a most valuable invention.

Monitory mechanisms operate in different ways, on different fronts. Some scrutinise power primarily at the level of *citizens' inputs* to government or civil society bodies; other monitory mechanisms are preoccupied with monitoring and contesting what are called *policy throughputs*; still others concentrate on scrutinising *policy outputs* produced by governmental or non-governmental organisations. Quite a few of the inventions concentrate simultaneously upon all three dimensions. Monitory mechanisms also come in different sizes and operate on various spatial scales, ranging from 'just round the corner' bodies with merely local footprints to global networks aimed at keeping tabs on those who exercise power over great distances.

Given such variations, it should not be surprising that a quick shortlist of the post-1945 inventions resembles – at first sight, to the untrained eye – a magpie's nest of randomly collected items. The list includes: citizen juries, bioregional assemblies, participatory budgeting, advisory boards, focus groups and networks of human rights organisations. There are think tanks, consensus conferences, teach-ins, public memorials, local community consultation schemes and open houses (developed for instance in the field of architecture) that offer information and advisory and advocacy services, archive and research facilities and opportunities for professional networking. Citizens' assemblies, democratic audits, brainstorming conferences, conflict of interest boards, global associations of parliamentarians against corruption and constitutional safaris (famously used by the drafters of the new South African constitution to examine best practice elsewhere) are on the list. So too are the inventions of India's banyan democracy: railway courts, *lok adalats*, public interest litigation and *satyagraha* methods of civil complaint and resistance. Included as well are consumer testing agencies and consumer councils, online petitions and chat rooms, democracy clubs and democracy cafés, public vigils and peaceful sieges, summits and global watchdog organisations set up to bring greater public accountability to business and other civil society bodies. The list of innovations extends to deliberative polls, accountancy boards, independent religious courts, experts' councils (such as the 'Five Wise Men' of the Council of Economic Advisers in Germany), public 'scorecards' – yellow cards and white lists – public planning exercises, public consultations, weblogs, electronic civil disobedience and websites dedicated to monitoring the abuse of power (such as Bully OnLine, a UK-based initiative that aims to tackle workplace bullying and related issues). And the list of new inventions includes self-selected listener opinion polls ('SLOPs') and unofficial ballots (text-messaged straw polls, for instance), international criminal courts, truth and reconciliation commissions, global social forums and the tendency of increasing numbers of non-governmental organisations to adopt written constitutions, with an elected component.

Let us pause, for evidently the list of inventions is disjointed, and potentially confusing. Clear-headed thinking is needed to spot the qualities that these inventions share in common. Monitory institutions play various roles. They are committed to providing publics with extra viewpoints and better information about the performance of various governmental and non-governmental bodies. And because they appeal to publics, monitory institutions (to scotch a possible misunderstanding) are not to be confused with top-down surveillance mechanisms that endanger democracy because they operate in secret for the private purposes of organisations of government or civil society (cf. Rosanvallon 2008). Monitory mechanisms are geared as well to the definition, scrutiny and enforcement of public standards and ethical rules for preventing corruption or the improper behaviour of those responsible for making decisions, not only in the field of elected government but in a wide variety of power settings. The new institutions of monitory democracy are further defined by their overall commitment to strengthening the diversity and influence of citizens' voices and choices in decisions that affect their lives – regardless of the outcome of elections.

Political geography

What is distinctive about monitory democracy is the way *all fields of social and political life* come to be scrutinised, not just by the standard machinery of representative democracy but by a whole host of *non-party, extra-parliamentary and often unelected bodies* operating within and underneath and beyond the boundaries of territorial states. There are

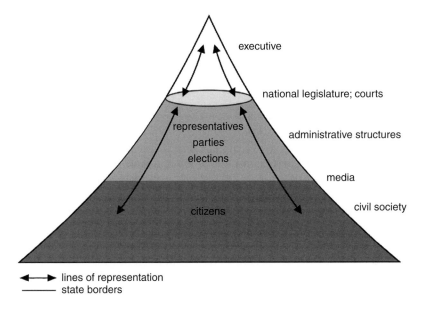

Figure 9.1. Territorially bound representative democracy

important exceptions to this trend – areas such as military weapons production and banking and investment – where monitory institutions are poorly developed. But in the era of monitory democracy, it is as if the principles of representative democracy – public openness, citizens' equality, selecting representatives – are superimposed on representative democracy itself. This has many practical consequences, but one especially striking effect is to alter the patterns of interaction – political geography – of democratic institutions.

Once upon a time, in the brief heyday of representative democracy, the thing called democracy had a rather simple political geography (Figure 9.1). Within the confines of any given state, democracy meant (from the point of view of citizens) following an election campaign and on the great day of reckoning turning out to vote for a party or independent candidate. He – it was almost always men – was someone local, a figure known to the community, a local shopkeeper or professional or someone in business or a trade unionist, for instance. Then came democracy's great ceremonial, the pause of deliberation, the calm of momentary reflection, the catharsis of ticking and crossing, before the storm of result. If blessed with enough votes, the local representative joined a privileged small circle of legislators, whose job was to stay in line with party policy, to support or oppose a government that used its majority in the legislature, to pass laws and to scrutinise their implementation, hopefully with results that pleased as many of the represented as possible. At the end of a limited stint as legislator, buck passing stopped. It was again time for the great choosing day. The representative either stepped down, into retirement, or faced the music of re-election.

This is obviously a simplified sketch of the role of elections, but it serves to highlight the different, more complex political geography of monitory democracy. Just as representative democracies preserved the assemblies of the ancient world, so monitory democracies depend upon legislatures, political parties and elections, which are often bitterly fought and closely contested affairs. But so complicated is the growing variety of interlaced, power-monitoring mechanisms that democrats from earlier times, if catapulted into the new world of monitory democracy, would find it hard to understand what is happening.

The new democracy demands a headshift, a break with conventional thinking in order to understand its political geography. For this purpose, let us imagine for a moment, as if from an aerial satellite, the contours of the new democracy. We would spot that its power-scrutinising institutions are less fixated on elections, parties and legislatures; no longer confined to the territorial state; and spatially arranged in ways much messier than textbooks on democracy typically suppose (see Figure 9.2). The vertical 'depth' and horizontal 'reach' of monitory institutions is striking. If the number of levels within any hierarchy of institutions is a measure of its 'depth', and if the number of units located within each of these levels is called its 'span' or 'width', then monitory democracy is the deepest and widest system of democracy ever known. In principle, in all settings, all relationships of power become publicly contestable by monitory institutions. The political geography of mechanisms like audit commissions, citizens' assemblies, web-based think tanks, local assemblies, regional parliaments, summits and global watchdog organisations defies simple-minded descriptions. So too does the political geography of the wider constellation of power-checking and power-disputing mechanisms in which they are embedded – bodies like citizens' assemblies and juries, audit and integrity commissions and many other watchdog organisations set up to bring greater public accountability to business and other civil society bodies.

Some misconceptions

Both the novelty and complexity of monitory democracy make it vulnerable to a handful of misunderstandings that need to be addressed in order better to understand, explain and judge its merits.

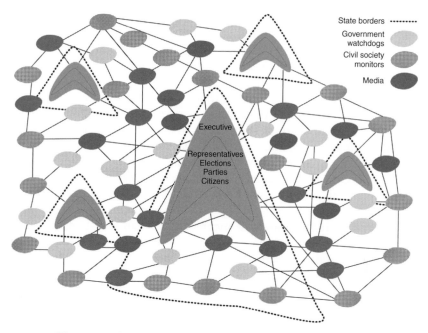

State borders ·········
Government watchdogs
Civil society monitors
Media

Executive

Representatives
Elections
Parties
Citizens

Figure 9.2. Monitory democracy

Representation

While it is often said that the struggle to bring greater public account-ability to government and non-government organisations that wield power over others is in effect a struggle for 'grass-roots democracy' or 'participatory democracy' or 'popular empowerment', the metaphors rest on a misunderstanding of contemporary trends. The age of moni-tory democracy is not heading backwards; it is not motivated by efforts to recapture the (imagined) spirit of assembly-based democracy – 'power to the people' – as some supporters of groups like Students for a Democratic Society (SDS) liked to say during the rebellions of the 1960s. Many contemporary champions of 'deep' or 'direct' democracy still speak as if they are Greeks, as if what really counts in matters of democracy is 'the commitment and capacities of ordinary people to make sensible decisions through reasoned deliberation and empowered because they attempt to tie action to discussion' (Fung and Wright 2003: 5). The reality of monitory democracy is otherwise, in that all of the new power-scrutinising experiments in the name of 'the people' or citizens' empowerment rely inevitably on *representation*. These experi-ments often draw their legitimacy from 'the people', but they are not understandable as efforts to abolish the gap between representatives and the represented, as if citizens could live without others acting on their behalf, and could find their true selves and express themselves as equals within a unified political community no longer burdened by miscommunication, or by misgovernment.

Monitory democracy in fact thrives on representation. Take the much-discussed example of citizens' assemblies (Keane 2009a: 699–701). In the early years of the twenty-first century, among the most talked about cases was the Citizens' Assembly on Electoral Reform in the Canadian province of British Columbia. Backed by the local legislature, the Citizens' Assembly worked for the best part of a year as an independent, non-partisan body charged with the task of casting a critical eye over the province's first-past-the-post electoral system. The Assembly had 161 members: it included 1 woman and 1 man drawn randomly from each of the province's 79 electoral districts, plus 2 aboriginal citizen representatives as well as 1 representative from the province's Legislative Assembly. The member representatives of the Citizens' Assembly were not elected, but drawn by lot. In contrast to the Greek trust in the deities as underwriters of decisions determined by lot, the Assembly members were chosen at random by a computer, from a pool of registered voters who were supposed to reflect the age, gender and geographical make-up of British Columbian citizens as a whole. Granted its own budget, the Citizens' Assembly was designed to operate outside the system of political parties, and to keep its distance from the legislature, organised lobby groups and journalists. Its duty was to act as an unelected body of temporary representatives of all British Columbians.

Elections

Another misconception, to do with the changing status and significance of elections, prevents many people from spotting the novelty of monitory democracy. Since 1945, when there were only a dozen democracies left on the face of the earth, party-based democracy has made a big comeback, so much so that it tricked scholars like Fukuyama and Huntington into thinking that nothing has changed, except for a large global leap in the number of representative democracies. They can be forgiven: following the widespread collapse and near extinction of democracy during the first half of the twentieth century, it is indeed true that most parts of the world have since become familiar with its basic governing institutions. Conventional party-centred forms of representation do not wither away. Millions of people have grown accustomed to competition among political parties, periodic elections, the limited-term holding of political office and the right of citizens to assemble in public to make their views known to their representatives in legislatures and executives, all of this operating within the container of law-bound territorial states. In contexts as different as Sri Lanka, Nigeria, Trinidad and Tobago, Malta and Botswana, the mechanisms of electoral democracy have taken root for the first time; while in other contexts, especially those where electoral democracy is well embedded, experiments have been conducted in their refurbishment, for instance by introducing primary elections into political parties, tightening restrictions on campaign fund-raising and spending, changing the rules of the electoral game, improving voting facilities for disabled citizens and banning party hopping (a decision taken by the Brazilian Supreme Court in 2007).

For all these reasons, it seemed perfectly reasonable for Huntington and other scholars to speak of the spectacular rebirth in recent decades of representative democracy as a 'third wave'. Enter monitory democracy: a brand new historical form of democracy that operates in ways greatly at variance with textbook accounts of 'representative' or 'liberal' or 'parliamentary' democracy, as it is still often called. In the era of monitory democracy, democracy is practised differently. Institutions like periodic elections, multi-party competition and the right of citizens to voice their public approval or disapproval of legislation remain familiar fixtures in the life of democracies. The issue of who is entitled to vote, and under which conditions, continues to stir up troubles (think of the bitter disturbances triggered by the disputed 2009 election results in Iran, or of the ongoing controversies about who owns the software of sometimes unreliable electronic voting machines manufactured by companies such as Election Systems and Software). In fact, some people, for instance felons, have their votes withdrawn; others, including diasporas, minority language speakers, the disabled and people with low literacy and number skills, are disadvantaged by secret ballot elections; still other constituencies, such as women, young people and the biosphere, are either poorly represented, or they are not represented at all.

Struggles to open up and improve the quality of electoral and legislative representation are by no means finished. But slowly and surely, the whole architecture of democracy has begun fundamentally to change. So too has the meaning of democracy. No longer synonymous with self-government by an assembly of male citizens (as in the Greek city states), or with party-based government guided by the will of a legislative majority of elected representatives, democracy comes to mean a way of life and a mode of governing in which power is everywhere subject to checks and balances, such that nobody is entitled to rule without the consent of the governed, or their representatives. A symptom of the redefinition of democracy is the advent of election monitoring. During the 1980s, for the first time in the history of democracy, founding elections in new or strife-torn polities began to be monitored systematically by outside teams of observers. 'Fair and open' methods – the elimination of violence, intimidation, ballot-rigging and other forms of political tomfoolery – are now expected of all countries, including the most powerful democracy on the face of the Earth, the United States, where Organization for Security and Co-operation in Europe (OSCE) observers played a role for the first time in the presidential elections of November 2004. In its 2008 elections, the competing sides proved once again that the campaign tool of legally monitoring elections is becoming as common as fund-raising and advertising. They did so by assembling literally thousands of lawyers at state level to protect their supporters at the polls, to help untangle ballot problems and to run to court should litigation be necessary (the campaign for Barack Obama sent 5,000 lawyers to Florida alone).

Civil society

In the era of monitory democracy, the franchise struggles that once tugged and tore apart whole societies have lost their centrality. As the culture of voting spreads, and as unelected representatives multiply in many different contexts (see Michael Saward's chapter), a brand new issue begins to surface. The old question that racked the age of representative democracy – *who* is entitled to vote and *when* – is compounded and complicated by a question for which there are still no easy answers: *where* are people entitled to vote, or to be represented, often by way of *unelected representatives*?

The intense concern with publicly scrutinising matters once thought to be non-political is unique to the age of monitory democracy. The era of representative democracy certainly saw the rise of self-organised pressure groups and schemes for 'socialising' the power of government, for instance through workers' control of industry. Few of these schemes survived the upheavals of the first half of the twentieth century, which makes the contrast with monitory democracy all the more striking. There is rising awareness of the need for users ('stakeholders') to exercise rights of criticism and cast votes within public service organisations in such fields as health care, education and transportation. The sea change is also evident in the unprecedented level of interest in the old eighteenth-century European term 'civil society'; for the first time in the history of democracy, these two words are now routinely used by democrats in all four corners of the earth. The change is manifest as well in the strong trend towards independent public scrutiny of all kinds of government policies covering (for instance) concerns about the maltreatment and legal rights of children, environmental protection plans and the need to take democracy 'upstream' by ensuring that the future development (say) of nanotechnology and genetically modified food is subject to laws that serve the interests of the many, not the few. Experiments with fostering new forms of citizens' participation and elected representation have even begun to penetrate markets; early innovations included the German system of co-determination known as *Mitbestimmung*, but today many businesses and market sectors have begun to feel the pinch of monitory mechanisms.

Watchdogs

The vital role played by civil societies in the invention of power-monitoring mechanisms seems to confirm what might be called James Madison's law of free government: no government can be considered free unless it is capable of governing a society that is itself capable of controlling the government. The law (famously sketched in the *Federalist Papers*, number 51) has tempted some people to conclude – mistakenly – that governments are quite incapable of scrutinising their own power. The truth is otherwise. In the era of monitory democracy, experience shows that governments sometimes vote to limit their arbitrary powers in favour of the good of their citizens, or in the name of the whole polity.

Government 'watchdog' institutions are a case in point. Their stated purpose is the public scrutiny of government by semi-independent agencies. Scrutiny mechanisms (it is worth remembering that the word scrutiny originally meant 'to sort rubbish', from the Latin *scrutari*, meaning 'to search', and from *scruta*, 'rubbish') supplement the power-monitoring role of elected government representatives and judges, even though this is not always their stated aim; very often they are introduced under the general authority of elected governments, for instance through ministerial responsibility. In practice, things often turn out differently than expected. Especially when protected by legislation, well resourced and well managed, government scrutiny bodies tend to take on a life of their own. Building on the much older precedents of ombudsmen, royal commissions, public enquiries and independent auditors checking the financial probity of government agencies – inventions that had their roots in the age of representative democracy – the new scrutiny mechanisms add checks and balances on the possible abuse of power by elected representatives. Often they are justified in terms of improving the efficiency and effectiveness of government, for instance through 'better informed' decision making that has the added advantage of raising the level of public trust in political institutions among citizens considered as 'stakeholders'. The process displays a double paradox. Not only are government scrutiny mechanisms often established by governments who subsequently fail to control their workings, for instance in cases of corruption and the enforcement of legal standards; the new mechanisms also have democratic, power-checking and hubris-preventing effects, even though they are normally staffed by unelected officials who operate at several arms' length from the rhythm of periodic elections.

The independent 'integrity systems' that came to enjoy an important public profile in various states in Australia from the 1970s are good examples. Following repeated media exposure of fraud and corruption among politicians and police, who in some cases had links with business and organised crime, monitory agencies were established to bring new eyes, ears and teeth to the public sector. The aim was to crack down on intentional wrongdoing or misconduct by elected representatives and appointed officials; fingers were pointed as well at the lax and self-serving complaints systems operated by the police, who are to democratic governments as sharp edges are to knives. Misgivings were also expressed about the reluctance of elected ministers to oversee publicly sensitive police operational matters. Two royal commissions in the state of South Australia during the 1970s led to the establishment (in 1985) of the first Police Complaints Authority. Other states followed suit, culminating in Queensland's Criminal Justice Commission (later the Crime and Misconduct Commission). Established in 1990 as a combined anti-corruption and criminal detection body, it was charged with the job of exposing corruption within the public sector, undertaking crime research, gathering evidence of organised crime, and tracking and recovering criminal proceeds. Its work subsequently led to the formation of an Office of Integrity Commissioner, a statutory body whose functions include the registration and monitoring of lobbyists and the provision of detailed advice to ministers, MPs and senior officials about ethics or integrity issues, including conflicts of interest.

Cross-border democracy?

In the age of monitory democracy, as Michael Zürn and Gregor Walter-Drop point out in their chapter, a great wall of prejudice surrounds the

whole idea of 'cross-border' or 'international' democracy. The prejudice dates from the era of territorially bound representative democracy,
and almost all leading scholars of democracy today defend the supposed
truth of this bias. One interesting thing about monitory democracy is
that it begins to confront the wall of prejudice with a hammer; its latticed patterns of power monitoring effectively pulverise the distinction
between 'domestic' and 'foreign', the 'local' and the 'global'. Like other
types of institutions, including business and universities, democracy
too is caught up in a process of 'glocalisation'. This is another way of
saying that its monitory mechanisms are dynamically inter-related, to
the point where these mechanisms function simultaneously, as both
part and whole of the overall system. In the system of monitory democracy, to put things a bit abstractly, parts and wholes in an absolute sense
do not exist. Its units are better described as sub-wholes – 'holons' is the
term famously coined by the Hungarian polymath Arthur Koestler –
that function simultaneously as self-regarding and self-asserting entities
that push and pull each other in a multi-lateral system in which all
entities play a part.

The example of summits, a remarkable mid-twentieth-century invention, helps bring this language down to earth. A strange fact is that
summits began as exercises in big power politics, as informal ad hoc
meetings of heads of state or leaders of government, or foreign ministers – the kind of meetings that first took place during the fragile Soviet/
American/British alliance against Hitler. From the end of World War
Two until the time of the famous Vienna Summit meeting between
Kennedy and Khruschev (in June 1961), there were well over a hundred
such summits, each using broadly similar methods. The meetings were
preoccupied with the dynamics of the Cold War, and so had both a global reach and a strong bipolarity about them. Whether used as tools of
amity or enmity, the early summits were also marked by a strong measure of predictability. The rule was that no statesman was willing to risk
the certainty of humiliation. Hence the great attention paid to drama-
turgy. The effect – like the old rituals of European monarchy – was to
reinforce the sense among audiences that these were top-down affairs,
instances of how the world was run by just a handful of men.

During the last decades of the twentieth century, the wholly surprising thing about summits was their dramatic transformation into sites
where the power of representatives was publicly contested. Summits
morphed into monitory mechanisms. The altered meaning and function of summits was evident at the series of high-level meetings between
Reagan and Gorbachev, including the 1986 Reykjavik gathering, where
without prior consultation with NATO and other bodies the aboli-
tion of ballistic missiles and strategic nuclear weapons – including all

nuclear weapons – was proposed. From thereon, summits began to be used by leaders to 'bounce' their bureaucracies into policy shifts, in a wide variety of contexts. That had the knock-on effect of politicising government, making it clear to wider audiences, both inside and outside government, that different political options existed.

The growth of summitry cloaked in secrecy and pageantry backfired. Summits began to attract the attention of thousands of journalists eager to report stories and images of exclusive and powerful clubs. Beginning with the Bonn G7 Summit in May 1985 (which attracted 30,000 demonstrators demanding global justice), its annual meetings provided an opportunity for civil society organisations and protesters to press their concerns related to matters as diverse as international trade and terrorism to energy development and cross-border crime – in effect, by turning rulers into culpable representatives. Similar trends were visible from the time of the 1988 IMF and World Bank meetings in Berlin, which attracted up to 80,000 well-briefed and well-organised protesters; and in the subsequent string of UN-sponsored summits that sparked off preparatory meetings, teach-ins and planned mobilisations that descended on the Children's Summit (1990), the Earth Summit (1992), the Conference on Human Rights (1993) and the Conference on Women (1995). Perhaps the most spectacular attempt so far to transform top-down governmental summits into new channels of bottom-up representation of the interests of civil society was the network (in July 2005) of Live 8 'global awareness' concerts calling upon political leaders to 'Make Poverty History'.

Political efficacy

It is sometimes said that the business of power scrutiny changes very little, that states and corporations are still the 'real' centres of power in deciding who gets what, when and how in this world. Empirical evidence that this is not necessarily so is suggested by the fact that all of the big public issues that have erupted around the world since 1945, including civil rights for women and minorities, American military intervention in Vietnam and Iraq, nuclear weapons, poverty reduction and global warming, have been generated not by political parties, elections, legislatures and governments, but principally by power-monitoring networks that run parallel to – and are often positioned against – the orthodox mechanisms of party-based representation.

The powerful civil rights movement that sprang up during the 1950s in the United States was among the pacesetters. Its inventive tactics – bus boycotts, improvement associations, coordinating committees, sit-ins, kneel-ins, 'jail-no-bail' pledges, freedom rides, citizenship schools, freedom singing, voter registration drives, mock elections – were proof positive that monitory bodies could have effects upon existing power relations by forcing many people to sense their contingency, often through bitter battles, sometimes resulting in surprising victories for those bent on humbling the powerful. The tactics eventually produced two historic pieces of legislation. The Civil Rights Act, signed by President Johnson on 2 July 1964, barred racial discrimination in public accommodations, education and employment. The Voting Rights Act, signed by Johnson on 6 August 1965, abolished literacy tests, poll taxes and other restrictions on voting, as well as authorised federal government intervention in states and individual voting districts that continued to use such tests to discriminate against African Americans. The enactment of the double-barrelled legislation was monitory democracy in action (further details are provided in Keane 2009a: 721–728). It proved that the powerless had power to change things, and that change had to begin in the home, the workplace and in other public fields of everyday life, before spreading across the whole of the political and social landscape of the American democracy.

Why monitory democracy?

Now that we have tackled some common misconceptions about the contours and main dynamics of monitory democracy, let us pause finally to ask one short question: how can its unplanned birth and subsequent growth be explained?

The motives behind the various power-scrutinising inventions described above are complicated; as in earlier phases of the history of democracy, generalisations are as difficult as they are perilous. But one thing is certain: the new type of democracy has had both its causes and causers. Monitory democracy is not a monogenic matter – a living thing hatched from a single cell. It is rather the resultant of many forces. Awareness of the dysfunctions and despotic potential of majority-rule democracy in representative form was an important early catalyst (as happened in post-1945 efforts to build human rights principles into democratic institutions). Monitory mechanisms (participatory budgeting and truth and reconciliation commissions are cases in point) usually happened only when cracks developed within ruling circles, so allowing the courage of citizens and the resolve of public-spirited leaders to do the rest. Personal ambition, monkey business, power games and the quest for more effective or cheaper government – and government eager to offload blame onto others for policy disappointments and failures – have all played their part. So too have conservative instincts, radical demands, geopolitical considerations and market pressures. Opportunities for building 'social capital' – cultivating the connections and skills among people at the local and regional levels – and the lure of winning power or revenue growth from the provision of outsourced government services have strongly motivated some organisations, especially NGOs, to push for stronger monitory institutions. Unintended consequences and plain good luck have also played their part; but no account of monitory democracy would be credible without taking into account the way power and conflict are shaped by new media institutions.

Think of their role like this: assembly-based democracy belonged to an era dominated by the spoken word, backed up by laws written on papyrus and stone, and by messages dispatched by foot, or by donkey and horse. Representative democracy sprang up in the era of print culture – the book, pamphlet and newspaper, and telegraphed and mailed messages – and fell into crisis during the advent of early mass communication media, especially radio and cinema and (in its infancy) television. By contrast, monitory democracy is tied closely to the growth of multi-media-saturated societies – societies whose structures of power are continuously 'bitten' by monitory institutions operating within a new galaxy of media defined by the ethos of communicative abundance.

Compared with the era of representative democracy, when print culture and limited spectrum audio-visual media were much more closely aligned with political parties and/or governments, the age of monitory democracy witnesses constant public scrutiny and spats about power, to the point where it seems as if no organisation or leader within the fields of government or social life is immune from political trouble. The change has been shaped by a variety of forces, including the decline of journalism proud of its commitment to fact-based 'objectivity' (an ideal born of the age of representative democracy) and the rise of adversarial and 'gotcha' styles of commercial journalism driven by ratings, sales and scandals. Technical factors, such as electronic memory, tighter channel spacing, new frequency allocation, direct satellite broadcasting, digital tuning and advanced compression techniques, have also been important. Chief among these technical factors is the advent of cable- and satellite-linked, computerised communications, which from the end of the 1960s triggered both product and process innovations in virtually every field of an increasingly commercialised media. This new galaxy of media has no historical precedent. Symbolised by one of its core components, the Internet, it is a whole new world system of overlapping and interlinked media devices that integrate texts, sounds and images and enable communication to take place through multiple user points, in chosen time, either real or delayed, within modular and ultimately global networks that are affordable and accessible to many hundreds of millions of people scattered across the globe.

All institutions in the business of scrutinising power rely heavily on these media innovations; if the new galaxy of communicative abundance suddenly imploded, monitory democracy would not last long. Monitory democracy and digital media networks behave as if they are conjoined twins. To say this is not to fall into the trap of supposing that computer-linked communications networks prefigure a brand new utopian world, a carnival of 'virtual communities' homesteading on the electronic frontier, a 'cyber-revolution' that yields equal access of all citizens to all media, anywhere and at any time. The new age of communicative abundance in fact produces various forms of media decadence: disappointments, instability and self-contradictions, for instance in the widening power gaps between communication rich and poor, who seem almost unneeded as communicators, or as consumers of media products (Keane 2009b). A majority of the world's people is too poor to make a telephone call; only a tiny minority has access to the Internet. The divide between media rich and media poor citizens blights all monitory democracies; it contradicts their basic principle that all citizens equally are entitled to communicate their opinions, and periodically to give elected and unelected representatives a rough ride.

Notwithstanding such worrying contradictions and disappointments, there are new and important things happening politically inside the swirling galaxy of communicative abundance. Especially striking is the way the realms of 'private life' and 'privacy' and wheeling and dealing of power 'in private' have been put on the defensive. Past generations would find the whole process astonishing in its global scale and democratic intensity. With the click of a camera, or the flick of a switch, the world of the private can suddenly be made public. Everything from the bedroom to the boardroom, the bureaucracy and the battlefield, seems to be up for media grabs. Thanks to stories told by professional and citizen journalists, who function as unelected representatives of publics, this is an age in which private text messages rebound publicly, to reveal the marital unfaithfulness and force the resignation of a government minister. It is an era in which Sony hand-held cameras are used by off-air reporters, known as 'embeds', to file ongoing videos and blogs featuring election candidates live, unplugged and unscripted; and this is the age in which video footage proves that soldiers in war zones raped women, terrorised children and tortured innocent civilians. In the age of communicative abundance, the private lives of elected politicians and unelected representatives (and in the case of celebrities their romances, parties, health, drug habits, quarrels and divorces) are potential talking points for millions of people. And thanks to talk shows, blogs and other media acts, there is an endless procession of 'ordinary people' talking publicly about their private fears, fantasies, hopes and expectations. Some of them are sometimes lucky enough to morph into media stars, thanks to simulated elections, in which audiences granted a 'vote' by media companies are urged to lodge their preference for the star of their choice, by acclamation, cell phone or the Internet.

Helped along by red-blooded commercial journalism that relies on styles of reporting concerned less with veracity than with 'breaking news' and blockbusting scoops, communicative abundance cuts like a knife into the power relations of government and civil society. It is easy to complain about the methods of the new journalism. It hunts in packs, its eyes on bad news, egged on by the newsroom saying that facts must never be allowed to get in the way of stories. It loves titillation, draws upon unattributed sources, fills news holes – in the era of monitory democracy news never sleeps – spins sensations, and concentrates too much on personalities, rather than time-bound contexts. The new journalism is formulaic and gets bored too quickly; and it likes to bow down to corporate power and government press briefings. But these accusations are only half the story. For in spite of everything, red-blooded journalism, now reinforced by the rapid growth of various forms of blogging and citizen journalism, helps keep alive the old utopias of shedding light on power, of 'freedom of information', 'government in the sunshine' and greater 'transparency' in the making of decisions. Given that unchecked power still weighs down hard on the heads of citizens, it is not surprising, thanks to the new journalism and the new monitory inventions, that public objections to wrongdoing and corruption are commonplace in the era of monitory democracy. There seems to be no end of scandals; and there are even times when scandals, like earthquakes, rumble beneath the feet of whole governments.

In the age of monitory democracy, some scandals become legendary, like the public uproar caused by the inadvertent discovery of evidence of secret burglaries of the Democratic Party National Committee headquarters in the Watergate Hotel in Washington DC, and the subsequent snowballing of events that became the Watergate affair, that resulted in threats of impeachment and the eventual resignation (in August 1974) of President Nixon in the United States. On the other side of the Atlantic, major scandals have included the nation-wide investigation by Italian police and judges of the extensive system of political corruption dubbed 'bribesville' (*Tangentopoli*) – an investigation that fuelled the *mani pulite*

(Italian for 'clean hands') campaign that led to the disappearance of many political parties and the suicide of some politicians and industry leaders after their crimes were exposed. There was, as well, the resignation of the French foreign minister and the admission by the French president on television that agents of the French secret service (DGSE) were responsible for the murder, in July 1985, of a Greenpeace activist and the bombing of their support vessel, the Rainbow Warrior, a boat that had been due to lead a flotilla of yachts to protest against French nuclear testing at Mururoa Atoll in the Pacific Ocean. And not to be forgotten were the whopping lies about the existence of 'weapons of mass destruction' spun by the defenders of the disastrous military invasion of Iraq in the early years of the twenty-first century.

Viral politics

These and other '-gate' scandals remind us of a perennial problem facing monitory democracy: there is no shortage of organised efforts by the powerful to manipulate people beneath them; and, hence, the political dirty business of dragging power from the shadows and uploading it, or flinging it into the blazing halogen of publicity, remains fundamentally important. Nobody should be kidded into thinking that the world of monitory democracy, with its many power-scrutinising institutions, is a level playing field – a paradise of equality of opportunity among all its citizens and their elected and unelected representatives. The combination of monitory democracy and communicative abundance nevertheless produces permanent flux, an unending restlessness driven by complex combinations of different interacting players and institutions, permanently pushing and pulling, heaving and straining, sometimes working together, at other times in opposition to one another. Elected and unelected representatives routinely strive to define and to determine who gets what, when and how; but the represented, taking advantage of various power-scrutinising devices, keep tabs on their representatives – sometimes with surprising success. The dynamics of monitory democracy are thus not describable using the simple spatial metaphors inherited from the age of representative democracy. Talk of the 'sovereignty' of parliament, or of 'local' versus 'central' government, or of tussles between 'pressure groups', political parties and governments, is just too simple. In terms of political geometry, the system of monitory democracy is something other and different: a complex web of differently sized and more or less interdependent monitory bodies that have the effect, thanks to communicative abundance, of continuously stirring up questions about who gets what, when and how, as well as holding publicly responsible those who exercise power, wherever they are situated. Monitory democracies are richly conflicted. Politics does not wither away.

There is something utterly novel about the whole trend. From its origins in the ancient assemblies of Syria-Mesopotamia, democracy has always cut through habit and prejudice and hierarchies of power (Keane 2009a). It has stirred up the sense that people can shape and reshape their lives as equals, and not surprisingly it has often brought commotion into the world. In the era of monitory democracy, the constant public scrutiny of power by hosts of differently sized monitory bodies with footprints large and small makes it the most energetic, most dynamic form of democracy ever. It even contains bodies (like the Democratic Audit network and Transparency International) that specialise in providing public assessments of the quality of existing power-scrutinising mechanisms and the degree to which they fairly represent citizens' interests. Other bodies specialise in directing questions at governments on a wide range of matters, extending from their human rights records, their energy production plans to the quality of the drinking water of their cities. Private companies are grilled about their services and products, their investment plans, how they treat their employees, and the size of their impact upon the biosphere. Various watchdogs and guide dogs and barking dogs are constantly on the job, pressing for greater public accountability of those who exercise power. The powerful consequently come to feel the constant pinch of the powerless.

When they do their job well, monitory mechanisms have many positive effects, ranging from greater openness and justice within markets and blowing the whistle on foolish government decisions to the general enrichment of public deliberation and the empowerment of citizens, either through meaningful schemes of participation and election, or by enabling them to identify publicly with their favourite unelected representatives, who are variously respected or revered because of their willingness to communicate with publics on the basis of their expertise, spirituality, lifetime achievements, their courage in the face of suffering and other qualities. Power monitoring by these elected and unelected representatives can be ineffective, or counterproductive, of course. Campaigns misfire or are poorly targeted; power wielders cleverly find loopholes and ways of rebutting or simply ignoring their opponents. There are times when large numbers of citizens find the monitory strategies of individuals, organisations and networks too timid, or confused, or simply irrelevant to their lives as consumers, workers, parents, community residents and younger and older citizens. And there are moments of grave danger – the post-2007 global recession is an example – when monitory mechanisms prove too weak or inept to prevent epidemics of bad decisions, blind folly and panic among elites.

Despite such setbacks, the political dynamics and overall 'feel' of monitory democracies are very different from the era of representative democracy. Politics in the age of monitory democracy has a definite 'viral' quality about it. The power controversies stirred up by monitory mechanisms follow unexpected paths and reach surprising destinations. Groups using mobile phones, bulletin boards, news groups, wikis and blogs sometimes manage, against considerable odds, to embarrass publicly politicians, parties and parliaments, or even whole governments. Power-monitoring bodies like Human Rights Watch or Amnesty International regularly do the same, usually with help from networks of supporters. Think for a moment about any current public controversy that attracts widespread attention: news about its contours and commentaries and disputes about its significance are typically relayed by many power-monitoring organisations, large, medium and small, in multiple locations. In the world of monitory democracy, that kind of latticed – viral, networked – pattern is typical, not exceptional. It has profound implications for the state-framed institutions of the old representative democracy, which find themselves more and more enmeshed in 'sticky' webs of power-scrutinising institutions that often hit their target, sometimes from long distances, often by means of boomerang effects.

In the age of monitory democracy, whenever things go well for the independent public monitors, bossy power can no longer hide comfortably behind private masks; power relations everywhere are subjected to organised efforts by some, with the help of media, to tell others – publics of various sizes – about matters that previously had been hidden away, 'in private'. This denaturing of power is usually a messy business, and it often comes wrapped in hype, certainly. Some people also complain about its effects, like 'information overload' and excessive 'distrust and suspicion', but from the point of view of monitory democracy communicative abundance on balance has positive consequences. In spite of all its hype and spin, the new media galaxy nudges and broadens people's horizons. It tutors their sense of pluralism and prods them into taking greater responsibility for how, when and why they communicate. The days when people had no choice but to listen to limited spectrum radio or watch television programmes alone, or with their families – the days of representative democracy and broadcasting and mass entertainment – are over. So, too, are the days when millions of people, huddled together as masses in the shadows of totalitarian power, found the skilfully orchestrated radio and film performances of demagogues fascinating, and reassuring.

Message-saturated democracies, by contrast, encourage people's suspicions of unaccountable power. All of the king's horses and all the king's men are unlikely to reverse the trend. Within the world of monitory democracies, growing numbers of people are coming to recognise that publicly unaccountable power often breeds hubris, lies, corruption, inefficient and ineffective decisions (Flyvbjerg *et al.* 2003). They are learning that they must therefore keep an eye on power and its representatives, that they must make judgements and choose their own courses of action. Citizens are thus tempted to think for themselves; to see the same world in different ways, from different angles; and to sharpen their overall sense that prevailing power relationships are not 'natural', but contingent. Communicative abundance and monitory institutions combine to promote something of a 'Gestalt switch' in the popular perception of power. The metaphysical idea of an objective, out-there-at-a-distance 'reality' is weakened; so too is the presumption that stubborn 'factual truth' is superior to power. The fabled distinction between what people can see with their eyes and what they are told about the emperor's new clothes breaks down. 'Reality', including the 'reality' of the powerful, comes to be understood as always 'produced reality', a matter of interpretation – and the power to force particular interpretations of the world down others' throats.

There is admittedly nothing automatic or magical about any of these positive effects. In the era of monitory democracy, communication is constantly the subject of dissembling, negotiation, compromise and power conflicts, in a phrase, a matter of politics. Communicative abundance for that reason does not somehow automatically ensure the triumph of either the spirit or institutions of monitory democracy. Message-saturated societies can and do have effects that are harmful for democracy. In some quarters, for instance, media saturation triggers citizens' inattention to events. While they are expected as good citizens to keep their eyes on public affairs, to take an interest in the world beyond their immediate household and neighbourhood, more than a few people find it ever harder to pay attention to the media's vast outpourings. Profusion breeds confusion. There are times, for instance when voters are so pelted with a hail of election advertisements on prime-time television that they react frostily. Disaffected, they get up from their sofas, leave their living rooms, change channels, or mute, concluding with a heavy sigh that the less you know, the better off you are. It is only a few steps from there to something more worrying: the unwitting spread of a culture of unthinking indifference. Monitory democracy certainly feeds upon communicative abundance, but one of its more perverse effects is to encourage individuals to escape the great complexity of the world by sticking their heads into the sands of wilful ignorance, or to float cynically upon the swirling tides and waves and eddies of fashion – to change their minds, to speak and act flippantly, to embrace or even celebrate opposites, to bid farewell to veracity, to slip into the arms of what some carefully call 'bullshit' (Frankfurt 2005).

Foolish illusions, cynicism and disaffection are among the biggest temptations facing citizens and their elected and unelected representatives. Whether or not monitory democracy will survive their deadly effects is for the future to tell us.

REFERENCES

Dunn, J. (2010) 'Democracy and its discontents', *The National Interest* 106 (March–April).

Eco, U. (1999) *Kant and the platypus: Essays on language and cognition.* London: Secker and Warburg.

Flyvbjerg, B., N. Bruzelius and W. Rothengatter (2003) *Megaprojects and risk: An anatomy of ambition.* Cambridge and New York: Cambridge University Press.

Frankfurt, H. G. (2005) *On bullshit.* Princeton and Oxford: Princeton University Press.

Fung, A. and E. O. Wright (2003) 'Thinking about empowered participatory governance', in A. Fung and E. O. Wright, *Deepening democracy: Institutional innovations in empowered participatory governance.* London and New York: Verso, pp. 3–42.

Hayek, F. von (1979) *Law, legislation and liberty: The political order of a free people.* London and Henley: Routledge.

Keane, J. (2009a) *The life and death of democracy.* London: Simon & Schuster.
(2009b) *Media decadence and democracy.* Senate Occasional Lecture. Canberra: Parliament of Australia.

Rosanvallon, P. (2008) *Counter-democracy: Politics in an age of distrust.* Cambridge and New York: Cambridge University Press.

10   Representing nature

Robyn Eckersley

Introduction

If I want to speak on behalf of orange-bellied parrots whose habitat
will be destroyed by a proposed development, in what sense can I act
as their political representative? I have no basis upon which to claim
I am their delegate because I have no mandate or authorisation from
parrots to speak on their behalf and I cannot justify my arguments or
actions to them. I have no expertise in ornithology and I do not (I hope)
resemble a parrot or share or understand a parrot's view of the world to
claim authority to speak on the basis of a common parrot identity. Nor
can I claim to be their trustee in the Burkean sense, because Burke dis-
ingenuously supposed that the trustee's authority to represent his/her
constituency was based upon common interests and sympathies that
were reciprocal, not one-way. All I can claim is that I care about the
fate of the parrots.

This chapter seeks to explore the idea of representing (non-human)
nature as a democratic task that involves persuading others to care
about not just parrots but non-human species in general in order to
support measures for their protection. Michael Saward has called this
discursive task 'representative claim making', but I shall call it 'nature
advocacy' (Saward 2006). Like the legal advocate, the nature advocate seeks to *speak for* someone or something by putting their case in
the best possible light. However, the nature advocate (unlike the legal
advocate) has an emotional investment in the subject matter, holds no
formal licence to act as an advocate, is not paid by his/her client and
has no legal tradition or specialised courts in which to operate. Nature
advocacy is a creative task that involves making present, introducing
or otherwise bringing into public view particular ecological concerns,
values, beings, entities and interests that the advocate believes have
been unfairly marginalised, 'misrecognised' or 'misrepresented' in political discourse and practice. Conventional forms of political representation rest on a special relationship between the representative and his/

her constituency, based on some kind of authorisation, accountability, expertise, or resemblance/common identity that confers legitimacy on the representative to speak or act in the name of the represented. However, the nature advocates I have in mind are self-appointed guardians or trustees of nature who want the community at large to share in the duty of care they feel towards their ward because that duty is most effectively discharged collectively, rather than individually.

Non-human species, along with future generations and non-citizens (persons living outside the polity), comprise a neglected constituency in liberal democratic states. All members of this constituency can be seriously affected by decisions made within the polity yet they have no formal representation in the making of those decisions. Nor are there any formal or direct mechanisms of accountability that require the political representatives of existing voters within a particular democratic polity to justify their decisions to, or to answer questions posed by, representatives of this constituency. Unlike some members of neglected constituencies within the polity (such as marginal social groups or minorities), members of the neglected environmental constituency *cannot* be physically present to make representations or call decision makers to account, because they cannot speak, do not yet exist or otherwise have no status as citizens.

Indeed, the transboundary character of many ecological problems, and the long lead-times taken for certain problems to become manifest, point to serious representation deficits in liberal democratic states. Political representatives in liberal democracies formally represent only the existing, voting citizens of territorially bounded nation states. This provides an incentive for representatives in the legislature and executive to avoid imposing ecological costs on producers and consumers within the polity by 'externalising' ecological costs (in time and space) in the same way that capitalist firms do. This is exacerbated by the fact that political parties and political leaders within liberal democracies typically formulate policies and make decisions within the temporal frame of electoral cycles, rather than long-range ecological horizons. Moreover, the specialised knowledge that is required to understand many ecological problems serves to disenfranchise the lay public (and sometimes elected political representatives themselves) from informed political debate about the wider consequences of decisions. The upshot of these representation deficits is a profound disconnect between those who make decisions that generate ecological risks (firms, consumers), those who have expert knowledge of such risks (scientists), the ecological victims who suffer (typically the least represented or those who are non-represented: marginalised social groups within the polity, future generations, non-citizens, and non-human species) and those who must take political responsibility for such risks (political representatives).

To be sure, the spectacular rise of environmental non-government organisations (NGOs) and the emergence of green parties in recent decades has helped to counteract this representational deficit by facilitating more nature advocacy in the public sphere, including in parliaments. However, these developments have yet to produce any kind of transformation of liberal democratic institutions in order to address this representational deficit. The problem for nature advocates is that any effort to renovate the institutions of representative, liberal democracy to enable more systematic representation of the neglected environmental constituency presupposes *recognition* of that constituency within the polity. Yet the case for recognition raises a host of difficult moral, political and epistemological challenges which vary for non-human species, future generations and non-compatriots. In this chapter I take on the particularly challenging task of exploring and arguing the case for the moral recognition of 'nature'. (Although humans are, of course, part of nature I use the term here as shorthand for non-human nature or non-human species.) My line of argument is as follows: if our political representatives should form a microcosm of our community, and if our understanding of the moral community is enlarged to include the ecological community, then the interests of non-human nature should be registered in a more formal way in our democratic institutional framework. However, 'greening democracy' is not as straightforward as, say, 'engendering democracy' along the lines discussed by Drude Dahlerup in Chapter 6 of this volume. Women have won the battle for recognition and they are now working to extend their political representation in the legislature. Nature advocates have yet to win the battle for the moral recognition of nature and, even if they had won, it is not obvious how this recognition should be institutionalised. I shall therefore focus most of the discussion on the necessary first step: the battle for recognition. This is still a matter of representative claim making since it requires making representations about nature and, by implication, human nature. The former will entail an exploration of how we might represent nature in ways that do not reduce it to a mere object, instrument or background stage upon which the human drama unfolds. The latter will entail exploring how we might provide an account of our human identity and role in the larger scheme of things that makes room for non-human flourishing. Representing nature therefore involves the making of both ethical and ontological claims. Assuming these representative claims are accepted (a big assumption), I shall then briefly explore the kinds of institutional innovations that might serve to represent, 'or make present', the particular interests, needs and requirements of non-human species and ecosystems in political decision making.

The challenge of nature advocacy

Nature advocacy has a long and varied history but I shall single out and take stock of the troubled evolution of certain discourses in western environmental philosophy that seek to defend non-human nature for its own sake, rather than only for its instrumental or aesthetic value. Variously referred to as ecocentric or biocentric, these discourses have mounted a critique of anthropocentrism or 'human chauvinism', which is the idea that humans are the only morally worthy beings on the planet, and the rest of nature is valuable only insofar as it is instrumentally valuable to humans but otherwise dispensable. Of course, nature advocates recognise that protecting the environment (including the climate) for the sake of humans will also bring indirect benefits for non-human species and this is a necessary and important part of the advocate's case. However, nature advocacy that is only concerned to protect nature for the sake of human well-being may not be enough to prevent the further extinction of non-human species or ensure the maintenance of biological diversity. The maintenance of viable and diverse populations and gene pools of non-human species is best achieved *in situ* rather than *ex situ*, by setting aside large tracts of relatively wild habitat rather than setting up zoos or gene banks. Without the recognition of non-human species for their own sake, and without seeing ourselves as part of, and sharing, a larger biotic community, there is no basis on which to redirect human development and need satisfaction in ways that make room for such habitat protection.

Nature advocacy is ultimately about winning hearts and minds through persuasion, but this is no easy matter in the face of unmet human need, our limited understanding of non-human species and the incommensurability of different cultural representations of nature. In exploring the problems and prospects of nature advocacy, I hope to weave my way towards an ideal of ecological democracy that is capable of embracing these challenges in ways that move beyond the zero-sum stalemate of 'people versus nature'.

Notwithstanding nearly three decades of development, ecocentric nature advocacy remains controversial (Eckersley 2004b). While it has attracted followers in the environment movement, it has failed to spread in popular culture or become part of the general *zeitgeist*. It has also drawn many criticisms within and beyond environmentalist circles. Some critics have accused ecocentric advocates of being misanthropic or even fascist while others have suggested that it is necessary to transcend what now seem fraught and old-fashioned distinctions between intrinsic and instrumental value, anthropocentrism and ecocentrism, culture and nature (for example, Norton 1991). Ecofeminists, environmental justice advocates, postcolonialists and post-structuralists have drawn attention to the role of class, gender, power and language in the social construction of nature and have deconstructed the concept of wilderness as an expression of western, patriarchal, neo-romantic and/or middle-class longings (Cronon 1996).

Even the more sympathetic social constructivists have taken issue with the idea of intrinsic value as an objective property of non-human life forms and have accused ecocentric advocates of naïve realism, pointing out that nobody can speak for 'nature in itself' because we have no way of knowing what that is. Rather, we can only speak about the nature we humans have socially constructed (Vogel 1995). This is true, of course, but only trivially so, since our concern is with *how* we construct or represent nature, not *that* we construct it. I also use the pronoun 'we' advisedly, since my concern is to defend and build neither a God-like objectivist nor an individual subjectivist construction of nature but rather an inter-subjective understanding of selves-in-communities that respects both human and biotic communities.

The problem with purely individual subjectivist or hyper-constructivist accounts is that they tend to reduce non-human species to a *tabula rasa* or mere passive recipients of human valuation, and thus fail to acknowledge non-human forms of agency (Norton 2002). A constructivist perspective need not deny the existence of nature as an extra-discursive reality; all it needs to claim is that we do not have any *shared* access to this reality other than through language. Moreover, our inter-subjective understandings about nature are provisional, and revisable, as scientific, cultural and moral understandings shift. While nature advocates are able to draw on all of these understandings, moral persuasion works best through the use of analogies and metaphor. Those philosophers who have taken 'the linguistic turn' have also emphasised the role of metaphor in moral progress, and the rhetorical nature of social reality (Rorty 1991). Efforts to persuade others typically require beginning from some common or familiar understanding and then moving, by analogy, to the less common and less familiar.

This focus on the social construction of nature through representative claim making also provides the opportunity to respond to the more troubling charge that is sometimes leveled against ecocentrism: that it is monistic or anti-pluralist and therefore anti-democratic (Norton 2002; Minteer and Pepperman Taylor 2002; Bowersox 2002). If we understand representative claim making on behalf of nature as ultimately an exercise in persuasion, concerned with exposing practices of exclusion and defending practices of inclusion, then it may be understood as an effort to extend or radicalise democracy rather than curtail it. This quintessential democratic task may be linked (structurally and historically) with the social and environmental justice movements. At the same time, I hope in this chapter to sensitise nature advocates to both the possibilities and limitations of some of the arguments that have thus far been deployed. As a democratic task, representing nature is necessarily a contingent exercise that must always remain open to, and reflect upon, ongoing criticism.

In modern times, it generally goes without saying that all humans already belong to Kant's 'kingdom of ends', that we all possess 'inherent dignity' and the right to self-determination and political representation. This was the basis upon which the political franchise was extended from propertied men, to working-class men and then to women, all of whom are recognised as entitled to vote for their political representatives or stand for office as political representatives. The quest for those who reject anthropocentrism has been to find ways of opening the moral door to non-human species *by analogy with the human case* so that they may also be represented 'in their own right', as it were. I shall argue that herein lies a conundrum: that the attempt to use the human case as a reference point invariably leads to invidious comparisons of the human and the non-human in ways that demean non-humans (and sometimes humans as well). However, I shall also argue that ultimately this is a problem that cannot be entirely avoided if we humans are to communicate with each other in ways that seek to extend well-established moral norms to new situations and thus stretch conventional moral horizons. I also suggest a less problematic basis for navigating these issues than traditional liberal moral or political philosophy; a basis which I call critical political ecology. Although both approaches are traceable to the Enlightenment quest for autonomy, liberalism has become complacent, while critical political ecology has continued to question the protocols of political representation and the boundaries of the moral and political community in space and time.

Back to the beginning[1]

Many of the early philosophical discourses concerned to 'liberate' all or some parts of non-human nature took the following form. While

---

[1] The next three sections incorporate revised sections from Eckersley (2004b).

recognising that non-human species are important resources for sustaining human livelihoods, the idea that non-human species should be considered valuable *only* as resources was rejected as one-dimensional, degrading of both human and non-human nature, and likely to sanction the accelerated extinction rates for redundant, 'useless', aesthetically unappealing, dangerous or inconvenient species. If a species had no use or appeal to humankind, or if technological substitutes could be found for the services they provided, then it would be 'no great mischief' if that species were to vanish from the earth. Resources, after all, are mere 'indices of utility to industrial society' (Evernden 1984: 10).

For all its problems, the intuitive appeal of the notion of intrinsic value in non-human species was one way of saying that non-human species, like human species, matter – that they are worthy, they have their own forms of agency, and they are valuable above and beyond their use to humans. Enlisting the notion of intrinsic value (or 'inherent value') was also a means by which to expose and challenge 'the arrogance of humanism' (Ehrenfeld 1981) or human chauvinism – the idea that humans are the crown of creation, the culmination of evolution, the only morally considerable beings entitled to a permanent place in the sun, as if the sole purpose of the rest of nature was merely to serve humanity.

For some non-anthropocentric theorists, if the welfare of non-human species was to be taken seriously and the destruction of their habitat considered a grave matter that should be non-negotiable (or at least much less negotiable than it currently is), then it also seemed necessary to defend an objectivist theory of intrinsic value that transcended the preferences and aesthetic tastes of humans (Regan 1981). After all, if human rights claims – based on the inherent dignity of the person – could trump competing arguments based on social utility, then so should the rights of non-human species. This was merely a case of rounding out the (liberal) rights revolution.

While the logic of the early argumentative strategy seemed straightforward enough, the task of articulating a theory of intrinsic value and defending an alternative biocentric or ecocentric philosophy has been anything but straightforward. Indeed, J. Baird Callicott (1985: 257) described this as the 'central and most recalcitrant problem for environmental ethics'. For example, environmental philosophers were divided over what the relevant properties of intrinsic value should be – was it sentience, aliveness, 'the subject of a life', autopoiesis? Was it individual organisms or ecological aggregations such as gene pools, populations or ecosystems? If environmental ethics was to have policy relevance, these matters had to be resolved in a practical, parsimonious and persuasive way. And the choice of relevant properties was not insignificant: it would determine how much of non-human nature would be included in the circle of moral and legal protection, and what character that protection would take.

Many of the early efforts to extend moral recognition to non-human species attempted to build up a larger, transhuman moral order through the extension of widely accepted, basic principles that underpin distinctly human emancipatory movements, most notably Kantian and utilitarian moral philosophy. In this sense, non-anthropocentric environmental ethics remained profoundly indebted to anthropocentric ethics, as Anthony Weston (1996: 139) has astutely observed. For Weston, 'the project of going beyond anthropocentrism still looks wild, incautious, intellectually overexcited' (Weston 1996: 143). He attributes this to the fact that this radical project is still in its 'originatory phase' – a phase of uncertainty and experimentation, with no secure foothold in dominant cultural understandings in the west. Indeed, Weston concedes that a great deal of exploration and metaphor is required in the early stages of the development of new values (Weston 1996: 147). Yet he also argues, perceptively, that the success of these explorations resides to a large extent 'in the way they open up the possibility of new connections, not in the way they settle or "close" any questions' (Weston 1996: 150). Weston's observations provide a good entry point for exploring both the discursive possibilities and problems associated with drawing analogies between the way we represent humans and non-humans.

Some of the most influential of the early efforts to extend moral considerability to non-human species involved the radical extension of *individualist* liberal moral philosophy to the environment. This form of moral extensionism found its classical expression in Peter Singer's *Animal Liberation* (1975) and Christopher Stone's legal essay 'Should Trees Have Standing?' (1974). It has since become part of the standard repertoire of those wishing to impugn human chauvinism. The argument runs as follows. An animal or 'natural entity' need not be a fully competent moral *agent* (equipped with Kantian powers of moral reasoning) in order to be recognised as a worthy moral *subject*, that is, as a being that is entitled to receive moral consideration. This is because, in the human domain, there are plenty of examples of individuals who do not possess any or full moral agency but who nonetheless deserve our respect and attentive care (infants, intellectually handicapped persons, the senile). We recognise these persons as morally considerable because they are ends-in-themselves and/or because they are beings capable of suffering or otherwise being harmed, even though they cannot necessarily return recognition in the way that fully competent moral agents can. It follows, once we accept that morally incompetent humans are nonetheless morally considerable, that there is no good reason for not accepting non-human others as morally considerable on the grounds that they too are ends-in-themselves or otherwise capable of suffering or being harmed. According to this line of argument, our failure to extend moral considerability to non-human species is symptomatic of speciesism or human chauvinism – an unwarranted prejudice against non-human others *just because they are not human.*

Now this strategy of progressive moral extensionism has been employed to defend quite different moral frameworks. Singer has used it to argue that not just humans but all *sentient* creatures (i.e., those with the capacity to suffer) ought to be treated as morally considerable, in the sense of having their particular 'interests' considered in the policy process. Whereas Singer's argument draws upon *moral* analogies and anomalies, Stone's argument rests upon *legal* analogies and anomalies. According to Stone, given that the Anglo-American legal system grants various sorts of rights to non-human entities (churches, corporations, ships, municipalities), there is no good reason for not extending legal rights to natural entities as well, such as mountains and rivers, to be enforced by human legal guardians when they can be shown to be harmed. While Stone's discussion mainly focuses on legal devices for protecting wild nature, an incipient ecocentric moral argument is nonetheless discernible in his discussion. For Stone, then, the creative and rhetorical possibilities in the rights discourse are far from exhausted.

Second thoughts

John Rodman was the first to warn of the dangers associated with the attempt to build up a larger, transhuman moral order through the extension of basic moral principles that underpin distinctly human emancipatory movements. In his lengthy review of Singer's and Stone's work he singled out for attention this method of argument from human analogy and anomaly (Rodman 1977: 87). Now the point of Rodman's critique was to show that, while Stone's and Singer's argumentative strategy is appealing, it unwittingly conveys a double message. On the one hand, it invites us to travel beyond the familiar by recognising the moral status of some or all members of the non-human world – essentially because there is no good reason not to, and to avoid inconsistency in our moral reasoning and behaviour. On the other hand, Rodman argues that this same process of morally elevating non-human others by analogy with *anomalous* human cases is degrading and patronising since it relegates non-human others 'to the status of inferior human beings, species anomalies ... moral half-breeds having rights without obligations' (Rodman 1977: 94). In the case of Singer's argument for animal liberation, Rodman suggests that what we have is 'not a revolution in ethics but something analogous to the Reform Bill of 1832, when the British aristocracy extended selected rights to the upper middle classes' (1977: 91). While Rodman accepts that we should not ignore suffering, he insists that it ought not to be the pivotal criteria in framing our moral relations with non-human (or indeed human) others. It is, after all, conceivable that humans may, through selective breeding and genetic engineering, produce domesticated animals that are no longer capable of suffering, thereby robbing animal liberationists of their grounds of objection to factory farming, vivisection and other cruel practices. Here I agree with Rodman that the real force of Singer's critique of factory farming stems not merely from the suffering it causes, but from an objection to our treatment of living organisms as machines, because, as he puts it, 'we react indignantly to the spectacle of external mechanical conditions being imposed upon natural entities that have their own internal structures, needs, and potentialities' (Rodman 1977: 100). For Rodman, what is missing from these early attempts to argue for the moral considerability of non-humans is any effort to regard such beings as 'having their own existence, their own character and potentialities, their own forms of excellence, their own integrity, their own grandeur' (1977: 94).

Rodman is careful to enlist a vocabulary that is not so obviously modeled on the human case, but can nonetheless encompass humans. Thus, humans, birds, bees, trees and micro-organisms all still have something in common, but these commonalities are formulated at a highly abstract level that tries to avoid reasoning *from* the human case by finding points of connection across all living beings. Yet to suggest that all beings have their own 'character', 'needs' and 'potentiality' can still be seen as betraying an underlying (liberal?) commitment to autonomy.

Nonetheless, Rodman's early critique has been echoed with increasing sophistication by a growing line of critical political ecologists who are sympathetic with the ecocentric project but sensitive to the problem of invidious comparison. Writing ten years later, for example, Neil Evernden argued that it is a fatal flaw for environmentalists to try to squeeze some of their moral constituency into the human prototype, reckoning that saving some is better than saving none (Evernden 1984: 10). This applies with special force to the Great Ape Project, which advocates the inclusion of chimpanzees, bonobos, gorillas and orang-utans in the human 'community of equals'.[2] Identifying only

---

[2] See *Declaration of Great Apes* at www.greatapeproject.org/declaration.php (retrieved 16 July 2008).

with those non-human species (such as apes) who are like us may serve to condemn those non-human species which are nothing like us.

Given that there are limits in the human capacity for *sympathetic* identification with non-human species that bear no resemblance to ourselves, we need to question whether this is an adequate basis upon which to ground moral recognition for non-human others. Indeed, the whole point of the contemporary debate about respecting difference (whether cultural or biological) is that 'the other' does not have to be 'like us' before we accord it any recognition and respect. If, as Todorov asks in exploring the relationship between self and other, loving the other means projecting ourselves or our own ideals onto the other, then does the other really need our love? (Todorov 1984: 168). Indigenous peoples certainly did not need the 'love' of Christian missionaries. Bears and lions do not need the love of circus audiences and many wild creatures could probably do without the love of ecotourists.

Val Plumwood (1993: 143) has shown how we must remain sensitive to the many ways in which the dualisms of self/other and human/non-human 'create a web of incorporations and inclusions'. Webs of inclusion and exclusion typically operate by the more powerful group excluding those who lack something that is possessed and deemed by the more powerful group to be the measure of worth (such as reason, civilisation, moral agency or language). According to Plumwood, this 'master consciousness' recognises the other 'only to the extent that it is assimilated to the self, or incorporated into the self and its system of desires and needs: only as colonised by the self. The master consciousness cannot tolerate unassimilated otherness' (Plumwood 1993: 52). Plumwood's notion of 'unassimilated otherness' attempts to break more decisively with any human analogies. Nonetheless, her argument is still indebted to, and builds upon, post-liberal emancipatory thought – most notably ecofeminism and postcolonialism.

One of the most difficult problems with any project of 'moral extensionism' is that there are numerous and obvious points at which the analogy with humans, with human autonomy and with human emancipatory struggles breaks down. For example, non-human species are not, so far as we know, rational moral agents capable of citizenship. They cannot return moral recognition, at least not in the way that humans can return recognition. They cannot organise or mobilise politically and, with the possible exception of certain mammals, they cannot communicate with us with the degree of precision necessary to enable humans to understand and formulate their needs, interests and strivings with any confidence and certainty.

Despite these obvious differences, it is extremely difficult and prob- ably impossible to avoid all resort to human reference points and human analogies if *human* advocates for the concerted protection of biological diversity are to communicate with, and enlist the understanding and support of, other *humans*. Indeed, it is precisely the communicative power of analogies that explains why many of the pioneering critics of human speciesism and anthropocentrism (such as Singer, Regan and the Routleys) began with the human case, employing (after Rodman) the 'progressive extension model of ethics' (Rodman 1977: 97). The point, after all, is to *persuade* other humans to reinterpret how we should collectively regard the rest of nature. One way of understanding the troubled history of this debate, then, is as a history of experiments with different vocabularies and analogies that are intended to *open up* new ways of thinking about, imagining, inhabiting and interacting with the rest of nature.

I believe these experiments ought to continue, especially given the significant wave of extinctions that are predicted to flow from climate change. And at the current juncture I would suggest that critical political ecology – which encompasses ecofeminist and postcolonial thought and the demands of the environmental justice movement – provides a prom- ising basis from which to explore both the continuities and differences between humans and other species, and between human autonomy and non-human agency, and what 'solidarity' and 'non-domination' might mean between humans and non-human species. A first step might be to rethink how we represent *ourselves* by acknowledging continuities and commonalities with the rest of nature in order to undermine the idea that the 'truly human' is somehow outside nature, the body and the bio- logical world (Plumwood 2000: 64).

In much traditional western ethics, philosophy and political the- ory, it has been common to begin by asking 'what does it mean to be human?' and to identify those features that distinguish humans from the rest of nature, such as sophisticated tool making, moral reasoning, language, (usually Judaeo-Christian) spirituality, and 'civilisation'. From these features were built ethical and political ideas that pro- moted whatever traits were selected as 'human-defining'. However, beginning in this way often meant, if we are to be fully human, that we must *promote* these uniquely human characteristics and thereby widen the existential gulf between humans and the rest of nature. To the extent to which we enlist these distinctive traits as the basis for progressive moral extensionism, then it becomes the basis of oppres- sion for those humans who lack such characteristics (women, non- Europeans, other species).

Framing the problem in terms of exclusionary dualisms (of self/other and human/non-human) provides a different way of highlighting the common logic between various forms of oppression and intolerance of difference, whether sexism, imperialism, racism *or* human chauvinism. Women, non-Europeans, and other species have been represented as less rational, less civilized, closer to nature and therefore less valuable to the extent that they lack or have less of the characteristics that are deemed to be 'human-defining' by those who possess the political power to represent human and non-human nature.

While there are countless ways in which we might distinguish humans from non-human species, there are also countless ways in which particular non-human species may be distinguished from both humans and other non-human species. To insist that only uniquely human traits should serve as the criteria of moral worthiness is nothing if not self-serving (Sterba 1994: 230).

Alongside the deepened sensitivity to the problem of invidious comparison it is also necessary to rethink the difficult (and sometimes faintly comical) attempt to draw a clear line between morally considerable beings, and morally inconsiderable ones – a task that has preoccupied objectivist non-anthropocentric applied ethicists. Whereas modernists such as Peter Singer once boldly drew the line between a shrimp and an oyster (the former were sentient and possessed interests that mattered, the latter were not sentient and therefore did not need to be considered in the moral calculus unless they were useful to sentient creatures), most critical and postmodern theorists have declined to embark upon such an exercise. Alternatively, they have preferred to employ looser metaphors and a vocabulary that accepts shadings and gradations in moral valuation, along with different cultural orientations and practices that are appropriate to different environments (e.g., why shouldn't Eskimos be allowed to eat whale meat if whales are not endangered?). Indeed, environmental monism, objectivist intrinsic value theories and abstract and universalist environmental philosophies have all been seriously challenged by the general anti-foundationalist movement in the social sciences and humanities, which has underscored the partial and situated nature of human knowledge and cultural understanding.

This search for a 'non-dualist' vocabulary from which to rethink cultural-ecological relations and develop a 'multicultural ecology'(Ivakhiv 2002) has been a necessary and important one, but the relativisation of environmental values that has necessarily accompanied this new direction of inquiry has raised new challenges for nature advocates, who are moral cosmopolitans. Whereas the early non-anthropocentric philosophers were strong advocates for the preservation of nature, aligned themselves with the wilderness and species preservation movement and trenchantly attacked capitalist development, consumerism and mass tourism, anti-foundationalist environmental philosophers have been primarily concerned to deconstruct meanings and dethrone what might be called conventional non-anthropocentric theory. The political motivations and implications of these critiques have not always been clearly discernible and they have attracted strong rejoinders from more conventional theorists (the so-called 'naïve realists') who have sought to reassert their scientific, philosophical and political project of saving nature, particularly Big Wilderness (Soulé and Lease 1995).

It is noteworthy that among those few critical post-structuralists who are still concerned to represent non-human nature other than as passive, meaningless and valueless material, awaiting inscription and valuation by human subjects, the use of analogies and metaphors has been unavoidable. For example, Jim Cheney (1989) has suggested that if we are to acknowledge the agency of nature, then we must think of it as a 'conversational partner'. Postmodern feminists such as Donna Harraway have sought to emphasise the agency of non-human nature by drawing on Native American wisdom. For Harraway (1988), we should think of nature as a coyote, or trickster, because it confounds our attempts to pin it down in terms of any neat set of dualisms, such as nature/culture. Similarly, her notion of humans as 'cyborgs' seeks to destabilise the dualisms of natural/unnatural and animal/machine (Harraway 1991).

The way forward is to recognise continuity, interdependence and some commonality to avoid hyper-separation between humans and the rest of nature, on the one hand, while also acknowledging the many areas of incommensurability, on the other. However, in the west at least, in view of the degree of hyper-separation, I would suggest that the best place to start is the broadest level of commonality (say the biological and ecological embeddedness of all life-forms, the common need for sustenance and security). From this basic commonality, and bearing in mind interdependence, we can then move to recognise the differences that need to be taken into account to enable mutual flourishing.

From liberalism to critical political ecology

Although my representation of nature is now couched in terms of a broader and less human-centred notion of autonomy or non-domination it still has roots in the Enlightenment ideals of autonomy and critique. However, for critical political ecologists, autonomy is a relational concept, something that is constituted by, and dependent upon, social structures and social meanings. Social and ecological communities are not constraints on individual autonomy but rather preconditions for human and non-human agency and flourishing. In this sense, critical political ecologists have sought to adjust autonomy to a world of more complex and intense economic, technological and ecological inter-dependence while also seeking to continue and extend the emancipa-tory project to human and non-human others.

Recognising the continuity in the struggle to emancipate both human and non-human nature provides the best reply to those critics who con-tinue to misrepresent ecocentric approaches as only concerned to res-cue nature *at the expense of* humanity, as if ecocentrics were indifferent or even hostile to human flourishing. The anthropocentric/ecocentric and instrumental/intrinsic value distinctions were never intended to drive a wedge between human and non-human interests. Quite the con-trary – the concern has always been to reconcile or mutually accommo-date these interests within a more encompassing moral framework. Yet these dualisms have been widely interpreted by critics as creating such a wedge, conveying the misleading impression of a necessary conflict and a zero-sum game between the interests and needs of the human and non-human worlds.

The anthropocentric/ecocentric dichotomy has also proved trouble-some in the way it has been taken to convey the (misleading) impression that the primary culprit for the ecological crisis is an arrogant, blanket humanity pitted against a defenceless non-human nature. Such a fram-ing (whether advanced mischievously or innocently) is clearly problem-atic in obscuring the fact that not all humans are equally responsible for, or equally troubled or affected by, environmental destruction. Indeed, a central insight of critical political ecology (particularly ecofeminism) is that the domination of nature is a complex phenomenon that has been managed and mediated by privileged social classes and imper-sonal social and economic systems that have systematically brought benefits to some humans at the expense of others. The result is that cer-tain privileged social classes, social groups and nations have achieved what Mary Mellor has called a 'parasitical transcendence' from human and non-human communities (Mellor 1997). In effect, a minority of the human race has been able to deny ecological and social responsi-bility and transcend biological embodiment and ecological limits (i.e., achieve greater physical resources, more time and more space) *only at the expense of others*, that is, by exploiting, excluding, marginalising and depriving human *and* non-human others. Val Plumwood has encap-sulated this problem in the idea of 'remoteness'. That is, privileged social classes have been able to remain remote (spatially, temporally,

epistemologically and technologically) from most of the ecological consequences of their decisions in ways that perpetuate ecological irration-
ality and environmental injustice (Plumwood 2002).

Critical political ecology, and the environmental justice movement
generally, have been in the vanguard of pointing to the historical and
ideological connections between the domination of non-human nature
and the domination of subaltern social groups – most notably women,
low-paid workers and indigenous peoples. While a closer inspection of
critical political ecology clearly reveals that the anthropocentric/eco-
centric distinction and the critique upon which it rests need not function in the blunt way in which critics have suggested, a reframing of the
fundamental principle of critical political ecology as 'respect for differently situated others', reinterpreted in an ecological context, might also
assist in foreclosing such misreadings.

Ultimately, critical political ecology seeks to locate and incorporate
the demand for social and environmental justice in the broader context
of the demand for dialogic or communicative justice. Environmental
justice is understood here in a distributive sense to include a fair distribution of the benefits and risks of social co-operation and the mini-
misation of those risks in relation to an expanded moral community.
Communicative justice is understood here as a fair/free communicative
context in which wealth and risk production and distribution decisions
take place in ways that are reflectively acceptable by 'differently situated others', or their representatives. Expressed in these terms, critical
political ecology is not merely compatible with democracy – it seeks the
expansion of democracy through the radicalisation of the idea of political representation in the risk society. This also provides the best reply
to the anti-foundationalist critique of ecocentrism.

Ecological democracy and the political representation of nature

If we accept the critical political ecology case for an expanded moral
community, then how might nature be included in an ecological democracy? Elsewhere I have formulated an ambit (representative) claim for
ecological democracy as follows: that all those potentially affected by
ecological risks should have some meaningful opportunity to participate or *otherwise be represented* in the making of the policies or decisions
which generate such risks (Eckersley 2004a). In one sense, this provides
no radical departure from existing representative democracy insofar as
the constituency of politically recognised subjects entitled to have their
interests represented and considered in democratic deliberation and

decision making is always larger than the class of political delibera-
tors and decision makers. The only difference here is that the constituency of politically recognised subjects is now much larger in including
the neglected environmental constituency. However, this enlargement
is important because it raises more challenging questions about the
motivation, knowledge and legitimacy of those who seek to represent
nature. While conventional political representatives never have perfect
motivation and perfect knowledge of the life-worlds, interests, values
and aspirations of the voters in their constituency, at least the voters
have the opportunity to put their case in their own terms, and also scrutinise decisions, ask questions, call their representative to account, and
vote him/her out of office if they perform their representative role badly.
In contrast, those who seek to represent nature, as we have seen, do not
have to answer to their constituency. Who, then, guards the ecological
guardians? How might monitory democracy (see Keane, Chapter 9 in
this volume) work in the case of nature advocates?

We have already noted that self-appointed nature advocates lack conventional sources of political legitimacy. According to John O'Neill
(2001: 496):

In the absence of authorisation, accountability, and presence, the remaining
source of legitimacy to claim to speak in such cases is epistemic. Those who
claim to speak on behalf of those without voice do so by appeal to their having
knowledge of the objective interests of those groups, often combined with special care for them.

O'Neill goes on to refer to natural scientists, biologists and ecologists
as legitimate representatives of nature. However, authority to represent
nature might also derive from traditional, local or vernacular knowledge (such as indigenous peoples or local fishers) or from other forms
of knowledge or 'moral capital'. For example, particular environmental non-government organisations (NGOs, such as Greenpeace or
Friends of the Earth) or environmental advocates (such as Al Gore)
might acquire 'moral authority' to speak for nature on the basis of a
reputation acquired through a long history of research and campaigning. Others might acquire authority on the basis of particular cultural
practices such as nature poetry, creative writing or the production of
nature documentaries.

Of course, not all nature advocates speak with one voice, and this
applies as much to scientists and environmental NGOs as to artists
and philosophers. Our brief, potted review of the history of ecocentric
nature advocacy has barely touched upon some of the deep disagreements within environmental philosophical and activist circles, not to

mention disagreement between nature advocates, on the one hand, and anthropocentric environmentalists and environmental sceptics, on the other. However, it is precisely this disagreement that provides the best answer to the question 'who guards the ecological guardians?' Ordinary processes of public democratic deliberation provide the best check upon nature advocacy. And no nature advocate should be above criticism. The implicit requirement that parties in deliberative exchanges reach mutual understanding through the public exchange of reasons has the effect of weeding out self-interested and partial arguments in favour of arguments that serve long-range, generalisable interests, such as environmental protection. Indeed, green political theorists have enthusiastically defended deliberative democracy as more conducive to protecting public interests than preference aggregration or bargaining. They have supported a proliferation of deliberative experiments in existing liberal democracies, including deliberative microcosms or mini-publics, such as citizens' juries, consensus conferences and deliberative polls that promote more environmentally informed representative claims and more environmentally informed preference formation.

Deliberation also provides an opportunity for those who care about orange-bellied parrots (and other species) to seek to persuade others. As Robert Goodin has suggested, those who have internalised the interests of nature may be said to engage in 'representative thinking', as if nature were an imaginary partner in conversation (Goodin 1996). But nature advocates must also be able to redeem their arguments in public in response to criticism. And as John O'Neill (2001: 483) reminds us, 'the virtue of deliberative democracy may lie not in claims that it resolves conflicts but that it reveals them'.

So what kinds of devices or institutions might serve to provide more systematic political representation of nature? Green political theorists have suggested a range of mechanisms that are conducive to 'giving nature a better hearing'. Some of these are familiar, others are novel and controversial. At the more conventional end of the spectrum, green political theorists favour proportional representation electoral systems because they provide more opportunity for green parties to gain seats in parliament than winner-take-all systems, which favour political parties that represent 'producer interests' (business and labour). More controversially, Andrew Dobson (1996) has taken this one step further by suggesting the reservation of a certain number of seats in parliament for nature's representatives (to be occupied by environmental NGOs). Elsewhere, I have suggested the establishment of an independent, statutory Environmental Defenders Office to bring legal actions on behalf of threatened species and habitats and to engage in advocacy work in the public sphere. The establishment of an independent Committee for the Future (as in Finland) or a Commission for the Future (as Australia once had), to promote research and debate about long-term interests also provides a means of representing future generations and indirectly, non-human species. The constitutional entrenchment of the precautionary principle as a simple and parsimonious measure to ensure risk-averse decisions by governments and public agencies would also protect both humans and non-human species from decisions that are likely to generate serious or irreversible harm to non-human species or others in the 'community-at-risk' (Eckersley 2004a). Others have explored the potential of environmental rights for both humans and non-humans as a supplement to human rights or as a means of qualifying existing human rights (Nash 1989; Eckersley 1995; Hayward 2005).

The foregoing suggestions for institutional reform are merely illustrative rather than exhaustive and they cannot themselves guarantee the protection of nature – after all, no democratic procedures (green or otherwise) can guarantee particular outcomes. However, they can enable more systematic opportunities for nature advocates to make their case and that is the best that any ecological democracy can offer.

Conclusion

Most of this chapter has been preoccupied with the representative claim making rather than with the procedures of political representation for nature advocacy. Surprisingly, this argumentative dimension has been given much less attention by green political theorists preoccupied with democratic innovation. While democratic procedures are necessarily open-ended, those who succeed in framing the terms of democratic discourse necessarily shape democratic debate and policy outcomes. Anti-environmentalists have been especially skilled at framing environmental problems in terms of slogans and overdrawn oppositions (such as 'people versus pandas', 'jobs versus the environment') that are designed to generate resentment towards environmental concerns and nature advocates among lay publics. Nature advocates must find ways of reframing our relationship with the non-human world that enables a reconciliation of human and non-human needs and interests.

In this chapter I have shown how some of the arguments have been formulated, and drawn out some of the problems and possibilities. In many ways, the task today is much more perilous than it was thirty years ago, given the global dimensions of so many ecological problems, and the need for nature advocates to communicate across class, gender and cultural boundaries in domestic and transnational public spheres.

Indeed, the challenges now facing the nature advocate in our global community could be seen as positively intimidating. The challenge is to develop arguments that encapsulate the idea of respect for non-human nature for its own sake; that do not privilege self-serving human attributes over non-human ones; that do not see nature as a mere passive substance to be acted on or valued by humans; that recognise some form of agency in nature; and that go beyond a mere instrumental valuation of nature's assets and services. Moreover, such arguments must not be narrowly confined to particular cultures (e.g., western) and linguistic (e.g., English) communities; but rather, they must speak across, and appeal to, a wide variety of human cultures (and languages) and recognise the needs of human communities to sustain their livelihoods from ecosystems.

In the light of these challenges it might seem tempting just to fall back on the vocabulary of prudence (let us look after nature since it looks after *us*) on the grounds that it is likely to reach across more cultures than the kind of nature advocacy I have articulated. These less controversial arguments based on prudence can sometimes achieve the same outcome, as Bryan Norton has long maintained in his so-called 'convergence hypothesis' (Norton 2002). However, instrumental arguments do not *always* lead to the same outcome and they also reinforce a particular way of seeing the world that has not always served humans well, as the early Frankfurt School has reminded us. Whenever we represent nature, we, unwittingly or otherwise, also represent ourselves and the sort of world we wish to inhabit. This is ultimately what nature advocacy is all about and why it remains vital to any democracy that is worthy of the name.

REFERENCES

Bowersox, J. (2002) 'Legitimacy crises: Why environmental ethics and environmental political thought must work together', in B. Minteer and B. Pepperman Taylor (eds.), *Democracy and the claims of nature: Critical perspectives for a new century*. Lanham, MD: Rowman and Littlefield, pp. 71–90.

Callicott, J. B. (1985) 'Intrinsic value, quantum theory and environmental ethics', *Environmental Ethics* 7(3): 257–75.

Cheney, J. (1989) 'Postmodern environmental ethics: Ethics as bioregional narrative', *Environmental Ethics* 11(2): 117–34.

Cronon, W. (1996) 'The trouble with wilderness, or, getting back to the wrong nature', *Environmental History* 1(1): 7–55.

Dobson, A. (1996) 'Representative democracy and the environment', in W. M. Lafferty and J. Meadowcroft (eds.), *Democracy and the environment: Problems and prospects*. Cheltenham, UK: Edward Elgar, pp. 124–39.

Eckersley, R. (1995) 'Liberal democracy and the environment: The rights discourse and the struggle for recognition', *Environmental Politics* 4(4): 169–98.

(2004a) *The Green state: Rethinking democracy and sovereignty.* Cambridge, MA: MIT Press.

(2004b) 'Ecocentric discourses: Problems and future prospects for nature advocacy', *Tamkang Review* 34(3–4): 155–86.

Ehrenfeld, D. (1981) *The arrogance of humanism.* New York: Oxford University Press.

Evernden, N. (1984) 'The environmentalist's dilemma', in *The paradox of environmentalism.* Downsview, Ontario: Faculty of Environmental Studies, York University.

Goodin, R. (1996) 'Enfranchising the earth, and its alternatives', *Political Studies* 44(4): 835–49.

Harraway, D. (1988) 'Situated knowledges: The science question in feminism and the privilege of partial perspective', *Feminist Studies* 14(3): 575–99.

(1991) *Simians, cyborgs and women.* New York: Routledge.

Hayward, T. (2005) *Constitutional environmental rights.* Oxford University Press.

Ivakhiv, A. (2002) 'Toward a multicultural ecology', *Organization and Environment* 15(4): 389–409.

Mellor, M. (1997) *Feminism and ecology.* New York University Press.

Minteer, B. and B. Pepperman Taylor (eds.) (2002) *Democracy and the claims of nature: Critical perspectives for a new century.* Lanham, MD: Rowman and Littlefield.

Nash, R. (1989) *The rights of nature: A history of environmental ethics.* Madison: University of Wisconsin Press.

Norton, B. (1991) *Toward unity among environmentalists.* New York: Oxford University Press.

(2002) 'Democracy and environmentalism: Foundations and justifications in environmental policy', in Minteer and Pepperman Taylor (eds.), pp. 11–31.

O'Neill, J. (2001) 'Representing people, representing nature, representing the world', *Environment and Planning C: Government and Policy* 19(4): 483–500.

Plumwood, V. (1993) *Feminism and the mastery of nature.* London: Routledge.

(2000) 'Deep ecology, deep pockets and deep problems: A feminist, ecosocialist analysis', in E. Katz, A. Light and D. Rothenberg (eds.) *Beneath the surface: Critical essays in the philosophy of deep ecology.* Cambridge, MA: MIT Press, pp. 59–84.

(2002) *Environmental culture: The ecological crisis of reason.* London: Routledge.

Regan, T. (1981) 'The nature and possibility of an environmental ethic', *Environmental Ethics* 3(1): 19–34.

Rodman, J. (1977) 'The liberation of nature?' *Inquiry* 20: 83–145.

Rorty, R. (1991) *Objectivity, relativism, and truth: Philosophical papers.* Cambridge University Press.

Saward, M. (2006) 'Representation', in A. Dobson and R. Eckersley (eds.), *Political theory and the ecological challenge*. Cambridge University Press, pp. 183–99.

Singer, P. (1975) *Animal liberation: A new ethics for our treatment of animals*. New York: The New Review.

Soulé, M. and G. Lease (1995) *Reinventing nature? Responses to postmodern deconstruction*. Washington DC: Island Press.

Sterba, J. (1994) 'Reconciling anthropocentric and nonanthropocentric environmental ethics', *Environmental Values* 3(3): 229–44.

Stone, C. (1974) *Should trees have standing? Toward legal rights for natural objects*. Los Altos, CA: Kaufman.

Todorov, T. (1984) *The conquest of America: The question of the other*. New York: Harper and Row.

Vogel, S. (1995) *Against nature: The concept of nature in critical theory*. Albany: State University of New York Press.

Weston, A. (1996) 'Before environmental ethics', in A. Light and E. Katz (eds.) *Environmental pragmatism*. London: Routledge, pp. 139–60.

11 Democracy and representation beyond the nation state

Michael Zürn and Gregor Walter-Drop

Introduction

If the EU were to apply for membership of the EU, it would not qualify because of the inadequate democratic content of its constitution. At the same time, a significant proportion of legislative activity in its member states is driven by decisions made in the opaque labyrinth of institutions in far-away Brussels.[1] So, are the member states democratically governed?

The picture is similar with respect to other international institutions in the OECD world. The WTO system of agreements, for instance, comprises almost 10,000 pages and is the result of marathon negotiations, lasting over a decade, involving over 150 states and thousands of experts. These agreements contain far-reaching implications for employees in crisis-prone industrial sectors, and in agriculture. To be sure, it was the democratically elected governments that participated in the negotiations. But did citizens really exercise recognisable influence over the decisions?

The problem behind these questions is clear. Although security and social welfare, two central aims of governance, can be better achieved with international institutions than without them, the mere existence of international institutions is no guarantee of good governance. Moreover, international institutions now truly exercise power. The rise of dispute settlement bodies, majority decisions rules, improved monitoring schemes, the role of transnational groups in 'enforcing' rules via naming and shaming, and, of course, a body of *ius cogens* in international law has led to an undermining of the consensus principle

---

[1] Majone (1996: 59) estimated this 'legislative Europeanisation' for France to be around 50 per cent. For Germany, von Beyme (1998) focused on key issues and arrived at smaller, but still significant percentages (cf. Tömmel 2006). König and Mäder (2008) critically re-evaluated the hypothesis but still arrived at figures showing between a quarter and a third of all legislative activity in Germany to be driven by EU impulses.

of international politics (Zürn *et al.* 2007). At least sometimes some national governments need to do things which they would not want to do without such international institutions. And if international institutions exercise power, they need to have legitimacy. Apart from producing effective solutions, governance must also fulfil certain procedural requirements in order to be rated as good. From the point of view of democratic theory, however, international institutions have very shaky foundations. The 'chain of representation' running from citizens to an international institution is very long and, at the same time, the possibilities of democratic control are obscure and do not follow a clear design. Against this background, Robert Dahl (1994) pointed almost paradigmatically to a fundamental dilemma of politics in the age of globalisation: the contradiction between 'system effectiveness and citizen participation'.

This chapter aims at questioning the notion of a contradiction – to use the terms of Fritz Scharpf (1997) – between *output legitimacy* (the acceptance of a political system created by system effectiveness) and *input legitimacy* (acceptance created by democratic procedures). We shall argue in the first section that viewing this issue as a choice between effective problem solving through international institutions and democratic political processes is already in normative terms a false approach. International institutions not only increase system effectiveness or output-legitimacy; they are also a normatively sensible response to the problems that are posed for democracy by globalisation. At the same time, it is indisputable that the actual functioning of these international institutions does not meet the democratic standards of representative democracy. In the second section of this chapter, we analyse the sceptical argument that insists that most deficits in the working of international institutions cannot easily be remedied, since democratic majority decisions in representative institutions depend – *in descriptive terms* – on a political community that is (among other things) based on trust and solidarity. For sceptics, the lack of a transnational *demos* poses a problem that cannot easily be overcome. Sceptics therefore see a structural dilemma: while international institutions may be necessary for effective policies, they are structurally undemocratic.

We consider this thesis to be too unsophisticated. In the third section of our chapter we challenge the sceptical argument by analysing the effect of globalisation on the formation of a *demos* and by disaggregating the *demos* itself into its elements. Based on this approach, we find, on the international level at least, a mixed picture. A short overview indicates that the willingness to form *associations* among *demos* members and to select representatives who are involved in decision making are of special interest. In modern territorial states this willingness to form associations constitutes the central mechanism by which a *demos* acquires the capacity to function as a democracy. Interest groups and elected representatives organised in parties together form the backbone of interest representation in modern nation states. In the fourth section we thus focus on associations and illustrate the different modes of representation underlying them. In modern democracies, all these modes of representation usually exist in a more or less balanced state. In the international sphere, however, the pattern deviates strongly from the familiar. This insight paves the way for some concluding remarks in the fifth section on how the democratisation of international institutions can proceed.

Denationalisation and democracy

In order to show how societal denationalisation – in our opinion a more precise term than globalisation – affects democracy, the terms 'democracy' and 'societal denationalisation' must first be clarified. The mechanism through which the latter affects the former will then be explained.

'Persons ... should be free and equal in the determination of the conditions of their own lives, so long as they do not deploy this framework to negate the rights of others' (Held 1995: 147). On the basis of this principle of autonomy, democracy, in very general terms, is a process of public will formation and decision making in which everybody affected by a decision has the same opportunity to participate actively and exert influence. Moreover, democracy – as understood here – is a "condition of possibility" of normatively justifiable solutions. Such a concept of democracy rejects purely procedural interpretations that reduce democracy to a decision-making system regardless of the content of decisions. At the same time, it challenges purely liberal or constitutionalist definitions which regard individual political rights as pre-politically given, and seek to protect them from the outcomes of the democratic process. This concept of democracy is reflective in the sense that the fundamental normative requirements of the democratic process, such as autonomous individuals with freedom of opinion and information, as well as the democratic process itself, are both seen as mutually reinforcing. Democracy consists of two components: a *democratic principle* – everyone affected by a decision should have a chance to participate – and a *deliberative principle* – any decision should be backed by arguments committed to values of rationality and impartiality (Habermas 1994; Elster 1998: 8; Schmalz-Bruns 1995). Whereas most theorists of democracy would agree on the first principle, the second is more contested. In order to show how globalisation is causing problems for national democracies, we will refer to the democratic principle. In order to show that the social conditions for democracy beyond the nation state are not impossible to fulfil, we shall also consider the deliberative principle, thus harnessing a more ambitious conception of democracy.

Instead of globalisation, we use the term denationalisation. Cross-referring to the classic works of Karl W. Deutsch (1969) and Eric Hobsbawm (1992) on nationalism, it sees a nation as a political community sustained by intensive interactions that stand in a mutually constitutive relationship to the nation state. Patterns of interaction, nation and nation state thus together form a national constellation (Habermas). Consequently, denationalisation is an indication of the weakening link between territorial states and their corresponding national societies, that is, a transformation of the contextual condition that made the national constellation possible.

Denationalisation can be defined as the extension of social spaces which are constituted by dense transactions that stretch beyond national borders without necessarily being global in scope. The degree of denationalisation can be measured by the extent of cross-border transactions relative to transactions taking place within national borders. Social transactions take place whenever goods, services and capital (economics), threats (security), pollutants (environment), signs (communication) or persons (mobility) are internationally exchanged or commonly produced. An empirical investigation carried out using this conceptualisation shows that denationalisation is not uniform, but rather a jagged process that differs markedly between issue areas and countries, and over time.[2] Denationalisation, defined in terms of the growing significance of cross-border transactions, has been taking place in mild forms since the 1950s. Accelerated denationalisation first occurred in the 1960s, with the massive deployment of nuclear weapons in the issue area of security. From the 1970s onward, the growth of cross-border exchanges accelerated in the fields of goods production and capital flows, information, travel, migration and regional environmental risks. Surprisingly, the growth of some of these exchange processes leveled off for a few years during the 1980s. Veritable denationalisation thrusts, however, occurred in a number of specific issue areas just as the growth of cross-border exchanges slowed down. The most notable

[2] In a research project funded by the German Research Association, we have developed seventy-two indicators to determine the extent of denationalisation in different issue areas and different OECD countries (Beisheim *et al.* 1999). For a similar undertaking with similar results, see Held *et al.* (1999).

developments took place in global financial markets, the growth of global environmental dangers, the Internet and organised crime. The common feature of all these more recent developments is that they concern the *integrated production* of goods and bads, rather than the mere *exchange* of goods and bads across national borders.

How does this process affect representative democracy? A logical corollary of the democratic principle is the congruence between social and political spaces (Scharpf 1993: 165–185; Held 1995: 16), which was for a long time not treated as a fundamental problem in modern democratic theory. The notion of a nation state consisting of a more or less circumscribed national society, a clearly demarcated territory and an administrative apparatus constituted to provide services for this society and territory, led theorists to treat congruence as a given. The notion of a territorially defined nation state was thus used as a shortcut to ensure the spatial congruence between rulers (the nation *state*) and subjects (the national *society*). This notion becomes problematic as soon as the nature of the relevant community is contested, as has happened in the course of societal denationalisation. Couched in different terms: the increase in cross-border transactions infringes on the normative dignity of political borders (Schmalz-Bruns 1998: 372; Held 1998).

From the standpoint of democracy, spatial congruence is necessary in two critical ways: first, between the people who are affected by a decision and their representatives in the decision-making system (input congruence); and, second, between the space in which regulations are valid and the space in which the social interactions to which the decision refers take place (output congruence). If there is no *input congruence*, then a group that is affected by a decision but does not participate in its making (either directly or though representatives) can be considered to have been determined by others, instead of being self-determined. As early as 1945, E. H. Carr saw the moral deficits in exclusive political communities whose privileges were established on the basis of exporting harm abroad (Carr 1945). What was true then is much truer today: in the age of denationalisation: the extension of the moral and political community that encompasses the interests of all those affected by decisions made within that community is a normative democratic requirement.

The congruence of the space for which regulations are valid and the boundaries of the relevant social transactions – *output incongruence* – is also significant for democratic legitimacy. According to Alexy (1985: 458) '*de jure* freedom, that is the legal authorisation to do or refrain from doing something, is worth nothing without *de facto* freedom, that is factual freedom of choice'. In a denationalised world ruled by a system of formally independent nation states, there is a danger that political communities cannot attain their desired goals due to conditions outside their jurisdiction. In this case, their political systems are unable to act on behalf of the collective.

Thus, the choice between the alternative of effective problem solving through international institutions and democratic political processes is not a particularly fruitful exercise. In democratic terms, international institutions are a sensible response to the problems facing democracy in times of denationalisation, especially because they help to redress the imbalance between social and political spaces. Theoretically, the 'emergence of denationalised governance structures' (Joerges 1996) helps to bring all those who are affected by a political decision into the decision-making system, thus observing the principle of 'no taxation without representation'. What is more, international institutions help to increase the real freedom of political communities because they allow for the implementation of policies that each state alone could not meaningfully pursue. Governance beyond the nation state can therefore improve both social welfare *and* representative democracy in the face of societal denationalisation. In this sense, international institutions are not the problem, but part of the solution to the problems of modern representative democracy in the age of denationalisation. The current major problem for modern democracy is not political integration, but societal denationalisation which undermines the normative dignity of political borders by increasing political externalities in integrated social spaces (due to input incongruence), and by reducing the autonomy of nation states (due to output incongruence).

The social prerequisites for democracy

Although, in principle, international institutions may compensate for democratic deficits brought about by input and output incongruence, they create at the same time new patterns of representation and new democratic deficits. And the greater the significance of international institutions, the greater the need for democratic legitimacy of their decisions. At the moment – on this point analysts are almost unanimous – this legitimacy is clearly inadequate.

There are two strands of thought to be found among those who identify a deficit in the way international institutions work; they differ mainly with respect to the question of whether in principle the democratic deficits of international institutions can be remedied. While some critics point to institutional deficits in the EU and other international institutions, they maintain that democratic reforms are possible, provided there is the appropriate political will. On the other hand, there are sceptics who consider these suggestions naïve, and question the very *possibility* of processes of democratic representation beyond the nation state. They argue that the EU and other international institutions cannot be democratically reformed because they do not meet the *social prerequisites* of democracy. We wish to introduce a third possibility, one that accepts the sceptics' focus on social prerequisites, but shows that the empirical complexity of these prerequisites reveals a much more varied picture than the sceptics suggest, a picture that has the potential to guide consideration of the social prerequisites of effective democratic governance beyond the nation state.

According to the sceptics, although democratic legitimacy may not be limited to ethnic communities it is only possible within the framework of a *demos*; or, in the words of Emerich Francis (1965: 77), a community which considers itself to be the 'legitimate bearer of political will'. We do not endeavour at this point to delve deeper into democratic theory; we use the term *demos* mainly to highlight the social, cultural and structural prerequisites of a functioning democracy. Beyond the nation state – so the sceptics' argument runs – these prerequisites are missing. Peter Graf Kielmannsegg (1994: 27) has eloquently summarised this point of view with respect to Europe:

Collective identities develop, become stable and are passed into tradition in communities of communication, of experiences and of memories. Europe, even within the narrower scope of Western Europe, has no communication community, hardly any common memories and only limited common experiences.

Seen in this way, the connection between nation and democracy is not an historical coincidence, but is systematic and indissoluble. Some have pushed this argument so far as to claim, for example, that direct elections to the European Parliament are a mistake because they are geared to the formation of a supranational *demos* – which is an impossible and counterproductive endeavour (Lepsius 1986). This is a strong argument that merits closer inspection. In which sense is a coherent *demos* necessary for the functioning of democratic institutions? It seems that without any form of *demos* international institutions will necessarily have deficits in legitimacy and efficiency. Without the appropriate social prerequisites majoritarian decision making is hardly achievable beyond the national level, and even negotiation systems based on argumentative consensus building will only work if they can at least build on a weak form of collective identity and some common values. It thus seems warranted to undertake a closer examination of the chances of forming a *demos* above the level of the nation state.

The *demos* beyond the nation state

In a first step, the broad rejection of a *demos* above the nation can be challenged from both an historical and a contemporary perspective. The challenge shows that there is no *a priori* reason not to believe that at least some elements of a *demos* are possible in the international sphere. Therefore, in a second step, we disaggregate the all-embracing term *demos* to establish which of its elements are required for what component of democracy, so enabling us to evaluate the current status of these components of the *demos* in international relations.

In the first place, it should be pointed out that a *demos* is never externally given, but always the result of political institutions and intensified transactions. The importance of political institutions is best exemplified by a look at modern European history. Historically, classic examples of the European nation state, such as France or Britain, illustrate that it was primarily the state that acquired a symbolic framework at an early stage of its history, and that this facilitated the development of an imagined community (Anderson 1991) marked by a strong national identity. It was this identity out of which the *demoi* eventually emerged, in the shape of political communities with the potential for democratic self-governance. In other words, political institutions fostered the emergence of an identity that paved the way to the formation of a *demos*, which in turn led to a democratisation of these institutions. Other cases in central Europe seem to suggest that community building preceded state building. However, in countries such as Germany or Italy, Poland and Czechoslovakia, national unity or independence were projects of relatively small elites that were supplemented by various measures of identity formation in the mass public once these elites had successfully taken over or established the respective national political institutions. Thus, even in these cases national collective identity achieved its ubiquity and paramount importance only *after* the respective institutions had been established, and because of activities initiated or fostered by these institutions.

The sceptics are right to point out that only when political communities have been established can the democratisation of the state institutions take place. Yet, state institutions in the national constellation typically have the power to shape the borders of areas of dense social transactions, and thus the limits of common communication, experience and memory. Consider examples such as the language policies of the emerging centralist France (Hobsbawm 1992), the unification of measurement units, currencies and time in the emerging Wilhelminian Empire (Hallerberg and Weber 2002) or the state-supported fabrication of national myths in Victorian Britain (Snyder 1993). The implication is that the borders of the communities themselves, and the process of identity formation, are strongly influenced by political institutions. These can of course be subject to change – provided there is the appropriate political will.

Against this background, it becomes obvious that any analysis of the state of transnational *demoi* involves the analysis of a moving target. The above-mentioned process of denationalisation suggests that transaction patterns have begun to change – not least because of the role of political institutions. In the field of communication, for instance, a number of indicators show significant tendencies of denationalisation. The tremendous facilitation of cross-border communication by the Internet is only one example. Equivalent developments can be seen in more traditional media, whether audio-visual, recorded or printed. A recent study of global book translations, for instance, shows a 50 per cent growth over the last three decades coupled with a significant increase in the diversity of languages subject to translation (Sapiro 2008). This development runs parallel to the spread of languages themselves, and in particular of English as a kind of 'lingua franca' of the denationalised world. According to Eurobarometer data, in 2006 more than 50 per cent of the population of the twenty-five European Union member states either spoke English as a native language or were able to hold a conversation in English. At the same time, 28 per cent identified themselves as having a working knowledge of at least two foreign languages (European Commission 2006). Cross-border communication within (and beyond) Europe has significantly increased and there are no signs of a reversal of this trend. Likewise, it is not far-fetched to assume that not only the denationalisation in communication and culture, but also denationalisation of trade, travel and even environmental problems, are leading to a convergence in the experiences of citizens inside the social spaces of dense social transactions. Without further empirical illustration it seems plausible to assume that this process is particularly strong within the European Union because of intensive patterns of denationalisation in this region.

In sum, the categorical distinction between the existence of such a community on the national level and the absence of such a community on a level beyond the nation state is becoming increasingly blurred. Even in the matter of common memories, which are among the core elements of national identity, it is interesting to note that there are projects such as the development of common French-German and Polish-German history textbooks for use in high schools on both sides of the border. Both cases are particularly noteworthy because for a long time collective memories in these countries were dominated by the traumatic experiences of multiple wars and were explicitly defined in contradistinction to their respective neighbours. Such examples suggest that even in difficult cases changes in the community of memory are not impossible.

It thus seems justified to conclude that the collective identity required for the formation of a *demos* is subject to change depending on (a) the political institutions fostering it and (b) the patterns of social transaction it reflects. Given current levels of political and social denationalisation there is no *a priori* reason for rejecting the possibility of forming a *demos* beyond the nation state.

Rights

It is helpful, at this point, to take a closer look at the term *demos* itself, to disaggregate it into its different components. A *demos* comprises at least six central elements that serve as the social prerequisites for democracy: rights, trust, public spirit, public discourse, solidarity and association.

The members of a demos acknowledge each other as autonomous individuals, each with a right to personal self-fulfilment. In this sense, civil liberty rights, including the right to physical integrity and the right to participate in will formation and decision-making processes, are constitutionally embodied in any democratic political community. However, at least within the OECD world, to some extent democracy also involves a transnational concern for such rights, in the form of support for human rights. Increasingly, civil society actors sue for human rights and protection from arbitrary violence on a transnational scale, and people organise themselves transnationally to prevent infringements of human rights 'abroad'. Societal denationalisation seems to have heightened the significance of these transnational monitoring activities. In Europe, individually actionable human rights are guaranteed in legally binding form by the European Human Rights Commission, and there are as well some indications of similar developments outside of Europe (Donnelly 1993; Evans 1997). In addition, if rights problems with clear transboundary implications arise, it is more or less accepted that all the affected countries are fully entitled to have their say, as long as they are represented by democratically elected politicians. This principle of cross-border representation is fostered by the transnational mutual acknowledgement of the importance of participation in decision-making processes at the national level. The steady increase in election monitoring, for example, shows that political rights, including those of people in other countries, are increasingly being defended on a transnational scale (Rosenau 1997: 259; Keane, Chapter 9). Some fundamental principles of a democratic political community thus seem to have begun to form across national borders in denationalised societies.

Trust

The members of a demos accept that once an obligation has been entered into, it must be complied with, and they believe that all other members should accept this as well. Again, it is possible to argue that this aspect of a democratic political community also appears to be relatively well established on the international level. According to the principle of *pacta sunt servanda* ('agreements must be kept'), it is generally accepted that international obligations should be fulfilled. Most western states do indeed comply with international contractual obligations (Henkin 1968; Chayes and Chayes 1995). The origins of this principle can be seen in the mutual obligation that arose in a society of states and may thus be construed as a sense of duty formed at the state (rather than the individual) level (Bull 1977). However, compliance is sometimes even demanded by national populations against executives who want to breach obligations; this 'compliance pull' of international regulations is strongest when obligations are politically, judicially and socially internalised (Zürn and Joerges 2005). It is thus safe to assume that a mutual obligation to follow rules once they have been agreed upon has developed in the OECD world beyond the level of governments. On this basis one may argue, against the sceptics, that political trust is today not restricted to the national and the inter-governmental sphere, but has also entered the transnational sphere.

Public spirit

Members of a fully developed *demos* show a sense of collective identity if their preferences as individuals include a concern for the well-being (or the suffering) of the collective. In its weak form, such a sense of collective identity (*Gemeinsinn*, or public spirit) is a precondition of public deliberations about the right solution for the community as a whole. Where there is no such public spirit, there is no reference point for arguing and, therefore, little transnational public debate on the 'right' policies for the whole. It seems nevertheless possible to argue that there are signs of public spirit developing in the OECD world. One can begin by referring to transnational sectoral publics and 'sectoral demoi' (Abromeit and Schmidt 1998) that roughly speaking hold deliberations about appropriate policies. Given this development, it comes as no surprise that in analyses of democratic legitimacy the focus has shifted to international political processes in which decision making is dominated by deliberative components that give priority to arguing over bargaining. Consider, for instance, the research on deliberation in the hundreds of European Union committees active in the implementation of Council decisions (cf. Joerges and Neyer 1997). Particularly within the field of environmental politics, similar developments can even be observed at the international level. After the admission of transnational non-governmental organisations (NGOs), international negotiations received an impetus that clearly distinguished them from conventional inter-governmental negotiations. The regime for the protection of the ozone layer as well as climate change politics illustrate that the inclusion of NGOs has elevated the status of epistemic communities (Adler and Haas 1992; Princen and Finger 1994), which in turn has helped strengthen deliberative elements at the expense of simple bargaining elements, and has also contributed to the relativisation of particular interests in favour of public interests (cf. Gehring 1995). To be sure, whenever fragmented national public opinions dominate national decision makers, as happened for instance in the various rounds of the BSE negotiations, deliberation at levels beyond the nation state dissolves (Neyer 2005). These developments can nevertheless be taken as an indicator of the presence of a weak form of collective identity outlined above, which is necessary for transforming inter-governmental bargaining into transnational negotiations, so enhancing their democratic quality.

Public discourse

Public spirit can be transformed into public discourse if most of the members affected by a decision have a capacity to communicate publicly. The participation of expert communities and the direct addressees of regulations in deliberative issue networks becomes possible because they are public spirited and possess the capacities and resources to communicate with each other in arenas beyond the nation state. Transnational sectoral publics (Eder et al. 1998) rest on social differentiation and stratification and evolve as issue networks around specific issue areas. These sectoral publics are dense communication networks with permeable borders, and they facilitate a more active participation than the broader public discourse. However, sectoral publics are always in danger of becoming captive to particular interests by developing rent-seeking behaviour, neglecting the public interests and detaching themselves from other issue networks (Zürn and Joerges 2005). However, in contrast to sectoral publics, the institutionalisation of a broader public discourse is dependent on a common language and media as well as a party system. While there are significant changes in the context of the denationalisation of communication and culture as outlined above, the infrastructure for a broader public discourse is still quite weak at the European level and hardly developed at all beyond that region.

Solidarity

In its stronger form, a sense of collective identity provides the basis for (re)distributive processes within a political community. Solidarity is the willingness of individuals to give up things they value for the sake of the collectivity, and the acceptance of redistributive policies is the best indicator of this. Although the EU's Regional and Structural Funds reflect some awareness of redistributive obligations at the European level, a recognisable sense of transnational social obligations is barely perceptible. While redistributive programmes to deal with catastrophes exist, they have an ad hoc character and are mainly aimed at rescuing people (Radtke 2007). Humanitarian activities of this sort are more accurately interpreted as evidence of support for the notion of a transnational concern for human rights. On the other hand, it is not clear whether a strong sense of collective identity, as suggested by the acceptance of redistributive measures, is necessary for democracy. National democracies differ widely in their use of redistributive policies, and even within individual nation states acceptance of such measures varies from one region to another.

Association

Based on mutual trust, solidarity and public spirit, members of a *demos* display a willingness to form associations to enter public discourse and to exercise their rights. They thus accept the principle of representation, which stipulates that other individuals or organisations can act on their behalf, or in the general interest. Associations take very different forms, ranging from 'big tent' or 'catch-all' political parties to highly specialised interest groups. The election of parliamentarians and the formation of different territorial levels of government in a federal system are also based on the principle of association and representation. Parliamentarians act on behalf of their constituencies while local or regional governments constitute a form of general territorial representation. In fact, the mechanisms of association and representation are central to any democratic territorial state because in large and functionally complex societies they are a necessary prerequisite for the aggregation, selection and formulation of interests – be they public or private (special) interests. It is interesting to note that as a political right the freedom of association is not only part of most Western constitutions but is also incorporated in such central human rights documents as the Universal Declaration of Human Rights and the European Convention on Human Rights. Cross-border consensus on certain intra-state norms, however, is clearly something else than the existence of elements of the *demos* on the international level itself.

The preceding analysis shows that the very strong claim that there is no *demos* beyond national borders needs differentiation. A *demos* consists of a number of analytically separable components that exist on the international level, albeit to varying degrees. For instance, the acceptance that all those affected by a denationalised issue must be represented in the process of international policy formulation seems relatively well developed. Mutual political rights and congruence are thus acknowledged as transnational normative criteria. Certain elements of a transnational political community with supervisory functions can also be identified in the monitoring of national governments' implementation of international policies, and in the cross-border recognition of individual human rights. These observations in no way suggest that the democratic legitimacy of governance beyond the nation state has already reached adequate levels. However, it does indicate that democratic processes beyond the nation state must not be ruled out as an unalterable matter of principle until all aspects of a *demos* are fully developed. Equally, there is no reason to assume that the appearance of a *demos* depends on a high degree of cultural homogeneity, and that it is thus feasible only within a national context. It seems much more practical to establish what kind of democratic processes can be generated on the basis of (partially) given components of a *demos*. To this end, more systematic research should focus on the question of which aspects of a transnational *demos* already exist and can be further developed within a democratic framework.

At the same time, the disaggregation of the term *demos* suggests that solidarity, public discourse and imbalances among different forms of representation are the weakest features of an emergent *demos* beyond the nation state. With respect to public discourse, it can reasonably be argued that this is not due to a lack of transnational public spirit, but rather to infrastructural difficulties that are vital for public discourse. The existence of transnational issue networks with deliberative elements nevertheless indicates that a lack of cultural homogeneity does not appear to be the major reason for the absence of a broader public discourse.

Cultural heterogeneity seems to be most relevant with respect to the development of a sense of solidarity. For many sceptics, democracy beyond the nation state is unthinkable because the central element of their notion of democracy is social rights. In their view, individual acts of solidarity depend on cultural integration (Streeck 1998). Solidarity, however, also implies the exclusion of others (Linklater 1998: 113). It can reasonably be assumed that here the sceptics confuse citizenship rights, which were 'extremely exclusive from the very origination of the concept' (Preuss 1998: 20) with democracy, which is an all-inclusive concept. The sceptics' argument and their tendency to over-generalise is driven by the fear of 'a liberal bias of intergovernmental and non-state political arenas' (Streeck 1998: 15). Even if there is no strong sense of collective identity in terms of solidarity and willingness to make sacrifices, this does not mean that the social prerequisites for democracy are completely lacking.

Representation in and above the nation state

We have argued above that one of the core elements of a *demos* is the willingness to form associations that represent citizens' interests through the democratic political process. In order to compare the different forms of representation in and above the nation state, it is helpful to introduce two categorical distinctions: one pertaining to the constitutive processes of a democracy, while the other is related to the type of organisation in which the members of a *demos* are willing to associate. We have already noted earlier that in addition to aggregation the democratic process also comprises deliberative elements, subject to the existence of certain social preconditions. While in aggregative processes participants try to assert their interests unconditionally, in deliberative processes participants have to justify their concerns as a matter of public interest: they argue instead of bargain with each other.

Turning to the second distinction, it can be argued that association and representation can be either issue-specific and, thus, functional, or they can happen on the basis of territorial structures that cut across the issue-specific networks. When both types of distinctions are acknowledged, four modes of representation can be identified, as in Table 11.1.

Interest groups can be distinguished from NGOs in that they are pursuing goals compatible with the short-term (economic) interests of their members while for NGOs normally no such compatibility exists.

Table 11.1. *Modes of representation*

	Aggregation of Interests	Deliberation
Functional organisation	Interest groups	NGOs
Territorial organisation	Regional political entities	Parliamentarians

Thus, interest groups might engage in debate and they will routinely cloak their interests as matters of public concern, but it is not their function to deliberate in the substantial sense introduced above. At the same time, NGOs will engage in interest-politics but they will do so normally for matters of public concern beyond the self-interest of their members. In a similar vein, it is the chief function of regional political entities to aggregate the interests of the units below them or within them and to represent them vis-à-vis the 'outside' while the parliament is *the* institution for the deliberation of public affairs above and beyond individual, institutional or group-specific self-interest.

Within a nation state, the four different modes of representation sketched above coexist in a more or less balanced relationship. To be sure, the exact balance that provides both legitimate and efficient governance is historically and geographically contingent, but in modern democracies all modes do exist to a certain degree. This is chiefly due to the fact, as argued above, that only aggregation and deliberation together make for a democracy that is more than just a set of procedures. At the same time, functional representation is best suited to problem solving, while territorial representation caters for the needs of maintaining collective identity and serves as a counterbalance to the dis-association of sectoral politics, which otherwise might lack coordination and overlook interests that are functionally difficult to organise.

Turning to the international level, it becomes apparent that representation does exist but that the four modes are not equally present. Broadly speaking, at levels beyond the nation state, bargaining trumps arguing and functional organisations are more important than broad institutions that build bridges between different sectors.

To clarify this point, it is helpful to distinguish between the European Union and functional international regimes. The former is marked by the fact that there are close political and institutional inter-linkages among diverse issue areas that are processed by a single institution covering the same territory. In functional international regimes, these same structures are lacking. On a more abstract level, the European Union can be called an 'omnibus institution', while functional international regimes are 'specialised institutions'. Let us turn first to these special-ised institutions.

When considering the above table, there is no doubt that the dom-inant mode of interest representation in the development of specialised international institutions that formulate policies is both aggregative and territorial. In other words, it is the bargaining of states within limited issue areas that forms the core of political processes on the international level. For very good reasons, these institutions are often labelled *inter-governmental* regimes. International institutions are most often designed by states. They quite often need the consent of all states for any kind of activity; and they also need the resources of nation states to implement any of their policies.

To be sure, some international institutions have moved beyond the mere aggregation of interests. For instance, the number of inter-national institutions with dispute settlement bodies and with some form of majority decision rules has grown over time. In this way, the dominance of the consensus principle has been undermined to some extent (Zürn *et al.* 2007). Majority decisions, for instance, can be found in the International Monetary Fund, the World Bank and many international environmental regimes. Examples of strong dispute-settlement bodies include the International Criminal Court, the World Trade Organization's 'Dispute Settlement Body', Mercosur's *Tribunal Permanente de Revisión* and, in a certain sense, even the UN Security Council.

NGOs also play a significant role in international politics. They incorporate a deliberative element as well. There are good reasons to suppose that this kind of transnationalisation has gained considerable quantitative momentum in recent decades. Today, the number of INGOs has surged to over 6,500 (Karns and Mingst 2004, 17); the change is not merely quantitative. In environmental matters alone, the number of transnational policy networks increased from two in 1953 to ninety in 1993 (Keck and Sikkink 1998, 10). With the increasing demand for privately-supplied knowledge and expertise, the number of accredited NGOs in the United Nations Economic and Social Council (ECOSOC) has continued to rise. In 1948, 50 NGOs were accredited; by 1996, their number had increased to 1041, and by 2005 to 2719. A similar trend can be observed in the field of humanitarian assistance. In the 1960s, the United Nations High Commissioner for Refugees (UNHCR) cooper-ated with between ten and twenty NGOs. By the 1990s the number of NGOs working with UNHCR had increased to several hundred. Moreover, NGOs that operate in the area of humanitarian relief dispose of more financial resources and take on far more complex tasks (Macrae

2002, 15). It thus seems safe to conclude that the influence of non-governmental organisations has significantly increased.

In addition, interest groups of different kinds also play a role in international politics. There are for instance a number of genuinely international interest organisations, such as the International Chamber of Commerce, or the multinational corporations which have significantly gained in number (the current count standing at an impressive 60,000) as well as political influence (Karns and Mingst 2004: 17). Even nationally constituted interest groups have begun to internationalise their activities in the context of denationalisation. A study of the political responses of such groups in highly denationalised issue areas, such as the Internet, migration and climate change politics, has shown that many of these groups not only demand international political action by states, but they themselves have begun to move beyond the nation state as the exclusive domain for political action (cf. Zürn and Walter 2005: 270 f.). This pattern becomes particularly visible wherever there exists a political opportunity structure that enables these groups to connect to pre-existing institutions. In other words, once policy-making processes have been initiated at levels beyond the nation state, even nationally constituted interest groups tend to follow the respective states to this level of activity.

Largely absent from the international level, however, is the parliamentarian mode of representation. To be sure, institutions such as the Council of Europe, NATO and the Organization for Security and Co-operation in Europe (OSCE) do have parliamentary assemblies. But without exception they are rather limited in their influence and they represent only parts of the national *demoi* on the international level, rather than operating as genuinely transnational bodies. This implies that the equalising effect of the principle of 'one person, one vote' is entirely missing from the field of international politics.

In spite of the changes described above, territorial representation remains (a) overwhelmingly in the hands of states (with only marginal forms of parliamentarian representation) and (b) largely dominated by functional forms of representation. In international institutions, the dominant mode of representation on the international level still functions via territorial states. Moreover, to the extent that deliberative aspects of decision making have gained some influence in sectorally limited institutions, the lack of regulation of clashes among different specialised international institutions is obvious. If it takes place at all, such regulation is left to inter-governmental conferences, again dominated by bargaining states. A public discourse that could serve as an instrument for balancing different sectoral regulations is largely absent.

Finally, it also has to be noted that in no small measure because of the absence of parliaments almost all modes of representation are heavily skewed towards powerful Western interests, even though the OECD countries represent less than a fifth of the world's population.

The situation differs to some extent when it comes to the European Union. It remains true that the member states, operating as the region's political entities, dominate the political process. The territorial mode of representation is still dominant – despite the existence of a coherent institutional setting that allows for (and fosters) functional organisations. But there are at least three structural differences between the EU and specialised international institutions. First, organisations that specialise in the functional mode of representation are relatively more powerful within the EU than beyond. There is a highly differentiated landscape of powerful interest groups and a significant number of financially well-supported NGOs. Second, within the EU the functional influence of NGOs is somewhat weaker than in specialised international institutions. A potential explanation lies in the fact that in the international realm NGOs offer unique possibilities to specialised institutions to overcome their governance deficits, and that they thus find themselves much more on a par with interest groups than is the case within the EU (Kellow 2002). Third, the European Parliament more closely resembles a transnational form of parliamentary representation than any other equivalent institution. There are no European parties and there is thus no truly European voting, but the MEPs are directly elected to serve at the European level. Coupled with the increasing influence of the European Parliament following the adoption of the Lisbon Treaty, this significantly adds to a more balanced picture of how the EU provides different modes of representation.

Summary and conclusions

In this chapter we have tried to analyse some familiar criticisms of the democratic deficit of international institutions. We have argued that in times of denationalisation, with regard to both the democratic legitimacy and efficiency of governance, international institutions are part of the solution rather than part of the problem. At the same time, we agree with the critics of international institutions that they indeed exhibit significant democratic weaknesses – specifically in the field of what Dahl has called 'citizen participation' (Dahl 1994). Sceptics maintain that these weaknesses are structural because of the absence of the social prerequisites for democracy on the international level. They draw the conclusion that efforts to democratise these institutions are in vain – ultimately because there cannot be a *demos* on the international level that could be the subject of any form of democratisation. We have claimed, however, that historically speaking, *demoi* have emerged in close proximity to political institutions that have fostered them and, in addition, that these *demoi* reflect areas of dense social transactions, of the kind that denationalisation is spreading beyond national borders. There is thus no *a priori* reason to reject the possibility of the formation of a *demos* beyond the nation state. In fact, a disaggregated analysis of the elements of a *demos* on the international level has shown that some components of a *demos*, such as the mutual acknowledgement of certain rights or the mutual trust in compliance, are already relatively well established. A sense of solidarity and a strong infrastructure of public discourse are still clearly deficient. In addition, the different forms of interest representation deviate from the national constellation. While all modes of interest aggregation clearly exist at the international level, the blend of these modes differs significantly from what we are accustomed to at the national level. In specialised international institutions there is a very strong dominance of states as territorial representative units functioning in a bargaining mode, with interests groups and NGOs slowly growing in importance and parliamentarian representation almost completely absent. In the case of the European Union, this dominance of the member states is muted. Functional modes of representation are stronger and there is a Parliament that, although still not on a par with national parliaments, nevertheless constitutes a significant improvement compared to the existing situation in specialised international institutions.

Based on these considerations, our analysis leads us to make certain suggestions about how the democratisation of international institutions could happen. At the European as well as at the international level, fostering transborder communication and discourse could go a long way toward strengthening the elements of a transnational *demos* that are still largely absent. Such discourse is not only a core component of the *demos* itself; it is also a necessary prerequisite for an increase in transnational solidarity that can only be based on common norms established through such discourse. While denationalisation in communications is already laying the ground for this, improvements of the necessary infrastructure would be a worthy political endeavour.

Core problems admittedly still exist concerning the different modes of representation. Strong state dominance in specialised international institutions is a severe impediment to the further democratisation of these institutions. It is thus centrally important to curb this dominance. While a strengthening of the parliamentarian mode of representation seems attractive but unlikely in the near future, there is reason to hope that the rise of transnational NGOs can counterbalance the dominance of states. International institutions should thus systematically permit NGO participation above and beyond the now common levels of recognition of these groups. What is missing, however, are mechanisms through which different sectoral subsystems can be coordinated with each other. It is here that the lack of a broad public debate extending across national and sectoral borders is most strongly felt. Our advice to international institutions is that they need actively to foster such debates by means of outreach programmes, public fora and other measures.

For the European Union, it has to be noted that while it may be true that it is a quite special and particularly powerful 'beast' among the international institutions, and that its legitimation requirements are therefore particularly challenging, it is also true that it fares much better in terms of balancing the different modes of representation than its international counterparts, and that it suffers much less from the dominance of a few states. Still, the Union could do much better in balancing NGOs versus interest groups; and it could certainly further strengthen the Parliament. This does not necessarily have to take the form of further enlarging its legislative powers, a move which in the past has not led to higher levels of popular support for the project of European unification (König and Mäder 2008: 445). Rather, the priority is to transform the European Parliament into a truly transnational institution based on transnational parties, truly transnational elections and cross-border political discourse (Lepsius 1986: 758). If that happened, even the Union might eventually become eligible for membership in the Union.

REFERENCES

Abromeit, H. and T. Schmidt (1998) 'Grenzprobleme der Demokratie', in B. Kohler-Koch (ed.) *Regieren in entgrenzten Räumen*. PVS-Sonderheft 29. Opladen: Westdeutscher Verlag, pp. 293–320.

Adler, E. and P. M. Haas (1992) 'Conclusion: Epistemic communities, world order, and the creation of a reflective research program', *International Organization* 46(1): 367–90.

Alexy, R. (1985) *Theorie der Grundrechte*. Baden-Baden: Nomos.

Anderson, B. (1991) *Imagined communities: Reflections on the origin and spread of nationalism*. 2nd edn. London: Verso.

Beisheim, M., S. Dreher, G. Walter, B. Zangl and M. Zürn (1999) *Im Zeitalter der Globalisierung? Thesen und Daten zur gesellschaftlichen und politischen Denationalisierung*. Baden-Baden: Nomos.

Beyme, K. von. (1998) 'Niedergang der Parlamente: Internationale Politik und nationale Entscheidungshoheit', *Internationale Politik* 53(4): 24–5.

Bull, H. (1977) *The anarchical society*. London: Macmillan.

Carr, E. H. (1945) *Nationalism and after*. London: Macmillan.

Chayes, A. and A. H. Chayes (1995) *The new sovereignty: Compliance with international regulatory agreements*. Cambridge, MA: Harvard University Press.

Dahl, R. A. (1994) 'A democratic dilemma: System effectiveness versus citizen participation', *Political Science Quarterly* 109(1): 23–34.

Deutsch, K. W. (1969) *Nationalism and its alternatives*. New York: Alfred Knopf.

Donnelly, J. (1993) *International human rights*. Boulder, CO: Westview Press.

Eder, K., K.-U. Hellmann and H. J. Trenz (1998) 'Regieren in Europa jenseits öffentlicher Legitimation? Eine Untersuchung zur Rolle von Öffentlichkeit in Europa', in B. Kohler-Koch (ed.) *Regieren in entgrenzten Räumen*. PVS-Sonderheft 29. Opladen: Westdeutscher Verlag, pp. 324–6.

Elster, J. (ed.) (1998) *Deliberative democracy*. Cambridge University Press.

European Commission (2006) 'Europeans and their languages: Summary', Special Eurobarometer 243, Brussels: European Commission.

Evans, T. (1997) 'Democratization and human rights', in A. McGrew (ed.) *The transformation of democracy*. Cambridge: Polity Press, pp. 122–48.

Francis, E. (1965) *Ethnos und Demos. Soziologische Beiträge zur Volkstheorie*. Berlin: Duncker and Humblot.

Gehring, T. (1995) 'Regieren im internationalen System. Verhandlungen, Normen und internationale Regime', *Politische Vierteljahresschrift* 36(2): 197–219.

Habermas, J. (1994) *Faktizität und Geltung*. Frankfurt am Main: Suhrkamp.

Hallerberg, M. and K. Weber (2002) 'German unification 1815–1871 and its relevance for integration theory', *Journal of European Integration* 24(1): 7–8.

Held, D. (1995) *Democracy and the global order: From the modern state to cosmopolitan governance*. Cambridge: Polity Press.

  (1998) 'Democracy and globalisation', in D. Archibugi, D. Held and M. Köhler (eds.) *Re-imagining political community: Studies in cosmopolitan democracy*. Cambridge: Polity Press, pp. 11–27.

Held, D., A. G. McGrew, D. Goldblatt and J. Perraton (1999) *Global transformations: Politics, economics and culture*. Cambridge: Polity Press.

Henkin, L. (1968) *How nations behave: Law and foreign policy*. London: Pall Mall Press.

Hobsbawm, E. J. (1992) *Nations and nationalism since 1780: Programme, myth, reality*. 2nd edn. Cambridge University Press.

Joerges, C. (1996) 'The emergence of denationalised governance structures and the European Court of Justice', Working Paper 16, Oslo: Center for European Studies (ARENA).

Joerges, C. and J. Neyer (1997) 'Transforming strategic interaction into deliberative problem-solving: European comitology in the foodstuff sector', *Journal of European Public Policy* 4(4): 609–25.

Karns, M. P. and K. Mingst (2004) *International organizations: The politics and processes of global governance*. Boulder, CO: Rienner.

Keck, M. E. and K. Sikkink (1998) *Activists beyond borders: Advocacy networks in international politics*. Ithaca, NY: Cornell University Press.

Kellow, A. (2002) 'Comparing business and public interest associability at the international level', *International Political Science Review* 23(2): 175–86.

Kielmannsegg, P. G. (1994) 'Lässt sich die Europäische Gemeinschaft demokratisch verfassen?', *Europäische Rundschau* 22(2): 22–33.

König, T. and L. Mäder (2008) 'Das Regieren jenseits des Nationalstaates und der Mythos einer 80-Prozent-Europäisierung in Deutschland', *Politische Vierteljahresschrift* 49(3): 438–63.

Lepsius, R. (1986) '"Ethnos" und "Demos"', *Kölner Zeitschrift für Soziologie und Sozialpsychologie* 38(4): 751–9.

Linklater, A. (1998) *The transformation of political community.* Cambridge: Polity Press.

Macrae, J. (ed.) (2002) *The new humanitarianisms: A review of trends in global humanitarian action.* Humanitarian Policy Group (HPG) Report 11, London: Overseas Development Institute.

Majone, G. (ed.) (1996) *Regulating Europe.* London: Routledge.

Neyer, J. (2005) 'Die Krise der EU und die Stärke einer deliberativen Integrationstheorie', *Zeitschrift für Internationale Beziehungen* 12(2): 377–82.

Preuss, U. K. (1998) 'The relevance of the concept of citizenship', in U. K. Preuss and F. Requejo (eds.) *European citizenship, multiculturalism, and the state.* Baden-Baden: Nomos.

Princen, T. and M. Finger (1994) *Environmental NGOs in world politics: Linking the local and the global.* London: Routledge.

Radtke, K. R. (2007) 'Ein Trend zu transnationaler Solidarität? Die Entwicklung des Spendenaufkommens in der Not und Entwicklungshilfe', Discussion Paper No. 304, Wissenschaftszentrum Berlin (WZB).

Rosenau, J. N. (1997) *Along the domestic-foreign frontier: Exploring governance in a turbulent world.* Cambridge University Press.

Sapiro, G. (ed.) (2008) *Translation. Le marché de la traduction en France à l'heure de la mondialisation.* Paris: CNRS-éditions.

Scharpf, F. W. (1993) 'Legitimationsprobleme der Globalisierung. Regieren in Verhandlungssystemen', in C. Böhret and G. Wewer (eds.) *Regieren im 21. Jahrhundert – Zwischen Globalisierung und Regionalisierung. Festgabe für Hans-Hermann Hartwich zum 65. Geburtstag.* Opladen: Leske & Budrich, pp. 165–85.

—— (1997) 'Economic integration, democracy, and the welfare state', *Journal of European Public Policy* 4(1): 18–36.

Schmalz-Bruns, R. (1995) *Reflexive Demokratie. Die demokratische Transformation moderner Politik.* Baden-Baden: Nomos.

—— (1998) 'Grenzerfahrungen und Grenzüberschreitungen: Demokratie im integrierten Europa', in B. Kohler-Koch (ed.) *Regieren in entgrenzten Räumen.* PVS-Sonderheft 29. Opladen: Westdeutscher Verlag.

Snyder, J. (1993) *Myths of empire: Domestic politics and international ambition.* New York: Cornell University Press.

Streeck, W. (1998) 'Einleitung', in W. Streeck (ed.) *Internationale Wirtschaft, nationale Demokratie? Herausforderungen für die Demokratietheorie.* Frankfurt/New York: Campus, pp. 11–58.

Tömmel, I. (2006) *Das politische System der EU*. Second completely revised edition. München and Wien: Oldenbourg.

Zürn, M. (2000) 'Democratic governance beyond the nation state: The EU and other international institutions', *European Journal of International Relations* 6(2): 183–221.

Zürn, M. and C. Joerges (eds.) (2005) *Law and governance in postnational constellations: Compliance in Europe and beyond*. Cambridge University Press.

Zürn, M. and G. Walter (eds.) (2005) *Globalizing interests: Pressure groups and denationalization*. Albany: State University of New York Press.

Zürn, M., M. Binder, M. Ecker-Ehrhardt and K. Radtke (2007) 'Politische Ordnungsbildung wider Willen', *Zeitschrift für Internationale Beziehungen* 14(1): 129–64.

General bibliography

Abromeit, H. and T. Schmidt (1998) 'Grenzprobleme der Demokratie', in B. Kohler-Koch (ed.) *Regieren in entgrenzten Räumen*. PVS-Sonderheft 29. Opladen: Westdeutscher Verlag, pp. 293–320.

Accarino, B. (1999) *Rappresentanza*. Bologna: Il Mulino.

Achen, C. H. (1978) 'Measuring representation', *American Journal of Political Science* 22(3): 475–510.

Achen, C. H. and L. Bartels (2004) 'Blind retrospection: Electoral responses to drought, flu and shark attacks', *Working Paper 2004/199*, Madrid: Instituto Juan March.

Adler, E. and P. M. Haas (1992) 'Conclusion: Epistemic communities, world order, and the creation of a reflective research program', *International Organization* 46(1): 367–90.

Aja, E. (2003) *El estado autonómico. Federalismo y hechos diferenciales*. Madrid: Alianza Editorial.

Alonso, S. (2011) *Challenging the State: Devolution and the Battle for Partisan Credibility*. Oxford University Press.

Anderson, B. (1991) *Imagined communities: Reflections on the origin and spread of nationalism*. 2nd edition. London: Verso.

Andeweg, R. B., R. Hillebrand, R. van Schendelen, J. Thomassen and M. L. Zielonka-Goei (1989) *Dutch parliamentary study 1990, manuskript für das symposium on parliamentary research*. Leiden.

Ankersmit, F. R. (2002) *Political representation*. Stanford University Press.

(2008) 'On the future of representative democracy', available at www.thefutureofrepresentativedemocracy.org

Anonymous (1816) *Réfutation de la doctrine de Montesquieu sur la balance des pouvoirs et aperçus divers sur plusieurs questions sur la droit publique*. Paris.

Bacchi, C. (1990) *Same difference: Feminism and sexual difference*. London: Allen & Unwin.

(2006) 'Arguing for and against quotas: Theoretical issues', in D. Dahlerup (ed.) *Women, quotas and politics*. New York/London: Routledge, pp. 32–51.

Bachrach, P. (1967) *The theory of democratic elitism*. Boston: Little, Brown.

Bachrach, P. and M. Baratz (1970) *Power and poverty*. Oxford University Press.

Baer, D. and S. Bryan (2005) *Money in politics*. Washington DC: National Democratic Institute.

Bailyn, B. (ed.) (1993) *The debate on the constitution: Federalist and antifederalist speeches, articles, and letters during the struggle over ratification.* 2 vols. New York: Library of America.

Barber, B. (1984) *Strong democracy: Participatory politics for a new age.* Berkeley: University of California Press.

Barker, R. (2001) *Legitimating identities.* Cambridge University Press.

Barley, S. R. (2007) 'Corporations, democracy, and the public good', *Journal of Management Inquiry* 16(3): 201–15.

Bastid, P. (1939) *Les discours de Sieyès dans les débats constitutionnels de l'An III (2 et 18 Thermidor): Édition critique avec une introduction et des notes.* Paris: Hachette.

Beetham, D. (1991) *The legitimation of power.* Basingstoke: Palgrave Macmillan.

(2005) *Democracy: A beginner's guide.* Oxford: Oneworld Publications.

(2006a) *Parliament and democracy in the twenty-first century: A guide to good practice.* Geneva: Inter-Parliamentary Union.

(2006b) 'Weber and Anglo-American democracy', in K.-L. Ay. and K. Borchardt (eds.) *Das Faszinosum Max Weber.* Konstanz: UVK Verlagsgesellschaft, pp. 343–51.

Beichelt, T. (2001) *Demokratische konsolidierung im postsozialistischen Europa. Die Rolle der politischen institutionen.* Opladen: Leske & Budrich.

Beisheim, M., S. Dreher, G. Walter, B. Zangl and M. Zürn (1999) *Im Zeitalter der Globalisierung? Thesen und Daten zur gesellschaftlichen und politischen Denationalisierung.* Baden-Baden: Nomos.

Benhabib, S. (2004) *The rights of others: Aliens, residents and citizens.* New York: Cambridge University Press.

Berlin, I. (1980) *Against the current.* New York: Viking Press.

(1992) 'Two concepts of liberty', in *Four essays on liberty.* Oxford University Press, pp. 118–72.

Betz, H.-G. (1994) *Radical right-wing populism in western Europe.* Houndsmill: Macmillan.

Beyme, K. von (1965) 'Repräsentatives und parlamentarisches regierungssystem. Eine begriffsgeschichtliche analyse', *Politische Vierteljahresschrift* 6(2): 145–59.

(1987) *America as a model: The impact of democracy in the world.* Aldershot: Gower.

(1988) 'Right-wing extremism in post-war Europe', *West European Politics* 11: 1–18.

(1998) 'Niedergang der Parlamente: Internationale Politik und nationale Entscheidungshoheit', *Internationale Politik* 53(4): 24–5.

(2000a) *Parliamentary democracy: Democratization, destabilization, reconsolidation, 1789–1999.* Houndsmill: Macmillan.

(2000b) *Parteien im Wandel. Von den Volksparteien zu den professionalisierten Wählerparteien.* Opladen: Westdeutscher Verlag, 2nd edition 2002.

Birch, A. H. (1993) *The concepts and theories of modern democracy.* London: Routledge.

Bjarnegård, E. (2009) *Men in politics: Revisiting patterns of gendered parliamentary representation in Thailand and beyond.* PhD thesis, Uppsala Universitet: Department of Government.

Bobbio, N. (1955) *Politica e cultura*. Turin: Einaudi.

(1999) *Teoria generale della politica*. Turin: Einaudi.

Böckenförde, E. W. (1991) *State, society and liberty: Studies in political theory and constitutional law*. New York and Oxford: Berg.

Bodin, J. (1992) *On sovereignty: Four chapters from the six books of the Commonwealth*. Cambridge University Press.

Brancati, D. (2007) 'The origins and strengths of regional parties', *British Journal of Political Science* 38: 135–59.

Brass, P. (1997) *Theft of an idol: Text and context in the representation of collective violence*. Princeton University Press.

Brubaker, R. (2004) *Ethnicity without groups*. Harvard University Press.

Bühlmann, M., W. Merkel and B. Wessels in collaboration with L. Müller (2008) *The quality of democracy: Democracy barometer for established democracies*. Zürich: National Center of Competence in Research (NCCR Democracy 21), Working Paper No. 10a, revised version March 2008.

Bull, H. (1977) *The anarchical society*. London: Macmillan.

Burke, E. (1834) *Thoughts on the cause of the present discontents*, in *The works of Edmund Burke*. London: Holdsworth and Ball, vol. I, pp. 124–53.

(1864) *To the electors of Bristol (1774)*, in Burke: *Works, Vol. 1*. London: Henry G. Bohn, pp. 442–9.

Butler, J. (1990) *Gender trouble: Feminism and the subversion of identity*. New York: Routledge.

(1997) *Excitable speech: Politics of the performative*. London and New York: Routledge.

Callicott, J. B. (1985) 'Intrinsic value, quantum theory and environmental ethics', *Environmental Ethics* 7(3): 257–75.

Caporaso, J. A. (ed.) (1989) *The elusive state*. London: Sage.

Carr, E. H. (1945) *Nationalism and after*. London: Macmillan.

Carré de Malberg, R. (1922) *Contribution à la théorie générale de l'État*, 2 vols., Paris: Librairie Recueil Sirey.

Chabal, P. and J.-P. Daloz (2006) *Culture troubles: Politics and the interpretation of meaning*. London: Hurst & Co.

Chandra, K. (2004) *Why ethnic parties succeed*. Cambridge University Press.

Chayes, A. and A. H. Chayes (1995) *The new sovereignty: Compliance with international regulatory agreements*. Cambridge, MA: Harvard University Press.

Cheney, J. (1989) 'Postmodern environmental ethics: Ethics as bioregional narrative', *Environmental Ethics* 11(2): 117–34.

Clarke, M. V. (1964) *Medieval representation and consent: A study of early parliaments in England and Ireland, with special reference to the modus tenendi parliamentum*. New York: Russell & Russell.

Cochin, A. (1979) *L'esprit du jacobinisme: Une interprétation sociologique de la révolution française*, Paris: Presses Universitaires de France.

Collier, D. and St. Levitsky (1997) 'Democracy with adjectives: Conceptual innovation in comparative research', *World Politics* 49(3): 430–51.

Committee on Political Parties of the American Political Studies Association (1950) *Toward a more responsible two-party system*. A Report of the APSR, Supplement 88.

Condorcet, Marquis de (1968) 'Lettres d'un bourgeois de New-Haven à un citoyen de Virginie', in Condorcet, Marquis de, *Oeuvres: nouvelle impression en facsimilé de l'édition Paris, 1847–1849*. 12 vols. Stuttgart-Bad Cannstatt: Friedrich Frommann.

Connor, W. (1967) 'Self-determination: The new phase', *World Politics* 20(1): 30–53.

Converse, P. E. and R. Pierce (1986) *Political representation in France*. Cambridge and London: Belknap Press.

Conversi, D. (1997) *The Basques, the Catalans and Spain*. London: Hurst & Company.

Cox, G. W. (1997) *Making votes count: Strategic coordination in the world's electoral systems*. Cambridge University Press.

(1999) 'Electoral rules and the calculus of mobilization', *Legislative Studies Quarterly* 24(3): 387–419.

Crahay, R. (1983) 'Jean Bodin aux Etats Généraux de 1576', in *Assemblee di Stati e istituzioni rappresentative nella storia del pensiero politico moderno (secoli XV–XX)*, vol. 1, 85–120. Università di Perugia, Annali della Facoltà di Scienze Politiche. Città di Castello: Maggioli Editore.

Croissant, A. and W. Merkel (eds.) (2004) 'Consolidated or defective democracy? Problems of regime change'. Special issue of *Democratization* 11(5).

Cronon, W. (1996) 'The trouble with wilderness, or, getting back to the wrong nature', *Environmental History* 1(1): 7–55.

Crouch, C. (2005) *Post-democracy*. Cambridge: Polity Press.

Dahl, R. A. (1970) *After the revolution?: Authority in a good society*. New Haven, CT: Yale University Press.

(1971) *Polyarchy: Participation and opposition*. New Haven, CT: Yale University Press.

(1983) *Dilemmas of pluralist democracy: Autonomy vs. control*. New Haven, CT: Yale University Press.

(1985) *A preface to economic democracy*. Cambridge: Polity Press.

(1989) *Democracy and its critics*. New Haven, CT: Yale University Press.

(1994) 'A democratic dilemma: System effectiveness versus citizen participation', *Political Science Quarterly* 109(1): 23–34.

(1996) 'The future of democratic theory', *Estudios. Working Papers* 90. Madrid.

(2000) *On democracy*. New Haven, CT and London: Yale University Press.

(2001) *How democratic is the American constitution?* New Haven, CT: Yale University Press.

(2006) *On political equality*. New Haven, CT: Yale University Press.

Dahlerup, D. (1978) 'Women's entry into politics: The experience of the Danish local and general elections 1908–20', *Scandinavian Political Studies* 1(2–3): 139–62.

(2004) 'Continuity and waves in the feminist movement", in H. R. Christensen, B. Halsaa and A. Saarinen (eds.), *Crossing borders: Re-mapping women's movements at the turn of the 21st Century*. Odense: The University Press of Southern Denmark, pp. 59–75.

(ed.) (2006) *Women, quotas and politics*. New York and London: Routledge.

(2007) 'Electoral gender quotas: Between equality of opportunity and equality of results', *Representation* 43(2): 73–92.

Dahlerup, D. and L. Freidenvall (2005) 'Quotas as a "fast track" to equal representation of women: Why Scandinavia is no longer the model', *International Feminist Journal of Politics* 7(1): 26–48.

Dahrendorf, R. (1968) *Homo sociologicus*. Köln, Opladen: Westdeutscher Verlag.

Dalton, R. (2004) *Democratic challenges, democratic choices: The erosion of political support in advanced industrial democracies*. New York and Oxford: Oxford University Press.

Decker, F. (2006a) 'Direkte demokratie im deutschen "Parteienbundesstaat"', *Aus Politik und Zeitgeschichte* 10: 3–10.

(ed.) (2006b) *Populismus. Gefahr für die demokratie oder nützliches korrektiv?* Wiesbaden: Verlag für Sozialwissenschaften.

Derathé, R. (1970) *Jean-Jacques Rousseau et la science politique de son temps*. Paris: Librairie Philosophique Vrin.

Derrida, J. (1998) *Limited Inc*. Evanston, IL: Northwestern University Press.

Deutsch, K. W. (1969) *Nationalism and its alternatives*. New York: Alfred Knopf.

Devlin, C. and R. Elgie (2008) 'The effect of increased women's representation in parliament: The case of Rwanda', *Parliamentary Affairs* 61(2): 237–54.

De Winter, L. and H. Türsan (1998) *Regionalist parties in western Europe*. London and New York: Routledge.

De Winter, L., M. Gómez-Reino and D. Lynch (eds.) (2006). *Autonomist parties in Europe: Identity politics and the revival of the territorial cleavage*. Barcelona: Institut de Ciènces Polítiques i Socials.

Dobson, A. (1996) 'Representative democracy and the environment', in W. M. Lafferty and J. Meadowcroft (eds.) *Democracy and the environment: Problems and prospects*. Cheltenham, UK: Edward Elgar, pp. 124–39.

Donnelly, J. (1993) *International human rights*. Boulder, CO: Westview Press.

Downs, A. (1957) *An economic theory of democracy*. New York: Harper and Row.

Doyle, W. (1987) 'The parlements', in K. M. Baker (ed.) *The French revolution and the creation of modern political culture*, vol. 1, *The political culture of the Old Regime*, Oxford: Pergamon Press, pp. 157–67.

Dunn, J. (2005) *Democracy: A history*. New York: Atlantic Monthly Press.

(2010) 'Democracy and its discontents', *The National Interest* 106 (March–April).

Easton, D. (1965) *A systems analysis of political life*. New York and London: John Wiley & Sons.

Eckersley, R. (1995) 'Liberal democracy and the environment: The rights discourse and the struggle for recognition', *Environmental Politics* 4(4): 169–98.

(2004a) *The Green state: Rethinking democracy and sovereignty*. Cambridge, MA: MIT Press.

(2004b) 'Ecocentric discourses: Problems and future prospects for nature advocacy', *Tamkang Review* 34(3–4): 155–86.

Eco, U. (1999) *Kant and the platypus: Essays on language and cognition*. London: Secker and Warburg.

Eder, K., K.-U. Hellmann and H. J. Trenz (1998) 'Regieren in Europa jenseits öffentlicher Legitimation? Eine Untersuchung zur Rolle von Öffentlichkeit in Europa', in B. Kohler-Koch (ed.) *Regieren in entgrenzten Räumen*. PVS-Sonderheft 29. Opladen: Westdeutscher Verlag, pp. 324–26.

Ehrenfeld, D. (1981) *The arrogance of humanism*. New York: Oxford University Press.

Elster, J. (ed.) (1998) *Deliberative democracy*. Cambridge University Press.

Esaiasson, P. and S. Holmberg (1996) *Representation from above: Members of parliament and representative democracy in Sweden*. Aldershot: Dartmouth.

Esman, M. (1977) *Ethnic conflict in the western world*. Ithaca, NY: Cornell University Press.

European Commission (2004) *Eurobarometer 61*. Brussels: EU Commission.
  (2006) 'Europeans and their languages. Summary', Special Eurobarometer 243, Brussels: European Commission.

Evans, R. (1977) *The feminists: Women's emancipation movements in Europe, America and Australasia, 1840–1920*. London: Croom Helm.

Evans, T. (1997) 'Democratization and human rights', in A. McGrew (ed.) *The transformation of democracy*. Cambridge: Polity Press, pp. 122–48.

Evernden, N. (1984) 'The environmentalist's dilemma', in N. Evernden (ed.) *Paradox of environmentalism*. Downsview, Ontario: Faculty of Environmental Studies, York University.

Faltin, I. (1990) *Norm, milieu, politische kultur*. Wiesbaden: DUV.

Fearon, J. and D. Laitin (2000) 'Violence and the social construction of ethnic identity', *International Organization* 54(4): 845–77.

Field, B. (2011) *Spain's 'Second Transition'? The Socialist Government of José Luis Rodríguez Zapatero*. New York: Routledge.

Filmer, R. (1991) 'Patriarcha', in J. P. Sommerville (ed.) *Patriarcha and other essays*. Cambridge University Press.

Fish, M. S. (2006) 'Stronger legislatures, stronger democracies', *Journal of Democracy* 17(1): 5–20.

Flyvbjerg, B., N. Bruzelius and W. Rothengatter (2003) *Megaprojects and risk: An anatomy of ambition*. Cambridge and New York: Cambridge University Press.

Forst, R. (2007) *Das recht der rechtfertigung*. Frankfurt: Suhrkamp.

Fralin, R. (1978) *Rousseau and representation: A study of the development of his concept of political institutions*. New York: Columbia University Press.

Franceshet, S. and J. M. Piscopo (2008) 'Gender quotas and women's substantive representation: Lessons from Argentina', *Politics & Gender* 4(3): 393–425.

Francis, E. (1965) *Ethnos und Demos. Soziologische Beiträge zur Volkstheorie*. Berlin: Duncker and Humblot.

Frankfurt, H. G. (2005) *On bullshit*. Princeton and Oxford: Princeton University Press.

Freidenvall, L. (2006) *Vägen till Varannan Damernas: Om kvinnorepresentation, kvotering och kandidaturval i svensk politik 1970–2002*. PhD thesis, Department of Political Science, Stockholm University.

Freitag, M. and U. Wagschal (eds.) (2007) *Direkte demokratie. Bestandsaufnahmen und wirkungen im internationalen vergleich*. Münster: LIT.

Friedman, R. B. (1990) 'On the concept of authority in political philosophy', in J. Raz (ed.) *Authority*. Oxford: Basil Blackwell, pp. 56–91.

Friedrich, C. J. (1963) *Man and his government: An empirical theory of politics.* New York: McGraw Book Company.

Fukuyama, F. (2006) *The end of history and the last man.* New York and London: Free Press.

Fung, A. and E. O. Wright (eds.) (2003) *Deepening democracy: Institutional innovations in empowered participatory governance.* London and New York: Verso.

Gadamer, H. G. (2004) *Truth and method.* London and New York: Continuum.

Gallant, N. (2008) 'Under what conditions can national minorities develop civic conceptions of nationhood?' Paper presented at the 18th Annual Association for the Study of Ethnicity and Nationalism Conference, London School of Economics, 15–16 April.

Galligan, Y. (2007) 'Gender and political representation: Current empirical perspectives', *International Political Science Review* 28(5): 557–70.

Gandhi, J. (2008) *Political institutions under dictatorship.* Cambridge University Press.

Gastil, J. and P. Levine (eds.) (2005) *The deliberative democracy handbook: Strategies for effective civic engagement in the 21st century.* San Francisco: Jossey-Bass.

Geertz, C. (2000) *Available light: Anthropological reflections on philosophical topics.* Princeton University Press.

Gehring, T. (1995) 'Regieren im internationalen System: Verhandlungen, Normen und internationale Regime', *Politische Vierteljahresschrift* 36(2): 197–219.

Giddens, A. (1994) *Beyond left and right: The future of radical politics.* Cambridge: Polity Press.

Gierke, von O. (1958) *Political theories of the middle age.* Cambridge University Press.

Ginsborg, P. (2005) *The politics of everyday life: Making choices, changing lives.* New Haven, CT and London: Yale University Press.

Goetz, A. M. and S. Hassim (eds.) (2003) *No shortcuts to power: African women in politics and policy making.* London: Zed Books.

Goodin, R. (1996) 'Enfranchising the earth, and its alternatives', *Political Studies* 44(4): 835–49.

Grotius, H. (1925) *De jure belli ac pacis libri tres,* 2 vols. Oxford: Clarendon.

Gurr, T., T. Robert, K. Jaggers and W. Moore (1991) 'The transformation of the western state: The growth of democracy, autocracy and state power since 1800', in A. A. Inkeles (ed.) *On measuring democracy.* New Brunswick: Transaction, pp. 69–104.

Habermas, J. (1987) *Theorie des kommunikativen Handelns (Vol. 2): zur kritik der funktionalistischen Vernunft.* Frankfurt am Main: Suhrkamp.

(1992) *Faktizität und geltung.* Frankfurt: Suhrkamp.

(1996) *Between facts and norms: Contribution to a discourse theory of law and democracy.* Cambridge, MA: MIT Press.

Hadenius, A. and J. Teorell (2005) 'Assessing alternative indices of democracy'. *Political concepts: IPSA Committee on Concepts and Methods Working Paper Series* (6). Mexico City.

Haider, J. (1994) *Die freiheit, die ich meine*. Frankfurt: Ullstein.

Hallerberg, M. and K. Weber (2002) 'German unification 1815–1871 and its relevance for integration theory', *Journal of European Integration* 24(1): 7–8.

Hamann, K. (1999) 'Federalist institutions, voting behaviour and party systems in Spain', *Publius: The Journal of Federalism* 29(1): 111–38.

Hardt, M. and A. Negri (2002) *Empire – die neue Weltordnung*. Frankfurt: Campus.

Harraway, D. (1988) 'Situated knowledges: The science question in feminism and the privilege of partial perspective', *Feminist Studies* 14(3): 575–99.

(1991) *Simians, cyborgs and women*. New York: Routledge.

Hartleb, F. (2004) *Rechts- und Linkspopulismus*. Wiesbaden: Verlag für Sozialwissenschaften.

Hayek, F. von (1979) *Law, legislation and liberty: The political order of a free people*. London and Henley: Routledge.

Hayward, J. (ed.) (1996) *The crisis of representation in Europe*. Abingdon, Oxon: Routledge.

Hayward, T. (2005) *Constitutional environmental rights*. Oxford University Press.

Hebbert, M. (1987). 'Regionalism: A reform concept and its application to Spain'. *Environment and Planning C: Government and Policy* 5: 239–250.

Hechter, M. (2000) *Containing nationalism*. Oxford University Press.

Held, D. (1993) *Political theory today*. Oxford: Polity Press.

(1995) *Democracy and the global order: From the modern state to cosmopolitan governance*. Cambridge: Polity Press.

(1998) 'Democracy and globalisation', in D. Archibugi, D. Held and M. Köhler (eds.) *Re-imagining political community: Studies in cosmopolitan democracy*. Cambridge: Polity Press, pp. 11–27.

Held, D., A. G. McGrew, D. Goldblatt and J. Perraton (1999) *Global transformations: Politics, economics and culture*. Cambridge: Polity Press.

Heller, W. (2002) 'Regional parties and national politics in Europe: Spain's Estado de las Autonomías, 1993 to 2002', *Comparative Political Studies* 35(6): 657–85.

Hemmati, M. (2002) *Multi-stakeholder processes for governance and sustainability*. London: Earthscan.

Henkin, L. (1968) *How nations behave: Law and foreign policy*. London: Pall Mall Press.

Hernes, H. (1982) *Staten – kvinner ingen adgang?* Oslo: Universitetsforlaget.

Herrera, C. L., R. Herrera and E. R. A. N. Smith (1992) 'Public opinion and congressional representation', *Public Opinion Quarterly* 56(2): 185–205.

Herzinger, R. (1997) *Die Tyrannei des Gemeinsinns. Ein Bekenntnis zur egoistischen Gesellschaft*. Berlin: Rowohlt.

Herzog, D., H. Rebenstorf, C. Werner and B. Wessels (1990) *Abgeordnete und Bürger*. Opladen: Westdeutscher Verlag.

Herzog, D., H. Rebenstorf and B. Wessels (eds.) (1993) *Parlament und Gesellschaft: Eine Funktionsanalyse der repräsentativen Demokratie*. Opladen: Westdeutscher Verlag.

Hirschman, A. O. (1970) *Exit, voice, and loyalty*. Cambridge, MA and London: Harvard University Press.

Hirst, P. (1994) *Associative democracy*. Cambridge: Polity Press.

(1997) *From statism to pluralism*. University College London Press.

Hobsbawm, E. J. (1992) *Nations and nationalism since 1780: Programme, myth, reality*. Cambridge University Press.

Holbach, P. H. T. Baron d' (1778–9) *Représentants*, in *Encyclopédie; ou, Dictionnaire raisonné des sciences, des arts et des métiers, par une société de gens de lettres. Mis en ordre & publié par M. Diderot; & quant a la partie mathématique, par M. D'Alembert*. 36 vols. Lausanne: Sociétés typographiques.

(1998) *La politique naturelle, ou Discours sur les vrais principes du gouvernement par un ancien magistrat* (1773). Paris: Fayard.

Holmberg, S. (1989) 'Political representation in Sweden', *Scandinavian Political Studies* 12: 1–36.

Holtmann, E. (2002) *Die angepassten Provokateure. Aufstieg und Niedergang der rechtsextremen DVU als Protestpartei im polarisierten Parteiensystem Sachsen-Anhalts*. Opladen: Westdeutscher Verlag.

Hooghe, L. (2004) 'Belgium: Hollowing the center'. In U. Amoretti and N. Bermeo (eds.) *Federalism and territorial cleavages*. Baltimore: Johns Hopkins University Press, pp. 55–92.

Horowitz, D. (1985) *Ethnic groups in conflict*. Berkeley: University of California Press.

Hough, D. and C. Jeffery (2006) *Devolution and electoral politics*. Manchester and New York: Manchester University Press.

Huber, J. D. and G. B. Powell, Jr. (1994) 'Congruence between citizens and policymakers in two visions of liberal democracy', *World Politics* 46(3): 291–326.

Hughes, J. and G. Sasse (2001) *Ethnicity and territory in the former Soviet Union*. London: Frank Cass Publishers.

Hughes, M. M. and P. Paxton (2008) 'Continuous change, episodes, and critical periods: A framework for understanding women's political representation over time', *Politics and Gender* 4(2): 233–64.

Informe sobre la Democracia en España 2007. Madrid: Fundación Alternativas.

Inglehart, R. (1990) *Culture shift in advanced industrial society*. Princeton University Press.

Ionescu, G. and E. Gellner (eds.) (1969) *Populism: Its meanings and national characteristics*. London: Weidenfeld & Nicolson.

Ishiyama, J. T. and M. Breuning (1998) *Ethnopolitics in the new Europe*. Boulder, CO and London: Lynne Rienner Publishers.

Ivakhiv, A. (2002) 'Toward a multicultural ecology', *Organization and Environment* 15(4): 389–409.

Jain, D. (2005) *Women, development, and the UN: The sixty-year quest for equality and justice*. Bloomington and Indianapolis: Indiana University Press.

Jalalzai, F. (2008) 'Women rule: Shattering the executive glass ceiling', *Politics and Gender* 4(2): 205–31.

Jewell, M. E. (1970) 'Attitudinal determinants of legislative behaviour: The utility of role analysis', in A. Kornberg and L. D. Musolf (eds). *Legislators in developmental perspective*. Kingsport: Kingsport Press, pp. 460–500.

Joerges, C. (1996) 'The emergence of denationalised governance structures and the European Court of Justice', Working Paper 16, Oslo: Center for European Studies (ARENA).

Joerges, C. and J. Neyer (1997) 'Transforming strategic interaction into deliberative problem-solving: European comitology in the foodstuff sector', *Journal of European Public Policy* 4(4): 609–25.

Kaase, M. (1984) 'The challenge of the "participatory revolution" in pluralist democracies', *International Political Science Review* 5(3): 299–318.

Kant, I. (1964) *Werke* (ed. Weisschädel) Wiesbaden: Insel-Verlag.

(1991) *The metaphysics of morals*. Cambridge University Press.

Karns, M. P. and K. Mingst (2004) *International organizations: The politics and processes of global governance*. Boulder, CO: Rienner.

Katz, R. S. and P. Mair (eds.) (1994) *How parties organize: Change and adaptation in party organizations in western democracies*. London: Sage.

Katz, R. S. and B. Wessels (eds.) (1999) *The European parliament, national parliaments, and European integration*. Oxford University Press.

Keane, J. (2008) 'Hypocrisy and democracy', *WZB-Mitteilungen* 120 (June): 30–2.

(2009a) *The life and death of democracy*. London: Simon & Schuster.

(2009b) *Media decadence and democracy*. Senate Occasional Lecture. Canberra: Parliament of Australia.

Keck, M. E. and K. Sikkink (1998) *Activists beyond borders: Advocacy networks in international politics*. Ithaca, NY: Cornell University Press.

Kellow, A. (2002) 'Comparing business and public interest associability at the international level', *International Political Science Review* 23(2): 175–86.

Kelsen, H. (1929) *Vom Wesen und Wert der Demokratie*. Tübingen: Mohr.

(1992) *Introduction to the problems of legal theory*. Oxford: Clarendon Press.

(1999) *General theory of law and state*. Union, NJ: The Lawbook Exchange.

Khasbulatov, R. I. (1993) 'Kakaya vlast' nuzhna Rossii', *Sotsiologicheskie issledovaniya* 11: 18–31.

Kielmannsegg, P. G. (1994) 'Lässt sich die Europäische Gemeinschaft demokratisch verfassen?', *Europäische Rundschau* 22(2): 22–33.

Kishlansky, M. A. (1986) *Parliamentary selection: Social and political choice in early modern England*. Cambridge University Press.

Klingemann, H.-D., R. Stöss and B. Wessels (eds.). *Politische Klasse und politische Institutionen: Probleme und Perspektiven der Elitenforschung*. Opladen: Westdeutscher Verlag.

Köchler, H. (ed.) (1985) *The crisis of representative democracy*. Frankfurt/M., Bern, New York: Lang.

Kohn, H. (1944) *The idea of nationalism*. New York: Macmillan.

König, T. and L. Mäder (2008) 'Das Regieren jenseits des Nationalstaates und der Mythos einer 80-Prozent-Europäisierung in Deutschland', *Politische Vierteljahresschrift* 49(3): 438–63.

Kraditor, A. S. (1965) *The ideas of the woman suffrage movement 1890–1920*. New York: Doubleday.

Kranenpohl, U. (2003) 'Verkürzen Verfassungsrichter Volksrechte?' *Gesellschaft–Wirtschaft – Politik* 52(1): 37–46.

(2006) 'Bewältigung des Reformstaus durch direkte Demokratie?' *Aus Politik und Zeitgeschichte* 10: 32–8.

Krohn, T. (2003) *Die Genese von Wahlsystemen in Transitionsprozessen. Portugal, Spanien, Polen und Tschechien im Vergleich.* Opladen: Leske & Budrich.

Krook, M. L. (2009) *Quotas for women in politics. Gender and candidate selection reform worldwide.* New York: Oxford University Press.

Küchenhoff, E. (1967) *Möglichkeiten und grenzen begrifflicher klarheit in der staatsformenlehre.* Berlin: Duncker and Humblot.

Kymlicka, W. (2003) 'Identity politics in multi-nation states', in Venice Commission (2005), *State consolidation and national identity.* Strasbourg: Council of Europe Publishing, Science and Technique of Democracy Series #38, pp. 45–53.

Lamennais, F. R. de (1823) *Extraits du drapeau blanc. Plan d'un libre intitulé: Observations sur le gouvernment de l'Angleterre, dit gouvernement représentatif constitutionnel.* Paris.

Lancaster, T. D. (1999) 'Complex self-identification and compounded representation in federal systems', *West European Politics* 22(2): 59–89.

Lane, J.-E., D. H. McKay and K. Newton (1991) *Political data handbook: OECD countries.* Oxford University Press.

Larserud, S. and R. Taphorn (2007) *Designing for equality: Best-fit, medium-fit and non-favourable combinations of electoral systems and gender quotas.* Stockholm: IDEA (The International Institute for Democracy and Electoral Assistance).

Laski, H. (1944) 'The parliamentary and presidential systems', *Public Administration Review,* Autumn: 347–59. See also D. K. Price, 'A response to Mr. Laski', *Public Administration Review,* Autumn: 360–63.

Latour, B. (1991) *Nous n'avons jamais été modernes.* Paris: La Découverte.

Laver, M. (1997) *Private desires, political action.* London: Sage.

Leibholz, G. (1967) *Strukturprobleme der modernen demokratie.* Karlsruhe: C. F. Müller, 3rd edition.

Lepsius, R. (1986) '"Ethnos" und "Demos"', *Kölner Zeitschrift für Soziologie und Sozialpsychologie* 38(4): 751–9.

Levine, A. (1981) *Liberal democracy: A critique of its theory.* New York: Columbia University Press.

Lijphart, A. (1984) *Democracies: Patterns of majoritarian and consensus government.* New Haven, CT: Yale University Press.

  (ed.) (1992) *Parliamentary versus presidential government.* Oxford University Press.

  (1994) *Electoral systems and party systems: A study of twenty-seven democracies.* Oxford University Press.

Lindberg, S. I. (2006) 'The surprising significance of African elections', *Journal of Democracy* 17(1): 139–51.

Linklater, A. (1998) *The transformation of political community.* Cambridge: Polity Press.

Linz, J. (1990) 'The perils of presidentialism', *Journal of Democracy* 1(1): 51–69.

Linz, J. and A. Stepan (1996) *Problems of democratic transition and consolidation: Southern Europe, South America, and post-communist Europe.* Baltimore: Johns Hopkins University Press.

Lipset, S. M. (1960) *Political man*. London: Mercury Books.

Llanque-Kurps, M. (2003) *Klassischer Republikanismus und moderner Verfassungsstaat*. HU Berlin: Habilitationsschrift.

Lovenduski, J. (2005) *Feminizing politics*. Cambridge: Polity Press.

Macrae, J. (ed.) (2002) *The new humanitarianisms: A review of trends in global humanitarian action*. Humanitarian Policy Group (HPG) Report 11, London: Overseas Development Institute.

Maffei, S. (1979) *Il Consiglio politico finora inedito presentato al governo veneto nell'anno 1736*. Venice: Palese.

Mair, P. (1990) *The West European party system*. Oxford and New York: Oxford University Press.

(1997) *Party system change*. Oxford University Press.

(2002) 'Populist democracy vs party democracy', in Y. Mény and Y. Surel (eds.) *Democracies and the populist challenge*. Houndsmill: Macmillan, pp. 139–54.

Majone, G. (1995) 'Independence versus accountability? Non-majoritarian institutions and democratic governance in Europe', in J. J. Hesse and T. A. J. Toonen (eds.), *The European yearbook of comparative government and public administration*, vol. 1. Baden-Baden and Boulder, CO: Nomos / Westview Press.

(ed.) (1996) *Regulating Europe*. London: Routledge.

Manin, B. (1997) *The principles of representative government*. Cambridge University Press.

Manin, B., A. Przeworski and S. Stokes (eds.) (1999) *Democracy, accountability and representation*. Cambridge University Press.

Mansbridge, J. J. (2003) 'Rethinking representation', *American Political Science Review* 97(4): 515–28.

Maravall, J. M. (2008) *La confrontación política*. Madrid: Taurus.

Maravall, J. M. and A. Przeworski (2003) *Democracy and the rule of law*. New York: Cambridge University Press.

Maritain, J. (1943) *Christianisme et démocratie*. New York: Éditions de la Maison française.

Marx, K. (1875) *Randglossen zum programm der deutschen Arbeiterpartei*, in *Marx-Engels Werke*, vol. 19. Berlin: Institut für Marxismus-Leninismus beim ZK der SED.

Mateo Diaz, M. (2005) *Representing women? Female legislators in West European parliaments*. University of Essex, European Consortium for Political Research Monographs.

Mayo, H. B. (1960) *An introduction to democratic theory*. New York: Oxford University Press.

McBride, D. and A. Mazur (1995) *Comparative state feminism*. New York: Routledge.

Meguid, B. (2008) *Party competition between unequals*. New York: Cambridge University Press.

Meier, C. (1995) *Athen. Ein neubeginn der weltgeschichte*. München: Goldmann Verlag.

Mellor, M. (1997) *Feminism and ecology*. New York University Press.

Merkel, W. (2004) 'Embedded and defective democracies', *Democratization* 11(5): 33–58.

Merkel, W., Sandschneider and D. Segert (eds.) (1996) *Systemwechsel 2. die Institutionalisierung der Demokratie*. Opladen: Leske & Budrich.

Michels, R. (1962) *Political parties? A sociological study of the oligarchical tendencies of modern democracy*. New York: The Free Press.

Mill, J. S. (1910) *Representative government* (1861). London: Dent.

(1928) *Autobiography* (1873). London: Oxford University Press.

Millar, F. (2002) *The Roman Republic in political thought: The Menahem Stern Jerusalem Lectures*. Hanover and London: University Press of New England.

Miller, W. E. (1988) *Without consent: Mass-elite linkages in presidential politics*. Lexington: University Press of Kentucky.

Miller, W. E. and D. E. Stokes (1963) 'Constituency influence in Congress', *American Political Science Review* 57(1): 45–56.

Miller, W. E., R. Pierce, J. Thomassen *et al.* (1999). *Policy representation in Western democracies*. Oxford University Press.

Minteer, B. and B. Pepperman Taylor (eds.) (2002) *Democracy and the claims of nature: Critical perspectives for a new century*. Lanham, MD: Rowman and Littlefield.

Montero, J., J. Ramón and J. Font (1991) 'El voto dual: lealtad y transferencia de votos en las elecciones autonómicas', *Estudis Electorals* 10: 183–211.

Montesquieu C. L. de S., Baron de (1989) *The spirit of the laws*. Cambridge University Press.

Moreno, L. (2001) 'Ethnoterritorial concurrence in multinational societies: The Spanish *comunidades autónomas*', in A. G. Gagnon and J. Tully (eds.) *Multinational democracies*. Cambridge University Press.

Mounier, J.-J. (1989) 'Rapport du comité chargé du travail sur la constitution', in F. Furet and R. Halévie (eds.) *Orateurs de la révolution française*, vol. 1: *Les constituants*, Paris: Pléiade.

Muirhead, R. (2006) 'A defense of party spirit', *Perspectives on Politics* 4: 713–27.

Mulgan, G. (1994) *Politics in an antipolitical age*. Cambridge: Polity Press.

Müller, W. C. (2000) 'Political parties in parliamentary democracies: Making delegation and accountability work', *European Journal of Political Research* 37(3): 309–33.

Münkler, H. (2006) 'Der Wettbewerb der Sinnproduzenten', *Merkur* 60(1): 15–22.

Nash, R. (1989) *The rights of nature: A history of environmental ethics*. Madison: University of Wisconsin Press.

Newman, S. (1994) 'Ethnoregional parties: A comparative perspective', *Regional Politics & Policy* 4(2): 28–66.

(1996) *Ethnoregional conflict in democracies: Mostly ballots, rarely bullets*. Westport and London: Greenwood Press.

(2000) 'Nationalism in postindustrial Societies: Why states still matter', *Comparative Politics* 33(1): 21–41.

Neyer, J. (2005) 'Die Krise der EU und die Stärke einer deliberativen Integrationstheorie', *Zeitschrift für Internationale Beziehungen* 12(2): 377–82.

Nohlen, D. (1978) *Wahlsysteme der Welt. Daten und analysen*. München: Piper.

Nohlen, D. and M. Fernández (eds.) (1991) *Presidencialismo versus parlamentarismo*. Cáracas: Nueva Sociedad.

Norris, P. (2006) 'The impact of electoral reform on women's representation', *Acta Politica* 41(2): 197–213.

(2007) 'Opening the door: Women leaders and constitution building in Iran and Afghanistan', in B. Kellerman and D. L. Rohde, *Women and leadership*. San Francisco: Jossey-Bass, pp. 197–225.

Norton, B. (1991) *Toward unity among environmentalists*. New York: Oxford University Press.

Núñez Seixas, X. M. (2005) 'De la región a la nacionalidad: Los neoregionalismos en la España de la transición y consolidación democrática', in C. H. Waisman, R. Rein and A. Gurruchaga (eds.) *Transiciones de la dictadura a la democracia: Los casos de España y América Latina*. Bilbao: Universidad del País Vasco.

Ober, J. (2008) 'The original meaning of "democracy": Capacity to do things, not majority rule', *Constellations* 15(1): 3–9.

Offe, C. (2001) 'The politics of parity: Can legal intervention neutralize the gender divide?' in J. Klausen and C. S. Maier (eds.) *Has liberalism failed women?* New York: Palgrave, pp. 39–54.

O'Neill, J. (2001) 'Representing people, representing nature, representing the world', *Environment and Planning C: Government and Policy* 19(4): 483–500.

Orriols, L. and A. Richards (2005) *Nationalism and the labour party: Differential voting in Scotland and Wales since 1997*. Estudio/Working Paper 213. Madrid: Instituto Juan March de Estudios e Investigaciones.

Paine, T. (1989) *The rights of man*, in B. Kuklick (ed.) *Political writings*. Cambridge University Press.

Painter, J. (2006) 'Prosaic geographies of stateness', *Political Geography* 25(7): 752–74.

Pallarés, F. and J. Font (1994) 'Las elecciones autonómicas en Cataluña 1980–1992', in P. del Castillo (ed.) *Comportamiento Político y Electoral*. Madrid: Centro de Investigaciones Sociológicas.

Palme, S. U. (1969) 'Vom Absolutismus zum Parlamentarismus in Schweden', in D. Gerhard (ed.) *Stände-Vertretungen in Europa im 17. und 18. Jahrhundert*. Göttingen: Vandenhoeck & Ruprecht, pp. 368–97.

Pateman, C. (1970) *Participation and democratic theory*. Cambridge University Press.

(1989) *The disorder of women*. London: Polity Press.

Pennock, J. R. (1983) 'Introduction' in J. R. Pennock and J. W. Chapman (eds.), *Liberal democracy. Nomos XXV*. New York: NYU.

Pérez-Nievas, S. and M. Fraile (2000) *Is the nationalist vote really nationalist? Dual voting in Catalonia, 1980–1999*. Estudio/Working Paper 147. Madrid: Instituto Juan March de Estudios e Investigaciones.

Pettit, P. (2003) 'Deliberative democracy, the discursive dilemma, and republican theory', in J. S. Fishkin and P. Laslett (eds.) *Debating deliberative democracy*. Oxford: Blackwell, pp. 138–62.

Phillips, A. (1995) *The politics of presence*. Oxford: Clarendon Press.

Pierson, P. (2004) *History, institutions, and social analysis*. Princeton and Oxford: Princeton University Press.

Pietilä, H. (2002) *Engendering the global agenda: The story of women in the United Nations*. Geneva: P. Imprinta.

Pitkin, H. (1967) *The concept of representation*. Berkeley: University of California Press.

(2004) 'Representation and democracy: Uneasy alliance', *Scandinavian Political Studies* 27(3): 335–42.

Pizzorno, A. (1993) *Le radici della politica assoluta e altri saggi*. Milan: Feltrinelli.

Plumwood, V. (1993) *Feminism and the mastery of nature*. London: Routledge.

(2000) 'Deep ecology, deep pockets and deep problems: A feminist, ecosocialist analysis', in E. Katz, A. Light and D. Rothenberg (eds.) *Beneath the surface: Critical essays in the philosophy of deep ecology*. Cambridge, MA: MIT Press, pp. 59–84.

(2002) *Environmental culture: The ecological crisis of reason*. London: Routledge.

Powell, G. B. (2000) *Elections as instruments of democracy: Majoritarian and proportional visions*. New Haven, CT and London: Yale University Press.

Powell, G. B. and G. Whitten (1993) 'A cross-national analysis of economic voting: Taking account of the political context', *American Journal of Political Science* 37(2): 391–414.

Powley, E. (2008) 'Defending children's rights: The legislative priorities of Rwandan women parliamentarians', *The Initiative for Inclusive Security. A Program of Hunt Alternatives Fund*. www.huntalternatives.org

Preuss, U. K. (1998) 'The relevance of the concept of citizenship', in U. K. Preuss and F. Requejo (eds.) *European citizenship, multiculturalism, and the state*. Baden-Baden: Nomos.

Priester, K. (2007) *Populismus. Historische und aktuelle Erscheinungsformen*. Frankfurt: Campus.

Princen, T. and M. Finger (1994) *Environmental NGOs in world politics: Linking the local and the global*. London: Routledge.

Przeworski, A. (ed.) (1996) *Sustainable democracy*. Cambridge University Press.

Przeworski, A., M. Alvarez, J. Cheibub and F. Limongi (2000) *Democracy and development: Political institutions and well-being in the world, 1950–1990*. Cambridge University Press.

Pulzer, P. (1988) 'When parties fail: Ethnic protest in Britain in the 1970s', in K. Lawson and P. Merkl (eds.) *When parties fail: Emerging alternative organizations*. Princeton University Press.

Radtke, K. R. (2007) 'Ein Trend zu transnationaler Solidarität? Die Entwicklung des Spendenaufkommens in der Not und Entwicklungshilfe', Discussion Paper No. 304, Wissenschaftszentrum Berlin (WZB).

Rawls, J. (1993) *Political liberalism*. New York: Columbia University Press.

Regan, T. (1981) 'The nature and possibility of an environmental ethic', *Environmental Ethics* 3(1): 19–34.

Rehfeld, A. (2005) *The concept of constituency: Political representation, democratic legitimacy and institutional design*. Cambridge University Press.

Revel, J. (1987) 'Les corps et communautés', in K. M. Baker (ed.) *The French revolution and the creation of modern political culture*: vol. 1, *The political culture of the Old Regime*. Oxford: Pergamon Press, pp. 225–42.

Riba, C. (2000) 'Voto dual y abstención diferencial. Un estudio sobre el comportamiento electoral en Cataluña', *Revista Española de Investigaciones Sociológicas* 91: 59–88.

Riker, W. H. (1986) '"Duverger's law" revisited', in B. Grofman and A. Lijphart (eds.) *Electoral laws and their political consequences*. New York: Agathon Press, pp. 19–42.

Rodman, J. (1977) 'The liberation of nature?' *Inquiry* 20: 83–145.

Roeder, P. G. (1999) 'Peoples and states after 1989: The political costs of incomplete national revolutions', *Slavic Review* 58(4): 854–82.

Rokkan, S. and D. Urwin (1983) *Economy, territory, identity*. London & Beverly Hills: Sage.

Roller, E. and P. van Houten (2003) 'National parties in regional party systems: The PSC-PSOE in Catalonia', *Regional and Federal Studies* 13(3): 1–22.

Rorty, R. (1989) *Contingency, irony, and solidarity*. Cambridge University Press.

(1991) *Objectivity, relativism, and truth: Philosophical papers*. Cambridge University Press.

Rosanvallon, P. (1992) *Le sacre du citoyen. Histoire du suffrage universel en France*. Paris: Gallimard.

(1998) *Le peuple introuvable. Histoire de la représentation démocratique en France*. Paris: Gallimard.

(2006) *La contre-démocratie: La politique à l'âge de la défiance*. Paris: Editions du Seuil.

(2008) *Counter-democracy. Politics in an age of distrust*. Cambridge and New York: Cambridge University Press.

Rosenau, J. N. (1997) *Along the domestic-foreign frontier: Exploring governance in a turbulent world*. Cambridge University Press.

(2000) 'Governance in a globalising world', in D. Held and A. McGrew (eds.) *The global transformations reader*. Cambridge: Polity Press, pp. 181–90.

Rousseau, J.-J. (1985) *The government of Poland*. Indianapolis: Hackett.

(1987) *On the social contract, or principles of political rights*, in *Basic political writings*. Indianapolis: Hackett, pp. 139–227.

Rudolf, J. (1977) 'Ethnic sub-states and the emergent politics of tri-level interaction in Western Europe', *The Western Political Quarterly* 30(4): 537–57.

Rudolf, J. and R. Thompson (1985) 'Ethnoterritorial movements and the policy process: Accommodating nationalist demands in the developed world', *Comparative Politics* 17(3): 291–311.

Runciman, D. (2007) 'The paradox of political representation', *Journal of Political Philosophy* 15(1): 93–114.

Rupnik, J. (2007) 'From democracy fatigue to populist backlash', *Journal of Democracy* 18(4): 17–25.

Rustow, D. (1970) 'Transitions to democracy: Toward a dynamic model', *Comparative Politics* 2(3): 337–63.

Sandel, M. J. (1995) *Liberalismus und Republikanismus: von der Notwendigkeit der Bürgertugend*. Vienna: Passagen.

Sapiro, G. (ed.) (2008) *Translation. Le marché de la traduction en France à l'heure de la mondialisation*. Paris: CNRS-éditions.

Sartori, G. (1976) *Parties and party systems.* Cambridge University Press.

Saward, M. (2006a) 'Representation', in A. Dobson and R. Eckersley (eds.) *Political theory and the ecological challenge.* Cambridge University Press, pp. 183–99.

   (2006b) 'The representative claim', *Contemporary Political Theory* 5(3): 297–318.

   (2009) 'Authorisation and authenticity: Representation and the unelected', *Journal of Political Philosophy* 17(1): 1–22.

   (2010) *The representative claim.* Oxford University Press.

Sawer, M., M. Tremblay and L. Trimble (2006) *Representing women in parliament: A comparative study.* New York: Routledge.

Schaffer, F. (1998) *Democracy in translation.* Ithaca, NY: Cornell University Press.

Scharpf, F. W. (1993) 'Legitimationsprobleme der Globalisierung. Regieren in Verhandlungssystemen', in C. Böhret and G. Wewer (eds.) *Regieren im 21. Jahrhundert – Zwischen Globalisierung und Regionalisierung. Festgabe für Hans-Hermann Hartwich zum 65. Geburtstag.* Opladen: Leske & Budrich, pp. 165–85.

   (1997) 'Economic integration, democracy, and the welfare state', *Journal of European Public Policy* 4(1): 18–36.

Schmalz-Bruns, R. (1995) *Reflexive demokratie. Die demokratische Transformation moderner Politik.* Baden-Baden: Nomos.

   (1998) 'Grenzerfahrungen und Grenzüberschreitungen: Demokratie im integrierten Europa', in B. Kohler-Koch (ed.) *Regieren in entgrenzten Räumen.* PVS-Sonderheft 29. Opladen: Westdeutscher Verlag.

Schmitt, C. (1923) *Die geistesgeschichtliche lage des heutigen parlamentarismus.* Berlin: Duncker & Humblot (7th edn. 1991).

   (2008) *Constitutional theory* (1928) Durham and London: Duke University Press.

Schmitt, H. and J. Thomassen (eds.) (1999) *Political representation and legitimacy in the European Union.* Oxford University Press.

Schmitter, P. (1995) 'The consolidation of political democracies', in G. Pridham (ed.) *Transitions to democracy: Comparative perspectives from southern Europe, Latin America and eastern Europe.* Dartmouth: Aldershot, pp. 535–69.

   (2000) *How to democratize the European Union – and why bother?* Lanham, MD: Rowman and Littlefield.

Schmitter, P. and T. Karl (1991) 'What *democracy* is ... and is not', *Journal of Democracy* 2: 75–88.

Schmitter, P. and G. Lehmbruch (eds.) (1979) *Trends toward corporatist intermediation.* London: Sage.

Schmitter, P. and A. Trechsel (2004) *The future of democracy in Europe: Trends, analyses and reforms.* A Green Paper for the Council of Europe. Strasbourg: Council of Europe Publishing.

Schrijver, F. J. (2004) 'Electoral performance of regionalist parties and perspectives on regional identity in France', *Regional & Federal Studies* 14(2): 187–210.

Schumpeter, J. (1942) *Capitalism, socialism, and democracy.* New York: Harper Torchbook.

Schwartzberg, M. (2007) *Democracy and legal change*. New York: Cambridge University Press.

(2010) 'Shouts, murmurs and votes: Acclamation and aggregation in ancient Greece', *Journal of Political Philosophy*, published online 3 March.

Sieyès, E.-J. (1985) *Écrits politiques*. Paris: Editions des archives contemporaines.

(1998) 'Bases de l'ordre social' in P. Pasquino, *Sieyes et l'invention de la constitution en France*. Paris: Odile Jacob.

Singer, P. (1975) *Animal liberation: A new ethics for our treatment of animals*. New York: The New Review.

Skinner, Q. (2002) 'Hobbes and the purely artificial person of the state', in Q. Skinner, *Visions of Politics*, 3 vols. Cambridge University Press, pp. 3, 177–208.

Skjeie, H. (1992) *Den politiske betydningen af kjønn: En studie av norsk topp-politikk*. Oslo: Institut for Samfunnsforskning.

Smith, A. (2000) *The nation in history*. Hanover: University Press of New England.

Smith, G. (2008) *Democratic innovations: Designing institutions for citizen participation*. Cambridge University Press.

Snyder, J. (1993) *Myths of empire: Domestic politics and international ambition*. New York: Cornell University Press.

Soulé, M. and G. Lease (1995) *Reinventing nature? Responses to postmodern deconstruction*. Washington DC: Island Press.

Southern African Development Community (SADC) (2008) *Protocol on gender and development*. Johannesburg.

Squires, J. (2007) *The new politics of gender equality*. New York: Palgrave Macmillan.

Stasavage, D. (2011) *States of Credit: Size, Power, and the Development of European Polities*. Princeton University Press.

Sterba, J. (1994) 'Reconciling anthropocentric and nonanthropocentric environmental ethics', *Environmental Values* 3(3): 229–44.

Stokes, S. C. (2003) *Mandates and democracy*. New York: Cambridge University Press.

Stone, C. (1974) *Should trees have standing? Toward legal rights for natural objects*. Los Altos, CA: Kaufman.

Stöss, R. (2000) *Rechtsextremismus im vereinten Deutschland*. Berlin: Friedrich Ebert Stiftung, 3rd edn.

Streeck, W. (1998) 'Einleitung', in W. Streeck (ed.) *Internationale Wirtschaft, nationale Demokratie? Herausforderungen für die Demokratietheorie*. Frankfurt/New York: Campus, pp. 11–58.

Strom, K. (2000) 'Delegation and accountability in parliamentary democracies', *European Journal of Political Research* 37(3): 261–90.

Sullivan, J. L. and R. E. O'Connor (1972) 'Electoral choice and popular control of public policy', *American Political Science Review* 66: 1256–68.

Taggart, P. (1995) 'New populist parties in western Europe', *West European Politics* 18(1): 34–51.

Tambini, D. (2001) *Nationalism in Italian politics: The stories of the Northern League 1980–2000*. London and New York: Routledge.

Thompson, D. F. (1987) *Political ethics and public office.* Cambridge, MA: Harvard University Press.

Thompson, G. (2008) *International quasi-constitutionalism and corporate citizenship: Language, troubles, dilemmas.* Milton Keynes: The Open University.

Tiryakian, E. (1994) 'Nationalist movements in advanced societies: Some methodological reflections', in J. Beramendi, R. Maiz and X. Núñez (eds.) *Nationalism in Europe: Past and present.* Universidad de Santiago de Compostela.

Todorov, T. (1984) *The conquest of America: The question of the other.* New York: Harper and Row.

Tömmel, I. (2006) *Das politische System der EU.* München and Wien: Oldenbourg.

Tully, J. (2001) 'Introduction', in A. G. Gagnon and J. Tully (eds.) *Multinational democracies.* Cambridge University Press.

Turkka, T. (2007) *The origins of parliamentarism: A study of Sandy's Motion.* Baden-Baden: Nomos.

Tuschhoff, C. (1999) 'The compounding effect: The impact of federalism on the concept of representation', *West European Politics* 22(2): 16–33.

United Nations Development Programme (UNDP) (2003) *Human development report for the Arab region.* New York: UNDP.

Urbinati, N. (1998) 'Democracy and populism', *Constellations* 5(1): 110–24.

(2005) 'Continuity and rupture: Political judgment in democratic representation', *Constellations* 12(1): 194–222.

(2006) *Representative democracy: Principles and genealogy.* University of Chicago Press.

Urbinati, N. and M. Warren (2008) 'The concept of representation in contemporary democracy', *The Annual Review of Political Science* 11: 387–412.

Urwin, D. (1983) 'Harbinger, fossil or fleabite? "Regionalism" and the west European party mosaic', in H. Daalder and P. Mair (eds) *Western European party systems.* London: Sage.

Vaughan, C. E. (1962) *The political writings of Jean-Jacques Rousseau,* 2 vols. New York: Wiley.

Vogel, S. (1995) *Against nature: The concept of nature in critical theory.* Albany: State University of New York Press.

Vorländer, H. (2003) *Demokratie.* München: Beck.

Wahlke, J. C., H. Eulau, W. Buchanan *et al.* (1962) *The legislative system: Explorations in legislative behavior.* New York, London: John Wiley & Sons.

Walzer, M. (1992a) *Zivile Gesellschaft und amerikanische Demokratie.* Berlin: Rotbuch Verlag.

(1992b) 'Comment', in C. Taylor, *Multiculturalism and the 'politics of recognition'.* Princeton University Press, pp. 99–103.

Wängnerud, L. (2009) 'Women in parliaments: Descriptive and substantive representation', *Annual Review of Political Science* 12: 51–69.

Waschkuhn, A. (1998) *Demokratietheorien.* München: Oldenbourg.

Weber, M. (1991, 1921) *From Max Weber: Essays in sociology.* London: Routledge.

(1994) *Political writings.* Cambridge University Press.

Werz, N. (ed.) (2003) *Populismus.* Opladen: Leske & Budrich.

Weston, A. (1996) 'Before environmental ethics', in A. Light and E. Katz (eds.) *Environmental pragmatism*. London: Routledge, pp. 139–60.

Wiles, P. (1969) 'A syndrome, not a doctrine: Some elementary theses on populism', in G. Ionescu and E. Gellner (eds.) *Populism. Its meanings and national characteristics*. London: Weidenfeld & Nicolson, pp. 166–79.

Wolin, S. S. (2004) *Politics and vision: Continuity and innovation in western political thought*. Princeton and Oxford: Princeton University Press.

(2008) *Democracy incorporated: Managed democracy and the specter of inverted totalitarianism*. Princeton and Oxford: Princeton University Press.

Wood, A. G. (1969) *The creation of the American revolution, 1776–1787*. Chapel Hill: University of North Carolina Press.

World Bank (2008) 'Report on engendering development', Washington DC: The World Bank Group.

Young, I. M. (1997) 'Deferring group representation', in I. Shapiro and W. Kymlicka (eds.) *Ethnicity and group rights. Nomos XXXIX* (ser.). New York University Press, pp. 349–76.

(1990) *Justice and the politics of difference*. Princeton University Press.

(2000) *Inclusion and democracy*. Oxford University Press.

Zakaria, F. (1997) 'The rise of illiberal democracy', *Foreign Affairs* 76(6): 22–43.

Zolo, D. (1997) *Die demokratische Fürstenherrschaft. Für eine realistische Theorie der Politik*. Göttingen: Steil.

Zürn, M. (2000) 'Democratic governance beyond the nation state: The EU and other international institutions', *European Journal of International Relations* 6(2): 183–221.

Zürn, M. and C. Joerges (eds.) (2005) *Law and governance in postnational constellations: Compliance in Europe and beyond*. Cambridge University Press.

Zürn, M. and G. Walter (eds.) (2005) *Globalizing interests: Pressure groups and denationalization*. Albany: State University of New York Press.

Zürn, M., M. Binder, M. Ecker-Ehrhardt and K. Radtke (2007) 'Politische Ordnungsbildung wider Willen', *Zeitschrift für Internationale Beziehungen* 14(1): 129–64.

WEBSITES

www.iKNOWPolitics.org International Knowledge Network of Women in Politics.

www.ipu.org The Inter-Parliamentary Union's website shows the world rank order in terms of women's representation in parliament.

www.quotaproject.org A website showing every country with gender quotas for parliament, by IDEA, The International Institute for Democracy and Electoral Assistance and Stockholm University.

www.terra.es/personal2/monolith/00women.htm Database on Women World Leaders.

www.unesco.org/education/information/nfsunesco/pdf/BEIJIN_E.PDF United Nations Fourth World Conference on Women (FWCW) (1995) 'Beijing Declaration and Platform for Action'.

www.wedo.org Women's Environmental and Development Organization.

www.womenslobby.org European Women's Lobby.

Index